IRELAND
BED & BREAKFAST
— *2003* —

Publisher: Tim Stilwell

Editor: Martin Dowling

STILWELL
Publishing

Distributed by Orca Book Services, Stanley House, 3 Fleets Lane, Poole, Dorset BH15 3AJ
(Tel: 01202 665432).
Available from all good bookshops.

ISBN 1-900861-33-X

Published by Stilwell Publishing,
59 Charlotte Road, Shoreditch, London, EC2A 3QW.
Tel: 020 7739 7179.

Publisher: Tim Stilwell
Editor: Martin Dowling
Typesetting: Tradespools Ltd, Frome, Somerset
Front Cover Design: Nigel Simpson & Crush Design Associates

Printed in Great Britain by Stephens & George Print, Merthyr Tydfil, Mid Glamorgan.

Contents

Introduction

This directory is really very straightforward. It sets out simply to list as many B&Bs in as many places in Ireland as possible, so that wherever you go, you know there is one nearby.

A few years ago my wife and I visited Ireland and decided to use B&Bs for accommodation on our trip. Like most visitors, our knowledge of Ireland's geography was reasonable but not brilliant. We had the Tourist Board's accommodation lists, but found it hard to match the listings to our road atlas - indeed, some places were impossible to find on any map, while others were miles away from the heading they were listed under. In the end, we just stayed in the big towns, missing out on the choice offered by the hundreds of B&Bs dotted all over the countryside.

We had had similar experiences in the UK as well. In 1993, I decided to set up a company devoted to publishing information about good, low-cost accommodation right across Britain, illustrated with proper maps and arranged in a way that everyone could understand without having to peer down narrow columns or interpret obscure symbols. The tenth edition of the British book appears this year. We finally turned our attention to Ireland in 1995 - this is the eighth edition of **Stilwell's Ireland: Bed & Breakfast**.

This is therefore a book to save the reader time and money: it suits anyone who wishes to plan a trip in Ireland, who appreciates good value and who is open to ideas. The directory is quite deliberately not a guidebook. Its aim is that of any directory in any field: to be comprehensive, to offer the widest choice. By this definition, **Stilwell's Ireland: Bed & Breakfast** outstrips any guidebook - we publish by far and away the largest number of B&Bs listed anywhere outside the Tourist Boards' lists. What we don't do is make up the reader's mind for them. There are plenty of other B&B books that push their particular premises as 'exclusive' or 'special'. We think that a simple glance over the salient details on any page and the reader will be his or her own guide.

We have two kinds of reader in mind. The first knows exactly where to go but not where to stay. The nearest B&B is the best solution; a quick look at the right county map gives the answer. The other reader is not so sure where to go. As they browse the pages, the short descriptions provide good ideas. All information here has been supplied by the B&B owners themselves. We should make it clear that inclusion in these pages does not imply personal recommendation. We have not visited them all individually; all we have done is write to them. The directory lists 1,300 entries in 550 locations throughout Northern Ireland and the Republic. The vast majority were included because they offered B&B for well under £25 (about €40) per person per night (in fact the average starting double rate per person per night in this book is £19.00 in Northern Ireland and €26.00 in the Republic).

Owners were canvassed in the summer of 2002 and responded by the end of October. They were asked to provide their range of rates per person per night for 2003. The rates are thus forecasts and are in any case always subject to seasonal fluctuation in demand. Some information may, of course, be out of date already. Grades may go up or down, or be removed altogether. The telephone company may alter exchange numbers. Proprietors may decide to sell up and move out of the business altogether. This is why the directory has to be a yearbook; in general, though, the information published here will be accurate, pertinent and useful for many a year. The pink highlight boxes are advertisements - the B&B has paid for some extra wordage and for their entry to stand out from the page a little more.

The main aim has been to provide details that are concise and easy to understand. The only symbols used are some conventional tourist symbols. There are some abbreviations, but it should be clear what they stand for without having to refer to the key on page vi. The grades are perhaps more difficult - each inspecting organisation has its own classification system with its own definition of merit. Once again, though, the reader will soon pick out the exceptional establishments - many have high grades from each organisation. The general rule is that more facilities mean higher prices. Do not be misled into thinking that an ungraded establishment is inferior. Many B&B owners never apply for grades or do not wish to pay for one. They thrive on business from guests who return again and again because the hospitality is excellent. My advice is: ring around. A simple telephone call and some judicious questions will give you an impression of your host very effectively. The largest collection of B&Bs in Northern Ireland and the Republic is now laid out before you - the greatest choice available in one book. We think that your tastes and preferences will do the rest.

We have deliberately arranged the book by administrative county in alphabetical order, listing all those in Northern Ireland first, followed by all those in the Republic. Another feature of the book is that we insist on using the proper postal address. Many entries thus carry a county name different from the one they are listed under or a 'post town' that is some miles from the village. These oddities arise from the postal service's distribution system. They should not, under any circumstances, be used as a directional guide. For example, the village of Carrigart in Donegal is a good 30km from Letterkenny, its quoted 'post town' - not a journey to make in error. Used on a letter though, it does speed the mail up. If you need directions to a B&B (especially if you are travelling at night), the best solution is to telephone the owner and ask the way.

The county maps are intended to act as a general reference. They present only the locations of each entry in the directory. For a more accurate idea of the location of a B&B, use the five-figure National Grid Reference published under each location's name. Used in tandem with an Ordnance Survey map or any atlas that uses the Irish National Grid, these numbers provide first-class route-planning references. The pubs and restaurants that appear beneath each location heading are included on the recommendation of B&Bs themselves. The tankard symbol shows that they are local establishments where one can get a decent evening meal at a reasonable price.

Throughout the book you will find boxes offering peremptory advice to readers. These may seem of little consequence; some may even annoy. We are sorry for intruding upon your sensibilities like this but the boxes actually neaten the page. Those that request courtesy and care for the customs of your hosts need no apology, however. Opening your home to strangers, albeit for payment, requires a leap of faith for most people; B&B owners are no exceptions. We simply ask everyone to observe the usual house rules. In this way, other guests will continue to meet with a welcome when they, too, pass through.

The Publisher, Stoke Newington, December 2002.

STILWELL'S

Key to Entries

🐴 Children welcome (from age shown in brackets, if specified)

🅿 Off-street car parking (number of places shown in brackets)

� No smoking

📺 Television (either in every room or in a TV lounge)

🐕 Pets accepted (by prior arrangement)

✗ Evening meal available (by prior arrangement)

Ⅴ Special diets catered for (by prior arrangement - please check with owner to see if your particular requirements are catered for)

▥ Central heating throughout

♿ Suitable for disabled people (please check with owner to see what level of disability is provided for)

✳ Christmas breaks a speciality

☕ Coffee/tea making facilities

cc Credit cards accepted

Use the National Grid reference with Ordnance Survey of Ireland and Ordnance Survey of Northern Ireland maps and atlases. The letter refers to a 100 kilometre grid square. The first two numbers refer to a North/South grid line and the last two numbers refer to an East/West grid line. The grid reference indicates their intersection point.

The location heading - every hamlet, village, town and city mentioned in this directory is represented on the local county map at the head of each section.

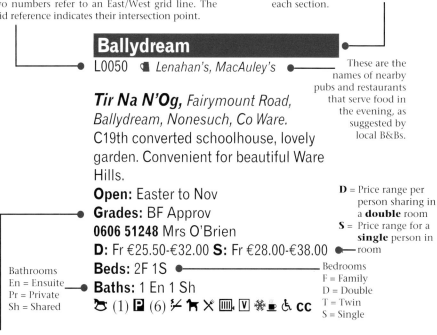

Ballydream

L0050 🍴 *Lenahan's, MacAuley's*

These are the names of nearby pubs and restaurants that serve food in the evening, as suggested by local B&Bs.

Tir Na N'Og, *Fairymount Road, Ballydream, Nonesuch, Co Ware.* C19th converted schoolhouse, lovely garden. Convenient for beautiful Ware Hills.

Open: Easter to Nov

Grades: BF Approv

0606 51248 Mrs O'Brien

D: Fr €25.50-€32.00 **S:** Fr €28.00-€38.00

Beds: 2F 1S

Baths: 1 En 1 Sh

🐴 (1) 🅿 (6) � 🐕 ✗ ▥ Ⅴ ✳☕ ♿ **cc**

D = Price range per person sharing in a **double** room

S = Price range for a **single** person in room

Bathrooms
En = Ensuite
Pr = Private
Sh = Shared

Bedrooms
F = Family
D = Double
T = Twin
S = Single

Grades - Bord Failte (**BF**, the Irish Tourist Board) grades guest houses in Stars (**1 Star** to **4 Star**); the Northern Ireland Tourist Board (**NITB**) rates them as Grade A (higher) or B. Both grade hotels in Stars (**1 Star** to **5 Star**). Both Tourist Boards for Ireland inspect B&B accommodation annually - such premises are entitled to show that they have been approved (**Approv**). The Automobile Association (**AA**) and Royal Automobile Club (**RAC**) both grade B&Bs for quality in Diamonds (**1 Diamond** to **5 Diamond**, highest) and hotels in Stars (**1 Star** to **5 Star**).

NORTHERN IRELAND

1   **County Antrim**
2   **County Armagh**
3   **County Down**
4   **County Fermanagh**
5   **County Londonderry**
6   **County Tyrone**

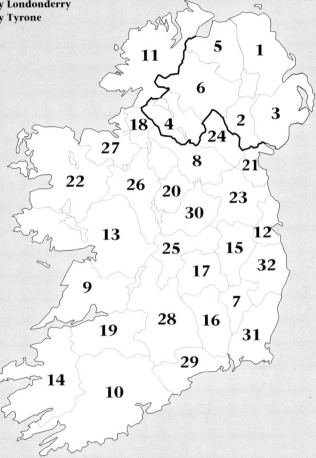

REPUBLIC OF IRELAND

7 **County Carlow**	16 **County Kilkenny**	25 **County Offaly**
8 **County Cavan**	17 **County Laois**	26 **CountyRoscommon**
9 **County Clare**	18 **County Leitrim**	27 **County Sligo**
10 **County Cork**	19 **County Limerick**	28 **County Tipperary**
11 **County Donegal**	20 **County Longford**	29 **County Waterford**
12 **County Dublin**	21 **County Louth**	30 **County Westmeath**
13 **County Galway**	22 **County Mayo**	31 **County Wexford**
14 **County Kerry**	23 **County Meath**	32 **County Wicklow**
15 **County Kildare**	24 **County Monaghan**	

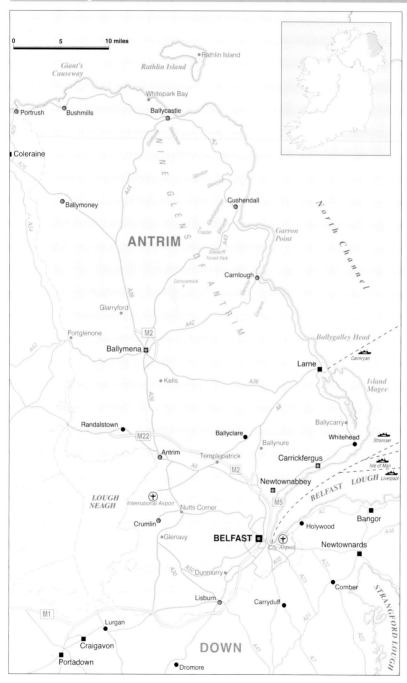

AIRPORTS ⊕

Belfast International Airport (Aldergrove) -
028 9442 2888.
Belfast City Airport - 028 9093 9093.

AIR SERVICES & AIRLINES ✈

From Belfast (International) to: **London
Heathrow, Manchester, Birmingham,
Glasgow, Sheffield, Cardiff, Southampton.**
British Airways Express (for **Logan Air**). In
Northern Ireland & the UK, tel. (local rate)
08705 511155. From the Republic, tel. (free-
fone) 1800 626747.

Belfast (International) to: **London Heathrow,
East Midlands. British Midland** - 08706
070555.

From Belfast (City) to: **Aberdeen,
Birmingham, Blackpool, Bristol, Guernsey,
Isle of Man, Jersey, Leeds-Bradford,
London City, London Gatwick, Newcastle.**
British European - 08705 676676.
British Airways Express (for **Manx Airlines**)
- in Northern Ireland & the UK, tel. (local rate)
08705 511155.
From the Republic, tel. (freefone) 1800 626747.

RAIL ⇌

The principal railway lines are: **Belfast** *to*
Londonderry and **Belfast** *to* **Dublin**.
For more information tel. **Northern Ireland
Rail** - 028 9089 9411.

FERRIES ⛴

Belfast to: **Stranraer**, *Dumfries & Galloway
(3 hrs) - and 1$^{1}/_{4}$ hrs (high speed).*
Stena Sealink - 028 9074 7747,
08705 707070
Larne to: **Cairnryan**, *nr Stranraer, Dumfries &
Galloway (2 hrs);* **Troon**, *Ayrshire (4 hrs);*
Fleetwood, *Lancs (8 hrs).*
P&O Irish Sea - 08702 424777.
Belfast to: **Troon**, *Ayrshire (2 $^{1}/_{2}$ hrs);*
Heysham, *Lancs (4 hrs).*
SeaCat - 08705 523523. From the Republic,
tel. (freefone) 1800 551743.
Belfast to: **Liverpool** *(8$^{1}/_{2}$ hrs).*
Norse Merchant Ferries - 08706 004321.
From the Republic, tel. 018 192999.

TOURIST INFORMATION OFFICES 𝒊

Belfast International Airport, **Aldergrove**,
Crumlin, Belfast, BT29 4AB, 028 9442 2888.

Pogue's Entry, Church Street, **Antrim**,
BT41 1BY, 028 9442 8331.

Sheskburn House, 7 Mary Street,
Ballycastle, County Antrim, BT54 6QH, 028
2076 2024.

76 Church Street, **Ballymena**, County Antrim,
BT43 6DF, 028 2563 8494.

35 Donegal Place, **Belfast**,
BT1 5AD, 028 9024 6009

Belfast City Airport, Sydenham Bypass,
Belfast, BT3 9JH, 028 9093 9093.

Knight Ride, Antrim Street, **Carrickfergus**,
County Antrim, BT38 7DG, 028 9336 6455.

Narrow Gauge Road, Larne Harbour, **Larne**,
County Antrim, BT40 3AW, 028 2826 0088.

Irish Linen Centre, Market Square, **Lisburn**,
County Antrim, BT49 0HA, 028 9266 0038.

Dunluce Centre, Sandhill Drive, **Portrush**,
County Antrim, BT56 8BT,
028 7082 3333 (Easter to Oct).

Antrim

J1587

Maranatha, 69 Oldstone Road, Antrim, Co Antrim, BT41 4SL. Situated 3 mins from Antrim Town.
Open: All year
028 9446 3150 Mr and Mrs Steele
D: Fr £18.00–£20.00
Beds: 3D **Baths:** 1 Sh
▣ (10) ⌦ ☒ ➤ ▥, ⬤

Ashcroft, 37 Thornhill Road, Antrim, BT41 2LH. Select accommodation near M2 motorway and airport. Central for touring.
Open: All Year (not Xmas)
028 9446 9117 (also fax) Mrs McKeown
D: Fr £17.50
Beds: 1F 1D 1T 1S **Baths:** 1 Ensuite 1 Private 1 Shared
⌂ ▣ (10) ⌦ ☒ ✗ ▥, ⬤

Ballycarry

J4494

Springbrook, 3 Island Road, Ballycarry, Carrickfergus, Co Antrim, BT38 9HB. Beautiful gardens and ponds. Home baking.
Open: All Year
028 9337 2329 Mr Beattie
D: Fr £20.00
Beds: 5D **Baths:** 2 Ensuite
▣

Ballycastle

D1241

Torr Brae, 77 Torr road, Ballycastle, Co Antrim, BT54 6RQ. Tranquil setting in a designated AONB overlooking Mull of Kintyre, Scotland.
Open: All year
028 2076 9625 (also fax) Mrs McHenry
torrbrae@lineone.net
D: Fr £17.50–£18.00 **S:** Fr £18.50
Beds: 1F 1D 1S **Baths:** 3 En
⌂ ▣ ⌦ ☒ ➤ ▥, ⬤ ❀ ⬤

Planning a longer stay?
Always ask for any special rates

All details shown are as supplied by B&B owners in Autumn 2002

Hillsea, 28 North Street, Ballycastle, Co Antrim, BT54 6BW. Lovely Victorian villa overlooking Sea of Moyle, large appetising breakfasts.
Open: Mar to Nov **Grades:** NITB Approv
028 2076 2385 Mr Jameson
D: Fr £20.00–£25.00 **S:** Fr £20.00–£25.00
Beds: 5F 5D 5T 2S **Baths:** 11 En 10 Pr 3 Sh
⌂ ▣ (70) ☒ ➤ ☒ ▥, ⬤ cc

Silversprings House, Ballycastle, Co Antrim, BT54 6ED. Family-run Dutch Colonial style house, quiet area midway sea front/town centre.
Open: Easter to end Sep
028 2076 2080 (also fax) Mrs Mulholland
D: Fr £16.00–£18.50 **S:** Fr £18.50
Beds: 1T 2D **Baths:** 2 En 1 Pr
⌂ ▣ ⌦ ☒ ▥, ⬤

Ballygalley

D3807

Halfway House Hotel, 352 Coast Road, Ballygalley, Larne, Co Antrim, BT40 2RA. Originally a coach house dating back to the early 1800s.
Open: All year (not Xmas) **Grades:** NITB 2 Star
028 2858 3265 Fax: 028 2858 3510
D: Fr £27.50–£30.00 **S:** Fr £35.00–£40.00
Beds: 1F 11D 3T **Baths:** 15 En
⌂ (2) ▣ (50) ☒ ✗ ▥, ⬤ cc

Ballymena

D1003   ⬤ *The Pavillion*

Neelsgrove Farm, 51 Carnearney Road, Ballymena, Co Antrim, BT42 2PL. Farmhouse set in rural area, convenient for touring Northern Ireland.
Open: All year (not Xmas/New Year)
028 2587 1225 Mrs Neely
maneely@brinternet.com
www.neelsgrove.freeserve.co.uk
D: Fr £16.00–£19.00 **S:** Fr £21.00–£24.00
Beds: 1F 1T 1D
▣ (6) ⌦ ➤ ▥, ⬤

Slemish House, 51 Albert Place, Ballymena, Co Antrim, BT43 6DY. Town house near shops and stations.
Open: All year
028 2564 7383 Miss Shaw
D: Fr £18.00 **S:** Fr £24.00
Beds: 1T 1D ☒ ☒ ▥, ⬤

Such Moor Stud, *94 Crankill Road, Ballymena, Co Antrim, BT43 5NW.* First class accommodation where guest will enjoy a warm friendly atmosphere.
Open: All Year (not Xmas/New Year)
028 2588 0521 Mrs Robinson
D: Fr £18.00–£21.00 **S:** Fr £21.00
Beds: 1F 1T 1D **Baths:** 1 En 1 Sh
🛏 🅿 (10) 🍴 📺 🛏 🔚

Ballymoney

C9425

Hob Green Country House, *41 Kirk Road, Ballymoney, Co Antrim, BT53 8HB.* Single-storey country home on south-facing hillside with 2 acres of superb mature gardens.
Open: All Year
028 2766 2620 (also fax) Mrs Johnston
D: Fr £20.00
Beds: 1F 2T 1D **Baths:** 4 Ensuite
🅿 (10) 🍴 📺 ✕ 📺 🔚 ❤ 🔳

Sandelwood, *98 Knock Road, Ballymoney, Co Antrim, BT53 6NQ.* Attractive, comfortable farmhouse convenient to Giant's Causeway - North Coast.
Open: Mar to Oct
028 2766 2621 Mrs Brown
D: Fr £16.00
Beds: 1F 2D **Baths:** 1 Pr 1 Sh
🛏 🅿 🍴 📺 🔚

Glen Lodge, *93a Frosses Road, Ballymoney, Co Antrim, BT53 7EJ.* Fresh, spacious home, all ensuite, gateway to Glens and Coast.
Open: All Year (not Xmas)
01726 890770 Fax: 01726 890774
info@surestay.com www.surestay.com
D: Fr £19.00
Beds: 2F 2D **Baths:** 4 Ensuite
🛏 🅿 (10) 📺 🔳

Ballynure

J3193

Rockbank, *40 Belfast Road, Ballynure, Ballyclare, Co Antrim, BT39 9TZ.* Quiet farmhouse located on main road 12 miles from Belfast.
Open: All year
028 9335 2261 Mrs Park
phildapark@aol.com
D: Fr £17.50–£20.00 **S:** Fr £20.00
Beds: 1F 1T 1D **Baths:** 2 En 1 Sh
🛏 (5) 🅿 (4) 📺 🛏 ✕ 📺 🔚 🔳

Belfast

J3374

Bowdens B & B,
17 Sandford Avenue, Cyprus Avenue, Belfast, BT5 5NW.
Open: All year
028 9065 2213 (also fax) Mrs Bowden
D: Fr £18.00 **S:** Fr £19.00
Beds: 1T 1D 1S **Baths:** 1 Sh
🛏 🅿 (3) 🍴 📺 🛏 🔚 🔳
Warm family-run town house in quiet cul-de-sac. Gardens, central heating, colour TV, complimentary tray. Convenient to bus routes, city airport, Seacat, Belfast Ferries, car parking. Try Bowden's famous Ulster Fry - free range eggs, dry cure bacon, organic or home-grown tomatoes in season, local potato bread and sausages, home-made jams.

Roseleigh House, *19 Rosetta Park, Belfast, BT6 0DL.* Luxurious ensuite accommodation in a restored Victorian house situated in residential South Belfast.
Open: All Year (not Xmas)
028 9064 4414 Ms Hunter
D: Fr £25.00–£27.00
Beds: 1F 2D 4T 2S **Baths:** 9 En
🛏 🅿 (6) 📺 ✕ 📺 🔚 🔳 cc

Eglantine Guest House, *21 Eglantine Avenue, Belfast, BT9 6DW.* Home from home welcome close to city centre. Personal attention.
Open: All Year
028 9066 7585 Mr & Mrs Cargill
D: Fr £20.00
Beds: 1F 3T 1D 3S **Baths:** 2 Shared
🛏 🛏 📺 📺 🔚 🔳

Lismore Lodge, *410 Ormeau Road, Belfast, BT7 3HY.* Comfortable family-run Victorian guest house, quiet area, near buses.
Open: All Year (not Xmas)
028 9064 1205 Mr & Mrs Devlin **Fax: 028 9064 2628**
D: Fr £25.00
Beds: 2D 3T 2S **Baths:** 7 En
🛏 (2) 🅿 (6) 📺 📺 🔚 🔳 cc

Please respect a B&B's wishes regarding children, animals and smoking

Planning a longer stay?
Always ask for any special rates

Old Rectory, *148 Malone Road, Belfast, BT9 5LH.* Breakfast: Ulster Fry, smoked salmon/scrambled eggs, venison sausages/mushrooms.
Open: All year (not Xmas)
028 9066 7882 Ms Callan **Fax: 028 9068 3759**
info@anoldrectory.co.uk
D: Fr £25.00–£30.00 **S:** Fr £36.00–£42.00
Beds: 1F 2D 4T 3S **Baths:** 2 En 3 Pr
⛺ (7) 🅿 (5) ⌇ 📺 ✕ Ⓥ ▥, ▪

Marine House, *30 Eglantine Avenue, Belfast, BT9 6DX.* Large detached villa, tree-lined avenue with gardens and car parking.
Open: All Year (not Xmas)
028 9066 2828 & 028 9038 1922 Mrs Corrigan
D: Fr £20.00–£22.50 **S:** Fr £27.00–£38.00
Beds: 11F 5D 2T 4S **Baths:** 3 En 4 Pr 2 Sh
⛺ 🅿 (4) 📺 ▥, ▪

Crecora, *114 Upper Newtownards Road, Belfast, BT4 3EN.* Victorian house on main road. Ferries & city airport nearby.
Open: All Year
028 9065 8257
D: Fr £18.00–£23.00
Beds: 2F 2D 4T 4S **Baths:** 3 En 3 Pr 3 Sh
⛺ 🅿 (15) ⌇ 📺 ♘ Ⓥ ▥, ⚒ ▪

Greenwood Guest House, *25 Park Road, Belfast, BT7 2FW.* 'Ulster Guest House of the Year 2000' finalist. Overlooking park.
Open: All year(not Xmas/New Year)
028 9020 2525 Mr Harris **Fax: 028 9020 2530**
info@greenwoodguesthouse.com
www.greenwoodguesthouse.com
D: Fr £27.50 **S:** Fr £37.50
Beds: 1F 2T 2D 2S **Baths:** 7 En
⛺ 🅿 (2) ⌇ 📺 ▥, ▪ cc

Bushmills

C9440   🍺 *Causeway Hotel*

Ardeevin, *145 Main Street, Bushmills, Co Antrim, BT57 8QE.* Comfortable family-run house convenient to Giant's Causeway and Bushmills Distillery.
Open: All Year
028 2073 1661 Mrs Montgomery
D: Fr £22.00
Beds: 2D 1T **Baths:** 2 Ensuite 1 Private
⌇ 📺 ▥, ▪

Craig Park, *24 Carnbore Road, Bushmills, Co Antrim, BT57 8YF.*
Open: All year (not Xmas)
028 2073 2496 Mrs Cheal **Fax: 028 2073 2479**
jan@craigpark.co.uk www.craigpark.co.uk
D: Fr £30.00 **S:** Fr £30.00–£50.00
Beds: 1F 1D 1T **Baths:** 3 En
⛺ 🅿 (8) ⌇ 📺 Ⓥ ▥, ▪ cc
A very comfortable Georgian-style country house offering superior accommodation, incredible views Bushmills and Giant's Causeway, Dunluce minutes away. Someone wrote about Craig Park - 'Heaven with a fence round it!'. Runner-up of 'Ulster Guest House of the Year' for 2 years running.

Knocklayde View, *90 Causeway Road, Bushmills, Co Antrim, BT57 8SX.* Country house with lovely view of countryside, near the beauty of the Giant's Causeway.
Open: All Year
028 2073 2099 Mrs Wylie
D: Fr £15.00–£16.00
Beds: 1F 1D **Baths:** 1 Shared
⛺ 🅿 📺 ▥, ▪

Carnlough

D2817

Bridge Inn (McAuleys), *2 Bridge Street, Carnlough, Ballymena, Co Antrim, BT44 0ET.* Traditional family-run hotel and pub ideally situated in picturesque surroundings.
Open: All year
028 2888 5669 Mr Davidson **Fax: 028 2888 5096**
the.bridge-inn@dnet.co.uk
www.welcometo/carnlough
D: Fr £18.00–£20.00 **S:** Fr £18.00–£20.00
Beds: 1F 3D 1T **Baths:** 2 Sh
⛺ (1) 🅿 (2) 📺 ♘ ✕ Ⓥ ▥,

BEDROOMS

D = Double   S = Single

T = Twin   F = Family

All details shown are as supplied by B&B owners in Autumn 2002

J4187

Beechgrove, *412 Upper Road, Carrickfergus, Co Antrim, BT38 8PW.* Friendly staff and friendly atmosphere, close to seaside and castle.
Open: All year
028 9336 3304 Mr & Mrs Barron
enquiries@beechgrovefarm.co.uk
www.beechgrovefarm.co.uk
D: Fr £16.00–£18.00 **S:** Fr £18.00–£20.00
Beds: 2F 1D 2T 1S **Baths:** 4 En 1 Sh
⛵ 🅿 (20) ⅍ 📺 ⊁ ✕ Ⓥ ▥ ⬛

Parklands, *320 Upper Road, Trooperslane, Carrickfergus, Co Antrim, BT38 8PN.* Stay with us in our traditional Ulster farmhouse, overlooking Belfast Lough.
Open: All Year
028 9336 2528 Mrs Sherratt
parklands@trooperslane.freeserve.co.uk
D: Fr £17.50–£20.00 **S:** Fr £20.00
Beds: 2D 1T **Baths:** 1 En 2 Sh
⛵ 🅿 ⅍ 📺 ⊁ ✕ Ⓥ ▥ ⬛ ❋ ⬛ cc

J1576

SURE STAY Belfast International Airport, *102 Moira Road, Crumlin, Belfast, BT29 4HG.* Award winning luxury guest-house, all facilities, 4 poster bed, jacuzzi.
Open: All year
028 9442 3099 (also fax)
info@caldhamellodge.co.uk
www.caldhamellodge.co.uk
D: Fr £20.00 **S:** Fr £40.00
Beds: 3D 3T **Baths:** 6 En
⛵ 🅿 (10) ⅍ 📺 ✕ ▥ ⬛

Crossroads Country House, *1 Largy Road, Crumlin, Belfast, BT29 4AH.* Victorian country house with resident reflexologist & day nursery in mature grounds.
Open: All Year
028 9445 2491 Mr Lorimer **Fax: 028 9442 3636**
crossroads@easynet.co.uk
D: Fr £15.00
Beds: 1F 1D 1T **Baths:** 2 Shared
⛵ 🅿 (16) ⅍ 📺 ⊁ ✕ Ⓥ ▥ ⬛

30 Crosshill Road, *Crumlin, Belfast, BT29 4BQ.* Comfortable farmhouse. Hearty breakfast. 5 minutes international airport. Lough Neagh.
028 9442 3674 (also fax) Mrs Harkness
D: Fr £25.00
Beds: 1F 1T **Baths:** 1 Shared
⛵ 🅿 📺 ⊁ ✕ Ⓥ ▥ ⬛

D2427

Cullentra House, *16 Cloghs Road, Cushendall, Ballymena, Co Antrim, BT44 0SP.* Award winning country house nestled amidst breathtaking scenery of Antrim coast/Glens.
Open: All Year
028 2177 1762 (also fax) Mrs McAuley
cullentra@hotmail.com
D: Fr £15.00–£17.00 **S:** Fr £20.00–£22.00
Beds: 1F 1D 1T **Baths:** 2 En 1 Sh
⛵ (4) 🅿 (6) ⅍ 📺 ✕ ▥ ⬛ cc

The Burn, *63 Ballyeamon Road, Cushendall, Ballymena, Co Antrim, BT44 0SN.* Peace, perfect peace - turf fire, books, tea and coffee.
Open: Easter to Easter
028 2177 1733 Mrs McAuley
D: Fr £16.00 **S:** Fr £18.00
Beds: 1F 1T 1S 1D **Baths:** 2 En 2 Sh
⛵ 🅿 (4) ⅍ 📺 ⊁ ✕ Ⓥ ▥ ⬛ cc

J2868

Warren House, *10 Thornhill Road, Kingsway, Dunmurry, Belfast, Co Antrim, BT17 9EJ.* Luxurious family home, set in rural surroundings on a mature site. Situated 4 miles from Belfast, 3 miles from Lisburn. Previous residence of DeLorean Motor Company. Winner of Holmes Guest House of the Year 1999. Convenient to buses and train station.
Open: All year
028 9061 1702 Ms Hughes **Fax: 028 9062 0654**
info@warrenhouseni.com *www.warrenhouseni.com*
D: Fr £25.00–£27.50 **S:** Fr £32.50–£35.00
Beds: 1F 1T 1D 1S
⛵ 🅿 ⅍ 📺 ⊁ ✕ Ⓥ ▥ ⬛ cc

Planning a longer stay?
Always ask for any special rates

Glarryford
D0512

The Firs, *86 Duneoin Road, Glarryford,*
Ballymena, Co Antrim, BT44 9HH. Bungalow in half
acre, lawns, shrubs, flowers. Convenient to
airport, seaport.
Open: All Year (not Xmas)
028 2568 5410 Miss Carson
D: Fr £13.00
Beds: 2D **Baths:** 1 Sh
🛏 (6) 🅿 (4) ⽄ 📺 ✕ 🆅 🎞 ⚈

Glenavy
J1672

Ashmore, *64 Main Street, Glenavy, Crumlin,*
Belfast, BT29 4LP. Modern bungalow. Large
garden. Parking.
Open: All Year
028 9442 2773 Mrs McClure
D: Fr £18.00
Beds: 2F 1D 1S **Baths:** 1 Ensuite 1 Private
🛏 🅿 (6) ⽄ 📺 🐾 🎞 ⚈

Kells
J1496

Springmount, *31 Ballygowan Road, Kells,*
Ballymena, Co Antrim, BT42 3PD. Friendly
farmhouse in quiet location.
Open: All Year
028 2589 1275 Mrs Bell
D: Fr £16.00
Beds: 3D **Baths:** 1 Shared
🛏 🅿 📺 🐾 ✕ 🎞 ⚈ ❋

Larne
D4002

Seaview Guest House,
156 Curran Road, Larne, Co
Antrim, BT40 1BX. Perfectly
situated for touring Antrim
Coast. Well established and
warm welcome.
Open: All year
028 2827 5397 Miss Muir **Fax: 028 2827 2438**
seaviewhouse@talk21.com www.seaviewlarne.co.uk
D: Fr £16.00–£22.00 **S:** Fr £16.00–£25.00
Beds: 4F 1D 2T 1S **Baths:** 5 En 5 Pr
🛏 (1) 🅿 (3) 📺 🐾 🎞 ⚈ cc

Derrin Guest House, *2*
Prince s Gardens, Larne, Co
Antrim, BT40 1RQ.
Open: All year (not Xmas)
028 2827 3269 (also fax)
Mrs Mills
info@derrinhouse.co.uk www.derrinhouse.co.uk
D: Fr £16.00–£22.00 **S:** Fr £20.00–£25.00
Beds: 2F 4D 1T **Baths:** 4 En 1 Sh
🛏 🅿 (3) 📺 🐾 🆅 🎞 ⚈ cc
Beautifully appointed Grade A guest house,
family run since 1964. Full fire certificate. Private
car park. Friendly welcoming atmosphere. Highly
Commended in 1994 Galtee Irish Breakfast
Awards. Finalist in 1997 British Airways Tourism
Awards. Ideal touring centre. 30 mins from
Belfast.

Manor Guest House, *23 Olderfleet Road,*
Larne, Co Antrim, BT40 1AS. Restored mid-
Victorian house situated two minutes walk from
Larne ferries and train station.
Open: All year (not Xmas/New Year)
028 2827 3305 Miss Graham **Fax: 028 2826 0505**
D: Fr £15.00 **S:** Fr £16.00
Beds: 1F 4D 2T 1S **Baths:** 8 En
🛏 🅿 (8) ⽄ 📺 🐾 🎞 ⚈ cc

Lisburn
J2664

Hillview Farm B&B, *35 Stoneyford Road,*
Lisburn, County Antrim, BT28 3RG. Country
farmhouse; warm, friendly, informal atmosphere.
Good home-cooked food.
Open: All Year
028 9264 8270 (also fax) Mrs Armstrong
geraldine@hillviewfarm.freeserve.co.uk
D: Fr £20.00–£25.00 **S:** Fr £20.00–£25.00
Beds: 2F 1T **Baths:** 2 En 1 Pr
🛏 🅿 (25) 📺 🐾 ✕ 🆅 🎞 ♿ ⚈

Newtownabbey
J3580

Iona, *161 Antrim Road, Newtownabbey, Belfast,*
BT36 7QR. Five minutes from restaurants, lounge,
bars and Ulster Way.
Open: All year (not Xmas)
028 9084 2256 Mrs Kelly
www.jonaguesthouse.co.uk
D: Fr £18.00–£20.00 **S:** Fr £20.00–£36.00
Beds: 1F 1D 2S **Baths:** 2 Sh
🛏 🅿 📺 🎞

J1977

Keef Halla, *20 Tully Road, Nutts Corner, Crumlin, Belfast, BT29 4SW.* Nearest 4 Star Guest House to Belfast International Airport. Rooms elegantly decorated, satellite TV.
Open: All Year
028 9082 5491 Mr & Mrs Kelly **Fax: 028 9082 5490**
info@keefhalla.com
D: Fr £25.00
Beds: 3F 2D 2T **Baths:** 7 En
🛏 (1) 🅿 (12) ⚲ 📺 ✕ 🎬 🛏 🐾 ✳ ♨ cc

C9703

Bannside Farmhouse, *268 Gortgole Road, Portglenone, Ballymena, Co Antrim, BT44 8AT.* Peaceful farmhouse near River Bann, forest park & marina nearby.
Open: All year
028 2582 1262 Misses Lowry
D: Fr £15.00 **S:** Fr £15.00
Beds: 1D 1T 1S **Baths:** 1 Sh
🛏 (3) 🅿 (5) ⚲ 📺 🎬

Sprucebank, *41 Ballymacombs Road, Portglenone, Ballymena, Co Antrim, BT44 8NR.* Relax in the tranquillity of our inviting old farmhouse.
Open: Mar to Oct
028 2582 1422 & 028 2582 2150 Mrs Sibbett **Fax: 028 2582 1422**
portglenone@nacn.org
D: Fr £17.00–£19.00
Beds: 1F 2D 1T **Baths:** 1 En 1 Sh
🛏 (3) 🅿 (6) ⚲ 📺 🐾 🎬 ♨

C8540

Hillrise Dhu Varren, *24 Dhu Varren, Portrush, Co Antrim, BT56 8EN.* Award winning guesthouse offering excellent service. Ideal centre golf & touring.
Open: Easter to Oct
028 7082 2450 Mrs Moore **Fax: 028 7082 2493**
d_moore@lineone.net www.hillrise-portrush.com
D: Fr £22.50–£25.00 **S:** Fr £28.00–£32.00
Beds: 1F 3T 1D **Baths:** 5 En
🛏 (1) 🅿 (6) ⚲ 📺 🎬 ♨ cc

Anvershiel, *16 Coleraine Road, Portrush, Co Antrim, BT56 8EA.*
Open: All year
028 7082 3861 Mrs Allen
enquiries@anvershiel.co.uk
www.anvershiel.co.uk
D: Fr £20.00–£30.00 **S:** Fr £25.00–£35.00
Beds: 3F 3D **Baths:** 6 En
🛏 🅿 (6) ⚲ 📺 🎬 ♨ cc
This delightful accommodation is situated in the beautiful Causeway coast area and is suitable for holidays by the sea or golfing. Anvershiel is situated in a quiet location only 5 mins from town centre and 2 mins from sandy beaches.

Maddybenny Farm House, *Atlantic Road, Portrush, Co Antrim, BT52 2PT.*
Open: All year (not Xmas)
028 7082 3394 & 07714 247560
(M) Mrs White
accommodation@maddybenny22.freeserve.co.uk
www.maddybenny.freeserve.co.uk
D: Fr £25.00 **S:** Fr £30.00
Beds: 2F 1T 1S **Baths:** 4 En
🛏 🅿 📺 ♨
Award-winning B&B and 4 star self catering cottages (6) sleep 6 or 8 persons. Own BHS approved riding centre, convenient to 7 golf course, University, Blue Flag beaches (strands) and Causeway coast. Off A29 2 Km from Portrush.

Abbeydean, *9 Ramore Avenue, Portrush, Co Antrim, BT56 8BB.* Family-run situated in select area. Convenient to all amenities.
Open: All Year (not Xmas)
028 7082 2645 Gary & Anne Boggs
D: Fr £16.00–£20.00 **S:** Fr £16.00–£18.00
Beds: 3F 2D 2T 2S **Baths:** 3 En 3 Pr
🛏 ⚲ 📺 ✕ 🎬 ♨

Arranmore House Lodge, *14 Coleraine Road, Portrush, Co Antrim, BT56 8EA.* Ideal base for golfing or visiting the attractions. Private parking.
Open: All year (not Xmas/New Year)
028 7082 4640 (also fax) Mr and Mrs Duggan
clarmont@talk21.com
D: Fr £20.00–£25.00 **S:** Fr £25.00–£30.00
Beds: 2T 1D **Baths:** 3 En
🅿 (5) ⚲ 📺 🎬 ♨ cc

Glencroft Guest House, *95 Coleraine Road, Portrush, Co Antrim, BT56 8HN*. Private garden. Private parking. Downstairs ensuite rooms. Enjoy Glencroft's special four course breakfast. Menu includes traditional Ulster fry and healthy fruit platter. Near Giant's Causeway, beautiful Blue Flag beaches. Convenient to Royal Portrush Golf Course and five other courses.
Open: All year (not Xmas)
028 7082 2902 Mr & Mrs Henderson
info@glencroft-bb.fsnet.co.uk
www.glencroft-bb.fsnet.co.uk
D: Fr £18.00–£22.50 **S:** Fr £20.00–£30.00
Beds: 2F 2D 2T **Baths:** 3 En 3 Sh
ॐ 🄿 (10) ⌿ 📺 ✕ Ⅴ ▥. ■

Beulah House, *16 Causeway Street, Portrush, Co Antrim, BT56 8AB*. Select accommodation, Good food, Private parking, rail, bus, golf, 5 mins.
Open: All Year (not Xmas)
028 7082 2413 & 028 7082 5900 Mr & Mrs Anderson
D: Fr £16.50–£20.00 **S:** Fr £16.50–£20.00
Beds: 1F 6D 3T 2S **Baths:** 3 En 3 Pr 2 Sh
ॐ 🄿 (10) ⌿ 📺 ✕ Ⅴ ▥. ■ cc

Brookhaven, *99 Coleraine Road, Portrush, Co Antrim, BT56 8HN*. Convenient to Giants Causeway, Royal Portrush Golf Course, Antrim Coast etc.
Open: All year
028 7082 4164 (also fax) D and M Agnew
info@brookhaven.org.uk *www.brookhaven.org.uk*
D: Fr £20.00–£23.00 **S:** Fr £25.00–£30.00
Beds: 1F 2D **Baths:** 3 En
ॐ 🄿 (8) 📺 Ⅴ ▥. ■ cc

Alexandra Guest House, *11 Lansdowne Crescent, Portrush, Co Antrim, BT56 8AY*. A charming period town house overlooking the bay. Ideally situated for exploring Giants Causeway.
Open: Jan to Dec
028 7082 2284 Mr McAlister
D: Fr £22.50
Beds: 3F 5D 2T **Baths:** 5 En 5 Pr 5 Sh
ॐ 🄿 ⌿ 📺 ▥. ■

D1452

Rathlin Guest House, *The Quay, Rathlin Island, Co Antrim, BT54 6RT*. Small family-run business, Northern Ireland's only inhabited island.
Open: Easter to Sep
028 2076 3917 Mr & Mrs McCurdy
D: Fr £16.00–£18.00
Beds: 2F 1D 1S **Baths:** 1 Shared
ॐ 🄿 📺 ✕ Ⅴ ▥. ■

J2486

Templeton Hotel, *882 Antrim Road, Templepatrick, Ballyclare, Co Antrim, BT39 0AH*. Modern rural hotel, 20 minutes from city centre and 10 from international airport.
Open: All Year
028 9443 2984 Mrs Kerr
D: Fr £55.00
Beds: 11D 12T 1S **Baths:** 24 Ensuite
ॐ 🄿 📺 ✕ Ⅴ ▥. ♿ ■

D0243

Whitepark House, *150 Whitepark Road, Whitepark Bay, Ballintoy, Ballycastle, Co Antrim, BT54 6NH*. Unique country house overlooking ocean near Giants Causeway. Warm welcome. Log fire.
Open: All year
028 2073 1482 Mr & Mrs Isles
bob@whiteparkhouse.com *www.whiteparkhouse.com*
D: Fr £27.50 **S:** Fr £30.00
Beds: 1T 2D **Baths:** 3 Sh
ॐ (10) 🄿 (5) Ⅴ ▥. ■ cc

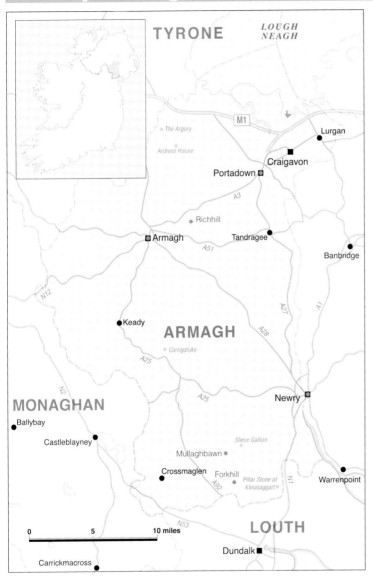

TYRONE

LOUGH NEAGH

M1

The Argory

Ardress House

Lurgan

Craigavon

Portadown

A3

Richhill

Armagh

Tandragee

Banbridge

A51

N12

A27

A1

Keady

ARMAGH

A28

Carrigatuke

A25

A25

Newry

MONAGHAN

N2

A25

Ballybay

Castleblayney

Slieve Gallion

Mullaghbawn

Crossmaglen

Forkhill

Pillar Stone of Kilnasaggart

Warrenpoint

A92

N1

N53

LOUTH

0   5   10 miles

Dundalk

Carrickmacross

RAIL ⇌

In Co Armagh, the main Belfast to Dublin line passes through **Lurgan**, **Portadown** and on towards **Newry**.
Tel. **Northern Ireland Rail** -
028 9089 9411 for timetable information.

BUS 🚌

The main bus links are: **Armagh** to **Belfast** (twice an hour) and **Armagh** to **Dublin** (once daily).

Tel. **Ulsterbus** for these and other destinations - 028 9066 6630.

TOURIST INFORMATION OFFICES 🛈

Old Bank Building, 40 English Street, **Armagh**, County Armagh, BT61 7BA, 028 3752 1800.

Armagh
H8745

Desart, *99 Cathedral Road, Armagh, BT61 8AE.*
Elegant detached family home convenient to Armagh city centre.
Open: All Year (not Xmas/New Year)
028 3752 2387 Mrs McRoberts
D: Fr £15.00–£20.00 **S:** Fr £15.00–£20.00
Beds: 1F 2T 2S **Baths:** 2 En 1 Sh
🛏 🅿 📺 ✕ ▥ ▦ ▪

Forkhill
J0115

Lakeview, *34 Church Road, Forkhill, Newry, Co Down, BT35 9SX.* Spacious modern home, scenic countryside. Forest/mountain rambling, golf, horse riding.
Open: All Year (not Xmas)
028 3088 8382 Mrs O'Neill
D: Fr £18.00–£20.00 **S:** Fr £18.00–£20.00
Beds: 2F **Baths:** 2 En 1 Sh
🛏 (5) 🅿 (8) 📺 ▦ ▪

Mullaghbawn
H9918

Adrigole House, *4 Bun Sleibhe, Mullaghbawn, South Armagh, BT35 0JN.* Situated in village of Mullaghbawn, South Armagh at the foot of Slieve Gullion mountain.
Open: All Year
028 3088 8689 & 07767 447010 (M) E & E Ryan
D: Fr £18.00 **S:** Fr £16.00
Beds: 2F 2S **Baths:** 2 En 1 Pr
🛏 🅿 📺 ♘ ✕ ▥ ▦ ❋ ▪

Portadown
J0053

Bannview Squash Club, *60 Portmore Street, Portadown, Craigavon, Co Armagh, BT62 3NF.* Situated within walking distance of town centre buses and trains.
Open: All Year (not Xmas)
028 3833 6666 (also fax) Mr Black
D: Fr £20.00–£25.00 **S:** Fr £25.00–£30.00
Beds: 20T **Baths:** 20 En
🛏 🅿 (17) 📺 ✕ ▥ ▦ ▪

SURE STAY The Cottage, *17 Gallrock Road, Portadown, Craigavon, Co Armagh, BT62 1NP.* Rural area. Family owned, friendly home cooking. 1 mile from exit 12 M1 motorway.
Open: All year
01762 852189 (also fax)
thecottage@btinternet.com
www.thecottage.btinternet.co.uk
D: Fr £20.00 **S:** Fr £22.00
Beds: 2F 3T 2D 1S **Baths:** 8 En
🛏 🅿 (12) ⊁ 📺 ✕ ▥ ▦ ♿ ❋ ▪

Richhill
H9447

Ballinahinch House, *47 Ballygroobany Road, Richhill, Armagh, BT61 9NA.* Victorian farmhouse, large garden. Ensuite rooms. Discount for extended stay.
Open: Easter to Oct
028 3887 0081 & 07713 085206 (M) Mrs Kee **Fax: 028 3887 0081**
D: Fr £17.00–£20.00 **S:** Fr £15.00
Beds: 3F 1T **Baths:** 3 En
🛏 ⊁ 📺 ✕ ▥ ▦ ▪ cc

County Down

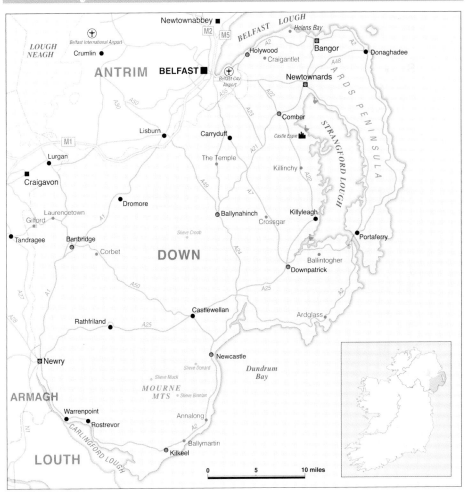

J3618

Heathdene, *76 Mill Road, Annalong, Newry, Co Down, BT34 4RH.* Modern bungalow. Beside famous Silent Valley. Amenities for all ages.
Open: All Year
028 4176 8822 Mrs Chambers
D: Fr £20.00 **S:** Fr £20.00
Beds: 1F 2D 1T **Baths:** 2 En 1 Sh
🛏 (2) 🅿 (3) 📺 🐾 Ⓥ ▥ ৬

The Sycamores, *52 Majors Hill, Annalong, Newry, Co Down, BT34 4QR.* Former farmhouse dating back to C18th. Situated in beautiful countryside with panoramic views.
Open: All year (not Xmas)
028 4376 8279 Mrs McKee
D: Fr £20.00–£22.00 **S:** Fr £25.00–£30.00
Beds: 1F 1D 1T **Baths:** 3 En
🛏 🅿 (6) ⚡ 📺 ▥ ৬ ▄

RAIL ⇌

The major rail service in County Down linked to the national network is the **Bangor** to **Belfast** commuter line running along the southern coast of **Belfast Lough**.
Tel. **Northern Ireland Rail** on 01232 899411 for timetable information.

BUS 🚌

There are good bus links to **Belfast** from all major towns in County Down.
Tel. **Ulsterbus** - 028 9066 6630.

TOURIST INFORMATION OFFICES 𝒊

Newry Road, **Banbridge**, County Down, BT32 3NB, 028 4062 3322.

34 Quay Street, **Bangor**, County Down, BT20 5ED, 028 9127 0069.

74 Market Street, **Downpatrick**, County Down, BT30 6LZ, 028 4461 2233.

The Square, **Hillsborough**, County Down, BT26 6AH, 028 9268 9717.

28 Bridge Street, Kilkeel, **Newry**, County Down, BT34 4AD, 028 4176 2525.

The Newcastle Centre, 10-14 Central Promenade, **Newcastle**, County Down, BT33 0AA, 028 4372 2222 (Easter to Oct).

Arts Centre, Bank Parade, **Newry**, County Down, BT35 6HP, 028 3026 8877.

31 Regent Street, **Newtownards**, County Down, BT23 4AD, 028 9182 6846.

The Stables, Castle Street, **Portaferry**, County Down, BT22 INZ, 028 4272 9882.

BATHROOMS

En = Ensuite

Pr = Private

Sh = Shared

Fair Haven, *16 Moneydarragh Road, Annalong, Newry, Co Down, BT34 4TY.* Modern bungalow in 'The kingdom of Mourne'. Peaceful area.
Open: All Year (not Xmas)
028 4376 8153 Mrs Jardine
D: Fr £17.00–£18.00 **S:** Fr £18.00–£22.00
Beds: 1F 1D 1T **Baths:** 2 En 1 Sh
🛏 🅿 ✂ 📺 🛏 Ⅴ Ⅲ, ♿

Ardglass
J5637

Strand Farm, *231 Ardglass Road, Ardglass, Downpatrick, Co Down, BT30 7UL.* Secluded farmhouse in peaceful surroundings. Warm welcome, refreshments on arrival.
Open: Mar to Oct
028 4484 1446 Mrs Donnan
D: Fr £16.50 **S:** Fr £18.00
Beds: 1F 1D 1T **Baths:** 1 En 1 Sh 1 Pr
🛏 🅿 (12) 📺 Ⅲ,

Ballintogher
J5147

Hillcrest, *157 Strangford Road, Ballintogher, Downpatrick, Co Down, BT30 7JZ.* Family-run farmhouse in the heart of Down.
Open: All Year (not Xmas)
028 4461 2583 Mrs Fitzsimons
D: Fr £20.00
Beds: 2D 1T **Baths:** 1 Ensuite 1 Shared
🛏 🅿 (6) 📺 🛏 ✗ Ⅲ,

Ballymartin
J3416

Wyncrest, *30 Main Road , Ballymartin, Kilkeel, Newry, Co Down, BT34 4NU.* Renowned for hospitality. Winner of All Ireland Breakfast Award.
Open: Easter to Nov
028 4176 3012 & 028 4176 5988 Mrs Adair **Fax: 028 4176 5988**
lorraine@kilkeel33.fsnet.co.uk
D: Fr £22.50 **S:** Fr £30.00
Beds: 1F 2D 2T 1S **Baths:** 4 En 1 Sh
🛏 🅿 (8) ✂ 📺 Ⅴ Ⅲ, ▪ cc

Planning a longer stay?
Always ask for any special rates

Please respect a B&B's wishes regarding children, animals and smoking

Ballynahinch

J3652

Bushymead Country House, 86 Drumaness Road, Ballynahinch, Co Down, BT24 8LT. Select accommodation in centre of historic County Down/main A24 road.
Open: All Year
028 9756 1171 (also fax) Mrs Murphy
bushmead@nireland.com
www.stayhereuk.com/wp/20789/index.html
D: Fr £16.00–£20.00 **S:** Fr £18.00–£25.00
Beds: 3F 1D 4T 2S **Baths:** 7 En 3 Sh
🛏 🅿 (32) ⅙ 📺 ⟟ ✕ Ⓥ ▥ ⚫ cc

Cornerhouse, 182 Dunmore Road, Ballynahinch, Co Down, BT24 8QQ. On a working farm, 4m Tropical Butterfly House, 9m Newcastle. Forest, parks, fishing.
Open: All year
028 9756 2670 Mrs Rogan
D: Fr £20.00 **S:** Fr £20.00
Beds: 4F **Baths:** 4 En
🛏 🅿 (10) 📺 ⟟ ✕ Ⓥ ▥ க ⚫

Number Thirty, 30 Mountview Road, Ballynahinch, Co Down, BT24 8JR. Modern chalet-bungalow in quiet country area overlooking Mourne Mountains.
Open: All Year (not Xmas)
028 9756 2956 Mrs Reid
D: Fr £18.00
Beds: 1F 1T 1D **Baths:** 1 Ensuite 1 Private 1 Shared
🛏 🅿 ⅙ 📺 ✕ ▥ க

Banbridge

J1245

Downshire Arms Hotel, 95 Newry Street, Banbridge, Co Down, BT32 3EF. Old coaching inn previously owned by Lord Downshire. Built in 1816. Listed building.
Open: All Year
028 4066 2638 Mr Heslip **Fax: 028 4062 6811**
D: Fr £32.50
Beds: 2F 1D 3T 3S **Baths:** 6 Ensuite 3 Shared
🛏 🅿 📺 ✕ Ⓥ ▥ ⚫

Bangor

J5081

Asda-Kern Bed & Breakfast, 18 Prospect Road, Bangor, Co Down, BT20 5DA. 4 mins from park, marina, shops, restaurants, train, bus stations.
Open: Easter to Oct
028 9146 1309 Mrs Graham
suangraham@nireland.com
www.asdakeran.20megsfree.com
D: Fr £18.00 **S:** Fr £18.00
Beds: 1F 1D 1S **Baths:** 1 Sh
🛏 (4) 🅿 (1) 📺 ✕ ▥ ⚫

Tara, 51 Princetown Road, Bangor, Co Down, BT20 3TA. In quiet area close to all amenities. All rooms ensuite, comfortably furnished.
Open: All Year (not Xmas)
028 9146 8924 Mr Spence **Fax: 028 9146 9870**
D: Fr £23.00 **S:** Fr £30.00
Beds: 3F 4D 1S
🛏 🅿 📺 ⟟ ✕ Ⓥ ▥ ⚫ cc

Bramble Lodge, 1 Bryansburn Road, Bangor, Co Down, BT20 3RY. Family-run guest house. Central location, comfort and a warm welcome assured.
Open: All Year (not Xmas)
028 9145 7924 Mrs Hanna
D: Fr £22.00
Beds: 1D 2T **Baths:** 3 Ensuite
🛏 (3) 🅿 (3) 📺 Ⓥ ▥ ⚫

Glendale House, 77 Southwell Road, Bangor, Co Down, BT20 3AE. Family-run guest house close to all amenities and marina.
Open: All Year (not Xmas)
028 9146 8613 Mrs Blachford
blachford@glendale77.freeserve.co.uk
www.glendale77.freeserve.co.uk
D: Fr £15.00 **S:** Fr £15.00
Beds: 1F 1D 1T **Baths:** 1 Sh
🛏 📺 ✕ Ⓥ ▥ ⚫

Comber

J4568

Old School House Inn, Castle Espie, 100 Ballydrain Road, Comber, Newtownards, Co Down, BT23 6EA. Enjoy Avril's cuisine grandmere in the Old Schoolhouse Inn. Also 12 presidential suites.
Open: All Year (not Xmas)
028 9754 1182 Mr & Mrs Brown **Fax: 028 9754 2583**
D: Fr £32.50
Beds: 6T 3D **Baths:** 9 Ensuite
🛏 🅿 ⅙ 📺 ✕ Ⓥ ▥ க ⚫

Corbet

J1644

Heathmar, *37 Corbet Road, Corbet, Banbridge, Co Down, BT32 3SH.* Comfortable beds, good food, friendly hospitality, convenient to all attractions.
Open: All Year (not Xmas)
028 4062 2348 Mrs Fleming
D: Fr £18.00
Beds: 2F 1T **Baths:** 2 Ensuite 1 Private
⌂ 🅿 (10) 📺 🏋 Ⓥ 🖳 ▪

Craigantlet

J4577

Beech Hill, *23 Ballymoney Road, Craigantlet, Newtownards, Co Down, BT23 4TG.* Country house in peaceful Hollywood Hills, 15 minutes from Belfast.
Open: All year **Grades:** AA 5 Diamond
028 9042 5892 (also fax) Mrs Brann
info@beech-hill.net www.beech-hill.net
D: Fr £30.00 **S:** Fr £40.00
Beds: 1T 2D **Baths:** 3 En
🅿 ⅍ 📺 🏋 Ⓥ 🖳 ▪ cc

Crossgar

J4552

Hillhouse, *53 Killyleagh Road, Crossgar, Downpatrick, Co Down, BT30 9LB.* Secluded Licensed Georgian guest house (Listed). Spacious accommodation. Belfast 12 miles.
Open: All Year (not Xmas)
028 4483 0792 Mrs Davison **Fax: 028 4483 0740**
D: Fr £25.00
Beds: 3F 23D 1T 44S **Baths:** 10 Ensuite 62 Private 34 Shared
⌂ (11) 🅿 (20) 📺 Ⓥ 🖳 ▪

Downpatrick

J4844

Pheasants' Hill Country House, *37 Killyleagh Road, Downpatrick, Co Down, BT30 9BL.* 1999 winner AA Best British Breakfast of the Year - Ireland.
Open: All Year
028 4461 7246 (also fax) Ms Bailey
pheasants.hill@dnet.co.uk
D: Fr £27.00
Beds: 2D 1T **Baths:** 2 En 1 Pr
⌂ 🅿 (10) ⅍ 📺 🏋 ✕ Ⓥ 🖳 ▪ cc

Gilford

J0648

Mount Pleasant, *38 Banbridge Road, Gilford, Craigavon, Co Armagh, BT63 6DJ.* Beautiful Georgian house in spacious grounds. Experience our special generous breakfast.
Open: All Year
028 3883 1522 (also fax) Mrs Buller
D: Fr £13.00–£15.00 **S:** Fr £15.00–£18.00
Beds: 1F 1D 1T 1S **Baths:** 2 Sh
⌂ 🅿 ⅍ 📺 🏋 🖳 ▪

Helens Bay

J4582

Carrig Gorm, *27 Bridge Road, Helens Bay, Bangor, Co Down, BT19 1TS.* Part Victorian and part C18th house, set in secluded gardens. Folk & Transport Museum nearby.
Open: All year (not Xmas/New Year)
028 9185 3680 (also fax) Mrs Eves
elizabeth@eeves.fsnet.co.uk
D: Fr £25.00–£30.00 **S:** Fr £30.00–£35.00
Beds: 1F 1T 1S **Baths:** 1 En 1 Sh
⌂ (1) 🅿 ⅍ 📺 Ⓥ 🖳 ▪

Holywood

J4078

Beech Hill, *23 Ballymoney Road, Craigantlet, Newtownards, Co Down, BT23 4TG.* Country house in peaceful Hollywood Hills, 15 minutes from Belfast.
Open: All year **Grades:** AA 5 Diamond
028 9042 5892 (also fax) Mrs Brann
info@beech-hill.net www.beech-hill.net
D: Fr £30.00 **S:** Fr £40.00
Beds: 1T 2D **Baths:** 3 En
🅿 ⅍ 📺 🏋 Ⓥ 🖳 ▪ cc

Kilkeel

J3014

Morne Abbey, *16 Greencastle Road, Kilkeel, Newry, Co Down, BT34 4DE.* The panoramic view of the Mourne Mountains is breathtaking.
Open: Easter to Oct
028 4176 2426 (also fax) Mrs Shannon
D: Fr £19.00–£19.50
Beds: 1F 1D 2T 1S **Baths:** 3 En 2 Sh
🅿 (10) ⅍ 📺 🖳

Kilmorey Arms Hotel, *41 Greencastle Street, Kilkeel, Newry, Co Down, BT34 4BH.* Long established hotel in centre of Kilkeel. Good food and accommodation.
Open: All Year
028 4176 2220 Giffen Family **Fax: 028 4176 5399**
D: Fr £23.50–£25.00
Beds: 1F 11D 10T 5S **Baths:** 27 Ensuite
⛇ �ᛈ (30) 🖵 ✕ 🛏 ᕼ ▪

Heath Hall, *160 Moyadd Road, Kilkeel, Newry, Co Down, BT34 4HJ.* Farmhouse overlooking Irish Sea with panoramic mountain view.
Open: All year
028 4176 2612 Mrs McGlue **Fax: 028 4176 4032**
D: Fr £17.00–£18.00 **S:** Fr £18.00–£20.00
Beds: 1F 1T 1D **Baths:** 1 En 1 Pr 1 Sh
⛇ ᛈ (10) ⚲ 🖵 ✕ 🆅 🛏 ▪

Killinchy
J5159

Barnageeha, *90 Ardmillan Road, Killinchy, Killinchy, Newtownards, Co Down, BT23 6QN.* Internationally important bird site, superb scenery.
Open: All Year
028 9754 1011 Mr & Mrs Crawford
D: Fr £25.00
Beds: 3T 1S **Baths:** 3 Ensuite
⛇ ᛈ (30) 🖵 ᕼ ✕ 🆅 🛏 ᕼ

Laurencetown
J1049

Mourneview, *32 Drumnascamph Road, Laurencetown, Gilford, Craigavon, Co Armagh, BT63 6DU.* Great place to see a lovely country.
Open: All Year (not Xmas)
028 4062 6270 & 028 4062 4251 Mrs Kerr **Fax: 028 4062 4251**
D: Fr £18.00
Beds: 1T 3D **Baths:** 4 Ensuite
⛇ ᛈ ⚲ 🖵 🛏 ᕼ ▪

All details shown are as supplied by B&B owners in Autumn 2002

Newcastle
J3731 ◀ *Burrendale Hotel, Briers', Harbour Inn, Mario's*

Beach House, *22 Downs Road, Newcastle, Co Down, BT33 0AG.* Sea front location. Convenient to RCD Golf Course and Slieve Donard Hotel.
Open: All Year (not Xmas/New Year)
028 4372 2345 Mrs Macauley **Fax: 028 4372 2817**
D: Fr £25.00–£27.50 **S:** Fr £25.00–£30.00
Beds: 2F 1D **Baths:** 2 En 1 Sh
ᛈ (2) ⚲ 🖵 🆅 🛏 ▪ **cc**

Grasmere, *16 Marguerite Park, Newcastle, Co Down, BT33 0PE.* Modern bungalow in quiet residential area. 10 minutes' walk to beach.
Open: All Year
028 4372 6801 Mrs McCormick
D: Fr £18.00–£20.00 **S:** Fr £22.50–£25.00
Beds: 1F 2D **Baths:** 1 Pr 1 Sh
⛇ ᛈ (2) ⚲ 🖵 ᕼ 🆅 🛏 ✳ ▪

Beverley, *72 Tollymore Road, Newcastle, Co.Down, BT33 0JN.* Self contained flatlet, panoramic view of Mourne Mountains, rural aspect.
Open: All year (not Xmas)
028 4372 2018 (also fax) Mrs McNeilly
tollymore@supanet.co
D: Fr £17.50 **S:** Fr £20.00
Beds: 1T **Baths:** 1 En
⛇ ᛈ (2) 🖵 ᕼ ✕ 🆅 🛏 ᕼ ▪ **cc**

Newry
J0826

Marymount, *Windsor Avenue, Newry, Co Down, BT34 1EG.* Bungalow with beautiful gardens, quiet location, walking distance town centre.
Open: All Year (not Xmas/New Year)
028 3026 1099 Mr & Mrs O'Hare
D: Fr £17.00–£19.00 **S:** Fr £22.00–£24.00
Beds: 3T **Baths:** 1 En 1 Sh
ᛈ ⚲ 🖵 🛏 ▪

Newtownards
J4874

Ard Cuan, *3 Manse Road, Newtownards, Co Down, BT23 4TP.* Victorian family home in acre of garden. Friendly informal welcome.
Open: All Year (not Xmas)
028 9181 1302 Mrs Kerr
D: Fr £22.00
Beds: 1F1D 1T **Baths:** 2 Shared
ᛈ 🖵 🛏 ▪

Edenvale, *130 Portaferry Road, Newtownards,*
Co Down, BT22 2AJ. Beautifully restored Georgian
farmhouse 2 miles from Newtownards in
secluded gardens.
Open: All Year (not Xmas/New Year)
028 9181 4881 Mrs Whyte **Fax: 028 9182 6192**
edenvalehouse@hotmail.com edenvalehouse.com
D: Fr £27.50 **S:** Fr £35.00
Beds: 1F 1D 1T **Baths:** 3 En
ﺡ ⊟ (6) ⌇ ▣ ↟ ▣ ▥ ▪ cc

Rostrevor
J1718

Fir Trees, *16 Killowen Old Road, Rostrevor,*
Newry, Co Down, BT34 3AD. Overlooking
Carlingford Lough. Forest walks from premises.
Open: All Year
028 4173 8602 Mr & Mrs Donnan
106666.3465@compuserve.com
D: Fr £23.00
Beds: 2D 1T **Baths:** 1 Ensuite 1 Shared
ﺡ ⊟ (4) ⌇ ▣ ↟ ▣ ▥ ▪

The Temple
J3660

Green Acres, *115a Carryduff Road , The Temple*
Lisburn, Co Antrim, BT27 6YL. Elegant bungalow
situated in an acre of beautiful gardens.
Open: All Year
028 9263 8631 Mr & Mrs Reid
D: Fr £20.00
Beds: 1F 1D 1T 1S **Baths:** 2 Ensuite 2 Private 1
Shared
ﺡ ⊟ (20) ▣ ↟ ▣ ▥ ✳ ▪

BATHROOMS

En = Ensuite

Pr = Private

Sh = Shared

STILWELL'S IRELAND: BED & BREAKFAST

BUS 🚌

Enniskillen to **Belfast** (6 a day) and
Enniskillen to **Dublin** (5 a day).
Tel. **Ulsterbus** - 028 9066 6630.

TOURIST INFORMATION
OFFICES ℹ️

Wellington Road, **Enniskillen**, County
Fermanagh, BT74 7EF, 028 6632 3110.

Belcoo

H0838

Corralea Forest Lodge, *Corralea, Belcoo,
Enniskillen, Co Fermanagh, BT93 5DZ.* Lakeside
purpose built guest house on lake shore in 34
acres.
Open: Easter to October
028 6638 6325 Mr & Mrs Catterall
D: Fr £21.00 **S:** Fr £21.00
Beds: 1D 3T **Baths:** 4 En
🛏️ 🅿️ 📺 ✕ 🏠 🍴

Brookeborough

H3840

Norfolk House, *Killykeeran, Brookeborough, Enniskillen, Co Fermanagh, BT94 4AQ.* Beautiful comfy house in peaceful countryside, guest rooms overlook garden.
Open: All Year
013655 31681 Mrs Norton
D: Fr £16.00–£20.00
Beds: 1F 1D 1T 1S **Baths:** 2 Ensuite 1 Shared
⏚ ▣ ⌇ ▥ ✕ Ⅴ ▥. ▪

Carrybridge

H2937

Aghnacarra House,
Carrybridge, Lisbellaw, Enniskillen, Co Fermanagh, BT94 5HX.
Open: Easter to Oct
Grades: AA 3 Diamond
028 6638 7077 Mrs Ensor **Fax: 028 6638 5811**
normaensor@talk21.com
D: Fr £19.00–£20.00 **S:** Fr £24.00–£25.00
Beds: 4F 2D 1T **Baths:** 7 En
▣ (8) ▥ ✕ ▥. ▪
Modern purpose-built, licensed, guesthouse. Picturesque setting 2.75 acres with small lake.

Derrygonnelly

H1252

Meadow View, *Sandhill, Derrygonnelly, Enniskillen, Co Fermanagh, BT93 6ER.* Modern, comfortable house. Peaceful setting.
Open: Easter to Sep
028 6864 1233 Mrs Wray
D: Fr £14.50–£16.50
Beds: 1F 2D **Baths:** 2 Ensuite 1 Shared
⏚ ▣ (6) ▥ ✕ Ⅴ ▥. ▪

Drumcrow

H1255

Bayview Guest House, *Tully, Church Hill, Derrygonnelly, Enniskillen, Co Fermanagh, BT93 6HP.* Farm guest house, friendly atmosphere. Overlooking Tully Bay, Lower Lough Erne.
Open: All year (not Xmas) **Grades:** NITB 2 Star
028 6864 1250 Mrs Hassard
dorothy.hassard@lineone.net
D: Fr £18.00–£20.00 **S:** Fr £23.00–£25.00
Beds: 4F 1T 1D 2S **Baths:** 2 En
▣ (6) ⌇ ▥ ☓ ✕ Ⅴ ▥. ▪ cc

Enniskillen

H2344

Willowbank, *Bellview Road, Dolan's Ring, Enniskillen, Co Fermanagh, BT74 4JH.*
Open: All year (not Xmas/New Year)
028 6632 8582 (also fax)
joan@willowbankhouse.com
www.willowbankhouse.com
D: Fr £20.00–£22.50 **S:** Fr £22.50–£27.50
Beds: 2F 2T 1D **Baths:** 5 En
⏚ ▣ (7) ⌇ ▥ ✕ Ⅴ ▥. ▪ cc
Located approx 3 miles from historic island town of Enniskillen. Purpose built on an elevated site overlooking the shores of Lough Erne. Centrally located for outdoor pursuits, sports, local attractions. NT properties. Marble Arch caves, Belleek Pottery, Ulster American Folk Park.

Mountview Guest House, *61 Irvinestown Road, Enniskillen, Co Fermanagh, BT74 6DN.* Victorian house, large ensuite. Half mile to town, Sky TV, snooker room.
Open: All year (not Xmas/New Year)
Grades: NITB 2 Star
028 6632 3147 Fax: 028 6632 9611
wendy@mountviewguests.com
www.mountviewguests.com
D: Fr £22.50 **S:** Fr £33.00–£34.00
Beds: 1F 1T 1D **Baths:** 3 En
⌇ ▥ ▥. ▪ cc

Drumcoo House, *32 Cherryville, Cornagrade Road, Enniskillen, Co Fermanagh, BT74 4FY.* Central lakeland base for fishing, walking, water sports, touring.
Open: All year (not Xmas/New Year)
028 6632 6672 (also fax) Mrs Farrell
farrellhj@btopenworld.com
D: Fr £20.00–£22.00 **S:** Fr £26.00–£28.00
Beds: 1F 1T 1D 1S **Baths:** 3 En 1 Sh
⏚ ▣ (10) ▥ Ⅴ ▥. ▪ cc

Abbeyville, *1 Willoughby Court, Portora, Enniskillen, Co Fermanagh, BT74 7EX.* Modern B&B, convenient to National Trust properties, leisure facilities and Marble Arch Caves.
Open: All Year (not Xmas)
028 6632 7033 Mrs McMahon
D: Fr £18.00–£22.00
Beds: 2T 1D **Baths:** 3 En
⏚ ▣ (6) ⌇ ▥ Ⅴ ▥. ▪

Belmore Court Motel, *Tempo Road, Enniskillen, Co Fermanagh, BT74 6HX.* Situated in the heart of the beautiful Fermanagh Lakelands.
Open: All Year (not Xmas)
028 6632 6633 Mr McCartney **Fax: 028 6632 6362**
book@motel.co.uk www.motel.co.uk
D: Fr £22.50–£27.50
Beds: 11F 13D 6T **Baths:** 30 En
⌂ P (30) 📺 🐾 🛏 ⑁ ■ cc

Florencecourt

H1734

Tullyhona House, *59 Marble Arch Road, Florencecourt, Enniskillen, Co Fermanagh, BT92 1DE.* Winner of 14 awards, Taste of Ulster Restaurant. Central for touring Ireland.
Open: All Year
028 6634 8452 Mr & Mrs Armstrong
tullyguest60@hotmail.com www.archhouse.com
D: Fr £19.00–£21.00 **S:** Fr £20.00–£25.00
Beds: 2F 2D 2T **Baths:** 2 En 2 Pr 2 Sh
⌂ P ✂ 📺 🐾 ✕ Ⓥ 🛏 ✱ ■ cc

Kesh

H1863

Muckross Lodge, *Muckross Quay, Kesh, Enniskillen, Co Fermanagh, BT93 1TZ.* Situated overlooking lake, beaches, public jetty at end of driveway.
Open: All Year
028 6863 1887 & 028 6863 1719 Mrs Anderson
muckross@lineone.net
D: Fr £16.00–£19.00 **S:** Fr £16.00–£19.00
Beds: 1F 1T 1D **Baths:** 3 En
⌂ P ✂ 📺 🐾 Ⓥ 🛏 ■

Letterbreen

H1840

Abocurragh Farmhouse, *Abocurragh, Letterbreen, Enniskillen, Co Fermanagh, BT94 9AG.* Farm guest house in picturesque setting.
Open: All Year
028 6634 8484 Mrs Mullally
D: Fr £22.50
Beds: 2F 1D **Baths:** 4 Ensuite
⌂ P ✂ 📺 ✕ Ⓥ 🛏 ■

Lisbellaw

H3041

Tatnamallaght House, *39 Farnamullan Road, Tatnamallaght, Lisbellaw, Enniskillen, Co Fermanagh, BT94 5DY.* Tat-na-Mallaght farm and guest house is situated in the heart of Fermagh Lakeland.
Open: All Year (not Xmas)
028 6638 7174 Mrs Dunlop
D: Fr £17.00–£19.00
Beds: 1F 1T 2D **Baths:** 2 Ensuite 1 Shared
✂ 📺 ✕ 🛏 ■

Maguiresbridge

H3438

Derryvree House, *200 Belfast Road, Maguiresbridge, Enniskillen, Co Fermanagh, BT94 4LD.* Comfortable farmhouse convenient to Upper and Lower Erne.
Open: All Year
028 8953 1251 Mr & Mrs Bothwell
D: Fr £18.00
Beds: 1F 1D 1T **Baths:** 1 Ensuite 1 Shared
⌂ P ✂ 📺 🐾 ✕ Ⓥ 🛏 ■

Tamlaght

H2741

Dromard House, *Tamlaght, Enniskillen, Co Fermanagh, BT74 4HR.*
Open: All year (not Xmas)
028 6638 7250 Mrs Weir
dromardhouse@yahoo.co.uk www.dromardhouse.com
D: Fr £20.00 **S:** Fr £25.00
Beds: 1F 2D 1T **Baths:** 4 En
⌂ P (4) ✂ 📺 🐾 🛏 ■
Beautifully situated on a hilltop, among mature woodland, 2 miles outside Enniskillen. Pretty, ensuite bedrooms, and attractive dining room overlooking the garden. There is a warm, relaxed atmosphere, and you can take the path through our woods, right to the lake.

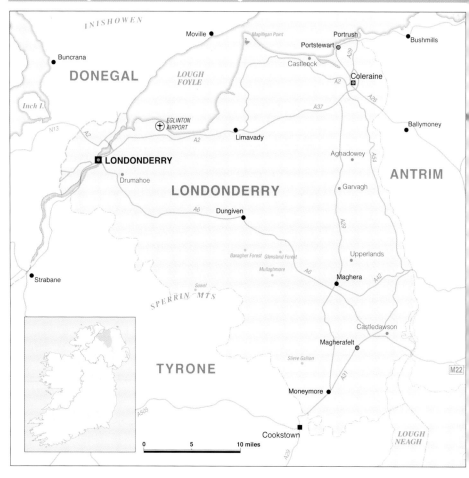

C8520

Greenhill House, *24 Greenhill Road, Aghadowey, Coleraine, Co Londonderry, BT51 4EU.* Award winning Georgian house. Base for touring, golfing, fishing.
Open: Mar to Oct
028 7086 8241 Mrs Hegarty **Fax: 028 7086 8365**
greenhill.house@btinternet.com
www.greenhill.house.btinternet.co.uk
D: Fr £25.00 **S:** Fr £30.00
Beds: 2F 2D 2T **Baths:** 6 En
ॐ ₽ (10) ⊁ ⚏ ✕ ▥ ▪ cc

C6221

Drummond Hotel, *481 Clooney Road, Ballykelly, Co Londonderry, BT49 9HP.* Family-run hotel, excellent cuisine, friendly atmosphere.
Open: All Year
028 7772 2121 Mr Peoples **Fax: 028 7772 2031**
D: Fr £30.00–£32.50
Beds: 3F 24D 15T **Baths:** 42 En
ॐ ₽ ⊁ ⚏ ⻏ ✕ Ⅴ ▥ ㊎ ✳ ▪

AIRPORTS ⊕
Eglinton Airport, tel. 028 7181 0784.

AIR SERVICES & AIRLINES ✈
Londonderry to **Glasgow, Manchester**.
British Airways Express. From the
Republic, tel. (freefone) 1800 626747.
In Northern Ireland & the UK, tel. (local rate) 08705 511155.
Also **British European** fly to many other UK mainland air-
ports, flying from **Londonderry** via **Belfast**,
tel. 08705 676676.

RAIL ⇌
Londonderry is at the end of the main line that leads to
Belfast, via **Coleraine, Ballymoney, Ballymena and Antrim**.
Change at **Antrim** for **Belfast International Airport**.
Tel. **Northern Ireland Rail** on 028 9089 9411 for timetable
information.

BUS ⊞
Ulsterbus run services from **Londonderry** to most large
towns
in Northern Ireland, tel 028 9066 6630.

TOURIST INFORMATION OFFICES 🛈
Railway Road, **Coleraine**, County Londonderry, BT52 1PE,
028 7034 4723.
Council Offices, 7 Connell Street, **Limavady**, County
Londonderry, BT49 0HA, 028 7776 0307.
44 Foyle Road, **Londonderry**, BT48 6PW, 028 7126 7284.

Castledawson
H9292

99 Old Town Road, Castledawson,
Magherafelt, Co Londonderry, BT45 8BZ. Modern
bungalow in rural setting. Friendly atmosphere,
good home cooking.
Open: All Year
028 7946 8741 (also fax) Mr & Mrs Buchanan
D: Fr £18.00 **S:** Fr £20.00
Beds: 1T 2D **Baths:** 1 Sh
⛺ ▣ ⌿ ⊡ ✕ Ⅷ ♿

Castlerock
C7736

Carneety House, 120 Mussenden Road,
Castlerock, Coleraine, Co Londonderry, BT51 4TX.
300-year-old farmhouse in beautiful countryside
by the sea.
Open: All Year (not Xmas)
028 7084 8640 Mrs Henry
D: Fr £16.00–£18.00 **S:** Fr £20.00
Beds: 2D 1T **Baths:** 1 Pr 1 Sh
⛺ (5) ▣ (4) ⌿ ⊡ ⌁ Ⅷ ♨

Coleraine
C8532

Coolbeg, *2e Grange Road,
Coleraine, Co Londonderry,
BT52 1NG.*
Open: All year (not Xmas)
028 7034 4961 Mrs Chandler
Fax: 028 7034 3278
dorothy@coolbeg.totalserve.co.uk
www.coolbeg.totalserve.co.uk
D: Fr £20.00–£22.00 **S:** Fr £25.00
Beds: 1F 3T 1S **Baths:** 4 En 1 Pr
⛺ (4) ▣ (5) ⌿ ⊡ Ⅷ ♿ ♨ cc
Modern bungalow set in pleasant gardens on
edge of town. TV and tea/coffee facilities. 2
ensuite bedrooms fully wheelchair accessible.
Ideal for touring North Antrim coast. Royal
Portrush and 4 other golf courses, fishing and
riding nearby.

Heathfield House, 31 Drumcroon Road,
Coleraine, Co Londonderry, BT51 4EB. Agri-Tourism
Award winner. Old world farmhouse. Convenient
to Giants Causeway on A29.
Open: All Year
028 2955 8245 (also fax) Mrs Torrens
D: Fr £23.00
Beds: 1D 2T **Baths:** 3 Ensuite
⛺ ▣ ⊡ ⌁ ✕ Ⅵ Ⅷ ♨

Clanwilliam Lodge, 21 Curragh Road,
Coleraine, Co Londonderry, BT51 3RY. Elegant
country home with stabling, riverside and forest
walks.
Open: All Year (not Xmas)
028 7035 6582 (also fax) Mrs McWilliam
clanwilliam21@hotmail.com
D: Fr £20.00–£22.50
Beds: 1F 1D 1T **Baths:** 3 En
⛺ ▣ (8) ⌿ ⊡ Ⅵ Ⅷ ♨ cc

Drumahoe
C4714

Killennan House, *40
Killennan Road, Drumahoe,
Londonderry, BT47 3NG.*
Beautiful country house, 10
mins from Derry, airport
nearby, welcoming atmosphere.
Open: All year (not Xmas/New Year)
Grades: NITB Approv
028 7130 1710 (also fax) Mrs Campbell
averil@killennan.co.uk www.killennan.co.uk
D: Fr £20.00 **S:** Fr £23.00
Beds: 1T 2D **Baths:** 3 En 1 Pr

Dungiven

C6809

Bradagh, *132 Main Street, Dungiven, Londonderry, Co Londonderry, BT47 4LG.* Detached town house, central location for touring, fishing, golf, walking.
Open: All Year (not Xmas)
028 7774 1346 (also fax) Mrs McMackens
D: Fr £14.00 **S:** Fr £14.00
Beds: 1F 1T 1S **Baths:** 2 Sh
☺ ▣ (3) 📺 🕭 🎟. ☕

Garvagh

C8315

Fairview, *53 Grove Road, Garvagh, Coleraine, Co Londonderry, BT51 5NY.* Farmhouse setting in quiet countryside with excellent view and parking.
Open: All year (not Xmas/New Year)
028 2955 8240 Mr & Mrs Stewart
D: Fr £14.00 **S:** Fr £18.00
Beds: 1F 1T **Baths:** 1 En 1 Pr
☺ ▣ ⅍ 📺 ✕ 🚻 🎟. ☕

Imperial Hotel, *38 Main Street, Garvagh, Coleraine, Co Londonderry, BT51 5AD.* Quiet family hotel 15 miles from Causeway Coast, ideal base touring, golfing, fishing, walking.
Open: All Year
028 2955 8218 & 028 2955 8643 Mr Mullan **Fax: 028 2955 7078**
D: Fr £25.00
Beds: 2F 5D 2T **Baths:** 8 Ensuite 1 Shared
☺ 📺 🕭 ✕ 🚻 🎟. ☕

Londonderry

C4316

Banks of the Faughan Motel, *69 Clooney Road, Londonderry, BT47 3PA.* Modern motel. Ideal base for touring Derry, Donegal, North Antrim.
Open: All Year
028 7186 0242 (also fax) Mrs Gourley
D: Fr £17.00–£19.00
Beds: 1F 5D 4T 2S **Baths:** 7 En 2 Sh
☺ ▣ (25) ⅍ 📺 🎟. ☕ cc

Braehead House, *22 Braehead Road, Londonderry, BT48 9XE.* Georgian farmhouse, spacious gardens, panoramic view. Five minutes to city centre.
Open: March to Nov
028 7126 3195 Mrs McKean
D: Fr £18.00–£20.00 **S:** Fr £16.00–£18.00
Beds: 1F 1T 1S **Baths:** 1 Sh
▣ ⅍ 📺 🕭 🎟. ☕

Groarty House, *62 Groarty Road, Londonderry, BT48 0JY.* Beautiful views overlooking Lough Foyle and city, in peaceful countryside.
Open: All Year
028 7126 1403 (also fax) Mrs Hyndman
groaty@btinternet.com
www.bandbnorthernireland.com
D: Fr £15.00–£17.50 **S:** Fr £17.50–£22.50
Beds: 1F 1D 1T **Baths:** 2 En 1 Pr
☺ ▣ (10) ⅍ 🎟. ☕ cc

Portstewart

C8137

Lis-Na-Rain, *6 Victoria Terrace, Portstewart, Co Londonderry, BT55 7BA.* Warm welcome guaranteed, incorporating licensed Ecosse Restaurant, with excellent sea view.
Open: All Year (not Xmas)
028 7083 3522 Miss Gardiner
D: Fr £18.00–£22.00 **S:** Fr £16.00
Beds: 1F 2D 3T 1S **Baths:** 5 En 2 Sh
☺ ⅍ 📺 ✕ 🎟 🎟. ☕ cc

Upperlands

C8704

Sperrin-View, *110a Drumbolg Road, Upperlands, Maghera, Co Londonderry, BT46 5UX.* Modern comfortable farmhouse in tranquil countryside.
Open: All Year (not Xmas)
028 2582 2374 (also fax) Mrs Crockett
sperinview@aol.com
D: Fr £19.00
Beds: 2F 1S **Baths:** 1 Shared
☺ ▣ (6) ⅍ 📺 🕭 ✕ 🎟 🎟. & ☕

C3800

Ballantines, *38 Leckpatrick Road, Artigarvan, Strabane, Co Tyrone, BT82 0HB.* Comfortable country home. Visitors' lounge/conservatory. Panoramic views, spacious garden.
Open: All Year (not Xmas)
028 7188 2714 Mrs Ballentine **Fax: 028 7138 2966**
D: Fr £15.00
Beds: 2D 1T 1S **Baths:** 1 Private 1 Shared
🛏 🅿 (20) ⅍ 📺 🖙 ✗ Ⅴ 🛋 ▪

H6256

The Grange, *15 Grange Road, Ballygawley, Dungannon, Co Tyrone, BT70 2HD.* Lovely old house, home cooking.
Open: All Year (not Xmas)
028 8556 8053 Mrs Lyttle
D: Fr £17.00
Beds: 1T 2D **Baths:** 3 Private

BUS 🚌

For information on buses from **Omagh**, tel. **Ulsterbus** on 028 9066 6630.

TOURIST INFORMATION OFFICES *i*

48 Molesworth St, **Cookstown**, County Tyrone, BT80 8TA, 028 8676 6727.
Killymaddy Amenity Centre, Ballygawley Road (M1 extension), **Dungannon**, County Tyrone, BT70 1TF, 028 8776 7259.
1 Market Street, **Omagh**, County Tyrone, BT78 1EE, 028 8224 7831.
Abercorn Square, **Strabane**, County Tyrone, BT82 8AG, 028 7188 3735.

Castlederg

H2684

Derg Arms, *43 Main Street, Castlederg, Co Tyrone, BT81 7AS.*
Open: All year (not Xmas/New Year)
028 8167 1644 Mr & Mrs Walls **Fax: 020 8167 0202**
dergarms@hotmail.com www.dergarms.com
D: Fr £20.00–£36.00 **S:** Fr £18.00–£20.00
Beds: 2F 1T 3D **Baths:** 5 En 1 Pr
🏝 🅿 (10) ⅍ 📺 ✕ Ⅴ ⅢⅢ. ⅙ ⬛ **cc**
Family-run guest house, which offers guests a number of services. Situated in the centre of town. Beautiful landscape gardens overlooking the castle ruins and River Derg. Private car park. Ideal base for touring North and South of Ireland.

BEDROOMS

D = Double   S = Single

T = Twin   F = Family

Clogher

H5351

Ratory, *Clogher, Co Tyrone, BT76 0UT.* Victorian farmhouse on Fintona road B168. One mile from village.
Open: All year (not Xmas)
028 8554 8288 Mr and Mrs Johnston
D: Fr £17.50 **S:** Fr £19.00
Beds: 1D **Baths:** 1 Pr
🅿 (6) ⅍ 📺 🏝 ✕ ⅢⅢ.

Coalisland

H8465

McGirr's, *11 The Square, Coalisland, Dungannon, Co Tyrone, BT71 4LN.* Fully refurbished licensed guest house, bar, lounge, off sales.
Open: All year
028 8774 7324 Mr McGirr
D: Fr £20.00 **S:** Fr £20.00
Beds: 1F 2D 3T 5S **Baths:** 11 En
🏝 🅿 ⅍ 📺 ✕ Ⅴ ⅢⅢ. ⬛

Cookstown

H8177

Royal Hotel, *64 Coagh Street, Cookstown, Co Tyrone, BT80 8NG.* Family owned town centre hotel, en suite bedrooms, friendly atmosphere throughout.
Open: All Year (not Xmas/New Year)
028 8676 2224 Mrs Henry **Fax: 028 8676 1932**
www.theroyal-hotel.com
D: Fr £25.00 **S:** Fr £30.00
Beds: 1F 5T 3D 1S **Baths:** 10 En
🏝 🅿 📺 ✕ Ⅴ ⅢⅢ. ⬛ **cc**

Dungannon

H7962

Cohannon Inn Autolodge, *212 Ballynakelly Road, Cohannon, Tamnamore, Dungannon, Co Tyrone, BT71 6HJ.* Motorway services motel accommodation, fully licensed, petrol station, supermarket, Post Office.
Open: All year
028 8772 4488 Miss Coyle **Fax: 028 8775 2217**
enquiries@cohannon-inn.com
www.cohannon-inn.com
D: Fr £20.00 **S:** Fr £40.00
Beds: 16F 12D 18T **Baths:** 46 En
🏝 🅿 ⅍ 📺 Ⅴ ⅢⅢ. ⅙ ⬛ **cc**

Gortaclare

H5164

Greenmount Lodge, *58 Greenmount Road, Gortaclare, Omagh, Co Tyrone, BT79 0YE.* Tennis court, laundry room for guests' use. Convenient touring Donegal, Fermanagh, Armagh.
Open: All Year
028 8284 1325 Mrs Reid **Fax: 028 8284 0019**
greenmountlodge@lineone.net
D: Fr £18.00–£20.00 **S:** Fr £19.00–£22.00
Beds: 2F 3D 2T 1S **Baths:** 8 En
ⓑ 🅿 (20) ⅍ 📺 📡 ✕ Ⓥ 🖼 ⅙ ⬛ cc

Moy

H8556 🍴 *The Ryandale, Sly Fox*

Muleany House, *86 Gorestown Road, Moy, Dungannon, Co Tyrone, BT71 7EX.* Perfectly situated for exploring Northern Ireland. Grade A Licensed guest house.
Open: All year
028 8778 4183 Mr and Mrs Mullen
mary@muleany.freeserve.co.uk
D: Fr £19.00
Beds: 3F 2T 3D 1S **Baths:** 9 En
ⓑ 🅿 (10) ⅍ 📺 📡 ✕ Ⓥ 🖼 ⬛ cc

Omagh

H4572

Four Winds, *63 Dromore Road (Old), Omagh, Co Tyrone, BT78 1RB.* Convenient Ulster History/ American Folk Parks. 10 mins' walk from town centre.
Open: All Year (not Xmas)
028 8224 3554 Mr & Mrs Thomas
D: Fr £18.00–£20.00
Beds: 2D 2T **Baths:** 1 Ensuite 1 Shared
ⓑ 🅿 (6) 📺 📡 Ⓥ 🖼 ⅙ ⬛

Sion Mills

H3493

Bide-a-Wee, *181 Melmount Road, Sion Mills, Strabane, Co Tyrone, BT82 9LA.* Friendly, comfortable Tudor house, tennis court, swimming pool, mature gardens.
Open: All Year (not Xmas)
028 8165 9571 Ms Fletcher
colin@cfhomes.freeserve.co.uk
D: Fr £18.00
Beds: 7F 5D 1T 2S **Baths:** 2 En 5 Pr
ⓑ 🅿 ⅍ 📺 ✕ Ⓥ 🖼 ⅙ ⬛

Strabane

H3497

Bowling Green House, *6 Bowling Green, Strabane, Co Tyrone, BT82 8AS.* Free car parking. Large breakfast served.
Open: All Year (not Xmas)
028 7188 4787 Mr & Mrs Casey
D: Fr £14.00–£15.00
Beds: 1F 1D 1T **Baths:** 1 Sh
ⓑ (1) 🅿 (30) 📺 🖼 ⬛

Tamnamore

H8761

Cohannon Inn Autolodge, *212 Ballynakelly Road, Cohannon, Tamnamore, Dungannon, Co Tyrone, BT71 6HJ.* Motorway services motel accommodation, fully licensed, petrol station, supermarket, Post Office.
Open: All year
028 8772 4488 Miss Coyle **Fax: 028 8775 2217**
enquiries@cohannon-inn.com
www.cohannon-inn.com
D: Fr £20.00 **S:** Fr £40.00
Beds: 16F 12D 18T **Baths:** 46 En
ⓑ 🅿 ⅍ 📺 Ⓥ 🖼 ⅙ ⬛ cc

County Carlow

RAIL ⇝

Carlow Town is on the **Dublin-Waterford** railway line.
Tel. **Irish Rail** 01 8366222 for timetable information.

Ballon

S8366

Sherwood Park House, *Kilbride, Ballon, Tullow, Carlow.* Timeless elegance and warm welcome await you. Listed period Georgian farmhouse.
Open: All year
0503 59117 Mrs Owens **Fax: 0503 59355**
info@sherwoodparkhouse.ie
www.sherwoodparkhouse.ie
D: Fr €45.00 **S:** Fr €55.00
Beds: 3F 2D **Baths:** 5 En
P (100) TV V cc

Borris

S7350

Breen's, *Main Street, Borris, Kilkenny.* Scenic village at foot of Mount Leinster, golf nearby.
Open: All year (not Xmas)
0503 73231 Mrs Breen
D: Fr €25.00 **S:** Fr €25.50
Beds: 1F 1D 2T **Baths:** 2 Sh
P TV V

Carlow

S7276

Barrowville Town House, *Kilkenny Road, Carlow Town, Co Carlow.*
Open: All year
0503 43324 Mr Dempsey **Fax: 0503 41953** www.barrowvillehouse.com
D: Fr €35.00-€37.50 **S:** Fr €40.00-€50.00
Beds: 3D 3T 1S **Baths:** 7 En
P (12) TV cc
Period Listed residence in own grounds. 3 mins walk to town centre. Well-appointed bedrooms. Antique furnishings. Traditional or buffet breakfast served in conservatory overlooking gardens. Perfectly situated for touring. Great golf nearby, visit our website.

B&B owners may vary rates – be sure to check when booking

Celtic Guest Accomodation, *34 Hillview Drive, Rathnapish, Carlow, Co Carlow.*
Open: All year
0503 35762 Margaret O'Brien
D: Fr €25.00-€32.00 **S:** Fr €23.00-€32.00
Beds: 1F 5D **Baths:** 5 En 1 Sh
(8) P (4) TV V
This recently refurbished house, tastefully decorated with quality furnishing and fabrics offers modern and comfortable accommodation with the emphasis on relaxation. Breakfast serves a fine selection of foods, continental and cooked. Irish hospitality assured.

Dolmen House, *Brownshill, Carlow.* Rural panoramic setting adjacent world famous Brownshill dolmen, golf nearby.
Open: Jul to Oct
0503 42444 (also fax) Mr Caesar
D: Fr €23.00 **S:** Fr €23.00
Beds: 2D **Baths:** 2 Sh
P (8) TV

Killamaster

S8080

Killamaster House, *Killamaster, Carlow.* Luxury farm bungalow, beautiful garden, wonderful mountain views, tea and scones on arrival.
Open: Mar to Oct
0503 63654 (also fax) Mrs Walsh
mairinwalsh@eircom.net
D: Fr €25.50-€28.00 **S:** Fr €23.00-€33.00
Beds: 2D 2T **Baths:** 3 En 1 Sh
P TV V cc

Rathvilly

S8782

Baile Ricead, *Ricketstown, Rathvilly, Carlow.* A homely farmhouse with beautiful view of the surrounding countryside and Wicklow Mountains.
Open: Mar to Oct
0503 61120 Mrs Corrigan **Fax: 0503 30477**
crt@indigo.ie
D: Fr €30.00
Beds: 1T 2D 1S **Baths:** 2 Ensuite
P (10) TV V

Tullow

S8573

Sherwood Park House, *Kilbride, Ballon, Tullow, Carlow.*
Open: All year
0503 59117
Mrs Owens **Fax: 0503 59355**

info@sherwoodparkhouse.ie
www.sherwoodparkhouse.ie
D: Fr €45.00 **S:** Fr €55.00
Beds: 3F 2D **Baths:** 5 En
➤ 🅿 (100) 📺 🛏 ✕ Ⓥ ▥ cc
Timeless elegance and warm welcome await you.
Listed period Georgian farmhouse.

Laburnum Lodge, *Bundody Road, Tullow, Carlow.* Elegant Georgian residence set in over one acre of landscaped gardens.
Open: All year
0503 51718 Mrs Byrne
lablodge@indigo.ie
D: Fr €28.00-€31.00 **S:** Fr €37.00-€39.00
Beds: 2F 2T 2D **Baths:** 6 Pr
➤ (2) 🅿 (6) ✂ 📺 🛏 Ⓥ ▥ ▪ cc

BATHROOMS

En = Ensuite

Pr = Private

Sh = Shared

BUS 🚌

Cavan to Belfast (2 daily). Cavan to Dublin (6 daily).

Tel. **Bus Eireann**, 01 8366111.

TOURIST INFORMATION OFFICES 🛈

Cavan, Farnham Street (open all year). Tel. 049 4331942.

Arva

N2797

Farrangarve, *Arva, Cavan.* Beautiful country residence in stunning Lakeland district. Warm, friendly atmosphere.
Open: Easter to Oct
049 4335357 Mrs Barry
D: Fr €23.50-€25.50 **S:** Fr €25.50
Beds: 1D 1T 1F **Baths:** 2 Sh
ॐ ▣ 🖵 ⌺ ✕ Ⓥ 🖿 ও ⚱

Ballinagh

N3998

Bavaria House, *Garrymore, Ballinagh, Cavan.* Well situated to discover the historical sites of Ireland. Relax in our ornamental gardens. Famous for fishing, boats for hire. Superb food served with own organically grown vegetables. We cater for veg/vegan, English/German spoken. Herbal advice.
Open: Easter to Oct
049 4337452 (also fax) Mrs Kiebler
t.i.kiebler@unison.ie
D: Fr €25.50-€28.00 **S:** Fr €32.00
Beds: 1F 1T 1D **Baths:** 1 En
ॐ (5) ▣ (5) ⅄ 🖵 ⌺ ✕ Ⓥ 🖿

Bawnboy

H2119

The Keepers' Arms, *Bawnboy, Ballyconnell, Belturbet, Co Cavan.* Come taste our wares.... in West Cavan. Day or evening cruising.
Open: All Year (not Xmas/New Year)
049 9523318 Mrs McKiernan **Fax: 049 9523008**
keepers@iol.ie
D: Fr €14.00-€19.00 **S:** Fr €32.00-€38.00
Beds: 3D 2T 6D **Baths:** 11 En
ॐ ▣ (15) ⅄ 🖵 ⌺ ✕ Ⓥ 🖿 ⚱ cc

Belturbet

H3617   🍵 *Erne Bistro, Four Horseshoes*

8 Church Street, *Belturbet, Co Cavan.* Newly-renovated town guest house within walking distance of shops, bars and restaurants.
Open: All year (not Xmas/New Year)
049 9522358 Mrs Hughes
D: Fr €25.39-€31.74 **S:** Fr €31.74
Beds: 3F 3T 2D **Baths:** 8 En
▣ (2) 🖵 ✕ Ⓥ 🖿 cc

Butlersbridge

H4110

Inishmore House, *Butlersbridge, Cavan.* Top fishing area, own boat jetty & boats for hire.
Open: Easter to Nov
049 4334151 Mrs Lynch
g.lynch@eircom.net
D: Fr €21.50-€28.00
Beds: 3F 1T **Baths:** 2 En
ॐ ▣ 🖵 ✕ Ⓥ 🖿 cc

Cavan

H4205

New County, *38 Farnham Road, Cavan.*
Open: All year
049 4361744 Mrs Dowling
D: Fr €21.50-€25.50
S: Fr €21.50-€32.00
Beds: 1F 1D 1T 1S **Baths:** 1 En 1 Sh
ॐ 🖵 ✕ Ⓥ 🖿 ⚱
5 mins from Cavan town and bus station. Golf, fishing - over 300 lakes in Cavan. Personal service guaranteed. Baby-sitting service. 2 hours Dublin/Belfast. Ideal base for touring Lakelands, close to Killykeen Forest.

Glendown, *33 Cathedral Road, Cavan.* Family home 400m to town centre. Great fishing, golf, horse riding & pubs.
Open: Mar to Dec
049 4332257 Mrs Flynn
tfflynn@eircom.net
D: Fr €27.00
Beds: 2F 1T 1D **Baths:** 4 Ensuite 4 Private
▣ (8) 🖵 Ⓥ 🖿 ⚱

Cloverhill

H4114

Fortview House, *Drumbran, Cloverhill, Belturbet, Co Cavan.* Beautiful country house. Excellent home cooking. Farm walks. First class fishing.
Open: Easter to Oct
049 4338185 Mrs Smith **Fax: 049 4338834**
fortviewhouse@hotmail.com
D: Fr €21.50 **S:** Fr €25.50
Beds: 3F 1D 2T **Baths:** 3 Pr 2 Sh 3 En
ॐ ▣ ⅄ 🖵 ✕ Ⓥ 🖿 ❋ ⚱

Cootehill

H6014

Riverside House, *Cootehill, Co Cavan.*
Victorian house set among mature trees
overlooking river. Five ensuite.
Open: All Year (not Xmas)
049 5559950 (also fax) Mrs Smith
D: Fr €23.50-€25.50 **S:** Fr €23.50-€25.50
Beds: 2F 1D 2T 1S **Baths:** 5 En
ॐ 🅿 (10) 🖤 ✕ Ⓥ ▥ cc

The Manse, *Bridge Street, Cootehill, Co Cavan.*
Beautiful spacious town house manse set in its
own mature gardens.
Open: All Year
049 5552322 Mrs Elliffe
D: Fr €23.00 **S:** Fr €25.50
Beds: 1D 1T **Baths:** 2 En
ॐ (4) 🅿 (6) Ⓣ 🖤 ✕ ▥

Crossdoney

H3701

Lisnamandra, *Crossdoney, Cavan.* Centuries-
old spacious farmhouse renowned for its charm,
comfort, delicious food.
Open: Easter to Oct
049 4337196 Mr & Mrs Neill **Fax: 049 4337111**
noelneill@eircom.net
D: Fr €26.00
Beds: 4F 1D 1S **Baths:** 4 Ensuite 1 Private
3 Shared
ॐ 🅿 (12) ✔ Ⓣ Ⓥ ▥ ▪

Mount Nugent

N4886

Ross Castle, *Mount Nugent, Oldcastle, Kells,
Co Meath.* Find exclusive retreat in C16th castle
on the shores of Lough Sheelin.
Open: All year
049 8540237 & 086 8242206 (M) Mrs Liebe-Harkort
book@rosscastle.com www.ross-castle.com
D: Fr €40.00 **S:** Fr €50.00
Beds: 2F 2D **Baths:** 4 En
ॐ 🅿 (5) 🖤 ▥ ▪ cc

Redhills

H4416

Hillside, *Shannon Wood, Redhills, Cavan.*
Beautiful modern home half mile Redhills village,
2 music pubs, horseriding, golf, fishing locally.
Open: Apr to Oct
047 55125 Mrs Smith
hillside@business-oz.com
D: Fr €21.50 **S:** Fr €25.50
Beds: 2T 1F **Baths:** 3 En
ॐ 🅿 Ⓣ ✕ Ⓥ ▥

All details shown are as supplied by
B&B owners in Autumn 2002

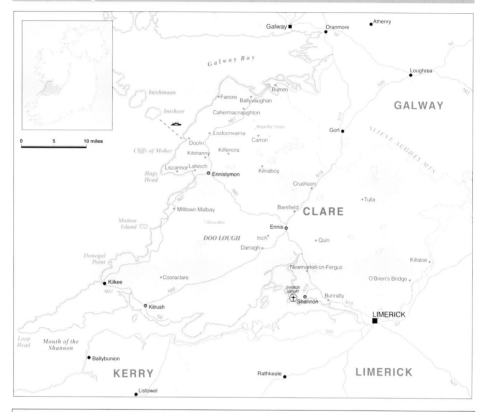

AIRPORT ⊕

Shannon Airport - tel. 061 471444.

AIR SERVICES & AIRLINES ✈

***Shannon** to **London Heathrow**:* **Aer Lingus**. In Ireland tel. 0818 365000; in Britain tel. 0845 084 4444

***Shannon** to **Manchester**:* **British Airways** (for Manx Airlines). In the Republic tel. (freefone) 1800 626747; in Northern Ireland & the UK tel. (local rate): 08705 511155.

FERRIES ⛴

You can get to the ***Aran Islands*** (see Galway chapter) from ***Doolin**, by **Doolin Ferries***, tel. 065 7074455/7074466.

TOURIST INFORMATION OFFICES 𝒊

Ennis (open all year), 065 6828366.
Kilkee (open Jun to Sep), 065 9056112.
Killaloe (open Jun to mid-Sep), 061 376866.
Kilrush (open Jun to Aug), 065 9051577.
Shannon Airport (open all year), 061 471664.

M2308

Rusheen Lodge,
Knocknagrough,
Ballyvaughan, Co Clare.
Open: Feb to Nov **Grades:** BF
4 Star, AA 4 Diamond, RAC 4
Diamond
065 7077092 Ms McGann **Fax: 065 7077152**
rusheen@iol.ie www.rusheenlodge.com
D: Fr €35.00-€45.00 **S:** Fr €50.00-€65.00
Beds: 3F 3D 3S **Baths:** 9 En
☎ (2) 🅿 (8) ⅍ 📺 ⅏ ⅋ 🍴 cc
Rusheen offers excellent and tastefully designed
ensuite bedrooms and suites with all modern
comforts ensuring a relaxing stay. Jameson
guide's Guest House of the Year, RAC small hotel
of the year. Non-smoking house.

Rockhaven,
Cahermacnaughton,
Ballyvaughan, Co Clare.
Family-run farmhouse with
scenic view. Ideal base for
touring the Burren, Cliffs of
Moher, Aran Islands.
Open: Apr to Sep **Grades:** BF Approv
065 7074454 Mrs McDonagh
rockhavenfarmhouse@eircom.net
www.tourclare.com/rockhaven
D: Fr €25.00-€27.00 **S:** Fr €25.00-€27.00
Beds: 1F 1D 1T **Baths:** 2 En 1 Pr
☎ 🅿 📺 🍴 ✗ � ⅏.

Merrijig Farmhouse, Lismactigue,
Ballyvaughan, Clare. Modern farmhouse set in a
beautiful valley in the heart of the Burren.
Open: Easter to Sep
065 7077120 (also fax) Mrs Keane
merrijig@eircom.net
D: Fr €25.50 **S:** Fr €29.00
Beds: 1F 1D 1T **Baths:** 3 En
☎ 🅿 (6) ⅍ 📺 ✗ � ⅏. ⅋

Dolmen Lodge Farmhouse, Town Ross,
Ballyvaughan, Galway. Elegant family home in
scenic setting. Panoramic views of Galway Bay
and the Burren.
Open: Apr to Oct
065 7077202 (also fax) Mrs Kyne
dolmenlodge@eircom.net
D: Fr €31.00
Beds: 1F 1T 1D **Baths:** 3 Ensuite
☎ 🅿 (4) 📺 � ⅏. ⅋ ⅋

Turlough House, Ballyvaughan, Co Clare.
Modern comfortable home. Well-appointed
bedrooms. Ideal for touring the Burren and
Connemara.
Open: All Year (not Xmas/New Year)
065 7077119 (also fax) Mrs Long
turlough@iol.ie
D: Fr €25.50-€32.00 **S:** Fr €32.00-€51.00
Beds: 1F 2D **Baths:** 3 En
☎ 🅿 (5) ⅍ 📺 ⅏. ⅋

R3683　⬛ Aubuln Lodge Hotel

Ashleigh, Cregard, Barefield, Ennis, Co Clare.
Convenient to Burren. Shannon Airport 30 mins.
Leisure activities nearby.
Open: Apr to Oct
065 6827187 Mrs Meaney
tommeaney@eircom.ie
D: Fr €26.00 **S:** Fr €29.00
Beds: 3F 2D **Baths:** 5 En
🅿 (5) ⅍ 📺 🐴 ✗ 📺 ⅏. ⅋ ⅋ cc

R4561　⬛ Durty Nellie's, Kathleen's Irish Pub, Medieval
Banquet

Innisfree, Bunratty East, Bunratty, Ennis, Co
Clare. Dormer bungalow. Scenic landscaped
gardens. Comfortable rooms, warm and
welcoming.
Open: All year
061 369773 Mrs McCarthy **Fax: 061 369926**
innisfree@unison.ie www.shannonheartland.ie
D: Fr €26.00-€28.00 **S:** Fr €39.00-€40.00
Beds: 1F 2T 1D **Baths:** 4 En
🅿 ⅍ 📺 📺 ⅏. ⅋ cc

Bunratty Woods House, Bunratty, Ennis, Co
Clare. Two minutes from Bunratty Castle and Folk
Park.
Open: All Year (not Xmas/New Year)
061 369689 Mrs O'Donovan **Fax: 061 369454**
bunratty@iol.ie
D: Fr €28.50-€35.00 **S:** Fr €38.00-€57.00
Beds: 3F 5D 6T 1S **Baths:** 15 En
☎ (12) 🅿 (20) ⅍ 📺 🐴 📺 ⅏. ⅋ cc

Planning a longer stay?
Always ask for any special rates

Rockfield House, *Hill Road, Bunratty, Co Clare.*
Overlooking River Shannon, surrounded by Folk
Park, 2 mins' drive from Durty Nellie's.
Open: All year (not Xmas/New Year)
061 364391 (also fax) Mrs Garry
D: Fr €28.00 **S:** Fr €41.00
Beds: 6D **Baths:** 6 En
🅿 (6) ⌿ 📺 ▥ ▪ cc

Bunratty Heights,
*Bunratty Road, Bunratty,
Ennis, Co Clare.* Only 10 min
drive to Shannon Airport, 1
mile to Bunratty Castle.
Open: All year (not Xmas)
061 369324 Mrs D'Arcy
bunrattyheights@eircom.net
D: Fr €25.50 **S:** Fr €32.00
Beds: 1F 2D 2T **Baths:** 5 En
ॐ (1) 🅿 (6) ⌿ 📺 ♉ ▣ ▥ ▪ cc

Ashgrove House, *Lower Road, Bunratty, Co
Clare.* Country home - 3 mins' drive Bunratty
castle & Durty Nellies pub, 10 mins Shannon
Airport.
Open: All Year (not Xmas/New Year)
061 369332 Mrs Tiernan
frashe@eircom.net www.ashgrovehouse.com
D: Fr €25.50 **S:** Fr €32.00-€38.00
Beds: 2F 4T 1D **Baths:** 4 En
ॐ 🅿 ⌿ 📺 ♉ ▣ ▥ ♿

M2811

Villa Maria, *Leagh South, The Burren, Clare.*
Quiet area, panoramic views of Galway Bay and
the Burren.
Open: Easter to Oct
065 7078019 Mrs Martin
vmaria@eircom.net
D: Fr €25.50
Beds: 1F 2D 2T **Baths:** 3 En 3 Pr 2 Sh
ॐ (1) 🅿 (1) ⌿ 📺 ♉ ♉

M2304

Rockhaven, *Cahermacnaughton,
Ballyvaughan, Co Clare.* Family-run farmhouse
with scenic view. Ideal base for touring the
Burren.
Open: Apr to Sep **Grades:** BF Approv
065 7074454 Mrs McDonagh
rockhavenfarmhouse@eircom.net
www.tourclare.com/rockhaven
D: Fr €25.00-€27.00 **S:** Fr €25.00-€27.00
Beds: 1F 1D 1T **Baths:** 2 En 1 Pr
ॐ 🅿 📺 ♉ ✕ ▣ ▥

R2799

Deelin House, *Carron, Ennis, Co Clare.*
Traditional farmhouse in the Burren, near
Poulnabrone Dolmen and Ailwee Caves.
Open: Mar to Oct
065 7089105 Mr & Mrs Linnane
D: Fr €23.00 **S:** Fr €32.00
Beds: 1F 2T **Baths:** 3 En
ॐ 🅿 📺 ✕ ▥

R0462

Old Parochial House, *Cooraclare, Kilrush, Co
Clare.* Welcome! Restored rectory (c1872). Village
2, beach 5 mins. Rural, quiet. Big breakfasts!
Open: Mar to Nov
065 9059059 (also fax) Mr & Mrs O'Neill
oldparochialhouse@eircom.net
www.oldparochialhouse.com
D: Fr €35.00-€45.00 **S:** Fr €45.00-€55.00
Beds: 1F 2D 1T **Baths:** 3 En 1 Pr
ॐ 🅿 (4) ⌿ ▥ ▪ cc

R3988

Lahardan House, *Crusheen, Ennis, Co Clare.*
Family residence in peaceful countryside. Ample
room to relax and dine.
Open: All Year
065 6827128 Mr & Mrs Griffey **Fax: 065 6827319**
D: Fr €27.50
Beds: 2F 3D 3T **Baths:** 8 En
ॐ 🅿 📺 ♉ ✕ ▣ ▥

R2972

Hawthorns, *Kilrush Road, Darragh, Ennis, Co
Clare.* Modern farmhouse - 30 minutes from
Shannon Airport, Cliffs of Moher, Burren,
Bunratty Castle.
Open: Mar to Nov
065 6838221 Mrs Nolan
D: Fr €24.00 **S:** Fr €32.00
Beds: 1F 1T 1D **Baths:** 3 En
🅿 📺 ▥

Planning a longer stay?
Always ask for any special rates

Doolin

R0897

Island View, *Cliffs of Moher Road, Doolin, Co Clare.* Modern warm bungalow on elevated site on R478. Family atmosphere. Non-smoking bedrooms.
Open: Apr to Nov
065 7074346 Mr & Mrs Sims **Fax: 065 7074844**
sims@iol.ie
D: Fr €28.00
Beds: 2F 2D **Baths:** 3 Ensuite 1 Private

Doolin Cottage, *Doolin, Ennis, Co Clare.* Situated beside Cliffs of Moher, Arran Islands, the Burren, traditional music pubs.
Open: Mar to Nov
065 7074762 Mrs Spencer
caroldoolin@hotmail.com
www.transatlan.com/ireland
D: Fr €19.00-€22.00 **S:** Fr €25.50-€32.00
Beds: 2F/D 2T/D **Baths:** 4 En

Glasha Meadows, *Glasha, Doolin, Co Clare.* Modern bungalow situated on Coast Road 479. Village near Cliffs of Moher, Aran ferries.
Open: All Year
065 7074443 Ms McDonagh
glameadows@eircom.net
D: Fr €28.00
Beds: 1F 2T 3D **Baths:** 6 Ensuite

Seacrest, *Ballaghaline, Doolin, Ennis, Co Clare.* Excellent, modern house. 100m from Doolin pier. Overlooking cliffs of Moher.
Open: May to Sept
065 7074458 Mrs Nagle **Fax: 065 7074936**
ken@doolincamping.com
D: Fr €23.00-€24.00 **S:** Fr €32.00-€33.00
Beds: 2F 2T **Baths:** 4 En
  cc

Riverfield House, *Doolin, Co Clare.* Century-old reconstructed home. Central to all amenities. Music pubs five mins' walk from house.
Open: All Year
065 7074113 (also fax) Mrs Garrahy
riverfield@eircom.net
D: Fr €28.00
Beds: 1F 3D **Baths:** 3 En 1 Pr

Atlantic Sunset House,
Cliffs of Moher Road, Doolin, Ennis, Co Clare.
Warm hospitable family-run B&B. Conveniently located on scenic cliffs of Moher Road.
Open: All year
065 7074080 Mrs Egan **Fax: 065 7074922**
sunsethouse@esatclear.ie
www.atlanticsunsetdoolin.com
D: Fr €26.00-€30.00 **S:** Fr €40.00
Beds: 2T 4D **Baths:** 6 En
  cc

Atlantic View, *Doolin, Ennis, Co Clare.*
Open: Easter to Oct
065 7074189 Mrs **Fax: 065 7074914**
atlanview@eircom.net
www.doolinferries.com
D: Fr €40.00 **S:** Fr €50.00
Beds: 1F 3T 7D 1S **Baths:** 12 En
  cc
Newly refurbished home with most bedrooms and the dining room offering spectacular ocean and cliff views. Situated within walking distance of the traditional Irish music pubs, restaurants and the pier where a daily ferry service operates to the Aran Islands.

Daly's, *Doolin, Ennis, Co Clare.*
Open: All year (not Xmas)
065 7074242 Mrs Daly **Fax: 065 7074668**
susan.daly@esatlink.com *www.dalys-house.com*
D: Fr €30.00
Beds: 4D 4T **Baths:** 5 En

Daly's House situated 150 yards from Doolin village, home of traditional Irish music. Panoramic views of the sea and the 'Cliffs of Moher', Burren Region. Just minutes walk to pubs, restaurants, craft shops and ferry service to the Aran Islands.

Ennis

R3377

Sunvill, *Lahinch Road, Claureen, Ennis, Co Clare.* Dormer bungalow. N85 to Cliffs of Moher & Burren. 20 mins Shannon Airport.
Open: All Year (not Xmas)
065 6828661 Mrs Canny
D: Fr €24.00
Beds: 4F 2D 2T **Baths:** 1 En

Lourdes, *Lifford Road, Ennis, Co Clare.* Five mins from town centre, 3 mins from swimming pool and 30 mins from Shannon Airport.
Open: All year (not Xmas/New Year)
065 6822578 Mr Shanahan
D: Fr €23.00-€25.00 **S:** Fr €32.00
Beds: 1F 1T 1D **Baths:** 1 Sh
⌂ ▣ (5) ⅍ 🖵 🐾 Ⅴ ▥. ▪

Shanlee, *Lohinch Road N85, Ennis, Co Clare.* N85. Convenient Burren, Cliffs of Moher. Shannon Airport 20 minutes.
Open: All Year
065 6840270 Mr & Mrs Connole
D: Fr €26.00
Beds: 1T 2D 1S **Baths:** 2 Ensuite
⌂ ▣ (7) 🖵 🐾 Ⅴ ▥. ▪

Ardilaun, *Galway Road, Ennis, Co Clare.* Modern architecturally designed 13 bedroom guest house in beautiful surroundings.
Open: All Year (not Xmas)
065 6822311 Mrs Purcell **Fax: 065 43989**
D: Fr €30.00
Beds: 4F 7D **Baths:** 11 Ensuite
⌂ ▣ (15) 🖵 ▥.

The Ashling Gheal Bed & Breakfast, *St Flannans Cross, Limerick Road, Ennis, Co Clare.* Newly built award-winning guest house. Situated in a peaceful setting with landscaped gardens.
Open: All Year
065 6823810 Mrs Flynn **Fax: 065 6829399**
D: Fr €28.00-€32.00 **S:** Fr €32.00-€38.00
Beds: 1F 2T 3D **Baths:** 6 En
⌂ ▣ (8) 🖵 Ⅴ ▥. ▪ cc

Glencar House, *Galway Road, Ennis, Co Clare.* Situated on N18 (Galway road) 1 km Ennis town, 20 metres Auburn Lodge Hotel.
Open: All Year (not Xmas/New Year)
065 6822348 Mr & Mrs Hoolihan **Fax: 065 6822885**
glencar.ennis@tinet.ie glencar.ennis.ie
D: Fr €25.50-€32.00 **S:** Fr €25.50-€32.00
Beds: 2F 1T 7D 2S **Baths:** 12 En 12 Pr
⌂ ▣ (13) ⅍ 🖵 ▥. ♿ ▪ cc

Planning a longer stay?
Always ask for any special rates

Cill Eoin House, *Clare Road, Ennis, Co Clare.* On the outskirts of the medieval town of Ennis, ideal centre for touring the Southwest of Ireland.

Open: All year (not Xmas)
065 6841668 & 065 6828311 Mr Lucey **Fax: 065 6841669**
cilleoin@iol.ie www.euroka.com/cilleoin/
D: Fr €32.00-€35.00 **S:** Fr €40.00-€45.00
Beds: 2F 6D 6T **Baths:** 14 En
⌂ ▣ (10) ⅍ 🖵 🐾 ▥. ▪ cc

St Patricks, *Corebeg, Doora, Ennis, Co Clare.*
Open: All year
065 6840122 (also fax) Mr & Mrs Grogan
D: Fr €26.50-€30.00 **S:** Fr €39.00-€42.50
Beds: 1D 2T 1F **Baths:** 3 En 1 Pr
⌂ ▣ (3) ⅍ 🖵 ✕ Ⅴ ▥. cc
Comfortable home in quiet scenic area. Ideal location for Knappogue, Cragganowen, Bunratty, Burren, Cliffs of Moher, golfing, fishing, traditional music. Off N18 at Clare Castle. Beside Doora Church.

St Martin's, *Ardlea Road, Ennis, Co Clare.*
Open: Easter to Nov
065 6824649 M Forde
fordeselfcatering@eircom.net
D: Fr €25.00-€30.00 **S:** Fr €34.00-€38.00
Beds: 2F 1T 1D 1S **Baths:** 3 En 1 Sh
⌂ ▣ (4) ⅍ 🖵 Ⅴ ▥. ▪ cc
Quiet select locality overlooking town. 80 metres off main Limerick Road, 500 metres to town centre. Central to traditional music, golf, pubs, and nightly entertainment. Shannon Airport 20 mins.

Newpark House, *Ennis, Co Clare.* Spacious old house with elegance of past and comfort of the present.
Open: Easter to Oct
065 6821233 Mrs Barron
newparkhouse.ennis@eircom.net
homepage.tinet.ie/~newparkhouse/
D: Fr €32.00-€38.00 **S:** Fr €38.00
Beds: 5F 1D **Baths:** 5 En 1 Pr
⌂ ▣ (10) 🖵 🐾 ✕ Ⅴ ▥. ▪

Druimin, *Golf Links Road, Ennis, Co Clare.*
Secluded setting beside Ennis Golf Club. Seems
like rural heartland.
Open: Apr to Sep
065 6824183 Mr & Mrs Finn **Fax: 065 6843331**
golfinn-ennis@eircom.net
D: Fr €28.00
Beds: 2D 3T **Baths:** 5 Ensuite
ॐ 🅿 (6) 📺 ✕ Ⅴ 🖩 ▪

Lakeside Country Lodge,
*Barntick (off Limerick Road),
Clarecastle, Ennis, Co Clare.*
Spacious lakeside home
(R473). Conservatory
overlooking lake. Convenient to airport.
Open: All year (not Xmas) **Grades:** BF Approv
065 6838488 (also fax) George & Joan Quinn
lakesidecountry@eircom.net www.lakeside.ie
D: Fr €26.50 **S:** Fr €35.00
Beds: 2F 2D **Baths:** 4 En
ॐ 🅿 (5) ⅙ 📺 ✕ 🖩 ▪ cc

Oakley, 10 Woodlawn, *Lahinch Road, Ennis,
Co Clare.* Spacious home with attractive front and
near gardens. Family-owned business offering
cosy, friendly atmosphere.
Open: May to Oct
065 6829267 Mrs Normoyle **Fax: 065 6845423**
oakley_house@hotmail.com
D: Fr €23.00-€25.50 **S:** Fr €29.50-€33.00
Beds: 2F 1D 1T **Baths:** 2 En 2 Sh
ॐ (7) 🅿 (7) 📺 Ⅴ 🖩 ▪ cc

Sunset Lodge, *Limerick Road, Ennis, Co Clare.*
Located on main Limerick-Ennis-Galway route,
ideal for touring the Burren.
Open: All Year
065 6842609 Mrs O'Sullivan
fionaosullivan.ennis@eircom.net
D: Fr €19.00-€23.00 **S:** Fr €21.50-€25.50
Beds: 5D 1T **Baths:** 4 En 1 Sh
ॐ 🅿 (4) 📺 🖩 ▪ cc

Moyville, *Lahinch Road, Ennis, Co Clare.*
Modern comfortable home on N85 to the Burren,
Cliffs of Moher. Ideally situated.
Open: Easter to Nov
065 6828278 (also fax) Mrs Finucane
D: Fr €25.50
Beds: 1F 2D 1T **Baths:** 4 Ensuite
ॐ (5) 🅿 (5) 📺 ✕ 🖩 ▪

Ryehill, *Tulla Road, Roslevan, Ennis, Co Clare.*
Family-run business. Ennis town centre and bus
stand 1.5km. Shannon Airport 35 minutes.
Open: All Year (not Xmas)
065 6824313 Mr O'Donnell
hughatredraven@eircom.net
D: Fr €28.00
Beds: 4F 4T 4D 1S **Baths:** 6 Ensuite
ॐ 🅿 (10) ⅙ 📺 🖩 ▪

Ennistymon
R1388

Station House, *Ennis
Road, Ennistymon, Co Clare.*
Open: All year (not New
Year)
065 7071149 Mrs Cahill **Fax:
065 7071709**
cahilka@indigo.ie www.bb-stationhouse.com
D: Fr €25.50 **S:** Fr €30.00
Beds: 4F 1T 1D **Baths:** 6 En
ॐ 🅿 ⅙ 📺 Ⅴ 🖩 ▪ cc
Spacious family home on Route N85. Hospitality
tray, hairdryers, direct dial telephone, TV in all
rooms. Cliffs of Moher, Burren, trips to Aran
Islands nearby. Breakfast Menu.

Callura Lodge, *Ennistymon, County Clare.*
Modern bungalow; nearby are Cliffs of Moher,
Burren, golf, fishing.
Open: Easter to Nov
065 707 1640 Mrs Scales
ura@eircom.net
D: Fr €25.50
Beds: 1F 2D 1T **Baths:** 2 En 1 Pr 2 Sh
🅿 (6) ⅙ 🖩

Hillbrook Farm, *Lahinch
Road, Ennistymon, Co Clare.*
Perfect for visiting Cliffs of
Moher, Burren, Aran Islands
and Bunratty.
Open: Mar to Nov **Grades:** BF Approv
065 7071164 Mrs Houlihan
hillbrookfarm@eircom.net www.hillbrookfarm.com
D: Fr €28.00-€32.00 **S:** Fr €40.00
Beds: 2F 2D **Baths:** 4 En
ॐ ⅙ 📺 ⛦ Ⅴ 🖩 ᵭ ▪ cc

Kilcornan, *Ennistymon, Co Clare.*
Panoramic views. Near Cliffs of Moher and the
Burren. Home baking.
Open: Apr to Sep
065 7071527 Ms McGuare
D: Fr €23.50-€25.50 **S:** Fr €36.00 **Baths:** 2 En
ॐ (2) 🅿 (4) ⅙ 📺 Ⅴ 🖩 ▪

Fanore

M1307

Admirals Rest, *Coast Road, Fanore, Ballyvaughan, Galway.* Overlooking Galway Bay. In the Burren. Close to nature reserve.
Open: Easter to Oct
065 7076105 Mr MacNamara **Fax: 065 7076161**
jdmn@iol.ie
D: Fr €15.00 **S:** Fr €20.00
Beds: 5T 4D 1S **Baths:** 10 En
🛏 (4) 🅿 (30) 🐎 ✕ ▥. ⚍ cc

Inch

R2975

Magowna House Hotel, *Inch, Ennis, Co Clare.* Superbly located family managed hotel with extensive gardens and lovely views.
Open: All Year (not Xmas)
065 6839009 Mr Murphy **Fax: 065 6839258**
magowna@iol.ie
D: Fr €42.00
Beds: 3F 5D 2T **Baths:** 10 Ensuite
🛏 🅿 (35) ▥ 🐎 ✕ ▣ ▥. & ⚍

Kilfenora

R1894

Main Street, *Kilfenora, Ennis, Co Clare.* Lovely old style village house. Close to sea and country.
Open: All Year (not Xmas/New Year)
065 7088040 Ms Murphy
D: Fr €20.50 **S:** Fr €21.50-€24.00
Beds: 3F 1T 2D **Baths:** 1 En 3 Pr
🛏 (1) 🅿 ⊁ ▣ 🐎 ▣ ▥. &

Killaloe

R7073

Rathmore House, *Ballina, Killaloe, Co.Clare.*
Open: All year (not Xmas)
061 379296 (also fax)
Mrs Byrnes
rathmorebb@oceanfree.net www.rathmorehouse.com
D: Fr €24.50-€30.00 **S:** Fr €37.00-€42.50
Beds: 4F 2D **Baths:** 4 En 2 Sh
🛏 (1) 🅿 (8) ▣ ▥. & ⚍ cc
Family home on R494, between Birdhill (N7) and Killaloe on the River Shannon. Ideal touring base for Limerick, Clare, Tipperary. Water sports centre and fishing nearby. Good selection of pubs, restaurants & hotels in village. A warm welcome awaits you.

Weldons Farmhouse, *Boher, Killaloe, Limerick.* Modern farmhouse set in countryside, ideal base for angling, very comfortable.
Open: All year (not Xmas/New Year)
061 379202 Mrs Weldon
margaretweldon@hotmail.com
D: Fr €25.50 **S:** Fr €32.00
Beds: 1F 1T 1D **Baths:** 2 En 2 Pr 1 Sh
🛏 🅿 (8) ▣ ▥. ⚍ cc

Kilnaboy

R2791

Burren House, *Kilnaboy, Corofin, Ennis, Co Clare.* Spacious house with Burren countryside views on R476 to Corofin/Kilfenora.
Open: Mar to Oct
065 6837143 Mr & Mrs Kierce
D: Fr €28.00
Beds: 1F 1D 1T **Baths:** 2 En 1 Pr
🛏 🅿 ⊁ ▣ ✕ ▥. ⚍

Fergus View, *Kilnaboy, Corofin, Ennis, Co Clare.* A teacher's residence built at the turn of the century.
Open: Easter to mid Oct
065 6837606 Mr & Mrs Kelleher **Fax: 065 6837192**
deckell@indigo.ie
D: Fr €30.50 **S:** Fr €42.00-€44.50
Beds: 1F 1T 4D **Baths:** 5 En 1 Sh
🛏 (4) 🅿 (7) ⊁ ▣ ✕ ▣ ▥.

Kilrush

Q9955

Bruach na Coille, *Killimer Road, Kilrush, Co Clare.* Kilrush 5 min walk. Car ferry 8 km. Frommer and AA recommended.
Open: All Year (not Xmas)
065 9052250 (also fax) Mrs Clarke
clarkekilrush@hotmail.com
D: Fr €30.50
Beds: 2D 2T **Baths:** 2 En 1 Sh
🛏 🅿 (6) ⊁ ▣ 🐎 ▣ ▥. ⚍

BATHROOMS

En = Ensuite

Pr = Private

Sh = Shared

Old Parochial House, *Cooraclare, Kilrush, Co Clare.* Welcome! Restored rectory (c1872). Village 2, beach 5 mins. Rural, quiet. Big breakfasts!
Open: Mar to Nov
065 9059059 (also fax) Mr & Mrs O'Neill
oldparochialhouse@eircom.net
www.oldparochialhouse.com
D: Fr €35.00-€45.00 **S:** Fr €45.00-€55.00
Beds: 1F 2D 1T **Baths:** 3 En 1 Pr
🛏 🅿 (4) ⌇ 🎦 💷, 🚲 **cc**

Kilshanny

R1293

Kilshanny Guest House, *Kilshanny, Ennistimon, Ennis, Co Clare.* The Burren National Park, the cliffs of Moher, Doolin and Liscannor fishing villages.
Open: All Year
065 7071660 A Galvin
D: Fr €23.00-€25.50 **S:** Fr €25.50-€28.00
Beds: 6T **Baths:** 5 Pr
🛏 🅿 🐾 ✕ 🎦 💷, 🚲 **cc**

Lahinch

R0988

Sandfield Lodge, *Lahinch, Ennis, Co Clare.* Charming period dwelling peacefully located on elevated wooded site, 700m off coast road.
Open: Mid-mar to Sep
065 81010 (also fax) Mr & Mrs Lucas
sandfield@eircom.net
D: Fr €28.00
Beds: 1F 2T 2D **Baths:** 4 Ensuite 1 Shared
🛏 🅿 (10) 🎦 💷,

Rozel, *Station Road, Lahinch, Ennis, Co Clare.* Superb accommodation set in pleasant garden surroundings offering panoramic views of sea and countryside.
Open: All Year
065 7081203 Mrs O'Dwyer **Fax: 065 7081505**
D: Fr €25.00
Beds: 2D 1T 1S **Baths:** 4 En
🅿 (4) ⌇ 🎦 💷, 🚲 **cc**

Sea Breeze, *Carrowgar, Lahinch, Ennis, Co Clare.* Family run bungalow. Peaceful, rural setting 2 km from Lahinch.
Open: May to Oct
065 7081073 Mrs White
mariantwhite@eircom.net
D: Fr €23.00-€24.00 **S:** Fr €27.00-€29.00
Beds: 1T 2D **Baths:** 3 En
🛏 🅿 ⌇ 🎦 💷, 🚲

Liscannor

R0688 ◀ *The Conch Shell, McHughs Pub, Liscanor Bay Hotel*

Harbour Sunset, *Cliffs of Moher Road, Liscannor, Ennis, Co Clare.* Charming old-style farmhouse on 86 acre dairy farm with friendly animals.
Open: May to Sep
065 7081039 (also fax) Mrs O'Gorman
harbsunfarmhse@eircom.net
D: Fr €28.00 **S:** Fr €37.00
Beds: 1F 2T **Baths:** 3 En
🛏 🅿 (6) 🎦 🐾 ✕ 🎦 💷,

Seascapes, *Rockmount, Liscannor, Ennis, Co Clare.* Spacious family home, sea views, main road to Cliffs of Moher and the Burren.
Open: Easter to Oct
065 7081550 Mr and Mrs Blake **Fax: 065 7081417**
princeblake@eircom.net
D: Fr €25.00 **S:** Fr €30.00
Beds: 2F 1T 1D **Baths:** 4 En
🅿 (4) 🎦 🐾 💷, 🚲

Carraig House, *Liscannor, Ennis, Co Clare.* Spacious house, rural setting, close to village, Cliffs of Moher - 4 km.
Open: All Year (not Xmas)
065 7081260 (also fax) Agnes & Noel Andrews
D: Fr €29.00
Beds: 3T 3D **Baths:** 6 En
🛏 🅿 (12) 🎦 💷, 🚲

Planning a longer stay?
Always ask for any special rates

BEDROOMS

D = Double   S = Single

T = Twin   F = Family

Lisdoonvarna

R1398   ◀ *Kincora, O'Connor's, McGann's*

Burren Haven, *St Brendan's Road, Lisdoonvarna, Ennis, Co Clare.* Central position, magnificent breakfast. Tea/coffee facilities. Vegans/vegetarians welcome.
Open: Apr to Oct
065 7074366 Mr & Mrs Purcell
kpurcell@tinet.ie
D: Fr €19.00 **S:** Fr €19.00
Beds: 2D 2T 2S
ॐ 🅿 🔲 ♔ ⊡ ▥ ⅃ ⚓

Lynch's Hotel, *Lisdoonvarna, Ennis, Co Clare.* Informal clean budget hotel, all usual facilities, in village square.
Open: Mid-may to Sep
065 7074010 Mr Lynch **Fax: 065 7074611**
lynchshotel@eircom.net
homepage.eircom.net/~joelynch/
D: Fr €30.00
Beds: 2F 5T 4D 1S **Baths:** 12 Ensuite
ॐ ⊡ ✕ ▥

Ore' A Tava, *Lisdoonvarna, Ennis, Co Clare.* Ideal base for touring Burren, Cliffs of Moher and Aran Islands.
Open: Easter to Oct
065 7074086 Mrs Stack **Fax: 065 7074547**
oreatava@eircomnet
D: Fr €19.00-€20.00 **S:** Fr €20.00-€26.00
Beds: 4D 2T **Baths:** 6 En
ॐ 🅿 (6) ⊡ ▥ cc

Benrue Farmhouse, *Lisdoonvarna, Ennis, Co Clare.* Modern family home with a 'home from home' atmosphere.
Open: Feb to Dec
065 7074059 Mr & Mrs Casey **Fax: 065 7074457**
benrue@eircom.net
D: Fr €28.00
Beds: 2F 2D 2T **Baths:** 4 En 2 Pr
ॐ 🅿 ⅃ ⊡ ♔ ✕ ▥ ⅃ ⚓

Slieve Elva, *Kilmoon, Lisdoonvarna, Ennis, Co Clare.* Award-winning spacious farmhouse in the Burren region, located 24km north of Lisdoonvarna.
Open: All Year
065 7074318 Mrs Donnellan **Fax: 065 74318**
slieveelva@eircom.net
homepage.eircom.net/~slieveelva/
D: Fr €25.50
Beds: 2F 2D 1T 1S **Baths:** 5 Ensuite 1 Private
ॐ 🅿 (6) ⊡ ♔ ✕ ⊡ ▥ ⅃ ⚓ ✳ ⚓

Fermona, *Bog Road, Lisdoonvarna, Ennis, Co Clare.* Modern bungalow in beautiful landscaped gardens in quiet area of the Burren, County Clare.
Open: Easter to Oct
065 7074243 Mrs Fitzpatrick
D: Fr €24.00-€27.00 **S:** Fr €32.50
Beds: 2T 3D **Baths:** 5 En
🅿 (6) ⅃ ⊡ ▥ ⚓ cc

Gleannbui, *Ballyconnoe, Lisdoonvarna, Ennis, Co Clare.* Friendly, peaceful, fishing, caving, walking, cycling, exploring heritage and scenery.
Open: Apr to Oct
065 7074352 Mrs Madigan
D: Fr €19.00 **S:** Fr €25.50
Beds: 2D 1T **Baths:** 1 En
ॐ 🅿 (5) ⊡ ⊡ ▥ ⚓

Woodview, *Coast Road, Lisdoonvarna, Ennis, Co Clare.* Lisdoonvarna warm welcome cottage gateway to Burren Doolin Cliffs, Moher.
Open: Easter to Oct
065 7074387 O'Halloran Family
D: Fr €16.00-€23.00 **S:** Fr €23.00-€34.50
Beds: 2D 1T 3F **Baths:** 3 En 1 Pr
🅿 (6) ⊡ ⊡ ▥ ⅃ ⚓

Milltown Malbay

R0579

Barker's, *Spanish Point, Milltown Malbay, Ennis, Co Clare.* Welcoming traditional music home within minutes of sandy beach, restaurants, pubs.
Open: Easter to Oct
065 7084408 (also fax) P Barker
barkers@eircom.net homepage.eircom.net/~barkers
D: Fr €25.00 **S:** Fr €30.00
Beds: 2F 1T 2D **Baths:** 5 En
ॐ 🅿 (8) ⅃ ⊡ ♔ ⊡ ▥ ⚓ cc

An Gleann, *Ennis Road, Milltown Malbay, Ennis, Co Clare.* Friendly family home, quiet location. Recommended in New York Times.
Open: All Year
065 7084281 M Hughes
angleann@bigfoot.com
D: Fr €28.00
Beds: 1F 1D 2T **Baths:** 4 En
ॐ (3) 🅿 (6) ⊡ ♔ ⊡ ▥ ⚓ cc

R3968

Ardkeen, *Monument Cross, Newmarket-on-Fergus, Ennis, Co Clare.* Warm, friendly home. Gardens and lawns. Ideal base for touring the West of Ireland.
Open: All Year (not Xmas)
061 368160 Mrs O'Shea
D: Fr €30.00
Beds: 1F 1D 1T 1S **Baths:** 2 Shared
🄿 📺 🐾 Ⓥ ▥ ♿

Tara Green Country Home, *Ballycally, Newmarket-on-Fergus, Ennis, Co Clare.* 3 miles Shannon Airport. Welcome to Irish/Polish home with organic garden.
Open: All Year
061 363789 (also fax) Ms O'Brien
tarag@iol.ie www.iol.ie/~tarag
D: Fr €30.00
Beds: 2F 1D 1T **Baths:** 4 Ensuite 1 Private
🛏 (1) 🄿 (6) ⊬ 📺 🐾 ✕ Ⓥ ▥ ♿ ▪

Golf View, *Latoon Cross, Newmarket-on-Fergus, Ennis, Co Clare.* New 3 Star guest house overlooking Dromoland Castle Golf Course.
Open: All Year
061 368095 Mrs Hogan **Fax: 065 6828624**
mhogangolfviewbandb@eircom.net
www.clarelive.com/golfview
D: Fr €32.00-€38.00 **S:** Fr €44.50-€51.00
Beds: 6F 4T 2D **Baths:** 6 Pr
🄿 ⊬ 📺 ▥ ♿ cc

Dormer, *Lisduff, Newmarket-on-Fergus, Ennis, Co Clare.* B&B in peaceful rural setting on airport side of Newmarket-on-Fergus.
Open: Easter to Oct
061 368354 Mrs Ryan
gerandsheilaryan@eircom.net www.web-ie/thedormer
D: Fr €25.00-€28.00 **S:** Fr €40.00
Beds: 1F 1D 1T **Baths:** 2 En 1 Pr
🛏 🄿 (4) ⊬ 📺 ▥ cc

R6667

Inishlosky, *O'Brien's Bridge, Co Clare.* Modern comfy family home on banks of River Shannon - bliss!
Open: All Year (not Xmas)
061 377420 Mrs Aherne
D: Fr €25.00
Beds: 3T **Baths:** 1 Ensuite 2 Shared
🛏 🄿 📺 🐾 ✕ Ⓥ ▥ ▪

Shannon Cottage, *O'Brien's Bridge, Killaloe, Limerick.* 200-year-old extended cottage on banks of River Shannon.
Open: Feb to Nov
061 377118 Mrs Hyland **Fax: 061 377966**
dave.hyland@camping-ireland.ie
D: Fr €40.00
Beds: 3F 3D **Baths:** 6 Ensuite
🛏 🄿 (6) 📺 ✕ Ⓥ ▥ ▪

R4174

Ardsollus Farm, *Quin, Ennis, Co Clare.*
Open: Feb to Nov
065 6825601
Mrs Hannon **Fax: 065 6825959**
ardsollusfarm@ireland.com
D: Fr €32.50-€35.00 **S:** Fr €45.00
Beds: 2D 2T **Baths:** 4 En
🛏 🄿 (6) 📺 ▥

Spacious agri-tourism award-winning farmhouse on 120-acre working farm fifth generation family home. This 300-year-old house while fully modernised, still retains it's old world charm, with antique furnishings throughout. Reduction on green fees at Dromoland Castle.

Castlefergus Farm Riding Stables, *Quin, Ennis, Co Clare.* Charming C19th farmhouse offering horseriding for all levels. Bunratty Banquets, Cliffs of Moher nearby. Shannon Airport 15 mins.
Open: Mar to Nov
065 6825914 (also fax) Mrs
D: Fr €25.50-€28.00 **S:** Fr €32.00-€38.00
Beds: 3F **Baths:** 3 En
🄿 (6) ⊬ 📺 ▥ cc

R4162

Valhalla, *Uranbeg, Shannon, Co Clare.* Modern house situated 10 minutes Bunratty/Knappogue Castles, 10 minutes Shannon Airport.
Open: All Year
061 368293 Mrs Collins **Fax: 061 368660**
valhalla@esatclear.ie
D: Fr €24.00 **S:** Fr €32.50
Beds: 3F 1D 2T **Baths:** 3 En
🛏 🄿 (6) 📺 ✕ Ⓥ ▥

Hillside, *16 Tullyglass Crescent, Shannon, Co Clare.* Family home situated in quiet cul-de-sac. 5 mins drive from Shannon Airport and famous Bunratty Castle. Rooms with television, hairdryer and tea/coffee making facilities. Ideally located for touring mid-west region. Warm welcome assured.
Open: All year
061 362103 A Murphy
hillsidebb@eircom.net
D: Fr €19.00-€23.00 **S:** Fr €23.00-€25.50
Beds: 1F 1D 2T **Baths:** 1 En 1 Pr 1 Sh
🛏 🅿 ⅄ 📺 ▥ cc

Avalon, *11 Ballycaseymore Hill, Shannon, County Clare.* 5 minutes' drive to airport. Ideally located for touring mid-west region.
Open: All Year (not Xmas)
061 362032 (also fax) M O'Loughlin
avalonbnb@eircom.net
D: Fr €25.50
Beds: 3D **Baths:** 2 Ensuite 1 Private
🛏 🅿 (4) ⅄ 📺 ▥

Tulla
R4979

Cragville, *Tulla, Ennis, Co Clare.* Situated in centre of Clare Lakelands, noted for fishing and near Bunratty folk park.
Open: Mar to Dec **Grades:** BF Approv
065 6835110 Mrs Culloo
annculloo@ireland.com
D: Fr €25.00 **S:** Fr €30.00
Beds: 1F 1T 1D **Baths:** 2 En 1 Pr
🛏 🅿 ⅄ 📺 🐾 Ⓥ ▥ ▪

BEDROOMS

D = Double   S = Single

T = Twin   F = Family

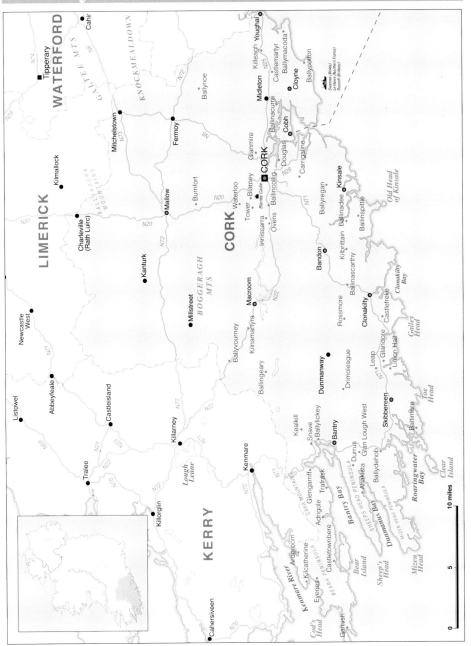

AIRPORT ⊕

Cork Airport - tel. 021 4313131.

AIR SERVICES & AIRLINES

Cork to: Heathrow, Manchester, Birmingham. **Aer Lingus** - in Republic tel. 0818 365000; in Northern Ireland & the UK tel. 0845 0844444.

Cork to Stansted.
Ryanair - in Republic - 0818 303030; in N Ireland & the UK - 0871 2460000.

RAIL ⇌

Cork City is at the end of a major line to *Dublin* via *Thurles* and *Portlaoise*.

There is also a branch line to *Youghal*. Phone **Irish Rail** - 01 8366222.

BUS 🚌

Cork to Dublin (6 daily). Cork to Limerick (6 daily). Phone **Bus Eireann** on 01 8366111.

For *Bantry*, *Castletownbere* and *Glengariff*, phone **O'Donoghues** on 027 70007.

FERRIES ⛴

Cork (Ringaskiddy) to: Swansea (10 hrs) **Swansea Cork Ferries**. In Republic, tel. 021 4271166. In UK, tel. 01792 456116.

TOURIST INFORMATION OFFICES *i*

Wolfe Tone Square, **Bantry** (Jun to Sep), 027 50229.

Clonakilty (Jul to Sep), 023 33226.

Spy Hill, **Cobh** (Easter to Sep), 021 4813301.

Grand Parade, **Cork** (open all year), 021 4255100.

Main St, **Glengarriff** (Jul to Aug), 027 63084.

Pier Road, **Kinsale** (Mar to Nov), 021 4772234.

North Street, **Skibbereen**, 028 21766.

Market Square, **Youghal**, 024 20170.

Adrigole

√8050

Ocean View Farm House, *Faha East, Trafrask, Adrigole, Bantry, Co Cork.*
Open: Easter to Oct
027 60069
Mrs O'Sullivan

oceanviewfarmhouse@eircom.net
www.beara.info.com/accomm/oceanview
D: Fr €23.00-€25.00 **S:** Fr €25.00-€30.00
Beds: 1F 1D 1T 2S **Baths:** 2 Sh
ॐ 🅿 (5) 📺 ✕ 🔽 🎞, ▪
Comfortable home in tranquil rural setting on scenic Ring of Beara. Adjacent to Beara Way walk & cycleway, West Cork sailing & leisure centre close by. Scenic walks, horseriding, angling, fishing, swimming, golfing. Near famous Healy Pass, Dunboy Castle and famed 'Garnish Island Italian Gardens'.

Ahakista

V8740

Hillcrest House, *Ahakista, Durrus, Bantry, Co Cork.* Traditional farmhouse, ensuite rooms, breakfast menu, large garden, beach, boating, Sheep's Head Way walking.
Open: Apr to Nov
027 67045 Mrs Hegarty
agneshegarty@oceanfree.net
D: Fr €30.00-€34.00 **S:** Fr €38.00-€44.00
Beds: 2F 1D 1T **Baths:** 3 En 1 Pr
ॐ (4) 🅿 (6) ✕ 📺 ╋ ✕ 🔽 🎞, ▪

Reenmore Farmhouse, *Ahakista, Durrus, Bantry, Co Cork.* Old style farmhouse in peaceful surroundings.
Open: Mar to Nov
027 67051 Mrs Barry
D: Fr €28.00
Beds: 1D
🅿 (8) 📺 ✕ 🔽 🎞, ▪

RATES

D = Price range per person sharing in a double or twin room

S = Price range for a single room

Ardgroom

V6955

Sea Villa, *Coast Road, Ardgroom, Bantry, Co Cork.* Situated in a beautiful and breathtaking rugged landscape. Surrounded by sea, mountains, hills.
Open: Mar to Nov
027 74369 (also fax) Mr and Mrs Sullivan
seavilla1@eircom.net
D: Fr €20.00 **S:** Fr €25.00
Beds: 3F **Baths:** 3 En
ॐ (6) 🅿

Canfie House, *Canfie, Ardgroom, Beara, Co Cork.* On Beara Way Path, magnificent views. Stone circle/village/restaurant 1km.
Open: Apr to Sep
027 74105 Mrs Leahy
hilaryleahy@eircom.net
D: Fr €15.50-€20.50 **S:** Fr €19.00-€25.50
Beds: 1F 1D 1T 1S **Baths:** 1 En 1 Sh
ॐ 🅿 📺 ✕ 🔽 🎞, ▪

O'Brien's, *Ardgroom, Bantry, Co Cork.* Family-run home in beautiful Ardgroom village. Glenbeg Lake, stone circle, within walking distance
Open: May to Oct
027 74019 Mrs O'Brien
ksobrien@eircom.net
D: Fr €22.50 **S:** Fr €20.50
Beds: 2D 1T **Baths:** 1 En 1 Sh
ॐ 📺 ✕ 🎞, ▪ cc

Harbour Scene, *Barrakilla, Ardgroom, Bantry, Co Cork.* Ring of Beara. Scenic views. Local stone circle and local fishing.
Open: Apr to Oct
027 74423 Mrs Hartnett **Fax: 027 74420**
harbourscene@eircom.net
D: Fr €19.00-€23.00 **S:** Fr €21.50-€25.50
Beds: 3D 1T **Baths:** 3 En 1 Sh
ॐ 🅿 (5) 📺 ╋ 🔽 🎞, ▪

Ballinacurra

W8871

Loughcarrig House, *Ballinacurra, Midleton, Co Cork.* Georgian house overlooking Cork Harbour estuary. Specialists in sea angling, birdwatching holidays and golfing.
Open: All year (not Xmas)
021 4631952 Brian & Cheryl Byrne **Fax: 021 4613707**
info@loughcarrig.com www.loughcarrig.com
D: Fr €35.00 **S:** Fr €39.00
Beds: 2F 2D 2T **Baths:** 6 En
ॐ 🅿 (30) 📺 ╋ 🔽 🎞, ▪

Ballinadee

W5651

Lochinver Farmhouse, *Ballinadee, Bandon, Co Cork.* Attractive farmhouse on dairy farm in scenic location, horseriding, beaches, golf nearby.
Open: Mar to Oct
021 4778124 Mrs Forde
hsforde@indigo.ie indigo.ie/~hsforde
D: Fr €25.00-€32.00 **S:** Fr €25.00-€44.00
Beds: 1F 2D 1T 1S **Baths:** 3 En 1 Sh
ॐ **P** (10) ⌇ 📺 Ⓥ ⅏ ■ cc

Ballinascarthy

W4046

Ard Na Greine, *Ballinascarthy, Clonakilty, Co Cork.* A warm welcome awaits you in this comfortable home with a spectacular view.
Open: All Year
023 39104 Mrs Walsh **Fax: 023 39397**
normawalsh1@eircom.net www.ardnagreine.com
D: Fr €28.50-€32.00 **S:** Fr €32.00-€37.00
Beds: 3D 1S 2F **Baths:** 5 En
ॐ **P** 📺 ⋔ ✕ Ⓥ ⅏ ✱ cc

Ballincollig

W5971

Westfield House, *West Village, Ballincollig, Cork.* Convenient to airport, ferryport, Blarney, Kinsale, Cobh & West Cork.
Open: All year (not Xmas/New Year)
021 4871824 Mrs Cotter **Fax: 021 4877415**
rosecotter@tinet.ie www.westfieldhousebandb.com
D: Fr €28.00-€32.00 **S:** Fr €30.00-€40.00
Beds: 2F 1D 1T **Baths:** 3 En 1 Pr
ॐ **P** (5) 📺 Ⓥ ⅏ ■ cc

Ballingeary

W1567

Cois Na Coille, *Gurteenakilla, Ballingeary, Macroom, Co Cork.* Modern bungalow in peaceful scenic location. Painters' & photographers' paradise only 4km Gougane National Park.
Open: All Year (not Xmas/New Year)
026 47172 (also fax) Mr & Mrs Kelleher
coisnacoille@eircom.net
D: Fr €23.00
Beds: 1F 2D 1T **Baths:** 1 Ensuite 1 Private 1 Shared
ॐ **P** 📺 ⋔ ✕ Ⓥ ⅏ ■

Ballinspittle

W5846

Raheen House, *Kilgobbin, Ballinspittle, Kinsale, Co Cork.* Luxury farmhouse. Views of the Old Head of Kinsale. Horseriding, beaches, golf
Open: May to Sep
021 4778173 (also fax) Mrs Sweetman
raheenhouse@eircom.ie
www.dragnet-systems.ie/dira/raheen
D: Fr €33.00 **S:** Fr €45.00
Beds: 3D 1T **Baths:** 4 En
ॐ **P** 📺 ⅏ ■

Silver Birch, *Kilgobbin, Ballinspittle, Kinsale, Cork.* Modern country home with panoramic views overlooking river. 10 mins' drive from Kinsale. Ideal base for touring and exploring the southern coastline. Peaceful and quiet. Comfortable rooms, plenty of parking, close to beaches. Excellent bar food nearby, family rooms Please ring for directions.
Open: Mar to Oct
021 4778111 (also fax) Mrs Collins
silverbirchkinsale@eircom.net
D: Fr €23.00-€30.00 **S:** Fr €38.00
Beds: 2F 4D 1S **Baths:** 4 En 1 Pr 2 Sh
ॐ **P** 📺 ⋔ ✕ Ⓥ ⅏ ■ cc

Ballycotton

W9963

Spanish Point Guest House, *Ballycotton, Midleton, Co Cork.*
Open: All year
021 4646177
Mrs Tattan **Fax: 021 4646179**
SpanishP@Indigo.ie
D: Fr €40.00 **S:** Fr €50.00
Beds: 2F 3D **Baths:** 5 En
ॐ **P** (15) 📺 ⋔ ✕ Ⓥ ⅏ ■ cc
We are a 3 Star B&B and restaurant specialising in local produce and fresh fish caught from our own trawler. This year we have built a wooden sun deck for our residents to relax on and enjoy the view. Superb food.

Planning a longer stay?
Always ask for any special rates

Ballydehob

√9835

Lynwood, *Schull Road, Ballydehob, Skibbereen, Co Cork.* On Mizen Ring, ideal for exploring. Breakfast menu, Ballydehob 300m.
Open: Easter to Oct
028 37124 (also fax) Mrs Vaughan
lynwoodbb@hotmail.com
D: Fr €27.50 **S:** Fr €35.00
Beds: 1F 3D **Baths:** 4 En
🛏 (1) 🅿 📺 🛏 Ⓥ 🖩 🛢

The Woodcock, *Ballydehob, Skibbereen, Co Cork.* Family business established over 20 yrs, refurbished March 1998, located in Main St.
Open: All Year
028 37139 Mrs Morris
D: Fr €21.50-€25.50 **S:** Fr €21.50-€25.50
Beds: 1F 1D 1T **Baths:** 3 En 2 Sh
🛏 (8) 🅿 (3) 🛏 ✕ Ⓥ 🖩 cc

Ballylickey

√0053

La Mirage, *Droumdaniel, Ballylickey, Bantry, Co Cork.* Country house overlooking Bantry Bay. Tea/coffee, home baking on arrival.
Open: Apr to Sep **Grades:** BF Approv
027 50688 Ms Lynch
lamirage@eircom.net
D: Fr €28.00-€30.00 **S:** Fr €43.00-€45.00
Beds: 2F 1T 1D **Baths:** 2 En 2 Pr
🛏 🅿 ⌇ 📺 🖩 🛢

Reendonegan House, *Reendonegan, Ballylickey, Bantry, Co Cork.* C18th Georgian country home overlooking Reendonegan Lough and Bantry Bay.
Open: Mar to Oct
027 51455 (also fax) Mrs Casey
reendonegan@eircom.net
D: Fr €32.00
Beds: 1F 2D **Baths:** 3 En
🛏 🅿 (6) 📺 🖩

Ballymacoda

X0471

Castle Farm, *Ballycrenane, Ballymacoda, Cork.* 1780 Georgian house overlooking Ballycotton Bay on 75 acre dairy farm.
Open: Apr to Oct
024 98165 Mrs Leahy
D: Fr €28.00
Beds: 2F 2D 1T **Baths:** 5 En
🛏 (3) 🅿 (5) ⌇ 📺 🛏 🖩 🛢

Ballynoe

W9389

Boulta House, *Ballynoe, Mallow, Co Cork.* 250-year-old farmhouse in idyllic surroundings on dairy/tillage farm, 12km Lismore Heritage Town.
Open: All year
058 59247 Mrs Mulcahy
D: Fr €30.00 **S:** Fr €25.00
Beds: 1F 1D 1S **Baths:** 1 En 1 Pr 1 Sh
🛏 🅿 🛏 ✕ Ⓥ 🖩

Ballyregan

W6154

Siroco, *Ballyregan, Kinsale, Co Cork.*
Open: May to Sep
Grades: BF Approv
021 4775129 (also fax) Mrs
D: Fr €25.00-€28.00
Beds: 3D
Baths: 2 En

⌇ 🖩 🛢

A modern bungalow in country area. Scenic views, car park. Bord Failte approved. Hairdryers, tea/coffee facilities in room. Kinsale 5 km, Innishannon 5 km. Close to amenities. Golf course, angling, horseriding, sailing, boat trips within 10 km. Airport 15 mins, ferry 25 mins.

Please respect a B&B's wishes regarding children, animals and smoking

B&B owners may vary rates – be sure to check when booking

Ballyvourney
W1977

The Mills Inn, *Ballyvourney, Macroom, Co Cork.*
One of Ireland's oldest inns (1755) set in acres of landscaped gardens.
Open: All Year
026 45237 Mr Scannell **Fax: 026 45454**
D: Fr €38.00
Beds: 2F 5T 5D **Baths:** 10 Ensuite
☎ 🅿 📺 🗙 🗸 🛏 ⅲ ⅲ & ▪

Baltimore
W0526

Rathmore House, *Baltimore, Skibbereen, Co Cork.*
Open: All year
028 20362 (also fax)
Mrs O'Driscoll

rathmorehouse@eircom.net
www.baltimore-ireland.com/rathmorehouse
D: Fr €27.00-€30.00 **S:** Fr €39.00-€42.50
Beds: 1F 2D 3T 1S **Baths:** 6 En
☎ 🅿 (10) 📺 🛏 🗙 🗸 ⅲ & ▪ cc
Georgian-style house sits on the outskirts of Baltimore with panoramic views over the harbour and islands. Hostess Marguerite O'Driscoll is noted for her warm Irish hospitality - she has a unique gift of making you feel at home.

Corner House, *Baltimore, Skibbereen, Co Cork.*
Family-run guest house situated in the centre of village.
Open: Easter to Oct
028 20143 Mr O Driscoll
D: Fr €25.00
Beds: 2F 2D 2T **Baths:** 6 En
☎ 📺 🗙 🗸 ⅲ

Channel View, *Baltimore, Skibbereen, Co Cork.*
Spacious House, spectacular sea views, scenic walks, Irish Tourist Board Approved.
Open: Mar to Oct
028 20440 Mrs Harrington
channelview@eircom.net
D: Fr €24.00-€28.50 **S:** Fr €38.00
Beds: 2F 2D 1T **Baths:** 4 En 4 Pr 1 Sh
☎ 🅿 (6) 📺 🗸 ⅲ & ▪ cc

Bandon
W4955

Oakgrove, *Kilbrogan, Bandon, Co Cork.*
Modern family home in beautiful countryside convenient for all amenities.
Open: All Year
023 41962 (also fax) Mrs O'Brien
D: Fr €29.00
Beds: 1F 2T 1D **Baths:** 2 Ensuite 2 Shared
☎ 🅿 (20) 🗸 📺 🛏 🗙 🗸 ⅲ

St Annes, *Clonakilty Road, Bandon, Co Cork.*
Georgian house, 0.5 miles from small county town. Nice gardens.
Open: All Year (not Xmas/New Year)
023 44239 (also fax) Mrs Buckley
D: Fr €25.50-€27.00 **S:** Fr €32.00
Beds: 2F 2D 1T 1S **Baths:** 6 En
☎ 🅿 🗸 📺 🛏 ⅲ ▪ cc

Bantry
W0048

Shangri La, *Glengarriff Road, Bantry, Co Cork.*
Open: Feb to Nov
027 50244 (also fax)
Mrs Schiesser

schiesserbb@eircom.net
D: Fr €28.00-€30.00 **S:** Fr €39.00-€42.50
Beds: 2F 2T 2D **Baths:** 6 En
☎ 🅿 (6) 📺 🗙 🗸 ⅲ ▪ cc
Friendly family home with magnificent views of Bantry Bay. On main Bantry-Glengarriff road (N71). Big garden, golf, riding, fishing, cycle hire nearby. Early breakfast available. Tea making facilities, light dinner on request. Near town. Credit cards, vouchers accepted. Private parking

Rocklands, *Gurteenroe, Bantry, Co Cork.* On Bantry-Glengarriff Road N71. panoramic views. Tea/coffee & home baking on arrival.
Open: Mar to Sep **Grades:** BF Approv
027 50212 Mrs Murray
D: Fr €27.00-€30.00 **S:** Fr €45.00
Beds: 1F 1T 1D **Baths:** 3 En
🅿 (5) 🗸 📺 🗸 ⅲ

Planning a longer stay?
Always ask for any special rates

La Mirage, *Droumdaniel, Ballylickey, Bantry, Co Cork.* Country house overlooking Bantry Bay. Tea/coffee, home baking on arrival.

Open: Apr to Sep **Grades:** BF Approv
027 50688 Ms Lynch
lamirage@eircom.net
D: Fr €28.00-€30.00 **S:** Fr €43.00-€45.00
Beds: 2F 1T 1D **Baths:** 2 En 2 Pr
⌂ ₧ ⅋ ⅏ ▥, ▪

Vickery's Inn Guest House, *New Street, Bantry, Co Cork.* Family-run guest house, restaurant/bar, with unique foyer in original 1850s courtyard.

Open: All year (not Xmas)
027 50006 (also fax) Ms Vickery
vickerys_lnn@westcork.com
www.westcork.com/vickerys-inn
D: Fr €33.00-€40.00 **S:** Fr €50.00-€58.00
Beds: 9D 2F 2T **Baths:** 13 En
⌂ ₧ (15) ⅏ ✕ �> ▥, ▪ cc

Dromcloc House, *Bantry, Co Cork.* Seaside dairy farm at Relane Point, signposted 2km west of Bantry off N71.

Open: Mar to Nov
027 50030 (also fax) Mrs Crowley
dromcloc@indigo.ie
cork-guide.ie/bantry/dromclochouse
D: Fr €26.00-€30.00 **S:** Fr €35.00-€40.00
Beds: 2F 2D 2T **Baths:** 5 En 1 Pr
⌂ ₧ (10) ⅋ ⅏ ✚ ✕ �> ▥,

Sea Mount Farmhouse, *Goats Path Road, Glan Lough West, Bantry, Co Cork.* Old-style farmhouse. 7 miles from Bantry. Hill walking, mountains and sea views.

Open: Apr to Oct **Grades:** BF Approv
027 61226 (also fax) Mrs McCarthy
info@seamountfarm.com www.seamountfarm.com
D: Fr €28.00
Beds: 6F 2T 4D
₧ (7) ⅋ ⅏ ▥, ▪ cc

Coulin, *Gurteenroe, Bantry, Co Cork.* Comfortable home. Ensuite rooms, TV in bedrooms. Electric blankets.

Open: May to Sep
027 50020 Mrs Cronin
D: Fr €25.00
Beds: 1T 2D
₧ ▥, ▪

Dunauley, *Seskin, Bantry, Co Cork.* Enjoy spectacular panoramic views overlooking Bantry Bay, Caha Mountains, town and islands.

Open: May to Sep
027 50290 (also fax) Mrs McAuley
rosemarymcauley@eircom.net www.dunauley.com
D: Fr €28.00-€38.00 **S:** Fr €32.00-€38.00
Beds: 1F 3D 2T **Baths:** 5 En
⌂ (12) ₧ (5) ⅋ ▥, ▪

Sonamar, *Dromleigh South, Bantry, Co Cork.* Distinctive bungalow and gardens, panoramic view of Bantry Bay, scenic location.

Open: Easter to Sep
027 50502 Mrs O'Sullivan
sonamar@iol.ie
D: Fr €21.50-€24.00 **S:** Fr €30.00-€32.50
Beds: 2F 2D 1T **Baths:** 3 En 2 Sh
₧ (8) ⅋ ⅏ ▥, ▪

Leyton, *23 Slip Lawn, Bantry, Co Cork.* Friendly, relaxing, home, quiet locality overlooking Bantry. All amenities nearby.

Open: May to Sep
027 50665 Mrs Harrington
leyton@iolfree.ie
D: Fr €23.00-€25.50 **S:** Fr €32.00
Beds: 1F 1D 1T **Baths:** 2 En 1 Sh
⌂ ₧ (3) ⅏ ✚ ▥, ▪ cc

The Mill, *Newtown, Bantry, Co Cork.* Luxurious home, ample parking. N71 Bantry-Glengarriff road, 1 km from town centre.

Open: Easter to 1 Nov
027 50278 (also fax) Mrs Kramer
Themill@eirecom.net
D: Fr €25.50-€29.00 **S:** Fr €38.00
Beds: 1F 3D 2T **Baths:** 6 En
⌂ (4) ₧ (10) ⅋ ⅏ ▥, ▪

Doire Liath, *Newtown, Bantry, Co Cork.* A family welcome awaits you. Five mins' walk from town centre. Private off-road parking. Beautiful views of nearby Seskin Mountain. Easy access to Beara, Sheep's Head and Mizen Peninsulas and local historical sites. Horse riding, fishing, golf and leisure centre all available locally.

Open: All year (not Xmas)
027 50223 Mrs Linehan
doireliath@eircom.net
D: Fr €17.00-€20.00 **S:** Fr €20.00-€25.00
Beds: 1F 2D 1S **Baths:** 3 En 1 Pr
⌂ ₧ (4) ▥,

Larchwood House, *Pearson's Bridge, Bantry, Co Cork.* Attractive modern house, warm welcome, beautiful riverside garden. Gourmet restaurant attached.
Open: All Year (not Xmas/New Year)
027 66181 S Vaughan
D: Fr €32.00 **S:** Fr €32.00
Beds: 2F 1T 1D
🛏 🅿 (20) ✕ 📺 ⛛ cc

Blarney
W6175

Garrycloyne Lodge, *Garrycloyne, Blarney, Cork.*
Open: Easter to Nov
021 4886214 Mrs Hallissey
garrycloynelodge@eircom.net
D: Fr €28.00-€30.00 **S:** Fr €40.00-€42.00
Beds: 1F 2D 1T **Baths:** 4 En
🛏 🅿 (6) 📺 🛏 ⛛ ⛬ cc
Comfortable old-style farmhouse situated 5km north of Blarney. Peaceful atmosphere and a reputation for hospitality. Working dairy farm on 145 acres. Large mature garden. Four bedrooms ensuite on ground floor. Tea/coffee on arrival. Signposted from Blarney on Waterloo Road.

Ashlee Lodge, *Tower, Blarney, Cork.* Luxury 4 Star guesthouse, situated on R617, leisure facilities, breakfast menu.
Open: All year (not Xmas)
Grades: BF 4 Star
021 4385346 & 087 2773449 (M) Mr & Mrs O'Leary
Fax: 021 4385726
info@ashleelodge.com www.ashleelodge.com
D: Fr €35.00-€70.00 **S:** Fr €65.00-€160.00
Beds: 10D **Baths:** 10 En
🛏 🅿 ⛛ 📺 ⛛ ⛬ cc

Travellers Joy, *Tower, Blarney, Cork.* Wonderful, warm home, highly recommended, award-winning gardens. Quality breakfasts.
Open: Feb to Dec
021 4385541 Mrs O'Shea
D: Fr €27.00-€31.00 **S:** Fr €38.00-€42.00
Beds: 2F 1T **Baths:** 3 En
🛏 🅿 ⛛ 📺 🛏 ⛬ cc

Yvory House, *Killowen, Blarney, Cork.* Luxurious modern bungalow set in scenic farming location.
Open: March to Nov
021 4381128 Mrs Sisk
D: Fr €21.50-€25.50 **S:** Fr €30.00-€35.50
Beds: 1T 3D **Baths:** 4 En
🛏 (9) 🅿 (6) ⛛ 📺 ⛛ ⛬ cc

Buena Vista, *Station Road, Blarney, Cork.* Beautiful luxrious bungalow, private gardens, golf course and pitch 'n' putt 250m.
Open: All Year (not Xmas)
021 4385035 Mr & Mrs Callaghan
D: Fr €24.00-€25.50 **S:** Fr €34.00-€38.00
Beds: 2F 2D 1T **Baths:** 5 Ensuite
🛏 🅿 (8) 📺 ⛬ ⛬

Rosemount, *The Square, Blarney, Cork.* Dormer bungalow, landscaped gardens, convenient to bus stop, castle and entertainment
Open: Easter to Nov
021 385584 Mrs Cronin
D: Fr €28.00
Beds: 1F 2D 2T **Baths:** 2 En 2 Pr 1 Sh
🛏 (4) 🅿 (10) ⛬ ⛬

Firgrove, *1 Castle Close Villas, Blarney, Cork.* Detached house, quiet area, minute's walk to bus, castle, restaurants.
Open: Mar to Nov
021 381403 Mrs O'Brien
D: Fr €28.00
Beds: 1F 2D 1T 1S **Baths:** 2 En 1 Pr 1 Sh
🛏 (8) 🅿 (3) ⛛ 📺 ⛬ ⛬

Allcorn's Country Home, *Shournagh Road, Blarney, Cork.* Really spacious riverside home & gardens, surrounded by woodlands & meadows on Killarney road (R617).
Open: Easter to Oct
021 385577 Mrs Allcorn **Fax:** 021 382828
D: Fr €30.00
Beds: 2F 1D 1S **Baths:** 3 Ensuite 1 Shared
🛏 🅿 (6) ⛛ 🛏 📺 ⛬ ⛬

Burnfort
W5990

Windwood, *Burnfort, Mallow, Co Cork.* Welcoming home in rural setting. Scenic walks along country lanes.
Open: All year
022 29417 Mrs Goodman
windwood@indigo.ie
D: Fr €20.00 **S:** Fr €20.00
Beds: 1D 1T **Baths:** 1 En 1 Pr
🛏 🅿 (4) ⛛ 📺 🛏 ✕ ⛬ ⛬ cc

Carrigaline
W7261

Willows, *Ballea Road, Carrigaline, Cork.*
Split level house, warm welcome, airport 3 miles, ferry port 3 miles.
Open: All year (not Xmas)
021 4372669 Mrs O'Leary
D: Fr €26.00-€30.00 **S:** Fr €35.00
Beds: 5F 1D 1T **Baths:** 3 En 1 Sh
⛵ 🅿 ✗ 📺 🛏, ▪

Castlefreke
W3336

Springfield House, *Kilkern, Castlefreke, Clonakilty, Co Cork.* Warm homely holiday awaits you. Beautiful Georgian farmhouse. Spacious rooms.
Open: Jan to Nov
023 40622 (also fax) Mr & Mrs Callanan
jandmcallanan@eircom.net
homepage.eircom.net/~springfieldhouse
D: Fr €30.00-€33.00 **S:** Fr €35.00-€39.00
Beds: 2F 2D **Baths:** 3 En 1 Pr
⛵ 🅿 📺 ✗ 🛏,

Castlemartyr
W9674

Kilamuckey House, *Castlemartyr, Midleton, Co Cork.* A period house on mature gardens, spacious rooms, good hospitality.
Open: May to Oct
021 4667266 The de Cogans
D: Fr €30.00 **S:** Fr €35.00
Beds: 3D
⛵ (10) 🅿 ✗ ✗ 📺 ▪ cc

Castletownbere
W6846

Massabielle, *Filane, Castletownbere, Bantry, Co Cork.* Perfectly situated for exploring the beautiful Ring of Beara. Warm welcome.
Open: Easter to Oct
027 70341 (also fax) Mrs Sheehan
massabielle@eircom.net
www.bearainfo.com/accom/massabielle
D: Fr €20.00-€23.00 **S:** Fr €24.00-€27.00
Beds: 1F 1D 1T **Baths:** 2 En 1 Pr
⛵ 🅿 📺 🛏 ✗ 📺 🛏, ▪ cc

Realt Na Mara, *Castletownbere, Bantry, Co Cork.* Comfortable home overlooking sea, popular walking route, personal attention.
Open: All Year
027 70101 Mrs Donegan
D: Fr €21.50-€24.00 **S:** Fr €30.00-€32.50
Beds: 1F 1D 3T **Baths:** 4 En
⛵ 🅿 (10) 📺 🛏 🛏, ✳ cc

Bay View House, *West End, Castletownbere, Bantry, Co Cork.* Nice old-fashioned house in the town centre, scenic surroundings everywhere.
Open: Jun to Sep
027 70099 Mrs Murphy
D: Fr €23.00
Beds: 3D **Baths:** 1 Sh
⛵ (12) 🛏,

Sea Breeze, *Derrymihan, Castletownbere, Bantry, Co Cork.* Comfortable modern home in a peaceful spot at sea shore.
Open: All Year (not Xmas/New Year)
027 70508 (also fax) Mrs McGurn
mcgurna@gofree.indigo.ie
D: Fr €21.50-€25.50 **S:** Fr €25.50-€29.00
Beds: 1F 2D **Baths:** 3 En
⛵ 🅿 ✗ 📺 📺 🛏, ▪

Clonakilty
W3841

Springfield House, *Kilkern, Castlefreke, Clonakilty, Co Cork.*
Open: Jan to Nov
023 40622 (also fax) Mr & Mrs Callanan
jandmcallanan@eircom.net
homepage.eircom.net/~springfieldhouse
D: Fr €30.00-€33.00 **S:** Fr €35.00-€39.00
Beds: 2F 2D **Baths:** 3 En 1 Pr
⛵ 🅿 📺 ✗ 🛏,
Warm homely holiday awaits you. Beautiful Georgian farmhouse. Spacious rooms. Peaceful location, dairy farm with panoramic view of Atlantic ocean. National awards of excellence. Delicious home cooking. Fresh farm produce. Signposted on Clonakilty - Rosscarbery N71. Activities nearby. Tea/coffee on arrival.

Please respect a B&B's wishes regarding children, animals and smoking

Hillcrest, *Desert, Clonakilty, Co Cork.* We offer a friendly comfortable home, but you will be stunned by the view.
Open: Easter to Sep
023 34799 Mr & Mrs Mullins
D: Fr €30.00 **S:** Fr €40.00
Beds: 2F 1T 1D **Baths:** 4 En
🛏 (4) 🅿 (10) ⊁ 📺 🐾 Ⓥ 🖩 🔥 🛁 ▪

Hillside Farm, *Kilgarriffe, Clonakilty, Co Cork.* Views of peaceful countryside, pub singing and entertainment, Lisnagun and Templeryan stone circles.
Open: Easter to Oct
023 33139 & 023 34588 Mrs Helen
Richardhelen@eircom.net
D: Fr €27.00-€29.00 **S:** Fr €33.00-€37.00
Beds: 4F 1D 2T **Baths:** 2 En 1 Pr 1 Sh
🛏 🅿 (10) ⊁ 📺 🐾 ✕ 🖩 ▪

Liscubba House, *Rossmore, Clonakilty, Co Cork.* Comfortable farmhouse in peaceful countryside, off the beaten track. Home cooking a speciality.
Open: All year
023 38679 Mrs Beechinor
beechal@eircom.net
D: Fr €25.00-€30.00 **S:** Fr €30.00
Beds: 1F 1D 1T **Baths:** 2 En 1 Sh
🛏 🅿 📺 🐾 ✕ Ⓥ 🖩

Fernhill House, *Clonakilty, Co Cork.* Family-run hotel in picturesque grounds, situated 1km from Clonakilty.
Open: All Year (not Xmas)
023 33258 Mrs O'Neill **Fax:** 023 34003
fernhillhh@eircom.net
D: Fr €45.00
Beds: 3F 1T 7D
🛏 🅿 📺 🐾 ✕ Ⓥ 🖩 ▪

Shalom, *Ballyduvane, Clonakilty, Co Cork.* Modern bungalow in rural setting, situated on the N71.
Open: Mar to Oct
023 33473 Mrs Moore
D: Fr €25.50
Beds: 3D **Baths:** 2 En 1 Pr
🛏 🅿 📺 🖩

Planning a longer stay?
Always ask for any special rates

B&B owners may vary rates – be sure to check when booking

Duvane Farm, *Ballyduvane, Clonakilty, Co Cork.* Scenic countryside view. Lovely woodland garden: sit and relax or stroll along paths.
Open: Easter to Oct
023 33129 (also fax) Mrs McCarthy
D: Fr €25.50-€32.00 **S:** Fr €25.50-€38.00
Beds: 1F 4D 1S **Baths:** 4 En 1 Pr
🛏 (5) ⊁ 📺 🐾 🖩 ▪

Nordav, *Western Road, Clonakilty, Co Cork.* Elegant family home surrounded by mature trees, very private, 200 metres town centre.
Open: Mar to Oct
023 33655 (also fax) Mrs McMahon
D: Fr €30.00
Beds: 1F 3D 1T **Baths:** 5 En
🛏 🅿 (4) 📺 🐾 Ⓥ 🖩 🔥 ▪

Melrose, *The Miles, Clonakilty, Co Cork.* Modern home, town outskirts. Gardens, near beach, golf, pitch & putt.
Open: All Year (not Xmas)
023 33956 (also fax) Mrs O'Brien
D: Fr €30.00
Beds: 2F 1T 2D **Baths:** 5 Ensuite 1 Private
🛏 🅿 (6) 📺 Ⓥ 🖩 ▪

Cobh

W8067

Glebe House, *Tay Road, Cobh, Co Cork.* Modern friendly home near Fota wildlife, Ringaskiddy ferries, golf, fishing, sailing, birdwatching.
Open: All year (not Xmas)
021 4811373 Mrs & Mrs Coughlan
glebehouse@eircom.net www.glebehousecobh.com
D: Fr €28.00-€32.00 **S:** Fr €38.00-€45.00
Beds: 4F 4D 4T **Baths:** 4 En 4 Pr
🛏 🅿 (6) 📺 Ⓥ 🖩 ▪ cc

Tearmann, *Ballynoe, Cobh, Co Cork.* Traditional farmhouse built 1860. Tranquil setting with large gardens.
Open: Mar to Oct
021 4813182 Mrs Maddox **Fax:** 021 814011
D: Fr €26.00
Beds: 1F 1D 1T **Baths:** 2 Ensuite 1 Private
🛏 🅿 (4) 📺 ✕ 🖩 ▪

W6571

Glenmalure, Carrigaline Road, Douglas, Cork.
Open: All year (not Xmas)
021 4894324 Mrs French
D: Fr €26.00-€30.00
S: Fr €32.00-€40.00
Beds: 1F 2D **Baths:** 2 En 1 Sh
 (8) TV 🖾 ⬛ 🐾

Enjoy friendly personal attention in modern comfortable family home. Ideal touring base close to ferryport, airport and hotels. Early breakfasts. Easily located off N25 at Douglas Exit.

Deaneville, Wellington Road, Cork.
Open: All year (not Xmas)
021 4506406 (also fax) B Madden
info@deaneville.com www.deaneville.com
D: Fr €26.00-€30.00 **S:** Fr €35.00-€40.00
Beds: 1F 2D 2T **Baths:** 2 En 2 Pr
  TV 🖾 ⬛ cc

Beautiful Georgian house situated in the city. Convenient for touring, 2 minutes bus and railway stations, airport 10 minutes, ferry 15 mins. Family home where guests come first. All rooms with tea/coffee facilities and hairdryers.

Lough Mahon House, Lower Glanmire Road, Tivoli, Cork. Family-run comfortable Georgian house with superb ensuite accommodation. Private floodlit car park.
Open: All year **Grades:** BF 3 Star, AA 3 Diamond
021 4502142 M Meagher **Fax:** 021 4501804
info@loughmahon.com www.loughmahon.com
D: Fr €35.00-€44.50 **S:** Fr €44.50-€57.00
Beds: 1F 2T 3D **Baths:** 6 En
  TV 🖾 ⬛ cc

Acorn House, 14 St Patrick's Hill, Cork.
City centre refurbished listed Georgian house, 5 minutes bus/rail.
Open: All year (not Xmas)
021 4502474 (also fax) Miss Boles
info@acornhouse-cork.com www.acornhouse-cork.com
D: Fr €32.00-€55.00 **S:** Fr €40.00-€60.00
Beds: 4F 2D 1T 2S **Baths:** 9 En
  (7) TV 🖾 ⬛ cc

St Kilda's, Western Road, Cork. Superb ensuite accommodation, just a 10-min walk to city centre, private off-street car parking, modern swimming/ leisure centre nearby, your host Gerald Collins.
Open: All year (not Xmas)
021 4273095 Mr Collins **Fax: 021 4275015**
gerald@stkildas.com www.stkildas.com
D: Fr €30.00-€45.00 **S:** Fr €40.00-€65.00
Beds: 11F 8D 2T **Baths:** 21 En
  (16) TV 🖾 ⬛ cc

Antoine House, Western Road, Cork.
Centrally located, 5 mins' walk city centre. Near airport, train station, bus station.
Open: All year
021 4273494 Mr Cross **Fax: 021 4273092**
info@antoinehouse.com www.antoinehouse.com
D: Fr €25.00-€40.00 **S:** Fr €40.00-€50.00
Beds: 2F 2T 2D 2S **Baths:** 8 En
  TV 🖾 ✳ ⬛ cc

Tara House, 52 Lower Glanmire Road, Cork.
Town house 100+ years old. Convenient city, and as base for touring South West.
Open: All Year (not Xmas)
021 500294 Mrs Chambers
D: Fr €28.00
Beds: 1F 2D 2T 1S **Baths:** 4 En 2 Sh
  TV 🐾 🖾 ⬛ cc

Fatima House, Grange Road, Douglas, Cork.
Modern warm comfortable home. Family run. Very easily located. Convenient Cork-Swansea ferry.
Open: All Year
021 362536 (also fax) Mrs O'Shea
D: Fr €32.50
Beds: 2F 2D **Baths:** 4 Ensuite
  (5) TV ⬛ ✳ ⬛

W5042

Travara Lodge, Courtmacsherry, Bandon, Co Cork. Comfortable Georgian house backed by woods overlooking Courtmacsherry Bay.
Open: All Year (not Xmas)
023 46493 R May & B Murphy
travaralodge@eircom.net
D: Fr €25.00-€32.00 **S:** Fr €25.00-€32.00
Beds: 2T 4D **Baths:** 6 En
  (6) 🐾 TV ⬛ cc

Crosshaven

W8060

Berminghams - Compass Rose, *Camden Road, Crosshaven, Cork.* Lovely country house convenient to fishing village. Central heating. Beautiful views of Cork Harbour and yachting marinas (3). Deep sea and shore angling. Golf and surfing. Cork Airport 9 miles. Cork-Swansea ferries 8 miles.
Open: All Year
021 4831181 Mr & Mrs Bermingham
compassrose@eircom.net
D: Fr €20.00-€25.00 **S:** Fr €25.50
Beds: 2F 2D 2T 1S **Baths:** 5 En 1 Sh
P (8) TV V

Douglas

W7069

Glenmalure, *Carrigaline Road, Douglas, Cork.* Enjoy friendly personal attention in modern comfortable family home. Ideal touring base.
Open: All year (not Xmas)
021 4894324 Mrs French
D: Fr €26.00-€30.00 **S:** Fr €32.00-€40.00
Beds: 1F 2D **Baths:** 2 En 1 Sh
P (8) TV

Drimoleague

W1245

Flower Lodge, *Caheragh North, Drimoleague, Skibbereen, Co Cork.* Flower Lodge is a comfortable family-run home with spacious ensuite bedrooms.
Open: May to Oct
028 31440 Mrs Collins
D: Fr €26.00
Beds: 1F 1T 1D **Baths:** 2 Ensuite
P (3) TV

Durrus

V9442

Rossmore House, *Durrus, Bantry, Co Cork.* Beautiful seaside bungalow overlooking Dunmanus Bay, 3km Durrus Village.
Open: Easter to Sep
027 61035 Mrs Dukelow
D: Fr €25.00 **S:** Fr €30.00
Beds: 1T 2D **Baths:** 2 Sh
P (6) TV

Avoca House, *Durrus, Bantry, Co Cork.* A haven for touring Sheeps & Mizen Head Peninsulas.
Open: Jan to Dec
027 61511 K Lynch
D: Fr €23.00-€25.50 **S:** Fr €25.50
Beds: 2F 1S 1D **Baths:** 4 En
P (3) TV **cc**

Eyeries

V6450

Formanes House, *Eyeries, Beara, County Cork.* Site on the Beara Way, spectacular view of sea and Kenmare River.
Open: All year (not Xmas)
027 74360 & 086 8334139 (M) Mrs O'Neill **Fax: 027 74360**
formaneshouse@eircom.net
D: Fr €22.50 **S:** Fr €27.00
Beds: 2F 2T **Baths:** 4 En
P TV V

Garnish

V5241

Windy Point House, *Garnish, Allihies, Bantry, Co Cork.* Overlooking cable-car to Dursey Island Luxurious rooms, panoramic views. Seafood a speciality.
Open: Apr to Oct
027 73017 (also fax) Mr & Mrs Sheehan
D: Fr €23.50 **S:** Fr €32.00
Beds: 3F 1D **Baths:** 4 En
P (10) TV V **cc**

Glan Lough West

V9741

Sea Mount Farmhouse, *Goats Path Road, Glan Lough West, Bantry, Co Cork.* Old-style farmhouse. 7 miles from Bantry. Hill walking, mountains and sea views.
Open: Apr to Oct **Grades:** BF Approv
027 61226 (also fax) Mrs McCarthy
info@seamountfarm.com www.seamountfarm.com
D: Fr €28.00
Beds: 6F 2T 4D
P (7) TV **cc**

Planning a longer stay?
Always ask for any special rates

Glandore

W2235

Kilfinnan Farm, *Glandore, Skibbereen, Co Cork.*
Picturesque location, stone circle 1 km, working
farm, sandy beaches nearby.
Open: All Year
028 33233 Mrs Mehigan
D: Fr €21.50-€25.50 **S:** Fr €29.00-€42.00
Beds: 2F 1D 1T **Baths:** 2 En 2 Sh
🛏 🅿 (6) ⅍ � ✗ ▥.

Glanmire

W7275

Kilmore, *Sallybrook, Glanmire, Cork.*
Modern comfortable family home in country,
convenient to Cork city.
Open: All year (not Xmas)
021 4821388 (also fax) Mrs Neary
D: Fr €25.00-€35.00 **S:** Fr €25.00-€35.00
Beds: 3F 1T **Baths:** 3 En 3 Pr
🛏 🅿 (10) ▥ � ▣ ▥.

Glengarriff

V9256

Cois Coille,
*Glengarriff, Bantry,
Co Cork.*
Open: Mar to Nov
Grades: BF Approv
**027 63202 & 086
8311293 (M)** R & N
Barry-Murphy

coiscoille@eircom.net
www.coiscoille.com
D: Fr €29.00 **S:** Fr €39.00
Beds: 2F 2D 2T **Baths:** 6 En
🛏 🅿 ⅍ ▣ ▣ ▥.
Warm hospitality in a modern comfortable home
overlooking Glengarriff Harbour, located 10 mins
walk from village. ITB approved with an award
winning garden in quiet woodland setting. Local
amenities include golf, hiking, fishing,
horseriding, garnish island, restaurants, pubs.

All details shown are as supplied by
B&B owners in Autumn 2002

B&B owners may vary rates – be sure to check when booking

Carraig Dubh House, *Droumgarriff,
Glengarriff, Bantry, Co Cork.* Family home,
peaceful location overlooking harbour and golf
club. Lovely gardens.
Open: Mar to Oct
027 63146 Mrs Connolly
Carraigdubhouse@hotmail.com
D: Fr €26.50 **S:** Fr €35.50
Beds: 1F 1T 2D **Baths:** 3 En 1 Pr
🛏 🅿 (4) ▣ ▥. ▪

Magannagan Farm, *Derryconnery, Glengarriff,
Bantry, Co Cork.* Working farm situated 3km from
Glengarriff village on Castlebere Road. Ideal
location for touring Rings of Beara and Kerry.
Perfect base for Beara Way Walk - passes
Magannagan Farm. Magnificent views of
Sugarloaf Mountain and scenic countryside.
Refreshments on arrival.
Open: Apr to Sep
027 63361 Mrs O'Shea
D: Fr €25.50 **S:** Fr €31.50
Beds: 3D **Baths:** 2 En 1 Pr
🛏 🅿 (5) ▣ ▥.

Island View House, *Glengarriff, Bantry, Co
Cork.* Comfortable home in quiet scenic area.
Most bedrooms overlooking Glengarriff Harbour.
Open: Easter to Nov
027 63081 Mrs O'Sullivan **Fax: 027 63298**
D: Fr €28.00
Beds: 2F 2D 2T **Baths:** 6 En
🛏 🅿 ▣ ▥. ⅙

Inniscarra

W5771

Knockawn Wood, *Curraleigh, Inniscarra,
Blarney, Cork.* Picturesque, peaceful, electric
blankets. Hot tea and scones on arrival. Fishing.
Lee Valley.
Open: All Year
021 4870284 (also fax) Mrs O'Donovan
odkmkwd@iol.ie homepages.iol.ie/~odkakwd
D: Fr €21.50-€24.00 **S:** Fr €25.50
Beds: 4F 1D 1T **Baths:** 3 En 1 Sh
🛏 🅿 (6) ▣ � ✗ ▥. ▪ cc

Chiriqui, *Canons Cross, Inniscarra, Co.Cork.*
Warm restful comfortable home, orthopaedic
beds, stimulating showers, Cork-Killarney route.
Open: Easter to Oct
021 871061 Mr & Mrs Roche **Fax: 021 871930 & 021
871061**
chiriqui@eircom.net
D: Fr €28.00
Beds: 1F 2D 1T **Baths:** 4 En
🅿 (4) ⅍ 📺 ▦, ▪ cc

Kealkill

W0456

Graceland, *Kealkill, Bantry, Co Cork.* Well-
established B&B. Choice of breakfast & a la Carte
evening meals. Wine licence.
Open: All Year
027 66055 Mrs Brennan **Fax: 027 66116**
gracelandbandb@hotmail.com
D: Fr €20.50-€23.00 **S:** Fr €27.00-€29.00
Beds: 1F 1D 2T **Baths:** 3 En 1 Pr
🅿 (4) ⅍ 📺 ✕ ▦, ✳ cc

Kilbrittain

W5247

Harbour Crest, *Rathclaren, Kilbrittain, Kinsale,
Co Cork.* Modern house convenient to Kinsale.
Elevated site overlooking Courtmacsherry Bay,
spectacular views. On R600.
Open: Mar to Nov
023 49676 (also fax) Mrs McCarthy
D: Fr €28.00
Beds: 2F 3T **Baths:** 4 En 1 Pr
⌂ 🅿 📺 ✕ ▦, cc

Kilcatherine

V6353

Glor na Mara, *Kilcatherine, Eyeries, Bantry, Co
Cork.* Oceanfront modern bungalow on Eyeries to
Ardgroom Coast Road. Spectacular sea/
mountain views.
Open: Apr to Oct
027 74012 (also fax) Mrs Crowley
D: Fr €19.00 **S:** Fr €23.00
Beds: 2D 1T **Baths:** 3 En
⌂ 🅿 📺 ✕ 🆅 ▦, ▪ cc

Planning a longer stay?
Always ask for any special rates

Killeagh (Youghal)

X0076

Bromley House, *Killeagh, Youghal, Co Cork.*
Modern home - 8km from Youghal on N25
Rosslare-Cork Road. 2 good pubs walking
distance.
Open: Mar to Oct
024 95235 Mrs Fogarty
D: Fr €28.00
Beds: 1F 1D 2T **Baths:** 4 Ensuite
🅿 📺 ▦, ▪

Tattans, *Killeagh, Youghal, Co Cork.* C18th pub
and guest house in scenic village near seaside or
N25.
Open: Mar to Oct
024 95173 (also fax) Mrs Tattan
D: Fr €32.00
Beds: 2F 2D 2T **Baths:** 5 Ensuite 1 Shared
⌂ (1) 🅿 (8) 📺 ♜ ✕ 🆅 ▦, ▪

Kilnamartyra

W2573

Hilltop Farmhouse, *Kilnamartyra, Macroom,
Co Cork.* Family-run in peaceful countryside. Idea
touring base for Cork or Kerry.
Open: Apr to 1 Oct
026 40154 Mrs Corkery
D: Fr €25.50
Beds: 1F 1T 2D **Baths:** 3 Ensuite 1 Shared
⌂ 🅿 📺 ♜ ✕ ▦,

Kinsale

W6450

Lighthouse, *The
Rock, Kinsale, Co
Cork.*
Open: All year
021 4772734
Mrs O'Gorman **Fax**
021 4773282
info@
lighthouse-kinsale.com www.lighthouse-kinsale.com
D: Fr €32.00-€51.00 **S:** Fr €63.50-€89.00
Beds: 1F 1T 2D 1S **Baths:** 5 En
⌂ (12) 🅿 (4) ⅍ 🆅 📺 ▦, ▪ cc
Tudor-style house. Antiques special feature. Four
poster and canopy beds. Highly recommended by
Sunday Times, Sunday Telegraph, Sunday
Express, Irish Examiner, Initials and Harpers &
Queen. The Lighthouse is easy to find, hard to
leave.

Danabel,
Sleaveen, Kinsale, Co Cork.
Open: All year (not Xmas/New Year)
021 4774087
Mrs Price
info@danabel.com
www.danabel.com
D: Fr €28.00-€40.00 **S:** Fr €50.00-€70.00
Beds: 1F 1T 3D **Baths:** 5 En
🛏 🅿 ⌇ 📺 🛏, ▪ cc
Modern house, quiet area. Town centre 3 mins' walk. Orthopaedic beds. Hairdryers, tea and coffee making facilities in bedrooms. Some bedrooms have harbour view. Airport/ferry 20 mins. Golf clubs 15 mins. Beach nearby, fishing, horseriding, yachting marina. Kinsale Harbour. Gourmet town. Frommer recommended.

Sceilig House, *Ardbrack, Kinsale, Co Cork.*
Open: All year (not Xmas)
021 4772832 (also fax)
Mrs Hurley
hurleyfamily@eircom.net
D: Fr €28.00-€40.00 **S:** Fr €50.00-€70.00
Beds: 2D 1T **Baths:** 3 En
🛏 🅿 (3) ⌇ 📺 📹 🛏,
All bedrooms enjoy panoramic views of harbour including Chales Fort on the left & James Fort across the bay on the right. Two rooms have either sunroom or private patio onto a rose garden. There are 3 pubs just 2 mins walk away.

Sea Gull House, *Cork Street, Kinsale, Co Cork.*
Open: Mar to Nov
021 4772240 Mr & Mrs O'Neill
marytap@iol.ie
www.seagullhouse.com
D: Fr €30.00-€33.00 **S:** Fr €40.00
Beds: 6F **Baths:** 5 En 🛏,
Family-run home in Kinsale Town. Next door to Desmond Castle and Wine Museum. Convenient to pubs, churches, beaches and golf courses. Visit Tap Tavern Bar and visit our medieval C11th well in our courtyard. Plenty of music and craic. Groups welcome.

B&B owners may vary rates – be sure to check when booking

River View, *Compass Hill, Kinsale, Co Cork.*
Modern comfortable home with panoramic view. 5 mins walk to town centre.
Open: Apr to Oct
021 4772794 M Roberts
D: Fr €28.00 **S:** Fr €40.00
Beds: 1F 1D 1T **Baths:** 2 En 2 Pr
🅿 ⌇ 📺 🛏, ▪ cc

Lochinver Farmhouse,
Ballinadee, Bandon, Co Cork.
Attractive farmhouse on dairy farm in scenic location, horseriding, beaches, golf nearby.
Open: Mar to Oct
021 4778124 Mrs Forde
hsforde@indigo.ie indigo.ie/~hsforde
D: Fr €25.00-€32.00 **S:** Fr €25.00-€44.00
Beds: 1F 2D 1T 1S **Baths:** 3 En 1 Sh
🛏 🅿 (10) ⌇ 📺 📹 🛏, ▪ cc

Cephas House, *Compass Hill, Kinsale, County Cork.*
Town house overlooking magnificent views of Kinsale Harbour and Bandon River.
Open: Mar to Oct
021 4772689 Mrs Hurley **Fax: 021 4772985**
thurley@boinet.ie
D: Fr €27.00-€40.00 **S:** Fr €60.00-€70.00
Beds: 1F 2D **Baths:** 3 En

Raheen House, *Kilgobbin, Ballinspittle, Kinsale, Co Cork.* Luxury farmhouse. Views of the Old Head of Kinsale. Horseriding, beaches, golf. Kinsale 10 km via Ballinadee road.
Open: May to Sep
021 4778173 (also fax) Mrs Sweetman
raheenhouse@eircom.ie
www.dragnet-systems.ie/dira/raheen
D: Fr €33.00 **S:** Fr €45.00
Beds: 3D 1T **Baths:** 4 En
🛏 🅿 📺 🛏, ▪

Ashling, *Bandon Road, Kinsale, Co Cork.*
Attractive modern ranch style bungalow with parking and garden.
Open: Easter to Oct
021 477 4127 Mrs McGlennon
D: Fr €25.50-€30.50
Beds: 1F 1T 3D **Baths:** 4 En 1 Pr
🛏 🅿 (5) 📺 🐴 🛏, ♿

The White House, *Pearse Street, Kinsale, Co Cork.* The White House epitomises Kinsale hospitality. Reputation for fine food and indulgent service.
Open: All year (not Xmas)
021 4772125 Mr Frawley **Fax: 021 4772045**
whitehse@indigo.ie www.whitehouse-kinsale.ie
D: Fr €44.45-€76.00 **S:** Fr €57.00-€95.00
Beds: 6D 4T **Baths:** 10 En
🛌 🅿 📺 ✕ Ⓥ ▥, ⬛ cc

Tesben House, *Ballinspittle Road, Barrells Cross, Kinsale, Co Cork.* Tranquil, unrivalled surroundings, picturesque view. 'Guide du Routard' recommended. Ferryport/airport 20kms.
Open: Mar to Nov
021 4778354 Mrs Murphy
tesbenhouse@eircom.net
homepage.eircom.net/~tenbenhouse
D: Fr €28.00-€31.00 **S:** Fr €40.00-€45.00
Beds: 2F 2D **Baths:** 2 En 2 Pr 2 Sh
🛌 🅿 ✁ 📺 ▥, cc

Rivermount, *Knockabinny, Kinsale, Co Cork.* Large house with excellent river views. Bedrooms with TV and tea/coffee.
Open: Mar to Nov
021 4778033 Mrs O'Sullivan
rivermnt@iol.ie
D: Fr €30.00-€35.00 **S:** Fr €55.00-€70.00
Beds: 3F 3D **Baths:** 6 En
🛌 🅿 (10) 📺 🕿 Ⓥ ▥, ⬛

Bayview, *Clasheen, Kinsale, Co Cork.* Panoramic view of bay and countryside from dining room. Breakfast menu 'Routard' recommended.
Open: April to Sep
021 4774054 Ms Cummins
D: Fr €24.00-€27.00 **S:** Fr €32.00-€35.00
Beds: 1T 2D **Baths:** 3 En
✁ ▥,

Hillside House, *Camphill, Kinsale, Co Cork.* Comfortable spacious home, lovely sea view, conservatory, landscaped gardens, Battle of Kinsale (1601) site.
Open: All year (not Xmas)
021 4772315 Mrs Griffin
D: Fr €26.00-€32.00
Beds: 2F 2D 2T **Baths:** 6 En 2 Sh
🛌 🅿 (8) ✁ 📺 ▥, ⬛ cc

Walyunga, *Sandycove, Kinsale, Co Cork.* Bright spacious modern bungalow, unique design. Quiet location. Panoramic ocean and valley views.
Open: Mar to Nov
021 774126 (also fax) Mrs Levis
D: Fr €38.00
Beds: 2F 2D 1T **Baths:** 4 Ensuite 1 Shared
🛌 (5) 🅿 (5) ✁ 📺 ▥, ⬛

Murphys Farm House, *Kinsale, Co Cork.* Our lavishly modernised farmhouse, offers you a mountain of facilities.
Open: Easter to Oct 31
021 4772229 Mrs Murphy **Fax: 021 4774176**
D: Fr €25.50-€32.00 **S:** Fr €29.00
Beds: 2T 2D **Baths:** 3 En 1Private
🅿 (6) ✁ 📺 🕿 ▥, ⬛

Setanta, *1 Haven Hill, Kinsale, Co Cork.* Modern bungalow with superb views of Kinsale town and harbour.
Open: May to Sep
021 4 772761 Mrs Allen
D: Fr €30.00-€35.00
Beds: 2T 1D **Baths:** 3 En
🅿 (3) 📺 🕿 Ⓥ ▥, ⬛ cc

The Gallery, *The Glen, Kinsale, Co Cork.* An award-winning town house located in the heart of Ireland's gourmet capital. The Gallery is noted for its atmosphere and charming decor. It is owned and run by two artists. The gallery has a fine selection of antique porcelain on view.
Open: All year (not Xmas)
021 4774558 & 021 4774990 Ms Crowley
carole@gallerybnb.com www.gallerybnb.com
D: Fr €35.00-€45.00 **S:** Fr €35.00-€45.00
Beds: 1F 3D **Baths:** 4 En
🛌 🅿 (10) ✁ 📺 🕿 ▥, ⬛ cc

Rockville, *The Rock, Kinsale, Co Cork.* Modern, comfortable bungalow with magnificent views of Kinsale town and harbour.
Open: Mar to Nov
021 772791 Mrs Gray
D: Fr €30.00
Beds: 1F 2D **Baths:** 3 Ensuite
🛌 🅿 (4) 📺 Ⓥ ▥, ⬛

Ardara

G7390

Rosemore House, *Wood Road, Ardara, Donegal.* Outskirts village, comfortable, friendly. Ideal for walking, cycling, touring, golfing.
Open: All year (not Xmas/New Year)
074 9541126 M Cunningham
rosmorehse@eircom.net
D: Fr €20.00-€23.00 **S:** Fr €17.00-€28.00
Beds: 1T 2D 2S **Baths:** 3 En 2 Sh
⏰ 🅿 (3) 📺 🐕 Ⓥ ⊞ ☛ cc

Woodhill House, *Ardara, Donegal.*
Historic coastal manor house with restaurant, bar & gardens.
Open: All year (not Xmas)
074 9541112 Mr Yates **Fax: 074 9541516**
yates@iol.ie www.woodhillhouse.com
D: Fr €45.00-€60.00 **S:** Fr €70.00-€100.00
Beds: 4D 3T 2S **Baths:** 9 En
⏰ 🅿 (20) 🐕 ✕ Ⓥ ⊞ ☛

Greenhaven, *Portnoo Road, Ardara, Donegal.*
Located on edge of heritage town of Ardara. Ideal centre Donegal's breathtaking scenic areas.
Open: Mar to Oct
074 9541129 (also fax) Mr & Mrs Molloy
D: Fr €28.00
Beds: 1F 3D 2T **Baths:** 6 Ensuite
🅿 (6) ⚒ 📺 ⊞ ☛

Brae House, *Front Street, Ardara, Donegal.*
In town, clean friendly family home. Orthopaedic beds. Easy to find, hard to leave.
Open: All Year
074 9541296 (also fax) Mrs Molloy
braehouse@tinet.ie
D: Fr €25.50
Beds: 1F 1T 2D 1S **Baths:** 4 Ensuite 1 Private
⏰ 🅿 ⚒ 📺 Ⓥ ⊞ ☛ ✳ ☛

RATES

D = Price range per person sharing in a double or twin room

S = Price range for a single room

Ballybofey

H1394

Steeple View, *Callan, Ballybofey, Lifford, Co Donegal.* Central location. Purpose built accommodation with guest lounge and kitchen.
Open: All year
074 9134229 Mrs Guthrie
steepleviewb&b@eircom.net www.steepleview.net
D: Fr €25.00 **S:** Fr €25.00
Beds: 1F 1T 1D 1S **Baths:** 4 En
⏰ 🅿 (10) 📺 🐕 ✕ Ⓥ ⊞ ✳ ☛ cc

Ballyhiernan

C1844

Fanad Lodge, *Ballyhiernan, Fanad Peninsula, Letterkenny, Co Donegal.* Lovely family home, Fanad Peninsula.
Open: All Year (not Xmas)
074 9159057 B McAteer
D: Fr €25.50
Beds: 6F 2T 3D 1S **Baths:** 1 Shared
⏰ 🅿 📺 ✕ Ⓥ ⊞

Ballyliffen

C3848

Castlelawn House, *Shore Road, Ballyliffen, Co Donegal.* Ideally situated in picturesque village of Ballyliffen. Warm and friendly welcome.
Open: All year
074 9376600 & 087 6166147 (M) Ms McGloughlin
D: Fr €30.00-€33.00 **S:** Fr €35.00-€45.00
Beds: 1D 2T **Baths:** 3 En
⏰ 🅿 ⊞ ✳

Carrick a Braghey House, *Shore Road, Ballyliffen, Co Donegal.* Village of Ballyliffen is home to some of the finest golf courses.
Open: All year
074 9376977 (also fax) Mrs Mofflin
mofflin@eircom.net
D: Fr €23.00-€25.50 **S:** Fr €28.00-€30.50
Beds: 1F 3D **Baths:** 4 En
⏰ 🅿 (6) 📺 ⊞ ✳ ☛ cc

Planning a longer stay?
Always ask for any special rates

Ballyshannon

G8761

Rath Caola, *Abbey Isle, Rosnowlagh Road, Ballyshannon, Co Donegal.* Clean/friendly, close to town; beaches, golf and surfing nearby.
Open: June to Oct
071 9851687 Mrs Lynch
gloriamarylynch@eircom.net
D: Fr €23.00-€25.00 **S:** Fr €30.00
Beds: 2D **Baths:** 2 En
⌂ ▣ (3) ⚞ ☒ ▥

Creevy Pier Hotel, *Ballyshannon, Donegal.* Comfortable family-run budget hotel/inn. Overlooking Donegal Bay. Special welcome for families/children.
Open: All Year
071 9851236 (also fax)
D: Fr €23.00 **S:** Fr €38.00
Beds: 5F 5D **Baths:** 10 En
⌂ ▣ (20) ☒ ✕ ▥

Buncrana

C3532

Lake of Shadows Hotel, *Grianan Park, Buncrana, Lifford, Co Donegal.* Traditional warm hospitality, family run.
Open: All Year (not Xmas)
074 9361005 Fax: 074 9362131
D: Fr €45.00
Beds: 23F 10T 10D 3S **Baths:** 23 Ensuite 23 Private
⌂ ▣ ☒ ✕ ☑ ▥ ⚐

Bundoran

G8259

Fitzgerald's, *Bundoran, Donegal.* Spacious bedrooms, many with sea views. Excellent bistro restaurant, secure parking.
Open: Mar to Nov
071 9841336 Mrs O'Donnell **Fax: 071 9842121**
info@fitzgeraldshotel.com www.fitzgeraldshotel.com
D: Fr €37.50-€57.00 **S:** Fr €50.00-€70.00
Beds: 2F 9D 5T **Baths:** 16 En
⌂ ▣ (16) ☒ ✕ ▥ cc

Bayview Guest House, *Main Street, Bundoran, Donegal.* Central location, seconds from all hotels and restaurants.
Open: All Year (not Xmas)
071 9841296 Mr Grath **Fax: 074 9141147**
D: Fr €28.00-€38.00 **S:** Fr €51.00
Beds: 10F 7D 2T **Baths:** 19 En
⌂ ▣ (10) ☒ ▥ cc

Killavil House, *Finner Road, Bundoran, Donegal.* New white 2-storey house, close to sea, on N17 route. All rooms ensuite.
Open: Mar to Nov
071 9841556 Mrs Davey
D: Fr €27.00
Beds: 2F 2D **Baths:** 4 Ensuite
⌂ (4) ▣ (4) ☒ ▥ ⚐

Carrick

G5878

Harmony Hill House, *Meenaneary, Carrick, Donegal.* Failte - families welcome, hill walking plentiful, Europe's highest sea cliffs, beaches, craic.
Open: Apr to Sep
074 9739304 Mr & Mrs Doherty
harmhill@indigo.ie
D: Fr €19.00-€23.00 **S:** Fr €38.00-€44.50
Beds: 2F 2D **Baths:** 4 En
⌂ ▣ (5) ⚞ ☒ ✕ ▥ cc

Carrigart

C1336

Sonas, *Upper Carrick, Carrigart, Letterkenny, Co Donegal.* Modern dormer bungalow, beautiful quiet countryside overlooking bay, home baking.
Open: All Year (not Xmas)
074 9155401 Mr & Mrs Gallagher **Fax: 074 9155195**
sonas1@indigo.ie www.ireland.travel.ie
D: Fr €19.00-€24.00 **S:** Fr €25.50-€32.50
Beds: 1F 3D 1T **Baths:** 5 En
⌂ (1) ▣ (6) ⚞ ☒ ✕ ☑ ▥ ⚐ cc

BATHROOMS

En = Ensuite

Pr = Private

Sh = Shared

Planning a longer stay?
Always ask for any special rates

Cavangarden

G8863

Cavangarden House, *Cavangarden, Ballyshannon, Donegal.* 1750 Georgian house in 380 acres. Private driveway, antique furniture, log fires, scenic views.
Open: Feb to Nov
071 9851365 Mrs McCaffrey
D: Fr €32.00
Beds: 2F 2D 2T **Baths:** 6 Ensuite
🛏 🅿 (10) ⅙ 📺 ✕ Ⅴ 🛏 ☎

Clonmany

C3746

Four Arches, *Urris, Clonmany, Inishowen, Co Donegal.* Surrounded by sea and mountains. Ideal for touring Inishowen Peninsula.
Open: All year (not Xmas)
074 9376561 Mrs McLaughlin
D: Fr €26.50 **S:** Fr €39.00
Beds: 3D 2T **Baths:** 5 En
🛏 🅿 (20) 🛏 ♿ ☎

Donegal

G9076

The Atlantic Guest House, *Main Street, Donegal.*
Open: All year (not Xmas)
074 9721187 Mr Browne
D: Fr €20.00-€30.00 **S:** Fr €30.00-€45.00
Beds: 3F 4D 4T 4S **Baths:** 7 En 8 Pr
🛏 🅿 (11) 📺 ★ Ⅴ 🛏 ☎ cc
Large family-run guest house right in the centre of historic Donegal town.

Island View House, *Ballyshannon Road, Donegal.* Georgian private house overlooking Donegal Bay - golfing, fishing, beaches nearby.
Open: All Year (not Xmas)
074 9722411 Mrs Dowds
dowdsb@indigo.ie
D: Fr €28.00
Beds: 4F 1D 2T 1S **Baths:** 4 En
🛏 🅿 (4) 📺 🛏 ☎

Maranatha, *The Glebe, Donegal.* 5 mins' walk to town centre. Quiet, tranquil setting, magnificent view over Donegal Bay.
Open: All Year (not Xmas)
074 9722671 Mrs Ryle
D: Fr €26.00
Beds: 2F 1D 1T **Baths:** 2 En 2 Sh
🛏 🅿 (4) ⅙ Ⅴ 🛏 ☎

The Waters Edge, *The Glebe, Donegal.* Spectacular waterside house off R267 - 5th house into secluded cul-de-sac.
Open: mid Jan to mid Dec
074 9721523 Mrs McGowan
thewatersedgebb2000@hotmail.com
D: Fr €23.50-€30.00 **S:** Fr €35.50-€44.50
Beds: 2D 1T 1F **Baths:** 4 En
🅿 (8) ⅙ Ⅴ 🛏

Quiet Water, *Muckross, St Ernan's, Donegal.* Hear birdsong, water lapping while enjoying good food, great company.
Open: All Year (not Xmas/New Year)
074 9723313 Mr & Mrs Campbell
D: Fr €24.00 **S:** Fr €30.50-€32.00
Beds: 2F 1T 1D **Baths:** 2 En 1 Sh
🅿 ⅙ 📺 Ⅴ 🛏 ☎

Bayview, *Golf Course Road, Donegal.* Overlooking Donegal Bay with excellent golfing, fishing, sandy beaches nearby.
Open: All Year (not Xmas)
074 9723018 Mrs McGuinness
D: Fr €25.50
Beds: 3D 1T
⅙ 📺 🛏 ☎

Dunfanaghy

C0137

Rosman House, *Figart, Dunfanaghy, Letterkenny, Co Donegal.* Beautiful modern comfortable bungalow with spectacular sea and mountain views.
Open: All Year
074 9136273 (also fax) Mrs McHugh
rossman@eircom.net
D: Fr €24.00-€28.00 **S:** Fr €32.00-€38.00
Beds: 2F 2D 2T **Baths:** 5 En 1 Pr
🛏 🅿 (8) ⅙ 📺 ★ 🛏 ☎ cc

Please respect a B&B's wishes regarding children, animals and smoking

Glencolumbkille
G5384

Scrigmor House, *Lower Dooey, Glencolumbkille, Donegal.* Scrigmor House overlooks the Atlantic Ocean. A modern bungalow with gardens and ponds.
Open: March to Oct
074 9730174 Mrs Doherty
scrigmor@infowing.ie
www.infowling.ie/donegal/ad/scrig.htm
D: Fr €20.50 **S:** Fr €23.00-€25.50
Beds: 5F 1T 4D **Baths:** 5 En
P (6) ⊡ ⅂ ⅴ ⅲ.

Ceathair Na Binne, *Doonalt, Glencolumbkille, Donegal.* Modern bungalow overlooking sea, peaceful scenic surrounding near beach.
Open: Jun to Sep
074 9730112 Ms McGlinchey
D: Fr €20.00 **S:** Fr €23.00-€25.00
Beds: 1F 1T 1D **Baths:** 3 En 1 Sh
⅍ P (5) ⊡ ⅲ. ⅀

Glenties
G8194

Oakdale Farmhouse, *Derries, N56 Route, Glenties, Donegal.* Comfortable farmhouse in scenic area 2km from Glenties on N56 road.
Open: Easter to Oct
074 9551262 Mrs O'Donnell
D: Fr €26.50
Beds: 2D 2T **Baths:** 3 Ensuite 1 Shared
P ⊡ ⅂ ⅹ ⅲ. ⅓

Killybegs
G7176

Cope House Ships Inn, *Main Street, Killybegs, Donegal.* The Cope House commands a towering view overlooking the busy harbour at Killybegs.
Open: All Year
074 9731834 Ms Barr **Fax: 074 9731646**
copehouse@ireland.com
D: Fr €25.50-€29.00 **S:** Fr €32.00-€35.50
Beds: 1F 4D 4T 2S **Baths:** 11 En
⅍ ⊡ ⅹ ⅲ. ⅀ cc

Lismolin Country Home, *Fintra Road, Killybegs, Donegal.* Modern family home with magnificent view of mountains. Quiet location.
Open: All Year (not Xmas)
074 9731035 & 074 9732310 Mrs Cahill **Fax: 074 9732310**
D: Fr €27.50
Beds: 3F 1D 1T **Baths:** 5 Ensuite
⅍ P (5) ⊡ ⅂ ⅹ ⅴ ⅲ. ⅀

Lough Head House, *Killybegs, Donegal.* Overlooking Killybegs Harbour lighthouse. Boats coming in - and out - visible from dining room.
Open: Easter to Oct
074 9731088 Mrs McKeever
D: Fr €21.50-€24.00 **S:** Fr €38.00
Beds: 1D 2T **Baths:** 2 En
P ⅍ ⅴ ⅲ.

Kilmacrenan
C1420

Fern House, *Lower Main Street, Kilmacrenan, Letterkenny, Co Donegal.* 10 mins drive from Letterkenny N56, bars/ restaurants walking distance.
Open: All year (not Xmas)
074 9139218 Mr & Mrs McElwee
mailto@fern-house.com *www.fern-house.com*
D: Fr €26.00-€30.00 **S:** Fr €35.00-€40.00
Beds: 2F 1D 2T **Baths:** 5 En
⅍ ⅍ P (6) ⊡ ⅲ. ⅓ ⅀ cc

Laghy
G9474

Bayside, *Mullinasole, Laghy, Donegal.* Comfortable, peaceful, country home. Coastal area off N15 overlooking inlet of Donegal Bay.
Open: Easter to Oct
074 9722768 Mrs Martin
D: Fr €25.50
Beds: 1F 1T 2D **Baths:** 4 Ensuite
P (6) ⊡ ⅴ ⅲ. ⅓ ⅀

BATHROOMS
En = Ensuite
Pr = Private
Sh = Shared

C1711

Glebe View, *The Glebe, Letterkenny, Co Donegal.*
Open: All year (not Xmas/ New Year)
074 9129701 & 086 1010732
(M) Sammy & Lorraine Wasson
D: Fr €22.00-€24.00 **S:** Fr €26.00-€28.00
Beds: 2F 1D 1T **Baths:** 2 En 2 Pr
➤ 🅿 (4) ✗ 📺 🕇 🕮 cc
Perfectly situated in a quiet location. First right off N13. Ideal touring base. Warm welcome assured with very comfortable accommodation. Close to Glenveigh National Park, local beaches and rugged coastline. Golfing amenities and shopping centres only a few minutes away.

Pennsylvania House B&B, *Curraghlea's, Mountain Top, Letterkenny, Co Donegal.*
Open: All year **Grades:** BF Approv, AA 4 Diamond
074 9126808 Mr & Mrs Duddy **Fax: 074 9128905**
pennsylvania.house@indigo.ie
www.accommodationdonegal.com
D: Fr €45.00-€51.00 **S:** Fr €44.50
Beds: 3F 3D 1S **Baths:** 7 En
➤ (12) 🅿 (10) ✗ 📺 📺 🕮 cc
The ultimate in sheer luxury, this American designed home has exquisite furnishings, plush decor, panoramic views and Irishness in abundance. Recent winners of AA 4 Diamonds award, off main N56 to Glenveigh National Park, smoke free home, American comforts at an Irish price.

Glencairn House, *Ramelton Road, Letterkenny, Co Donegal.*
Open: All year (not Xmas)
074 9124393 & 074 9125242 Mrs McCleary
glencairnbb@hotmail.com
www.glencairnhousebb.com
D: Fr €24.50-€30.00 **S:** Fr €37.00-€42.50
Beds: 3D 3T **Baths:** 5 Pr
➤ 🅿 📺 📺 🕮 cc
Panoramic view from patio on R245 2 km from Letterkenny. Near Mount Errigal Hotel/Silver Tassie and 5 minutes' drive to Holiday Inn. Central for all routes, Glenveagh National Park and Giant's Causeway. Golf, pitch & putt close by. ALL ground floor.

Ballyraine Guest House, *Ramelton Road, Letterkenny, Co. Donegal.*
Open: All year **Grades:** BF Approv, AA 3 Diamond
074 9124460 Mrs Smith **Fax: 074 9120851**
ballyraineguesthouse@eircom.net
homepage.eircom.net/~ballyraineguesthouse
D: Fr €28.00-€35.00 **S:** Fr €35.00-€45.00
Beds: 1F 3T 4D **Baths:** 8 En
➤ 🅿 (14) 📺 📺 🕮 cc
New purpose-built guest house on R245 to Ramelton. Walking distance to Letterkenny town centre. Active night life, theatre, cinema, leisure centre, pitch and putt and golf nearby. Central location for touring the North West, Glenveigh National Park, Inishowen, Fanad and the Giant's Causeway.

Oaklands, *8 Oakland Park, Letterkenny, Co Donegal.*
Excellent location for touring NW Donegal. 5 mins from town and bus station.
Open: All year
074 9125529 Mrs Leonard **Fax: 074 9125205**
oaklands@unison.ie www.bandbdonegal.net
D: Fr €24.50 **S:** Fr €33.00
Beds: 2D 2T **Baths:** 4 En
➤ 🅿 ✗ 📺 🕮

Belvedere House, *Ballaghderg, Kilmacrenan Road, Letterkenny, Co Donegal.*
Bungalow situated in quiet countryside, overlooking Errigal and Muckish mountains.
Open: Easter to Oct
074 9123031 Mrs Duggan
D: Fr €21.50 **S:** Fr €25.50-€29.00
Beds: 2D 1T **Baths:** 3 En 2 Pr
➤ 🅿 (5) 📺 🕮 ♿

Altan, *Ballaghderg, Letterkenny, Co Donegal.*
Modern house, commanding best panoramic views of Donegal Mountains.
Open: Easter to Oct
074 9121641 Mrs Gallagher
D: Fr €20.50-€23.00 **S:** Fr €32.00
Beds: 1F 1D 1T **Baths:** 4 En
🅿 (10) 📺 📺 🕮 cc

Pine Trees, *Gortlee, Letterkenny, Co Donegal.*
Bungalow walking distance to town and bus station, all amenities nearby, breakfast menu.
Open: Easter to Oct
074 9124111 Ms Murray
D: Fr €25.50
Beds: 2F 2D 1S **Baths:** 2 En 1 Pr
➤ 🅿 ✗ 📺 📺 🕮 ♿

Whitepark, *Ballyraine, Letterkenny, Co Donegal.*
Comfortable spacious home. Situated R245
Ramelton Road. Large garden and patio area to
relax. Quiet rooms facing the back, ground floor
rooms available. 5 mins' walk to Errigal Hotel,
music there most evenings. 30 mins' drive to
Glenveagh National Park and to beach.
Open: All year (not Xmas)
074 9124067 Mr and Mrs O'Donnell **Fax: 074
9167597**
D: Fr €25.50 **S:** Fr €38.50
Beds: 1F 2D 3T **Baths:** 6 En
⌂ 🅿 (8) 📺 ▥, ▪

Killererin House, *N56, Ballaghderg, Mountain
Top, Letterkenny, Co Donegal.* Family-run B&B.
Private car parking. Warm Irish welcome. Tea/
coffee served on arrival.
Open: All Year (not Xmas)
074 9124563 Mrs McGrath
kerin@indigo.ie www.indigo.ie/~kerin
D: Fr €20.50-€22.50 **S:** Fr €28.50
Beds: 2F 1T 1D 1S **Baths:** 3 En 2 Sh
⌂ 🅿 (6) 📺 ▥, ▪ cc

Lifford

H3398

Haw Lodge, *The Haw,
Lifford, Co Donegal.*
Open: Mar to Nov
**074 9141397 & 074 9141985 &
087 9818794 (M)**
Mrs Patterson **Fax: 074
9142894**
D: Fr €27.50-€30.00 **S:** Fr €34.00-€36.50
Beds: 1F 2D 1T **Baths:** 2 En 2 Sh
⌂ 🅿 (4) ✕ 📺 ▥, ▪
Restored farmhouse of character & warmth.
Spectacular views, clean & comfortable. Large
family suite. Central for touring Donegal,
Northern Ireland, Derry City & Giants Causeway.
Close to Lifford/Derry cycle route. Fishing,
walking, leisure centre nearby. On N15 road.

Hall Greene, *Porthall,
Lifford, Co Donegal.*
C17th farmhouse with an
uninterrupted view for miles.
Open: All year (not Xmas/
New Year)
074 9141318 Mr & Mrs McKean
hallgreenfarmhouse@eircom.net
www.geocites.com/thehallgreen
D: Fr €26.00-€30.00 **S:** Fr €40.00-€42.00
Beds: 2F 1D 1T **Baths:** 2 En 2 Sh
⌂ 🅿 📺 🍴 ▥, ▪ cc

Malin Head

C3958

Whitestrand B&B, *Crega,
Malin Head PO, Co Donegal.*
Open: All year
074 9370335 Mary Houghton
whitestrand@eircom.net
www.eircom.net/~whitestrand
D: Fr €23.00 **S:** Fr €23.00
Beds: 3T 1D **Baths:** 4 En
⌂ 🅿 (15) 📺 ▥, ▪
Enjoy a warm welcome, home baking, in family-
run dormer, close to beautiful views of hills and
sea. Near friendly pubs, restaurants, beaches,
walks, fishing, diving and golf courses to the
sound of the sea on white strand pebble beach.

Mountcharles

G8677

Coast Road Guest House, *Main Street,
Mountcharles, Donegal.* Coast Road Guest
House. Ideal centre for touring Donegal. Golf,
fishing, beach, walks.
Open: All year (not Xmas)
074 9735018
peggycleary@eircom.net
D: Fr €25.00 **S:** Fr €38.00
Beds: 3D 1T 1S **Baths:** 2 En 2 Sh 📺 Ⅴ ▥, ▪

Naran

G7098

Thalassa Country Home, *Naran, Portnoo,
Donegal.* Warm comfortable home in magnificent
scenic coastal location.
Open: Feb to Nov
074 9545151 Mrs Friel
D: Fr €24.00-€25.50 **S:** Fr €29.00-€32.00
Beds: 2F 1T 1D **Baths:** 4 En
🅿 📺 ✕ ▥,

Pettigoe

H1066

Hill Top View, *Pettigoe, Donegal.*
Spectacular view of Lough Erne. Anglers',
walkers' paradise. Lough Derg pilgrimage.
Open: All Year (not Xmas)
071 9861535 Mrs O'Shea
donegal@infowing.ie www.infowing.ie
D: Fr €25.50
Beds: 1F 1T **Baths:** 4 Ensuite
⌂ (1) 🅿 (6) ✕ 📺 🍴 ✕ Ⅴ ▥,

Ramelton

C2221

Ardeen, *Ramelton, Letterkenny, Co Donegal.*
Period house, quiet surroundings, tennis court,
scenic walking and cycling.
Open: Easter to Oct
074 9151243 Mrs Campbell
ardeenbandb@eircom.net www.ardeenhouse.com
D: Fr €30.00-€35.00 **S:** Fr €35.00-€45.00
Beds: 1F 2D 1T 1S **Baths:** 4 En 1 Pr
❥ ▣ (6) ⊡ ▦ cc

Raphoe

C2503

Strabane Road, *Raphoe,
Lifford, Co Donegal.*
Distinctive bungalow 200
metres from Raphoe, central
for touring, Giants Causeway,
Letterkenny.
Open: Apr to Oct
074 9145410 Mrs Chambers
D: Fr €26.50 **S:** Fr €35.00
Beds: 1F 1T 1D 1S **Baths:** 4 En
❥ (2) ▣ (4) ⊡ ▦ ▪

Rathmullan

C2927

Carriglough House, *Saltpans, Rathmullan,
Letterkenny, Co Donegal.* Tranquil old farmhouse.
Turf fires, electric blankets, super breakfasts.
Beaches, golf, horseriding, fantastic scenery.
Open: Mar to Nov
074 9158197 Mrs Hodgson
D: Fr €23.00-€25.50 **S:** Fr €25.50-€32.00
Beds: 2D 1T **Baths:** 2 En 1 Pr
❥ ▣ (3) ⊡ ★ ✕ Ⅴ ▦ ▪

Redcastle

C5535

Fernbank, *Redcastle PO, Redcastle, Lifford, Co
Donegal.* Overlooking beautiful Lough Foyle,
Inishowen.
Open: All Year
074 9383032 Mrs McLaughlin
D: Fr €25.50 **S:** Fr €25.50
Beds: 4F 1T 2D 1S **Baths:** 4 Pr
❥ ▣ ⊡ ✕ ▦

County Dublin

Balbriggan

Skerries

Rush

COUNTY
DUBLIN

Lambay
Island

Swords

MEATH

DUBLIN
AIRPORT

Malahide   Portmarnock

N3

N2

M50

M4

Santry   M1

Castleknock   Whitehall   Beaumont   Sutton

Lucan   Glasnevin   Raheny

Celbridge   Cabra   Drumcondra

Palmerstown   DUBLIN   Clontarf

Holyhead
(Anglesey, N. Wales)

Ranelagh   Sandymount

Clondalkin   Rathmines

Ballsbridge   Donnybrook   Holyhead
(Anglesey, N. Wales)

Rathfarnham

N7   Tallaght   Rathgar

Templeogue   Monkstown   Dun Laoghaire

Saggart   Sandyford   Killiney

Stepaside

M11

N81   Shankill

WICKLOW   Bray

0   5   10 miles

AIRPORTS ⊕
Dublin Airport - 01 8141111.

AIR SERVICES & AIRLINES ✈

Dublin to Birmingham, Bradford, Bristol, Edinburgh, Glasgow, London Heathrow, London Gatwick, Manchester, Newcastle.
Aer Lingus - in Republic, tel. 0818 365000; in UK tel. 0845 0844444.

Dublin to Birmingham, Bournemouth, Bristol, Cardiff, Glasgow (Prestwick), Leeds-Bradford, Liverpool, London (Gatwick), London (Luton), London (Stansted), Manchester.
Ryanair - In Republic, tel. 0818 303030; in UK, tel. 0871 2460000.

RAIL ⇌
Dublin (Connolly) serves the North, North West and East Coast with lines to *Belfast, Londonderry, Sligo, Wexford and Rosslare.*
Dublin (Heuston) serves the West, South and South West with lines to *Galway, Westport (Mayo), Limerick, Cork, Tralee and Waterford.*
For timetable details phone **Irish Rail** on 01 8366222.

FERRIES ⛴
Dun Laoghaire to Holyhead (Car Ferry 3¹/₂ hrs, High Speed Sea 99 mins, Catamaran 1³/₄ hrs) -
Stena Sealink - tel. in Republic 01 2047777, in UK 0870 5707070.
Dublin to Holyhead (3¹/₂ hrs) -
Irish Ferries - in Republic, tel. 01 6610511; in UK tel. 0870 5171717.
Dublin to Liverpool (4 hrs) - **SeaCat** - in Republic, tel. (freefone) 1800 551743; in UK, tel. 08705 523523. **P&O Irish Sea** -
Dublin to Mostyn (6hrs) - Dublin to Liverpool (7¹/₂ hrs) - in Republic, tel. 01 800409049; in UK tel. 0870 2424777

BUS 🚌
There are bus services to all major towns in the Republic and Northern Ireland.
Tel. **Bus Eireann** on 01 8366111.

TOURIST INFORMATION OFFICES ℹ
Dublin Airport (open all year), 1850 230330.
14 Upper O'Connell Street, **Dublin** 1 (open all year), 1850 230330.
Baggot Street, **Dublin** 2 (open all year), 1850 230330.
New Ferry Terminal, **Dun Laoghaire** (open all year), 1850 230330.
Skerries, 01 8495208.
The Square, **Tallaght**, 1850 230330.

O1831

Aona House, *48 Merrion Road, Ballsbridge, Dublin 4.* Beautiful Victorian townhouse near ferries, museums, galleries, transport. City 2km.
Open: All year
01 6684349 Mr & Mrs McKiernan **Fax: 01 6684988**
aonahse@indigo.ie indigo.ie/~aonahse
D: Fr €38.00-€45.00 **S:** Fr €45.00-€50.00
Beds: 2F 1T 2D 1S **Baths:** 6 En
➳ 🅿 (6) 📺 🛏 & ■ cc

Linaveagh House, *73 Anglesea Road, Ballsbridge, Dublin 4.* Family-run Edwardian home, excellent location for Dublin's principal events & business venues.
Open: All Year
01 6608867 Mrs Kelly
D: Fr €38.00-€44.50 **S:** Fr €44.50
Beds: 2F 1D 2T 1S **Baths:** 6 En
➳ 🅿 (4) ⅟ 📺 🛏 ✻ ■ cc

23 Waterloo Road, *Ballsbridge, Dublin 4.*

Waterloo Lodge is ideally located on the South side of Dublin's city centre. Just minutes walk from St Stephen's Green, Temple Bar, the RDS, Lansdowne Road. There are many fine bars and restaurants in the immediate vicinity. See you soon.

Open: All year
01 6685380 Mr Daly **Fax: 01 6685786**
info@waterloolodge.com www.waterloolodge.com
D: Fr €45.00-€70.00 **S:** Fr €60.00-€80.00
Beds: 4F 3T 6D 1S **Baths:** 14 En
⊠ (2) 🅿 (6) ⅍ 📺 ✈ Ⓥ 🔟, ♨ cc

DUBLIN — **Beaumont**

O1738

St Rita's Guest House, *11 Coolatree Close, Beaumont, Dublin 9.* Close to airport, city centre, golf, coast line, restaurants, many other attractions.

Open: All year
01 8360760 Mrs McLoughlin
D: Fr €23.00-€25.50 **S:** Fr €28.00-€32.00
Beds: 1F 1D 1T 1S **Baths:** 1 Pr 1 Sh
🅿 📺 ✕ Ⓥ 🔟,

Crannog, *168a Beaumont Road, Beaumont, Dublin 9.* Dormer bungalow. 3 miles airport, 20 mins centre. Buses outside door. Ensuite, TV.

Open: All year
01 8377660 Ms Doyle
doyle2002@eircom.net
D: Fr €38.00 **S:** Fr €40.00
Beds: 1F 2D 1T 1S **Baths:** 2 En 1 Pr
⊠ (9) 🅿 ⅍ 📺 🔟,

171 Beaumont Road, *Beaumont, Dublin 9.*

Situated on the main Beaumont Road with bus to city centre.

Open: All year
01 8369469 (also fax) Mr Costelloe
D: Fr €30.00-€35.00 **S:** Fr €35.00-€40.00
Beds: 2F 1T 4D 1S **Baths:** 4 En
⊠ 🅿 (6) ⅍ 🔟, ♨ cc

All details shown are as supplied by B&B owners in Autumn 2002

DUBLIN — **Cabra**

O1237

Wyoming, *173 Navan Road, Cabra, Dublin 7.*

Comfortable town house on main road three miles from Dublin.

Open: All Year (not Xmas)
01 8380154 Mrs Dexter
D: Fr €35.00
Beds: 2D 1S **Baths:** 2 En 1 Sh
⊠ 🅿 (3) 📺 🔟, ♨

DUBLIN — **Castleknock**

O0837

Deerpark House, *Castleknock Road, Phoenix Park Gates, Castleknock, Dublin 15.* Large detached old world house, completely restored to high standard.

Open: All year (not Xmas)
01 8207466 Mrs McKay
D: Fr €35.00-€37.50 **S:** Fr €45.00-€50.00
Beds: 2F 2D 2T **Baths:** 6 En
⊠ 🅿 (8) 📺 🔟, ♨ cc

DUBLIN — **Central**

O1634

The Old Dubliner Guest House, *62 Amiens Street, Dublin 1.*

Open: All year (not Xmas/New Year)
01 8555666 Fax: 01 8555677
dublinerbb@aol.com
www.olddubliner.com
D: Fr €50.00-€60.00
Beds: 4F 2T 8D
Baths: 14 En
⊠ 🅿 (3) 📺 🔟, ♨ cc

In the heart of the city, a listed Georgian town house. The Old Dubliner offers a warm welcome and comfortable stay with ensuite rooms, TV and a renowned Irish breakfast. Just a 15 min walk to the thriving Temple Bar area.

RATES

D = Price range per person sharing in a double or twin room

S = Price range for a single room

The Parkway, 5 *Gardiner Place, Dublin 1.*
Open: All year
01 8740469 & 01 8748084
Mr Heffernan
parkway@eircom.net
D: Fr €28.00-€40.00
S: Fr €32.00-€36.00
Beds: 2F 4T 3D 2S
Baths: 8 En 1 Pr 2 Sh
☎ 🅿 (4) 📺 Ⅴ 🛏 ♨

Family-run original late C18th Georgian house in city centre. Very clean and comfortable rooms. A warm welcome and help with any query or problems you may have anytime. Close to swimming pools, music venues, full Irish Breakfast.

Huband House, 10 Warrington Place, Mount Street, Dublin 2.
Open: All year (not Xmas)
01 6785767 & 01 6629060 Mr McCourt **Fax: 01 6629060**
hubandhouse@eircom.net www.hubandhouse.ie
D: Fr €35.00-€50.00 **S:** Fr €45.00-€60.00
Beds: 2F 1T 2D 1S **Baths:** 6 En
☎ 🅿 (4) 📺 🛏 ♨ **cc**

City centre Victorian house, newly renovated with ensuite rooms.

BATHROOMS

En = Ensuite

Pr = Private

Sh = Shared

Harrington House, 21 *Harrington Street, Dublin 2.*
Open: All year
01 4780877 & 01 4754008 Mr McCourt
Fax: 01 4780877
hubandhouse@eircom.net www.hubandhouse.ie
D: Fr €25.00-€45.00 **S:** Fr €40.00-€55.00
Beds: 3F 3T 4D 1S **Baths:** 11 En
☎ 📺 🛏 ♨ **cc**

Delightful residence for tourists and business travellers alike. Situated 10-15 mins' walk from the heart of the city and vibrant Temple Bar, with its restaurant, pubs and clubs. Trinity College, National Concert Hall, Dublin Castle, Cathedrals, Christchurch and shopping districts.

Kingfisher Restaurant & Apartments, 166 Parnell *Street, Dublin 1.*
Open: All year
01 8728732 Mr Drake **Fax: 01 8782978**
info@kingfisherdublin.com
www.kingfisherdublin.com
D: Fr €35.00-€55.00 **S:** Fr €45.00-€60.00
Beds: 6F 1T 6D **Baths:** 12 En
☎ 🅿 (2) 📺 ✕ Ⅴ ❋ ♨ **cc**

City centre location. Restaurant, wine bar and cyber café. Beside many famous cultural sights of Dublin, famous Temple Bar and shops. All rooms ensuite, colour TV & video, some with kitchenettes. Prices include selection of award-winning breakfasts served in air-conditioned restaurant.

Lynams Hotel, 63-64 *O'Connell Street, Dublin.*
Open: All year (not Xmas/ New Year)
01 8880886 Fax: 01 8880890
lynams.hotel@indigo.ie www.lynams-hotel.com
D: Fr €49.00-€65.00 **S:** Fr €70.00-€90.00
Beds: 1F 13T 15D 5S **Baths:** 42 En
☎ (3) ⅙ 📺 ✕ Ⅴ 🛏 ♨ **cc**

Lynam's enjoys a superb location on Ireland's main street, O'Connell Street. A boutique style hotel, decorated with individuality & elegance, respecting it's original Georgian architecture. Lynam's is located central to Dublin's main shopping & entertainment areas. We cater to the needs of the modern traveller.

Planning a longer stay?
Always ask for any special rates

Baggot Court, *92 Lower Baggot Street, Central Dublin, Dublin 2.*
Open: All year (not Xmas)
01 6612819 Roxanne Mooney
Fax: 01 6610253

baggot@indigo.ie
www.ebookireland.com/baggot-court.htm
D: Fr €45.00-€80.00 **S:** Fr €70.00-€100.00
Beds: 3F 4D 2T 2S **Baths:** 11 En
🛏 (10) 🅿 (6) ⅍ 📺 📺 🛋, ▬ **cc**
Beautifully refurbished Georgian house situated only a 5 min walk to city centre. Luxurious accommodation with tastefully decorated rooms, each with quality furnishings. Full breakfast with a selection of foods, we offer a friendly and informal atmosphere with the emphasis on relaxation.

Harcourt Inn, *27 Harcourt Street, Dublin 2.*
Open: All year (not Xmas/ New Year)
01 4783927 Mrs Mooney
Fax: 01 4782550

harcourt@indigo.ie
D: Fr €40.00-€80.00 **S:** Fr €50.00-€100.00
Beds: 3F 8D 3T 1S **Baths:** 15 En
🛏 (5) ⅍ 📺 📺 🛋, ▬ **cc**
An elegant yet homely feel, this Georgian house has all to offer. Located just off St. Stephen's Green, surrounded by all the main tourist attractions & finest restaurants. Relax over breakfast with a selection of foods, continental & cooked.

Kellys Hotel, *36 South Great George's Street, Dublin 2.* Heart of Dublin, beside fashionable Grafton Street. Few minutes walk Trinity College, Temple Bar.
Open: All year (not Xmas)
01 6779277 Mr Lynam **Fax: 01 6713216**
kellyhtl@iol.ie *www.kellyshtl.com*
D: Fr €35.00-€60.00 **S:** Fr €40.00-€65.00
Beds: 3F 7D 7S **Baths:** 17 En
🛏 (12) 📺 ☂ ✕ 📺 🛋, **cc**

New Belvedere Hotel, *Great Denmark Street, Central Dublin, Dublin 1.* Fully licensed offering every modern amenity.
Open: All Year (not Xmas)
01 8728522 Fax: 01 8728631
D: Fr €63.50
Beds: 30T 10D **Baths:** 40 Ensuite
🛏 🅿 📺 ☂ ✕ 📺 🛋, ▬

O'Shea's Hotel, *19/20 Talbot Street, Central Dublin, Dublin 2.* Traditional Irish music nightly. Warm, friendly atmosphere. Near many attractions.
Open: All year (not Xmas)
01 8365670 Fax: 01 8365214
osheashotel@eircom.net
D: Fr €32.00-€44.50 **S:** Fr €38.00-€51.00
Baths: 34 En
🛏 🅿 📺 ✕ 🛋, **cc**

Leeson Inn Downtown, *24 Lower Leeson Street, Central Dublin, Dublin 2.* On the fashionable South Side, close to all amenities.
Open: All year (not Xmas)
01 6622002 Mr Magauran **Fax: 01 6621567**
leesonin@iol.ie
D: Fr €40.00-€50.00 **S:** Fr €50.00
Beds: 6F 10T 8D 1S **Baths:** 25 En
🛏 🅿 (4) 📺 🛋, ▬ **cc**

DUBLIN   **Clontarf**
O2036

Ferryview House, *96 Clontarf Road, Clontarf, Dublin 3.* Located in the exclusive coastal suburb of Clontarf. Refurbished family-run guest house.
Open: All year (not Xmas) **Grades:** BF Approv, AA 4 Diamond
01 8335893 Ms Allister **Fax: 01 8532141**
ferryview@oceanfree.net *www.ferryviewhouse.com*
D: Fr €28.00-€57.00 **S:** Fr €57.00-€76.00
Beds: 6D 2T **Baths:** 8 En
🛏 🅿 (8) 📺 🛋, ▬ **cc**

BATHROOMS

En = Ensuite

Pr = Private

Sh = Shared

Bayview, *98 Clontarf Road, Clontarf, Dublin 3.* Beautiful home overlooking Dublin Bay. Comfortable and friendly. Close to city centre.
Open: Easter to Nov
01 8333950 Mrs Barry
D: Fr €35.00-€37.00 **S:** Fr €45.00-€47.00
Beds: 1F 2D **Baths:** 3 En
⏰ (1) 🅿 (3) ⌁ 📺 Ⓥ ⛆, ⬛

Aishling House, *19/20 St Lawrence, Clontarf, Dublin 3.* Elegant Victorian Grade II residence. Convenient for city, port and airport.
Open: All year (not Xmas)
01 8339097 Mr & Mrs English **Fax: 01 8338400**
info@aishlinghouse.com aishlinghouse.com
D: Fr €45.00-€55.00 **S:** Fr €60.00-€75.00
Beds: 5F 1T 3D **Baths:** 9 En
⏰ 🅿 (5) ⌁ 📺 Ⓥ ⛆, ✳ ⬛ cc

Hollybrook Park House, *10 Hollybrook Park, Clontarf, Dublin 3.* Secluded period house, private grounds, convenient city airport, ferry, seafront.
Open: Mar to Oct
01 8339656 Mrs Shouldice
D: Fr €32.00-€35.50 **S:** Fr €33.00-€35.50
Beds: 1F 1D 1T **Baths:** 2 En
⏰ (8) 🅿 (4) 📺 ⛆, ⬛

Hedigans, *14 Hollybrook Park, Clontarf, Dublin 3.* Hedigans is a late Victorian residence in Clontarf, centrally located.
Open: All Year (not Xmas)
01 8531663 Mr Hedigan **Fax: 01 8333337**
D: Fr €45.00
Beds: 2F 4D 3T **Baths:** 9 En
⏰ 🅿 (12) ⌁ 📺 Ⓥ ⛆, ♿ ⬛ cc

Annagh House, *301 Clontarf Road, Clontarf, Dublin 3.* Charming Victorian house completely refurbished to a high standard.
Open: All Year (not Xmas)
01 8338841 (also fax) Mr & Mrs Devlin
D: Fr €34.50
Beds: 1F 1D 1T **Baths:** 3 En
⏰ 🅿 (5) ⌁ 📺 Ⓥ ⛆, ⬛ cc

BEDROOMS

D = Double   S = Single

T = Twin   F = Family

O1931

Herbert Lodge, *65 Morehampton Road, Donnybrook, Dublin 4.*
Open: All year
01 6603403 Mr O'Feinneadha **Fax: 01 6688794**
herbertl@indigo.ie
D: Fr €32.00-€40.00 **S:** Fr €39.00-€50.00
Beds: 4D 2T 1S **Baths:** 5 En 1 Pr
⏰ (10) 🅿 (2) 📺 ⛆, ⬛ cc
Charming Victorian house offering friendly service and quality accommodation. Situated in fashionable Dublin 4, close to RDS, Lansdowne rugby stadium. Only a short walk to St Stephen's Green and Grafton Street. A haven for the discerning traveller.

Donnybrook Lodge, *131 Stillorgan Road, Donnybrook, Dublin 4.* Relax in comfortable surroundings in the heart of Dublin's most exclusive area.
Open: All Year
01 2837333 Ms O'Rourke **Fax: 01 2604770**
D: Fr €60.50
Beds: 2F 3D 2S **Baths:** 7 Ensuite
⏰ 🅿 (8) 📺 Ⓥ ⛆, ⬛

O1636

Lydon House, *200 Clonliffe Road, Drumcondra, Dublin 3.* Elegant Georgian family home close to Dublin city centre.

Open: All year (not Xmas/New Year)
01 8570192
seanaibanai2@eircom.net www.lydonhouse.com
D: Fr €30.00-€35.00 **S:** Fr €40.00-€55.00
Beds: 3F 1T 1D **Baths:** 5 En
🅿 (6) 📺 ⛆, ⬛ cc

St Andrew's, *1/3 Lanbay Road, Drumcondra, Dublin 9.* Convenient for city centre, airport and ferry port.
Open: All Year
01 8374684 Mr Lynch **Fax: 01 8570446**
info@dublinbed.com www.dublinbed.com
D: Fr €41.00 **S:** Fr €44.50
Beds: 2F 4T 4D 2S **Baths:** 12 En
⏰ (8) 🅿 (4) 📺 ♘ Ⓥ ⛆, ♿ ⬛ cc

Avoca House, *112-114 Home Farm Road, Drumcondra, Dublin 9.* Quality accommodation convenient to airport, ferry, city centre & Temple Bar.
Open: All Year (not Xmas)
01 8375769 & 087 2312725 (M) Mrs Farry **Fax:** 01 8375769
D: Fr €32.00
Beds: 3D 1T **Baths:** 3 En 1 Sh
🄿 ⌁ 📺 ▥, ▪

Muckross House, *Claude Road, Drumcondra, Dublin 9.* Situated just off main airport road (N1). Convenient to airport and car ferry.
Open: All Year (not Xmas/New Year)
01 8304888 Mrs Griffin
muckrosshouse01@eircom.net
D: Fr €28.50-€32.00 **S:** Fr €38.00
Beds: 2F 2T 1D **Baths:** 5 En
⌂ 🄿 (6) 📺 ▥, ▪ cc

Parknasilla, *15 Iona Drive, Drumcondra, Dublin 9.* Edwardian detached house off main M1 airport road. Convenient to city.
Open: All year (not Xmas/New Year)
01 8305724 Mrs Ryan
D: Fr €25.00-€29.00 **S:** Fr €32.00
Beds: 2F 1T 1D **Baths:** 2 En 2 Sh
⌂ (12) 🄿 (1) ⌁ 📺 📹 ▥,

DUBLIN · Dun Laoghaire
O2327

Ophira, *10 Corrig Avenue, Dun Laoghaire, Co Dublin.*
Open: All year (not Xmas)
Grades: BF Approv
01 2800997 (also fax) Mr & Mrs O'Connor
johnandcathy@ophira.ie www.ophira.ie
D: Fr €32.50-€65.00 **S:** Fr €32.50-€65.00
Beds: 2F 2D 1S **Baths:** 4 En 1 Sh
⌂ 🄿 (3) ⌁ 📺 ▥, ▪ cc
150-year-old Victorian house, near restaurants, bars, harbour and People's Park. 5 mins walk from Holyhead Ferry, 15 mins from Dublin city (DART). Secure car parking. Angling, sailing, golf, swimming, scuba diving, water skiing. Perfect for trips to Dublin city/Wicklow Mountains.

Tara Hall, *24 Sandycove Road, Dun Laoghaire, Co Dublin.*
Open: All year
01 2805120 Mr O'Feinneadha
charcon@gofreeindigo.ie
D: Fr €22.00-€32.00 **S:** Fr €22.00-€36.00
Beds: 1F 3D 3T **Baths:** 5 En 1 Sh
⌂ 🄿 (6) 📺 📹 ▥, ▪ cc
This refurbished Regency-style house, once the former residence of William Monk Gibbon, poet is ideally situated by the beach, a short walk to Dun Laoghaire harbour, a haven for any discerning traveller. Full Irish breakfast included

Belmont, *3 Mulgrave Terrace, Dun Laoghaire, Co Dublin.* Cinema complex, two shopping centres, golf courses nearby, 300 metres town centre.
Open: All year (not Xmas)
01 2801422 (also fax) Mrs Di Felice
cdifelice@esatclear.ie
D: Fr €25.00-€29.00 **S:** Fr €32.00-€45.00
Beds: 2F 2T 1S **Baths:** 3 En 2 Sh
⌂ (1) 🄿 (5) 📺 ▥, ▪ cc

Ariemond, *47 Mulgrave Street, Dun Laoghaire, Co Dublin.* Centre of town, by the sea. Car parking available.
Open: All year (not Xmas)
01 2801664 (also fax)
Mrs Power
ariemond@hotmail.com
D: Fr €25.00-€30.00 **S:** Fr €50.00-€58.00
Beds: 3F 1D 1T **Baths:** 3 En 2 Sh
⌂ (3) 🄿 (4) 📹 ▥, cc

Kilteely House, *1 Johnstown Road, Dun Laoghaire, Co Dublin.* Comfortable refurbished family home near ferry, transport, golf clubs.
Open: All year (not Xmas) **Grades:** BF Approv
01 2853394 (also fax) Mrs McGovern
kilteelyhouse@eircom.net
D: Fr €70.00 **S:** Fr €50.00
Beds: 1D 2T **Baths:** 3 En
⌂ (1) 🄿 (5) 📺 ▥, ▪ cc

Claremont Villas, *off Adelaide Road, Dun
aoghaire, Co Dublin.* Victorian home, built 1876.
Good family rates. Near Dart (train).
Open: All year (not Xmas/New Year) **Grades:** BF
Approv
01 2805346 (also fax) Mrs Harkin
arkinann@hotmail.com www.claremonthouse.net
D: Fr €30.00-€36.00 **S:** Fr €38.00-€46.00
Beds: 2F 1T 2D **Baths:** 4 En 1 Sh
➳ ⅄ 📺 Ⅴ ▥, ■ cc

Avondale, *3 Northumberland Avenue, Dun
Laoghaire, Co Dublin.* A warm welcome to our 100-
year-old spacious and comfortable Victorian
home.
Open: All Year (not Xmas)
01 2809628 Mrs Gorby
D: Fr €25.00
Beds: 1F 2D 3T **Baths:** 3 Sh
➳ ⅄ 📺 Ⅴ ▥,

The House of Reaney, *16 Clarinda Park West,
Dun Laoghaire, Co Dublin.* 3 story Regency
terrace house with many fine architectural
details.
Open: Mar to Oct
01 2805394 Mr Reaney
D: Fr €48.00 **S:** Fr €82.50
Beds: 1F 2D 1T **Baths:** 4 En
➳ (12) ⅄ Ⅴ ▥, ■ cc

Lissadell, *212 Glenageary Road Upper, Dun
Laoghaire, Co Dublin.* Luxurious warm, friendly
house, in conservation area 5 mins' walk DART
station.
Open: All Year
01 2350609 Mrs Goldrick **Fax: 01 2350454**
D: Fr €25.50-€38.00 **S:** Fr €32.00-€38.00
Beds: 2F 2D 1T 1S **Baths:** 6 En
➳ 🄿 (6) ⅄ 📺 Ⅴ ▥, ⅌ ❋ ■ cc

O1537   ⅃ *Botanic House*

Botanic View, *25 Botanic Road, Glasnevin,
Dublin 9.* Freshly refurbished Edwardian house.
All ensuite, 10 minutes from city centre.
Open: All Year
01726 890770 (UK) Fax: 01726 890774 (UK)
info@surestay.com www.surestay.com
D: Fr €35.00
Beds: 1F 2T 2D **Baths:** 5 Ensuite
➳ 🄿 (5) 📺 ▥, ■ cc

Egan's House, *7/
9 Iona Park,
Glasnevin, Dublin 9.*
Open: All year (not
Xmas)
01 8303611
Fax: 01 8303312
info@eganshouse.com
www.eganshouse.com
D: Fr €32.00-€69.00 **S:** Fr €39.00-€75.00
Beds: 2F 8T 8D 5S **Baths:** 23 En
➳ 🄿 (10) 📺 ▥, ■ cc
Edwardian, quiet, near city centre/airport,
historic, family-run, Irish breakfast. Near Croke
Park, botanic gardens, Dublin Zoo, point depot,
championship golf courses, Landsdowne Road.
Warm friendly atmosphere. Refurbished,
includes 2 large family suites.

Gartan House, *44 Iona Road, Glasnevin, Dublin
9.* Gartan House is 3km from city centre. Bus 41
from airport.
Open: All Year
01 8305906 Mrs Tarrant
D: Fr €31.00
Beds: 1F 1T 1D 1S **Baths:** 3 Ensuite
➳ ⅄ 📺 ▥,

Hydra House, *61 Iona Road, Glasnevin, Dublin
9.* Elegant Edwardian family-run guest house,
close Botanic Gardens, Dublin Airport, Croke
Park.
Open: All Year (not Xmas)
01 8306253 Mrs O'Connor
D: Fr €24.00-€29.00 **S:** Fr €29.00-€35.50
Beds: 2F 1T 1S **Baths:** 2 En 1 Pr 1 Sh
➳ (7) ⅄ 📺 Ⅴ ▥,

O2624

70 Avondale Road, *Killiney, Dun Laoghaire, Co
Dublin.* Family run house - easy reach of Dublin
City and Wicklow.
Open: All year
01 2859952 (also fax) Mrs McAnaney
mcananey@hotmail.com www.macananey.com
D: Fr €30.00-€33.00 **S:** Fr €38.00-€45.00
Beds: 1F 2D 1T **Baths:** 3 En 1 Pr
➳ 🄿 (4) 📺 ⅄ Ⅴ ▥, ■ cc

National Grid References given are
for villages, towns and cities – not
for individual houses

Please respect a B&B's wishes regarding children, animals and smoking

O2327

46 Windsor Park, *Monkstown, Co Dublin.*
Friendly home convenient to 46a bus and Salthill
DART station.
Open: Apr to Oct
01 2843711 Mrs Corbett Monaghan
monaghanwindsor@eircom.net
D: Fr €26.00-€30.00 **S:** Fr €36.00-€45.00
Beds: 2T 1D 1S **Baths:** 2 En 1 Sh

O0735

62 Wheatfield Road, *Palmerstown, Dublin 20.*
Comfortable, quiet house just off N4. Excellent
Irish breakfast.
Open: All year (not Xmas)
01 6265279 Mrs Moorhead
cmoorhead@oceanfree.net
D: Fr €30.00 **S:** Fr €35.00
Beds: 2F 1T **Baths:** 2 Sh

O2237   Station House

Rathmullan, *110 Bettyglen, Raheny, Dublin 5.*
Convenient to airport, car ferry, DART-rail, buses,
golf, city and sea.
Open: All Year
01 8318463 Mrs Patton
D: Fr €25.50 **S:** Fr €32.00
Beds: 1D 2T **Baths:** 2 Sh

Eden Lodge, *44 Edenmore Crescent, Raheny,
Dublin 5.* Comfortable family home. Situated in
the village.
Open: All year
01 8671415 (also fax) Mrs Costellue
D: Fr €30.00-€35.00 **S:** Fr €35.00
Beds: 1F 1T 1D 1S

O1531

102 Sandford Road, *Ranelagh, Dublin 6.*
Detached red brick home. Excellent location -
Ranelagh - near city centre.
Open: All year
01 4976059 Mrs McGrath
D: Fr €45.00 **S:** Fr €50.00
Beds: 1F 1D 1T 1S **Baths:** 3 En

Northbrook Hotel, *22 Northbrook Road,
Leeson Park, Ranelagh, Dublin 6.* Family-run hotel
warm welcome.
Open: All Year
01 6688951 Fax: 01 6604251
D: Fr €56.00
Beds: 10T 2S

Avonlee House, *68 Sandford Road, Ranelagh,
Dublin 9.* Freshly refurbished Victorian house,
luxury ensuite rooms. 15 mins centre.
Open: All Year (not Xmas)
01726 890770 (UK) Fax: 01726 890774 (UK)
info@surestay.com www.surestay.com
D: Fr €50.00
Beds: 2F 2T 2D **Baths:** 6 Ensuite
cc

O1428

Little Silver, *2 Fonthill Park, Rathfarnham,
Dublin 14.* Quiet family home near restaurants,
sport facilities. Wicklow Way nearby.
Open: Mar to Oct
01 4931677 Mrs Byrne
D: Fr €32.00
Beds: 1T 1D 1S **Baths:** 1 Shared

O1429

Ardagh House, *1 Highfield Road, Rathgar,
Dublin 6.* Conveniently located & beautifully
refurbished in this premier residential area.
Open: All Year (not Xmas)
01 4977068 Mr Doyle **Fax: 01 4973991**
enquiries@ardagh-house.ie www.ardagh-house.ie
D: Fr €33.00-€44.50 **S:** Fr €42.00-€51.00
Beds: 6F 6D 4T 3S **Baths:** 19 En

)1531

URE STAY Rathmines, *23 Leinster Road,*
Rathmines, Dublin 6. Superb Georgian town
ouse, all ensuite, generous breakfasts, 15 mins
centre.
Open: All year
1726 890770 **(UK) Fax: 01726 890774 (UK)**
nfo@surestay.com www.surestay.com
): Fr €44.45-€51.00 **S:** Fr €51.00-€57.00
Beds: 6T 7D **Baths:** 13 En

)1826

Pinehill, *Sandyford, Dublin 18.* Quaint cottage-
tyle residence with all modern conveniences.
Open: All Year (not Xmas)
1 2952061 Mrs Martini www.martini.pair.com
): Fr €44.50
Beds: 1F 2T 1S **Baths:** 3 Ensuite 1 Private
(3) 🅿 📺 📺 ▥ 🚫 ♿ 🚭

)1932

Dromard Terrace, *Sandymount, Dublin 4.*
Period style house in village, 2 miles centre.
Open: Easter to Nov
1 6683861 Mrs Bermingham
): Fr €28.00
Beds: 1D 1T 1S **Baths:** 1 Private
📺 ▥ 🚫

)1740

32 Santry Close, *Santry, Dublin 9.*
Comfortable family home, 2 km from airport, 5 km
rom city centre.
Open: Mar to Oct
1 8424515 Mrs Levins
): Fr €24.00-€28.00 **S:** Fr €30.50
Beds: 1F 1D 1T **Baths:** 1 En 2 Sh
(10) 🅿 (2) 🚫 📺 ▥ 🚫

B&B owners may vary
ates – be sure to check when
ooking

O2539

Suttons B&B, *154 Sutton*
Park, Sutton, Dublin 13.
Excellent accommodation,
close to DART, airport,
seafront, ideal base for
sightseeing.
Open: All year (not Xmas)
01 8325167 Ms Sutton **Fax:** 01 8395516
suttonsbandb@iol.ie
D: Fr €28.00-€34.00 **S:** Fr €36.00-€39.00
Beds: 1F 1D 1T 1S **Baths:** 3 En 1 Sh
🅿 (4) 🚫 📺 ▥

O1227   🚩 Spawell, Little Venice, The Morgue

28 Rossmore Grove, *Templeogue, Dublin 6.*
Luxury home less than five minutes from exit 11,
M50.
Open: Jan to Dec
01 4907286 **(also fax)** Mrs McGreal
mcgreal_28@yahoo.co.uk
D: Fr €28.00-€33.00 **S:** Fr €38.00-€40.00
Beds: 1F 1T 1D **Baths:** 2 En 1 Sh
🅿 (2) 🚫 📺 ▥ 🚫

O1538

Almara Guest House, *226 Collins Avenue*
West, Whitehall, Dublin 9. Superb location 5 mins
from city centre, airport and ferry.
Open: All year (not Xmas)
01 8510512 **& 087 2222929 (M)** Mrs Fanning
Fax: 01 8510512
almara@oceanfree.net www.almarabb.com
D: Fr €29.00-€37.00 **S:** Fr €45.00-€64.50
Beds: 1F 2D 1T **Baths:** 4 En
🛏 (6) 🅿 (8) 🚫 📺 📺 ▥ 🚫 cc

O2246

Maywood House, *13 St Andrews Grove,*
Malahide, Co Dublin. Quiet house in Malahide.
TV, tea/coffee. Beside restaurants and public
transport.
Open: All Year
01 8451712 **(also fax)** Ms Dagg Hanley
maywood@indigo.ie
D: Fr €35.00
Beds: 1F 3D 1T **Baths:** 3 En 1 Pr 2 Sh
🛏 🅿 (5) 📺 🐾 ▥ 🚫

Hazelgrove,
Blackwood Lane, Malahide, Co Dublin.
Open: Apr to Sep
01 8462629 (also fax) Mrs O'Leary
oleary@ hazelgrove.iol.ie
D: Fr €32.50
S: Fr €50.00
Beds: 1F 1D 1T **Baths:** 3 En
⌂ (7) ▯ (10) ⌽ ▭ ▦ ▪ cc
Delightful Georgian style home on private grounds, where discerning guests can enjoy peace and tranquillity. Dublin Airport 9km. Attractive marina village of Malahide 2km. Close to golf clubs, Castle, ferryport, City 13km. Breakfast menu, T/C facilities.

Aishling, *59 Biscayne, Malahide, Co Dublin.*
Excellent accommodation overlooking beach with breakfast menu and homemade bread.
Open: Apr to Sep
01 8452292 Mrs Handley
D: Fr €29.00
Beds: 1D 2T **Baths:** 2 En 1 Pr
▯ (3) ⌽ �V ▦ ▪

O2444

Steiermark, *13 Beach Park, on Strand Road, Portmarnock, Co Dublin.*
Open: All year (not Xmas)
01 8462032 (also fax)
Mrs Grabner
grabnerg@hotmail.com
D: Fr €30.00-€32.00 **S:** Fr €43.00-€45.00
Beds: 1D 2T **Baths:** 3 En
▯ (6) ⌽ ▭ �V ▦ ▪ cc
Complete comfort and full Irish/continental breakfast. Opposite beautiful beach, hotel, golf links.

Robinia, *452 Strand Road, Portmarnock, Co Dublin.* Modern house, overlooking the Irish Sea. Wonderful location.
Open: All year (not Xmas)
01 8462987 Mrs Creane
D: Fr €32.00-€35.00
Beds: 3F **Baths:** 3 En
▯ (3) ⌽ ▦ ▪

Vermont, *29 Martello Court, Portmarnock, Co Dublin.* 15 mins Dublin Airport, 10 mins from beautiful scenic views, golf courses/sandy beach
Open: Jan to Nov
01 8461500 Mrs Tonkin
D: Fr €32.00 **S:** Fr €38.00
Beds: 1F 1D 1T **Baths:** 1 En
⌂ ▯ (4) ⌽ ▭ ▦ ▪

Oakleigh, *30 Dewberry Park, Portmarnock, Co Dublin.* Overlooking the sea. Close to ferry, airport, city centre, golf and park.
Open: All Year (not Xmas)
01 8461628 Mr & Mrs Lynch
D: Fr €30.00
Beds: 1T 1D 1S **Baths:** 2 Ensuite 1 Shared
▯ (4) ⌽ ▭ ▦ ▪

O0326

The Old Forge, *Saggart, Co Dublin.* The Old Forge B&B, built in 1747, comprises four 2-store cottages.
Open: All Year (not Xmas)
01 4589226 Ms Burns **Fax: 01 4587592**
D: Fr €32.00
Beds: 2T 4D **Baths:** 4 Ensuite 2 Shared
⌂ (1) ▯ (15) ⌽ ▭ ⌖ ▭ ▦ ⌾ ▪

O2421

Brides Glen House, *Loughlinstown, Shankill, Co Dublin.* Extended farmhouse overlooking gle with stream. 2kms off main N11 Dublin-Wicklow road.
Open: Apr to Sep
01 2822510 Mrs Srevenson **Fax: 01 2827485**
D: Fr €27.00
Beds: 6F 3T 2D 1S **Baths:** 2 Ensuite 3 Private
▯ ⌽ ▦

O2560

Redbank House, *5-7 Church Street, Skerries, Co Dublin.* Old sea captain's house attached to award-winning Redbank Restaurant (sea fish dishes our speciality).
Open: All year (not Xmas)
01 8491005 Mr & Mrs McCoy **Fax: 01 8491598**
redbank@eircom.net www.redbank.ie
D: Fr €50.00-€60.00 **S:** Fr €60.00-€70.00
Beds: 9D 3T **Baths:** 12 En
⌂ ▯ ⌽ ▭ ⌖ ✕ ▭ ▦ ⌾ ▪ cc

Hill House, *Milverton, Skerries, Co Dublin.* luxury bungalow in quiet scenic area. Airport, Dublin and beaches nearby.
Open: May to Oct
01 8491873 Mrs Swan
D: Fr €23.00-€25.50 **S:** Fr €32.00-€38.00
Beds: 2F 1T **Baths:** 1 En
⊃ P (8) TV ⅢⅢ ⅙ ⅱ

Woodview Farmhouse, *Margaretstown, Skerries, Co Dublin.* Large comfortable farmhouse adjacent to beautiful Ardgillan Castle and seaside town of Skerries.
Open: Apr to Oct
01 8491528 Mrs Clinton
clintonj@indigo.ie
D: Fr €21.50-€24.00 **S:** Fr €28.00-€32.00
Beds: 1F 3D 2T **Baths:** 4 En
⊃ P (6) ⅙ TV ⊁ × V ⅢⅢ ⅙ ⅱ cc

Stepaside

①1923

Three Rock View, *8 Kilgobbin Road, Stepaside, Dublin 18.*
Open: All year (not Xmas)
01 2956780 (also fax)
Mrs Naismith
owen_naismith@stepaside.net www.stepaside.net/trv
D: Fr €45.00-€50.00 **S:** Fr €45.00-€50.00
Beds: 1D 2T 1S **Baths:** 2 En 2 Sh
⅟ (8) TV ⅢⅢ, ⅱ
Welcome to the quiet foothills of the Dublin mountains, where we have all the amenities and comforts to make your visit a pleasant experience. A homely setting where guests are greeted as friends.

Swords

①1846

Ard Cill, *The Rath, Swords, Co Dublin.* Spacious dormer bungalow in quiet country surroundings. Adjacent to airport/golf.
Open: All year
01 8405172 Mrs White **Fax:** 01 8451716
D: Fr €30.00 **S:** Fr €45.00
Beds: 1F 1T 1D **Baths:** 1 En 1 Sh
⊃ P (6) ⅢⅢ.

Lissadell, *Balheary Avenue, Swords, Co Dublin.*
Open: All year (not Xmas/New Year)
01 8404109
Mrs Cavanagh
mcavanagh@ oceanfree.net
D: Fr €28.00-€30.00 **S:** Fr €45.00
Beds: 1F 1D **Baths:** 2 En
P (4) ⅙ TV ⅢⅢ, ⅱ
Quiet country location, 10 mins north of Dublin Airport. Dublin City 30 mins. Ensuite rooms, comfortable beds. Tea and coffee-making facilities. Ideal touring base for North Country including famous Newgrange. A warm welcome assured.

Evergreen, *Balheary Avenue, Swords, Co Dublin.*
Open: All year
01 8403886 & 087 2516371 (M)
Mr & Mrs Canavan
jcanavan@tinet.ie
www.evergreenireland.net
D: Fr €28.00-€32.00 **S:** Fr €44.00
Beds: 1F 1T 1D **Baths:** 3 En
⊃ P TV ⊁ V ⅢⅢ, ⅱ cc
Luxurious accommodation, 3km from Swords. Ideal touring base. Warm welcome. Directions: N1 from Dublin past Airport towards Swords. Take LEFT at Estuary Roundabout onto R125. RIGHT at traffic lights out Balheary Road. 2nd LEFT towards Swords Open Golf. On left past Balheary Church.

Annacurra, *4 Dale View, Rathbeale Road, Swords, Co Dublin.* Modern town house, 3 miles from airport, adjacent golf/beaches.
Open: All year
01 8401990 Mrs Collins
annacurrahouse@eircom.net
D: Fr €30.00 **S:** Fr €45.00
Beds: 1T 2D 1S **Baths:** 3 En 2 Pr
⊃ ⅢⅢ.

Please respect a B&B's wishes regarding children, animals and smoking

Riversdale, *Balheary Road, Swords, Co Dublin.*
Quiet location, airport 10 mins, city 20 mins,
parking.
Open: All Year (not Xmas/New Year)
01 8404802 (also fax) Mrs Cavanagh
michaelc@indigo.ie
D: Fr €25.50-€32.00
Beds: 4F 1D **Baths:** 4 En
🛏 (3) 🅿 ⅄ 📺 ▥ ▪ cc

Ananda B&B, *Malahide Road, Swords, Co.
Dublin.* Family-run B&B, 5 mins from airport.
Excellent restaurants in Swords and the seaside
town of Malahide. Also excellent golfing.
Open: All year
01 8603516 Mrs O'Shea **Fax: 01 8902100**
D: Fr €30.00 **S:** Fr €48.00
Beds: 1F 2T 1D **Baths:** 4 En
🅿 (6) ⅄ 📺 Ⓥ ▥ ▪

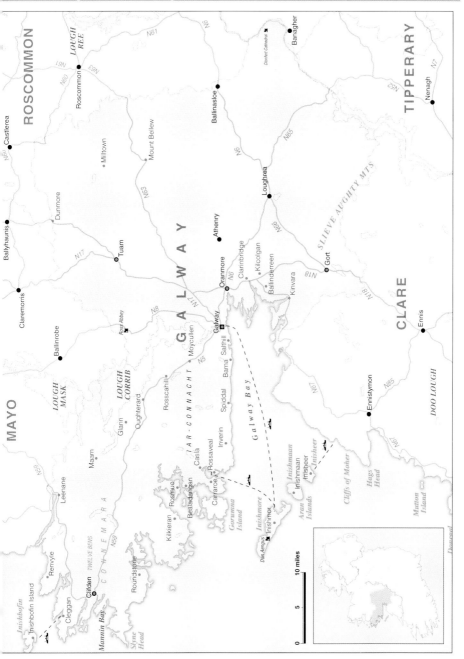

RAIL 🚆

Galway City is on the end of the main line to **Dublin (Heuston)**, via **Athlone**. For timetable details phone **Irish Rail** on 01 8366222.

FERRIES 🛳

Boats to the **Aran Islands** run all the year round from **Rossaveel** or **Galway City.**

Island Ferries - 091 568903.
O'Brien Shipping - 091 567283.

BUS 🚌

Galway to **Dublin** (6 daily) - **Bus Eireann** - 01 8366111.

TOURIST INFORMATION OFFICES ℹ

Ballinasloe (Jul to Aug), 0905 42131.

Market Street, **Clifden**, 095 21163.

Eyre Square, **Galway City** (open all year), 091 537700.

Mill Museum, **Tuam** (Jul to Sep), 093 25486.

ARAN ISLANDS — Inisheer

L9702

Ostan Inis Oirr, *Inisheer, Aran Islands, Galway.*
Open: Easter to Oct
Grades: BF Approv
099 75020 & 099 75046
Fax: 099 75099
inisoirrhotel@eircom.net www.inisoirrhotel.com
D: Fr €30.00-€35.00 **S:** Fr €35.00-€40.00
Beds: 2F 7T 4D 1S **Baths:** 14 En
🛏 ⅍ 📺 🕇 ✕ Ⅴ 🖿 ⅙ cc
Hotel Inis Oirr, owned & run by the Flaherty family is situated close to sandy beach and pier. Facilities include a restaurant, bar and lounge on the premises. Great atmosphere with traditional Irish music and fresh local seafood everyday.

Sharry's B&B, *West Village, Inisheer, Aran Islands, Galway.* A centrally located two-storey house with rooms overlooking Galway Bay.
Open: Mar to Oct
099 75024 Mrs Sharry
maire.searraigh@oceanfree.net
D: Fr €22.00-€25.00 **S:** Fr €25.50-€32.00
Beds: 2D 2T **Baths:** 3 En 1 Sh
🛏 🖿 cc

Planning a longer stay?
Always ask for any special rates

ARAN ISLANDS — Inishmaan

L9305

Creigmore, *Inishmaan, Aran Islands, Galway.* Breathtaking views Cliffs of Moher, County Clare. Beautiful flowers, nature walks. Home-cooked food.
Open: All year (not Xmas)
099 73012 Mrs Faherty **Fax: 099 73111**
D: Fr €25.00 **S:** Fr €25.00
Beds: 1T 1D 1S **Baths:** 3 Sh
🛏 ⅍ 📺 ✕ Ⅴ 🖿 ▪ cc

Ard Alainn, *West Village, Inishmaan, Aran Islands, Galway.* Comfortable.
Open: Easter to Sept
099 73027 (also fax) Mrs Faherty
D: Fr €21.50-€25.50 **S:** Fr €21.50
Beds: 3T 3S 1D **Baths:** 3 En
🛏 🖿

ARAN ISLANDS — Inishmor

L8408

Beach View House, *Oatquarter, Kilronan, Inis Mor, Aran Islands, Galway.* Walking distance to one of the oldest and most famous European Forts - Dun Aengus. Two minutes to a beautiful blue flag beach.
Open: May to Sep
099 61141 (also fax) Mrs Conneely
beachviewhouse@eircom.net
D: Fr €27.50 **S:** Fr €40.00
Beds: 3D 2T 1F **Baths:** 2 Sh
🛏 🄿 ⅍ 📺 🕇 ▪

RATES
D = Price range per person sharing in a double or twin room
S = Price range for a single room

Ard Einne Guest House, *Inishmor, Aran Islands, Galway.* High quality accommodation and food. Scenic views on historical island.
Open: Feb to Dec
099 61126 Enda and Clodagh Gill **Fax: 099 61388**
ardeinne@eircom.net
www.galway.net/pages/ardeinne
D: Fr €36.00 **S:** Fr €50.00-€70.00
Beds: 4D 10T **Baths:** 14 En
⊟ (8) ⅍ 📺 ✕ 🔽 ▥. ▪ cc

An Crugan, *Kilronan, Inishmor, Aran Islands, Galway.* Situated Kilronan Village, credit cards accepted, convenient all amenities.
Open: Mar to Nov
099 61150 Mr & Mrs McDonagh **Fax: 099 61468**
ancrugan@eircom.net
D: Fr €30.00
Beds: 1F 2D 3T **Baths:** 5 En
⊳ 🄿 ⅍ 📺 ▥. ▪ cc

Atlantic House, *Manister, Inishmor, Aran Islands, Galway.* Comfortable family run guest house in Scenic surroundings.
Open: Mar to Sept
099 61185 Mrs Connolly
D: Fr €19.00
Beds: 3D 2T **Baths:** 2 Sh
⊳ ⅍ ▥. ▪

Realog B&B, *Manister, Kilronan, Inishmor, Aran Islands, Galway.* Friendly family-run B&B, panoramic views. Ideal for relaxing and exploring local sites.
Open: May to Sep
099 61159 A O'Flaherty
D: Fr €226.00 **S:** Fr €26.00
Beds: 1T 3D **Baths:** 3 En 1 Sh
⊳ (10) ⅍ 📺 ▥.

M3915

Noel Jordan's Bar, Lounge & B&B, *Ballinderreen, Kilcolgan, Galway.*
Open: All year
091 796400 Mr & Mrs Jordan
jordanspub@hotmail.com
D: Fr €20.00-€25.00 **S:** Fr €25.00-€30.00
Beds: 2T 2D **Baths:** 4 En
⊳ 🄿 (20) 📺 ✕ ▥. ▪
A friendly family-run pub/B&B on the Galway/Clare coast. Area renowned for oysters, restaurants, fishing, golf, riding, sea-angling. Ideal for touring Connemara & the Burren Beaches nearby. Galway City 12 miles.

M2222 🍴 *Donnelly's, O'Grady's, Twelve Pins*

Abbeyville, *Freeport, Barna, Co Galway.* Beside village restaurants, pubs, beaches, golf club, Connemara, Aran Islands.
Open: All year
091 592430 Mrs Ryan
ryanbearna@eircom.net
D: Fr €28.00-€30.00 **S:** Fr €38.50
Beds: 1F 1T 2D **Baths:** 4 En
⊳ 🄿 ⅍ 📺 ⋔ 🔽 ▥. ▪

L9231

The Lodge, *Bealadangan, Lettermore, Galway.* Beautifully renovated C19th home by the sea. Set in spacious grounds.
Open: June to Sep
091 572434 (also fax) MR O'Malley
D: Fr €25.00
Beds: 1F 2T 2D 1S **Baths:** 1 Ensuite 1 Private
⊳ (10) 🄿 (7) 📺 ▥.

L9325

Donaghue's, *Carraroe, Galway.* Country family home. Remote area. Boat trips to Aran Islands.
Open: Easter to Nov
091 595174 (also fax) Mrs Donaghue
donaghuec@estatclear.ie
D: Fr €23.00 **S:** Fr €23.00
Beds: 3F 1T 1D 1S **Baths:** 1 En 2 Pr 1 Sh
⊳ 🄿 📺 ⋔ ▥. ▪ cc

Casla
L9624

Derrykyle Country House, *Casla, Galway.*
Spacious country home, ideal for angling,
walking & touring the Aran Islands.
Open: May to Oct
091 572412 Ms Mullin
D: Fr €25.50
Beds: 1D 1T **Baths:** 2 En
☎ (5) 🅿 (8) ⊬ 📺 🛏

Clarinbridge
M4120

Rock Lodge, *Stradbally, Clarinbridge, Galway.*
Quiet location; private walkway to seashore,
Central to Burren/Connemara/Aran Islands.
Open: Mar to Nov
091 796071 Mrs Diskin
johndiskin@eircom.com
D: Fr €21.50-€24.00 **S:** Fr €30.00-€32.50
Beds: 1F 2D 1T **Baths:** 2 En 1 Sh
🅿 (8) 📺 🛏 ⬤

Cleggan
L6057

Oliver's, *Cleggan,
Galway.*
Open: All year
**095 44640 Fax: 095
44605** www.
oliversconnemara.
com
D: Fr €22.00-€25.00
S: Fr €22.00-€25.00
Beds: 2F 3D 1S
Baths: 6 En
☎ 🅿 (10) ⊬ 📺 ✕ 🛏 ⬤ cc
Located in the picturesque fishing village of
Cleggan and the stunning scenery of Connemara.
10 km from Clifden. Warm, comfortable
accommodation. Friendly pub offering home
cooking, including fresh seafood & live music.
Horse-riding, sea-angling and hill walking in the
village.

Planning a longer stay?
Always ask for any special rates

Cnoc Breac, *Cleggan, Galway.*
Peaceful surroundings, convenient to beaches,
Inishbofin ferries, angling, pony trekking.
Open: May to Sep **Grades:** BF Approv
095 44688 Mrs King
tking@gofree.indigo.ie
D: Fr €24.00-€26.50 **S:** Fr €32.00-€39.00
Beds: 3D 1T **Baths:** 4 En
☎ 🅿 (4) 🛏 ⬤ cc

Cois Na Mara, *Cleggan, Galway.* Family home
in scenic area near safe sandy beaches.
Open: May to Sep
095 44647 Mrs Hughes **Fax: 095 44016**
D: Fr €25.50
Beds: 2F 2T 2D **Baths:** 3 Ensuite 2 Shared
☎ 🅿 (8) 🛏 ⬤

Clifden
L6550

**Buttermilk
Lodge Guest
House,** *Westport
Road, Clifden,
Galway, Co Galway*
Open: Feb to Jan
Grades: BF 3 Star
095 21951
Mrs O'Toole
Fax: 095 21953
buttermilk@anu.ie www.buttermilklodge.com
D: Fr €30.00-€50.00 **S:** Fr €40.00-€60.00
Beds: 2F 8D 1T **Baths:** 11 En 1 Pr
☎ (5) 🅿 (14) 📺 📹 🛏 ⬤ cc
Warm friendly home-from-home, 5 mins' walk
from town centre. Spacious ensuite rooms with
satellite TV, phone, hairdryer. Extensive breakfast
menu, home-baking, tea/coffee facilities,
mountain views, turf fires, laundry facilities and
many extra touches.

White Heather House, *The Square, Clifden,
Galway.* Ideally sited in Clifden town centre, all
amenities at our doorstep.
Open: Mar to Oct
095 21655 & 086 8182715 (M) Mr King **Fax: 095
21655**
D: Fr €20.50-€25.50
Beds: 4F 2T **Baths:** 6 En
☎ ⊬ 📹 🛏 cc

Clifden House, *Clifden, Galway.*
Open: Mar to Jan
095 21187
Mr Prendergast
Fax: 095 21701
resv@clifden.info
www.clifden.info
D: Fr €30.00-€60.00 **S:** Fr €40.00-€50.00
Beds: 9D 3T **Baths:** 12 En
🛏 🅿 📺 Ⓥ 🖳.
This period town house of almost 200 years offers spacious airy rooms with views over the Twelve Bens. Newly renovated in 2001, it is an ideal base for touring Connemara, golfing, fishing or enjoying the delights of Clifden's bars and restaurants.

Cregg House, *Galway Road, Clifden, Galway.*
Open: Easter to Nov
095 21326 (also fax)
Mrs O'Donnel
cregghouse1@eircom.net
D: Fr €30.00 **S:** Fr €40.00
Beds: 2F 2D 2T **Baths:** 6 En
🛏 🅿 📺 ✈ 🖳 ♿ 🐾
An immaculate dormer bungalow standing in an elevated position in its own landscaped gardens with spacious bedrooms, breakfast menu, fishing river nearby. It's an ideal base for touring Connemara and beyond. Recommended by Elsie Dillard: 'Best B&B in Ireland'.

Benbaun House, *Westport Road, Clifden, Galway.*
Open: Easter to Nov
095 21462 (also fax) Dr Lydon
benbaunhouse@eircom.net
www.connemara.net/benbaunhouse
D: Fr €25.00-€35.00 **S:** Fr €30.00-€40.00
Beds: 3F 3T 3D 1S **Baths:** 10 En
🅿 (10) 📺 ✕ Ⓥ 🖳 ♿ 🐾 cc
Affordable luxury, set well back from the road in mature, leafy gardens, 2 mins' walk from Clifden town centre. Newly refurbished to a very high standard. Whether you're sightseeing, fishing, rambling or golfing, Benbaun House is where you'll find a home away from home.

B&B owners may vary rates – be sure to check when booking

Ardmore House, *Sky Road, Fahy, Clifden, Galway.* Modern farmhouse, situated 5km west of Clifden, signposted on Sky road.
Open: Easter to Sep
095 21221 Mrs Mullen **Fax: 095 21100**
info@ardmore-house.com www.ardmore-house.com
D: Fr €28.00-€32.00 **S:** Fr €40.00
Beds: 2F 2D 2T **Baths:** 6 En 1 Pr
🛏 🅿 (6) ✈ 📺 🖳 ♿ 🐾

Sunnybank, *Church Hill, Clifden, Galway.* Sunnybank is a uniquely situated Georgian house, in its own calm and tranquil grounds.
Open: Easter to Nov
095 21437 Shane O'Grady **Fax: 095 21976**
www.connemara.net/sunnybankhouse
D: Fr €25.50-€51.00 **S:** Fr €51.00
Beds: 5D 4T 1S **Baths:** 10 En
🛏 (7) 🅿 (12) 📺 🖳 🐾 cc

Mallmore House, *Ballyconneely Road, Clifden, Galway.* Lovingly restored Georgian house in 35-acre wooded grounds on shores of Clifden Bay.
Open: Apr to Oct
095 21460 Mrs Hardman
mallmore@indigo.ie
D: Fr €24.00-€27.00 **S:** Fr €38.00
Beds: 2F 3D 1T **Baths:** 6 En
🛏 🅿 (15) 📺 Ⓥ 🖳 🐾

Failte, *Ardbear, Clifden, Galway.* Overlooking town and bay. Breakfast award-winner.
Open: Apr to Sep
095 21159 (also fax) Mrs Kelly
kelly-failte@iol.ie www.connemara.net/failte
D: Fr €21.50-€24.50 **S:** Fr €27.00-€32.50
Beds: 2F 1D 1T 1S **Baths:** 2 En 2 Pr 3 Sh
🛏 🅿 (15) 📺 🖳 cc

Lakeside B&B, Goulane, *Galway Road, Connemara, Clifden, Co Galway.* Restful and peaceful location near mountains, lakes and beautiful beaches.
Open: Easter to Nov
095 21168 Mrs Kirby
D: Fr €23.00-€25.50 **S:** Fr €29.00-€32.00
Beds: 3D 1T **Baths:** 3 En 1 Sh
🅿 (6) ✈ 📺 ✈ 🖳

National Grid References given are for villages, towns and cities – not for individual houses

Ocean Villa, *Sky Road, Clifden, Galway.*
Beautiful split - level seaside bungalow.
Panoramic views of sea and landscapes.
Open: Mar to Oct
095 21357 Mrs Murray **Fax: 095 21137**
oceanvilla@eircom.net
connemara-tourism.org/oceanvilla
D: Fr €23.00-€25.50 **S:** Fr €25.50-€32.00
Beds: 2F 2T 2D **Baths:** 4 En 2 Sh
🛏 🅿 📺 ✕ Ⓥ ⊞ ▪

River View, *Galway Road, Clifden, Galway.*
Comfortable friendly home only 5 minutes from
town, beautiful scenery.
Open: May to Oct
095 21067 Mrs Long
D: Fr €19.00-€21.50 **S:** Fr €25.50-€33.00
Beds: 1F 2D 1T **Baths:** 3 En 1 Pr
🛏 🅿 (10) 🔭 Ⓥ ⊞ ☖ ▪

Waterfront Rest, *Derreen, Streamstown Bay,*
Clifden, Galway. Our stress-free zone includes
private beach and golf course - paradise.
Open: Easter to Oct
095 21716 (also fax) Mrs Corbett
waterfrontrest@eircom.net
D: Fr €23.00-€25.50 **S:** Fr €25.50-€32.00
Beds: 2F 6D 1T **Baths:** 8 En 1 Pr
🛏 🅿 (12) ✂ 📺 Ⓥ ⊞ ▪ cc

The Wilderness, *Emloughmore, Ballinahinch,*
Clifden, Galway. Modern farmhouse, located in
peaceful, scenic wilds of Connemara.
Open: Feb to Nov
095 21123 Mr & Mrs Joyce
D: Fr €27.00
Beds: 1F 2D 1T **Baths:** 4 En
🛏 🅿 📺 🔭 Ⓥ ⊞ ▪ cc

Carraig na Greine, *Westport Road, Clifden,*
Galway. Modern bungalow, Clifden 5 mins' walk,
first B&B on first right off N59.
Open: Apr to Oct
095 21435 Mrs Nolan **Fax: 095 21648**
D: Fr €19.00-€20.50 **S:** Fr €20.50
Beds: 1F 2D 1T **Baths:** 4 En
🛏 🅿 (4) ⊞ ▪

BATHROOMS

En = Ensuite

Pr = Private

Sh = Shared

Smugglers Lodge, *Bridge Street, Clifden,*
Galway. Smugglers is a charming old world style
town house, situated in the centre of Clifden. We
have off-street private parking and are within 2
mins' walk of bars and restaurants. Our rooms are
large and spacious. Welcome to Smugglers.
Open: Mar to Jan
095 21391 Mrs Prendergast **Fax: 095 21212**
smugglers@cliften.com www.cliften.com
D: Fr €25.50-€38.00 **S:** Fr €44.50
Beds: 3D 1T **Baths:** 4 En
🛏 🅿 (8) 📺 Ⓥ ⊞

Dunmore

M5163   🍴 *Piper Reilly, PJ's*

Little Castle House, *Little Castle, Dunmore,*
Tuam, Co Galway. Modern farmhouse in rural
setting. Warm welcome and comfortable
accommodation.
Open: Easter to Oct
093 38236 Mr and Mrs Healy **Fax: 093 38833**
D: Fr €26.00-€26.80 **S:** Fr €32.00
Beds: 2F 1D **Baths:** 2 En 1 Pr
🛏 🅿 (10) 📺 ⊞ ▪

Galway

M2925

Drumlin View, *6*
Knocknacarra
Cross, Galway.
Open: All year (not
Xmas)
091 529513 (also
fax) Mr & Mrs Glynn
cglynn@iol.ie
D: Fr €27.00-€50.00 **S:** Fr €30.00-€50.00
Beds: 3F 2T 2D **Baths:** 7 En
🛏 🅿 ✂ 📺 Ⓥ ⊞ ▪
Overlooking Galway Bay near Leisureland, warm
comfortable home away from home. Ideal base
for touring cliffs Moher, Connemara, home
cooking and baking, tea making facilities. 'One of
the finest breakfasts in Ireland,' said the Brooklyn
Spectator. Recommended by 'Hidden Ireland
Guide'.

Please respect a B&B's wishes
regarding children, animals and
smoking

Planning a longer stay?
Always ask for any special rates

Flannery's, *54 Dalysfort Road, Salthill, Galway.*
Open: All year (not Xmas) **Grades:** BF Approv
091 522048 (also fax) Mrs Flannery

phil.flannery@iol.ie
www.flannerysbedandbreakfast.com
D: Fr €25.00-€32.00 **S:** Fr €28.00-€38.00
Beds: 1F 2D 1T **Baths:** 3 En
✿ (4) ▯ (4) ⊬ 📺 🐾 Ⅴ 🎞 cc
Award-winning house with charming garden in quiet area. Great breakfasts, comfortable beds, private off-street parking. German spoken. Follow signs to Salthill. On the sea front, between the Waterfront Hotel and Leisureland, turn into Dalysfort Road.

Sea Breeze Lodge, *9 Cashelmara, Knocknacarra Cross, Salthill, Galway.*
Open: All year
091 529581 (also fax) Mr Atal
seabreeze.lodge@oceanfree.net
D: Fr €25.00-€50.00 **S:** Fr €28.00-€44.00
Beds: 3F 3T 4D 1S **Baths:** 11 En
✿▯⊬📺Ⅴ🎞❋ cc
Overlooking Galway Bay, 1 mile to 2 beaches. Close to all amenities. Pubs, restaurants, very high standard swimming pool, surfing, horse riding centre, 2 miles from city centre, very high standard. Pine beds, wooden floors. Probably the best B&B in Galway!

Newcastle Lodge, *28 Lower Newcastle, Galway.* Beside NUIG and 10 mins walk Galway City. Ideal for touring.
Open: All year (not Xmas/New Year) **Grades:** BF Approv
091 527888 (also fax) Mrs Burke
D: Fr €27.50-€40.00 **S:** Fr €37.50-€55.00
Beds: 2F 2D 3T 1S **Baths:** 6 En 2 Sh
✿▯ (6) ⊬📺Ⅴ🎞 cc

Bohola House, *1 Westbrook, Barna Road, Salt Hill, Galway.*
Open: All year
091 591349
Mrs Moran

boholahouse@hotmail.com galway.net/pages/bohola
D: Fr €30.00-€45.00 **S:** Fr €30.00-€45.00
Beds: 2F 3D **Baths:** 5 En
✿ ▯ (5) ⊬ 📺 Ⅴ 🎞 cc
Luxurious home with balconies in quiet cul-de-sac overlooking Galway Bay on coast road. Rooms with king-size beds, hairdryers, multi-channel TV tea/coffee. Breakfast include full Irish, smoked salmon, fruit, yoghurts, fresh coffee. Ideal for touring Connemara, Aran Islands, the Burren and Cliffs of Moher.

Marian Lodge Guesthouse, *Knocknacarra Road, Upper Salthill, Galway.*
Open: All year
091 521678
Mrs Molloy
Fax: 091 528103
celine@iol.ie www.marian-lodge.com
D: Fr €28.00-€44.00 **S:** Fr €38.00-€75.00
Beds: 2F 2D 2T **Baths:** 6 En
✿ (3) ▯ (10) 📺 🎞 cc
Home from home beside Galway Bay. Daily tours arranged Connemara/Burren/Aran Islands. City bus route. Rooms ensuite, cable TV, tea/coffee, telephone. Convenient to city, Aquarium, Leisureland. Beside golf course/driving range, hotel, pub, shops.

Tysons, *Rockbarton Park Hotel, 5/7 Rockbarton, Salthill, Galway.* Cosy, intimate family establishment, chef proprietor - fresh seafood, 200 metres from seafront.
Open: All Year (not Xmas/New Year)
091 522018 & 091 522286 Mr Tyson **Fax: 091 522286 & 091 527692**
tysonshotel@eircom.net
D: Fr €38.00-€44.50 **S:** Fr €44.50-€57.00
Beds: 11F 5T 6D **Baths:** 11 En
✿▯ (11) ⊬📺✕Ⅴ🎞 cc

Atlantic Heights,
2 Cashelmara, Knocknacarra Cross, Salthill, Galway.
Open: All year (not Xmas) **Grades:** AA 4 Diamond
091 529466 & 091 528830 Mrs Mitchell
Fax: 091 529466
atlanticheights@galway.iol.ie
www.galway.net/pages/atlantic-heights
D: Fr €25.00-€42.00 **S:** Fr €30.00-€57.00
Beds: 3F 2D 1S **Baths:** 6 En
☼ (1) 🄿 (7) 📺 🛪 📺 🛏. ▪ cc

Luxurious, homely, award-winning home with balcony overlooking Galway Bay. Rooms with telephone, multichannel TV, hairdryers, tea/coffee facilities, guest lounge, private parking, laundry service, e-mail facilities, extensive breakfast menu, chef owners, pubs, restaurants, golf, beach, riding, swimming pool nearby.

Ward's Hotel, Lower
Salthill, Galway.
Open: All year (not Xmas)
091 521956 Mr Ward
D: Fr €35.00-€50.00 **S:** Fr €38.00-€55.00
Beds: 7D 1T 2S **Baths:** 10 En
☼ 🄿 (10) 📺 ✕ 🛏.

A distinctive, family-run ITB Approved small hotel, centrally located 5 mins from Galway's city centre and also Salthill's picturesque promenade. All modern facilities. Secure car park, cosy bar. All rooms are ensuite, have multi-channel TV and direct-dial telephone.

Seashore Lodge, No 4,
Cashelmara, Knocknacarra Cross, Salthill, Galway.
Open: All year
091 529189 & 091 590051
Mrs Costello **Fax: 091 529189**
ncostello@eircom.net
www.galway.net/pages/seashore-lodge
D: Fr €30.00-€40.00 **S:** Fr €32.00-€45.00
Beds: 3F 3D 3T **Baths:** 8 En
☼ 🄿 (8) 📺 📺 🛏. ❋ ▪ cc

New luxury purpose-built B&B overlooking Galway Bay, cable TV, spacious rooms, convenient for golf, horse riding, surfing, tennis, gateway to Connemara touring. B&B highly recommended in ADAC Book. Owner recommended in travel section of the LA Times.

Carraig Beag, 1 Burren
View Heights, Knocknacarra Road, Upper Salthill, Galway.
Open: All year (not Xmas)
091 521696 Mrs Lydon
D: Fr €30.00-€38.00 **S:** Fr €38.00-€68.00
Beds: 1F 2D 2T **Baths:** 5 En
☼ 🄿 (8) ✂ 📺 🛏. ▪

Luxurious brick house, walking distance to sea front, Leisureland, tennis, golf. Ideal base for touring Connemara, Cliffs of Moher, Aran Islands, Mayo. 2km Galway city. Recommended Dillard/Causin and Rick Steeves B&B Guides. Hairdryers, tea/coffee facilities in rooms.

The Forge, 42 New Road, Galway. Failte! City
centre location beside traditional pubs and restaurants.
Open: All year (not Xmas)
091 561446 D O'Connell
theforge42@yahoo.co.uk
D: Fr €25.00-€30.00 **S:** Fr €30.00-€40.00
Beds: 1F 1D 1T **Baths:** 2 En 1 Sh
☼ 🄿 (4) 📺 📺 🛏. ♿ cc

Ard Mhuire, Knocknacarra Road, Galway.
Attractive, comfortable home close to seaside and all amenities.
Open: All year (not Xmas)
091 522344 Mrs McDonagh **Fax: 091 529629**
teresa@ardmhuire.com www.ardmhuire.com
D: Fr €30.00-€38.00 **S:** Fr €43.00-€50.00
Beds: 2F 2D 2T **Baths:** 6 En 1 Pr
☼ (1) 🄿 (8) ✂ 📺 🛏. ▪

Anna Ree House, 49 Oaklands, Upper Salthill,
Galway. Warm comfortable seaside house, convenient to all amenities. Excellent breakfast. Private parking.
Open: All year (not Xmas)
091 522583 Mrs Hannify
D: Fr €23.00-€28.00 **S:** Fr €25.00-€32.00
Beds: 1F 2D 2T 1S **Baths:** 6 En
☼ 🄿 📺 🛏. ▪

Bologna, 30 Lower Newcastle, Galway.
Situated beside NUI within walking distance of city centre. Modern comfortable home.
Open: All year
091 523792 Mrs Drummond
g70@familyhomes.ie
D: Fr €22.00-€27.00 **S:** Fr €27.00-€32.00
Beds: 1F 1T 1D 1S **Baths:** 2 Sh
☼ 🄿 (3) 📺 🛏. cc

Anno Santo, *Threadneedle Road, Salthill, Galway.* Perfect blend of personal attention plus the amenities and facilities the seasoned traveller expects.
Open: All Year
091 523011 Mrs Vaughan **Fax: 091 522110**
annosant@iol.ie
D: Fr €40.00-€60.00
Beds: 10F 7T 3D 1S **Baths:** 21 Ensuite
☎ 🅿 📺 🍴 ✗ 🆅 ⅢⅢ 🛋

Kilbree, *Circular Road, Dangan Upper, Galway.* Luxurious home en route to Connemara, overlooking River Corrib. Convenient to city.
Open: All Year
091 527177 Mike & Annette O'Grady **Fax: 091 520404**
kilbree@eircom.net
D: Fr €33.50
Beds: 1F 3D 2T **Baths:** 6 En
☎ 🅿 (10) 📺 ✗ 🆅 ⅢⅢ ✻ 🛋 cc

Ardawn, *31 College Road, Galway.* First class 4 Star family-run guest house. Friendly atmosphere. Five-minute walk from city centre.
Open: All Year (not Xmas)
091 568833 Mrs Guilfoyle **Fax: 091 563454**
D: Fr €45.00
Beds: 2F 3D 1T **Baths:** 6 En
☎ 🅿 (7) ⅄ 📺 ⅢⅢ 🛋 cc

Snaefell, *6 Glenina Heights, Salthill, Galway.* Friendly home on main bus routes. Tea/coffee any time. Most vouchers acceptable.
Open: Easter to Oct
091 751643 Mrs Beatty
D: Fr €30.00
Beds: 1F 1T 1D **Baths:** 3 Ensuite
☎ 🅿 (4) ⅄ 📺 ✗ ⅢⅢ 🛋

Seacrest, *Roscam, Merlin Park, Galway.* Spacious bungalow overlooking Galway Bay and the Burren. Peaceful scenic area.
Open: Feb to Oct
091 757975 Mrs Connolly **Fax: 091 756531**
D: Fr €30.00
Beds: 1F 2T 3D **Baths:** 5 Ensuite 1 Shared
🅿 (10) ⅄ 📺 🆅 ⅢⅢ ♿ 🛋

Lissadell, *9 Glenina Heights, Dublin Road, Galway.* Family-run modern, comfortable home. Tea/coffee on arrival.
Open: All Year (not Xmas)
091 755851 Mrs Egan
D: Fr €30.00
Beds: 1F 1D 1T **Baths:** 2 En 1 Sh
☎ ✗ 🆅 ⅢⅢ

Dunguaire, *8 Lurgan Park, Murrough, Galway.* Warm friendly family-run home, cable TV in bedrooms.
Open: All Year
091 757043 Mrs Cawley
ccawley@eircom.net
D: Fr €32.00
Beds: 1F 2D 1S **Baths:** 2 Ensuite
☎ 🅿 📺 ⅢⅢ 🛋

Woodhaven Lodge, *20 Woodhaven Merlin Park, Galway.* Pleasantly disposed visitor-friendly family-run house.
Open: All Year (not Xmas/New Year)
091 753806 Mr & Mrs Kenny
woodhavenlodge@eircom.net
D: Fr €25.50-€32.00 **S:** Fr €32.00-€35.00
Beds: 1F 1T 2D **Baths:** 4 En
☎ (5) 🅿 (4) ⅄ 📺 ⅢⅢ 🛋 cc

Corrigeen, *4 Woodhaven, Dublin Road, Merlin Park, Galway, Galway City East.* Delightful purpose-built B&B, main approach road Galway city. Ideal Burren, Aran Islands, Connemara.
Open: All Year (not Xmas)
091 756226 Mrs Sweeney **Fax: 091 756255**
dess@eircom.net www.galway.net/pages/corrigeen
D: Fr €25.50-€38.00 **S:** Fr €32.00-€38.00
Beds: 2D 2T **Baths:** 4 En
☎ 🅿 (4) 📺 ⅢⅢ 🛋

Greenways, *9 Glenard Crescent, Salthill, Galway.* Elevated view of Galway Bay. Prize-winning garden. Close to Leisureland.
Open: Easter to Nov
091 522308 Mrs Carey
D: Fr €24.00-€28.50 **S:** Fr €32.50-€34.50
Beds: 1F 1T 2D **Baths:** 4 En
☎ (4) 🅿 (4) ⅄ 📺 ⅢⅢ 🛋

Baywood, *30 D'Alton Drive, Salthill, Galway.* Ideal for touring Connemara, the Aran Islands or the Burren in Co Clare.
Open: All Year
091 521076 Mrs Gallen
D: Fr €24.00-€28.50 **S:** Fr €32.00
Beds: 1F 1T 2D **Baths:** 3 En

Sulbea, *4 Lower Canal Road, Galway.* Quiet area, overlooking river bank, adjacent to city centre.
Open: All year (not Xmas)
091 521253 Mrs O'Sullivan
D: Fr €20.32-€22.86 **S:** Fr €20.32-€22.86
Beds: 2D 1T 1S **Baths:** 2 Sh ⅢⅢ

Ross House, 14 Whitestrand Avenue, Salthill, Galway. Ross House - comfortable town home in quiet cul-de-sac.
Open: All Year
091 587431 Mrs Davy **Fax: 091 581970**
rosshousebb@eircom.net
D: Fr €24.00-€25.50
Beds: 2D 2T **Baths:** 4 En
🅿 (4) ⚲ 📺 Ⓥ 🛏. 🖭 **cc**

Clare Villa, 38 Threadneedle Street, Galway. Ideal base for touring Connemara, the Burren and Aran Islands or shopping in Galway.
Open: Feb to Oct
091 522520 Mrs Connolly
clarevilla@yahoo.com
D: Fr €27.00-€30.00 **S:** Fr €39.00-€45.00
Beds: 3F 2D 1T **Baths:** 6 En
🔽 🅿 (6) 📺 🛏. 🖭

Padua, Threadneedle Street, Galway. Spacious family residence beside beach, tennis, golf, Leisureland, on bus route, private rear parking.
Open: All Year (not Xmas)
091 529252 & 087 2234285 (M) Mrs Staunton
D: Fr €23.00-€25.50 **S:** Fr €23.00-€32.00
Beds: 4F 2D 2T **Baths:** 4 En
🔽 🅿 (4) 📺 🐕 🛏. ♿ 🖭

St Martins, 26 Rockbarton Road, Upper Salthill, Galway. Near beach, restaurants, pubs. On bus route to Galway City.
Open: Jul to Aug
091 521310 Mrs Murray
D: Fr €23.00-€25.50
Beds: 3D **Baths:** 3 En
🅿 (4) ⚲ 📺 🛏.

Lockerbie, 3 Rockbarton Green, Galway. A warm welcome awaits you in a comfortable home in beautiful tree-lined surroundings.
Open: Easter to November
091 521434 Mrs Patton
D: Fr €24.00-€28.00 **S:** Fr €32.00
Beds: 4F 1T 2D 1S
🔽 🅿 ⚲ 🛏. 🖭

BEDROOMS

D = Double   S = Single

T = Twin   F = Family

Liscarra House, 6 Seamount, Threadneedle Road, Galway. Luxurious home on R338 overlooking Galway Bay, beside beach, tennis, golf, Leisureland, swimming pool.
Open: Mar to Oct
091 521299 Mrs Regan
eregan@eircom.net
D: Fr €30.00
Beds: 3D 2T **Baths:** 4 En 1 Pr
🔽 (8) 🅿 (5) ⚲ 📺 Ⓥ 🛏. 🖭

Chateau, 1 Woodfield, Barna Road, Galway. Modern home on Coast Road overlooking Galway Bay. Quiet location.
Open: Easter to Oct
091 590732 Mrs Reidy
D: Fr €23.00-€28.00 **S:** Fr €29.00-€32.00
Beds: 1T 2D **Baths:** 2 En 1 Pr
🅿 (3) ⚲ 📺 Ⓥ 🛏. 🖭 **cc**

Trieste, 12 Forster Park, Dalysfort Road, Upper Salthill, Galway. Bungalow - near beach, golf, tennis, leisure land. City 1 km. On bus route.
Open: Easter to Oct
091 521014 (also fax) Mrs Barry
maryba@indigo.ie
D: Fr €21.50-€25.50 **S:** Fr €30.00-€34.50
Beds: 1F 2D 1T 1S **Baths:** 3 En 2 Sh
🔽 🅿 (3) 📺 🛏. 🖭 **cc**

Lakelands, Limnagh, Corrandulla, Co Galway. Country residence overlooking Lough Corrib. Base: Connemara, Mayo, Cong. Fishing & shooting in season.
Open: Easter to Sept
091 791852 Mrs Keane
D: Fr €25.50-€28.00 **S:** Fr €25.50-€28.00
Beds: 4F 1T 1D 1S **Baths:** 3 En 3 Pr 1 Sh 📺 🛏. 🖭

Heron Lodge, 11 Lough Atalia Road, Galway. Elevated bungalow with charming decor, beautiful views over Loch Atalia and Clare Hills.
Open: Feb to Nov
091 561076 S & C Langan
slangan@iol.ie
D: Fr €23.00-€28.00 **S:** Fr €25.50-€38.00
Beds: 1F 1D 1T 1S **Baths:** 4 En
🔽 (10) 🅿 (6) 📺 Ⓥ 🛏.

The Stables, College Road, Galway. Centrally located. 5 mins' walk from city centre. Modern accommodation.
Open: All year
091 539630 Mr Ward
D: Fr €26.00-€32.00 **S:** Fr €32.00-€38.00
Beds: 1T 2D 1S **Baths:** 4 En
🅿 (8) 📺 🛏. ✱ **cc**

Planning a longer stay?
Always ask for any special rates

M0747

Glann House, *Glann, Oughterard, Galway.*
Old style Connemara farmhouse. Fisherman's/
walkers' lodge. Lakeside angling facilities.
Open: March to Oct
091 552127 Mrs Clancy **Fax: 091 552538**
wander@gofree.indigo.ie
D: Fr €23.00-€29.00 **S:** Fr €23.00-€29.00
Beds: 2F 2T 3D **Baths:** 3 En 2 Sh
🛏 🅿 (12) ⌿ 📺 🛏 🗺 ⬛ cc

M0422

Ard Mhuirbhi, *Inverin, Spiddal, Galway.*
Spacious seaside accommodation in peaceful
location. Superb views. Family suites.
Open: All year (not Xmas/New Year)
091 593215 Mrs Feeney **Fax: 091 593326**
ardmhuirbhi@eircom.net
D: Fr €27.00-€30.00 **S:** Fr €39.00-€42.00
Beds: 2F 2T 1D **Baths:** 4 En 1 Pr
🛏 (5) 🅿 (5) ⌿ 📺 🗺 ⬛ cc

Clai-ard, *Cornarone East, Inverin, Spiddal,
Galway.* New bungalow, friendly home
overlooking Galway Bay. Sandy beaches.
Delightful gardens.
Open: Jan to Dec
091 593488 (also fax) Mrs Folan-Burke
D: Fr €25.50
Beds: 1F 2D **Baths:** 3 En 1 Sh
🛏 🅿 (6) 📺 ✕ 🗺 ❋ ⬛

M4217

Ashgrove, *Newtown, Kilcolgan, Galway.*
Friendly home. Ideal touring base - Burren, Cliffs
of Moher, Connemara.
Open: Apr to Oct
091 796047 Mr & Mrs Murphy
ashgrovebandb@eircom.net
D: Fr €24.00 **S:** Fr €24.00
Beds: 1F 2D **Baths:** 3 En
🛏 (2) 🅿 (8) ⌿ 🗺 cc

L8431

Hillside House, *Kylesalia, Kilkieran,
Connemara, Galway.* Comfortable family home
situated off main road on R340 towards Carna.
Open: Easter to Nov
095 33420 Mrs Madden **Fax: 095 33624**
hillsidehouse@oceanfree.net
D: Fr €30.00
Beds: 1F 2D 1T **Baths:** 4 En
🛏 🅿 (6) 🗺 ⬛

M3512

Burren View, *Doorus, Kinvara, Galway.*
Beautifully situated on scenic, serene, healthy
peninsula off N67 on N18.
Open: Easter to Oct
091 637142 Mr & Mrs O'Connor
D: Fr €26.00
Beds: 5F 2T 2S **Baths:** 2 Ensuite 2 Private 2
Shared
🛏 🅿 ⌿ 📺 ✕ 🗺 ⬛

Fortview House, *Lisheeninane, Kinvara,
Galway.* Ideal base for touring the Burren,
Connemara and Galway city. Beach 3 km.
Open: Mar to Oct
091 637147 Mrs Silke
fortviewhousebandb@eircom.net
D: Fr €24.00 **S:** Fr €32.50
Beds: 2F 2D 1T 1S **Baths:** 6 En
🛏 🅿 (6) ⌿ 📺 🗺 ⬛

Cois Cuain, *Kinvara, Galway.* Dormer bungalow
overlooking Kinvara Bay and Dungory Castle;
beside the Burren.
Open: Easter to Nov
091 637119 Mrs Walsh
D: Fr €25.50 **S:** Fr €38.00
Beds: 1F 1D 1T **Baths:** 2 En 1 Pr
🅿 (6) ⌿ 🗺

BATHROOMS
En = Ensuite
Pr = Private
Sh = Shared

All details shown are as supplied by B&B owners in Autumn 2002

Leenane

L8761

Killary Lodge, *Derrynasliggaun, Leenane, Galway.*
Open: Feb to Nov
095 42276 Mr Young
Fax: 095 42314
lodge@killary.com
www.killary.com
D: Fr €43.00-€53.00 **S:** Fr €43.00-€78.00
Beds: 7F 3D 6T 5S **Baths:** 21 En
cc
Located directly on the shores of Killary Harbour, Killary Lodge offers friendly atmosphere, comfortable, stylish, ensuite rooms, evening meals and lunch packages. Wonderful area for walking and cycling, many other activities are also available. Egon Ronay and AA recommended.

Portfinn Lodge, *Leenane, Galway.*
Open: Easter to Oct
095 42265 Mr Daly **Fax: 095 42315**
rorydaly@anu.ie www.portfinn.com
D: Fr €24.00-€32.00 **S:** Fr €51.00-€64.00
Beds: 2F 3D 3T **Baths:** 8 En
(20) cc
Portfinn Lodge set among the magnificent scenery of the Killary and the Mweelrea Mountains. An ideal centre for the walker and rambler, our seafood restaurant is internationally acclaimed, offering the best of local produce.

Maam

L9553

Leckavrea View Farmhouse, *Maam, Galway.* Lakeside house in picturesque surroundings.
Open: All Year (not Xmas)
094 9548040 Mrs Gavin
D: Fr €26.00
Beds: 3F 2D 1S **Baths:** 6 Ensuite

Milltown

M4162

St Anns, *Milltown, Tuam, Co Galway.* Friendly family farmhouse in wooded surroundings on N17 Galway-Sligo.
Open: Mar to Oct
093 51337 Mrs Birmingham
st_annes_bb@hotmail.com
D: Fr €26.00-€27.00 **S:** Fr €32.00-€35.00
Beds: 2F 1T **Baths:** 3 En 3 Pr
(10)

Mount Bellew

M6746

St Anns, *Lake View Restaurant, Mount Bellew, Ballinasloe, Co Galway.*
Open: All year
0905 79239 Mrs Briggs
D: Fr €20.00-€25.00 **S:** Fr €25.00-€30.00
Beds: 2F 5T **Baths:** 5 En
Two-storey building off the square. Five bedrooms ensuite with tea/coffee facilities. Meals in restaurant daily. Car park. Garden for visitors use overlooking lake. Golf course nearby. TV lounge for visitors & TV in every room.

Moycullen

M2132 *The Ferryman*

Ave Maria, *Moycullen, Galway.* Split level bungalow in N59 Galway-Clifden Road overlooking Lough Corrib.
Open: Apr to Oct
091 555133 Mrs Kelly
Larmoy@eircom.net
D: Fr €23.00 **S:** Fr €30.50
Beds: 1F 2D **Baths:** 3 En
(7) (5)

French Ville, *Moycullen, Galway.* Ideal for salmon and trout fishing. 2 miles from Lough Corrib.
Open: Easter to Oct
091 555229 Mr McDonagh
D: Fr €22.00-€25.00 **S:** Fr €22.00-€25.00
Beds: 1T 2D 2S **Baths:** 1 Pr 1 Sh
(4)

Oranmore

M3824

Son Amar, Coast Road, Oranmore, Galway.
Open: All year
091 794176 (also fax)
Mrs Leyne
sonamar@indigo.ie www.sonamargalway.com
D: Fr €27.00-€35.00 **S:** Fr €38.50
Beds: 6F 4D 2S **Baths:** 4 En 1 Sh
ॐ (10) ᗰ (12) ⌇ ☲ ☑ ▥ ❈ ▪
Gracious Georgian home, overlooking Galway Bay and Burren Mountains. Golf, surfing and horseriding nearby. Residents spacious TV lounge. Smoke free home, within view of C11th Oranmore Castle - a haven of peace and quiet. Oranmore, private car hire available, at Son Amar.

Castle View, Galway Coast Road, Oranmore, Galway. Spacious neo-Georgian home, overlooking Galway Bay and Burren mountains.
Open: All Year
091 794648 Mrs Collins
D: Fr €26.00
Beds: 4F **Baths:** 4 Ensuite
ᗰ (10) ☑ ▥

Oughterard

M1143

Corrib Wave,
Portacarron,
Connemara,
Oughterard,
Galway.
Open: Mar to Dec
091 552147
Mr & Mrs Healy
Fax: 091 552736
cwh@gofree.indigo.ie www.corribwave.com
D: Fr €32.50-€35.00 **S:** Fr €50.00
Beds: 2F 8T **Baths:** 10 En
ᗰ (30) ⌇ ☑ ☲ ☑ ▥
The home of Michael & Maria Healy. Panoramic lakeside setting. Beautiful bedrooms, superb home cooking. Warm welcome. Peace & quiet, turf fire, angling specialists, boats for hire, lakeside walk. 18 hole golf course 1km. Wine licence.

Pine Grove, Lake Shore,
Hill of Doon Road, Glann, Oughterard, Galway.
Open: Mar to Oct
091 552101 Mrs Maloney
pgrove@eircom.net
D: Fr €26.00-€30.00 **S:** Fr €35.00-€40.00
Beds: 3F 1T **Baths:** 4 En
ᗰ (6) ☑ ▥
Quiet home on Western Way, 5 min walk Lough Corrib, famous for game angling, coarse angling within 15 mins. Ideal for touring Connemara & Arran Islands. Golf, pitch & putt, swimming, pubs & restaurants 10 mins. Travel Agents Vouchers accepted.

Fough East, Oughterard, County Galway.
Friendly, welcoming, home. Beautifully decorated with idyllic gardens, conveniently located in the village.
Open: Easter to Oct
091 552614 & 091 552957 Mr & Mrs McGeough
Fax: 091 552465
fougheast@iolfree.ie
D: Fr €24.00 **S:** Fr €30.00
Beds: 2F 2D 1T **Baths:** 5 En
ॐ ᗰ (10) ⌇ ☑ ▥ ♿ ▪

Lakeland Country House, Portacarron, Oughterard, Galway. Lakeside home just 5-min drive from the village, tranquil setting on Lough Corrib.
Open: All Year (not Xmas)
091 552146 & 091 552121 (also fax) Mrs Faherty & the Costelloes
mayfly@eircom.net
D: Fr €32.00
Beds: 1F 4D 4T **Baths:** 8 En 1 Pr
ॐ ᗰ (20) ⌇ ☑ ✕ ☑ ▥ ♿ ▪ cc

Portumna

M8504

Oakpark Lodge, Portland, Lorrha, Portumna, Co Galway. Beautiful riverside country house. Guest rooms overlook lawn & garden to the majestic River Shannon.
Open: All Year (not Xmas)
0509 47143 Mr & Mrs O'Carroll **Fax: 0509 47222**
oakpark@eircom.net
D: Fr €26.00
Beds: 1F 3T **Baths:** 2 En 1 Pr 1 Sh
ᗰ (6) ☑ ♘ ▥

Birch Cottage, St Joseph's Road, Portumna, Ballinasloe, Co Galway.
Open: All year (not Xmas/New Year) **Grades:** BF Approv
0509 41625 Mrs Carty
D: Fr €25.00-€30.00 **S:** Fr €35.00-€40.00
Beds: 1F 1T 3D **Baths:** 1 En 4 Pr
🛏 🅿 (8) 📺 ✕ Ⅴ ▥.
ITB Approved B&B located in Portumna, adjacent to 18 hole championship golf course, forest, park, Lough, Derg, Galway City, Limerick & the Burren one hour drive. Ideal for touring, being so centrally located. Excellent coarse, game and fly fishing.

Renvyle

L7664 🍺 Renvyle Inn, Veldon's

Fuchsia House, Curragh, Renvyle, Connemara, Galway. Nestled between mountains and Atlantic. Traditional decor. Fishing, horseriding, walking.
Open: Easter to Oct
095 43502 Mrs Walsh
fuchsiahouse@esatclear.ie
D: Fr €23.00 **S:** Fr €29.00
Beds: 1F 1T 1D **Baths:** 3 En
🛏 🅿 (6) 📺 ✕ Ⅴ ▥. ▪

Sunnymeade, Tully, Renvyle, Galway.
Renvyle's longest established B&B - stress-free. Situated above sandy beaches.
Open: All Year (not Xmas)
095 43491 (also fax) Conneely Family
sunny@eircom.net
D: Fr €26.00
Beds: 1F 3D 2T **Baths:** 6 En
🛏 (12) 🅿 (6) ⊱ ▥. ▪ cc

Inishkeen House, Tooreena, Renvyle, Connemara, Galway. Comfortable country home with warm relaxed atmosphere, superbly located beside sea and mountains.
Open: All Year (not Xmas)
095 43521 (also fax) Mrs Flaherty
inishkee@gofree.indigo.ie
www.connemara.net/inishkeen-house
D: Fr €27.00-€32.00 **S:** Fr €25.50
Beds: 1F 1D 1T **Baths:** 2 En 1 Pr
🛏 🅿 (3) 📺 ⊀ ✕ ▥. ▪

Rosmuc

L9233

Dun Manus, Glencoh, Screebe, Rosmuc, Galway. Modern country home overlooking Atlantic, friendly atmosphere, home cooking, mountain walks.
Open: Mar to Oct
091 574139 & 087 6360039 (M) Mrs Conroy
D: Fr €25.00-€30.00 **S:** Fr €35.00
Beds: 2D 1T **Baths:** 3 En
🛏 🅿 (6) 📺 ✕ Ⅴ ▥.

Rossaveal

L9625

Hernon's Bungalow, Rossaveal, Galway.
5 minutes from Rossaveal harbour, where ferries leave for the Aran Islands.
Open: Easter to Oct
091 572158 Mrs Hernon **Fax:** 091 572656
D: Fr €27.00
Beds: 1F 2D 1T **Baths:** 2 En 2 Pr
🅿 ⊱ 📺 ✕ ▥. ▪ cc

Rosscahill

M1838 🍺 Boat Inn, Ferryman Inn

Garrynagry, Rossacahill, Co Galway.
Dormer bungalow, ideal for fishing, walking or sightseeing. Warm welcome.
Open: All year (not Xmas/New Year)
091 550446 Mrs McDonough
D: Fr €25.00-€38.00 **S:** Fr €25.00-€320.00
Beds: 1F 1T 1D **Baths:** 3 En
🛏 🅿 (4) ⊱ 📺 Ⅴ ▥.

Roundstone

L7240 🍺 Roundhouse Hotel, Harbour View, Ryan's Bar, O'Dowd's, Eldon's, Keogh's

Heatherglen, Roundstone, Galway.
Overlooking Roundstone Bay with panoramic views. Beaches, pony-trekking, tennis courts, golf, angling.
Open: All Year (not Xmas)
095 35837 Mrs Keane **Fax:** 095 35793
spkeane@eircom.net
D: Fr €30.00
Beds: 1F 1D 2T **Baths:** 4 Ensuite
🛏 🅿 (8) 📺 ▥. ⅋ ▪

Seagrove House, *Letterdyse, Roundstone, Galway.* Perfectly situated for exploring Connemara's beauty and charms. You are assured of a warm welcome and restful nights at Seagrove House. Fishing, golf and mountain climbing close by. Seagrove House provides the perfect location for a holiday to remember.
Open: All year (not Xmas)
095 35810 Mrs McDonagh **Fax: 095 35003**
D: Fr €27.00 **S:** Fr €30.00
Beds: 3F 1T 1D **Baths:** 5 En 1 Pr
🐾 (5) 🅿 (7) 📺 🐕 🛏️ 🚿 ■

Salthill

M2723

Woodville, *Barna Road, Salthill, Galway.* Friendly, welcoming home with spectacular views of Galway Bay.
Open: Easter to Oct
091 524260 (also fax) Ms Wheeler
D: Fr €32.00
Beds: 1F 2D 1T **Baths:** 4 En
🐾 🅿 (4) 🚫 📺 🛏️ ■

Achill Bed & Breakfast, *9 Whitesand Road, Salthill, Galway.* Convenient B&B. Private car park, TV in rooms, 5 mins walk city centre.
Open: All Year (not Xmas)
091 589149 Mrs Donaghue
D: Fr €29.00
Beds: 1F 3D **Baths:** 4 En
🐾 🅿 (6) 🚫 📺 ✕ 🛏️ ■

3 Cashelmara Lodge, *Salthill, Galway.* New luxury accommodation overlooking Galway Bay with breathtaking interior.
Open: Feb to Nov
091 520020 Mrs Fahey
cashelmara@eircom.ie
www2.wombat.ie/pages/cashelmara/
D: Fr €25.50-€32.00 **S:** Fr €32.00-€38.00
Beds: 2F 2T 2D **Baths:** 6 Ensuite 6 Private
🅿 (7) 🚫 📺 📺 🛏️ ■ cc

Spiddal

M1222

Ard Mhuirbhi, *Inverin, Spiddal, Galway.* Spacious seaside accommodation in peaceful location. Superb views. Family suites.
Open: All year (not Xmas/New Year)
091 593215 Mrs Feeney **Fax: 091 593326**
ardmhuirbhi@eircom.net
D: Fr €27.00-€30.00 **S:** Fr €39.00-€42.00
Beds: 2F 2T 1D **Baths:** 4 En 1 Pr
🐾 (5) 🅿 (5) 🚫 📺 📺 🛏️ ■ cc

Sliabh Rua House, *Salahoona, Spiddal, Galway.* Spacious seaside home, amidst the wilds of Connemara. Magnificent walks, island and mountain views. Situated in extremely cultural, historic and tranquil region, we offer the perfect relaxing get away. Ideal for touring Aran Islands and Connemara. BF Approved.
Open: May to Oct
091 553243 Mrs Curran
sliabhrua@eircom.net
D: Fr €25.50 **S:** Fr €38.00
Beds: 4F **Baths:** 4 En
🅿 🚫 📺 🛏️ ■

Ard Aoibhinn, *Connemara, Spiddal, Galway.* 1km west of village. Many guide book recommendations. Convenient Aran Islands Ferry.
Open: All Year
091 553179 (also fax) Mrs O'Malley Curran
D: Fr €25.50
Beds: 3F 2D 1S **Baths:** 5 Ensuite
🐾 🅿 (10) 📺 🐕 ✕ 🛏️ 🚿 ❄ ■

Ardmor Country House, *Greenhill, Spiddal, Galway.* Country home, seaside location, spectacular views, picturesque gardens. Spacious bedrooms, tastefully decorated.
Open: Mar to Dec
091 553145 Mrs Feeney **Fax: 091 553596**
D: Fr €30.00
Beds: 4F 1T 2D **Baths:** 7 Ensuite
🅿 🚫 📺 📺 🛏️ 🚿 ■

BEDROOMS

D = Double	S = Single
T = Twin	F = Family

Planning a longer stay?
Always ask for any special rates

Sailin, *Coill Rua, Spiddal, Galway.* Bungalow in quiet location, sea side of coast road overlooking Galway Bay, Aran Islands.
Open: Easter to Oct
091 553308 Mrs McCarthaigh
D: Fr €21.50-€24.00 **S:** Fr €28.00-€33.00
Beds: 1F 2D 1T 1S **Baths:** 1 En 4 Pr
ॐ 🅿 ⌦ 📺 ▦

Ard Eoinin Bed & Breakfast, *Spiddal, Galway.*
Modern comfortable home beside Spiddal Village - its fine restaurants, great pubs, Blue Flag beach.
Open: All Year (not Xmas/New Year)
091 553234 Mrs Naughton
naughtonc@eircom.net www.geocities.com/ardeoinin
D: Fr €23.00-€24.00 **S:** Fr €32.00-€34.50
Beds: 1F 2D 3T **Baths:** 6 En
ॐ 🅿 (8) ⌦ 🐾 📺 ▦ ▪

Please respect a B&B's wishes regarding children, animals and smoking

Ard Na Greine, *Cre Dhubh, Spiddal, Galway.*
Friendly, comfortable house. Beaches/restaurants/pubs/music/bog walks/horseriding all close by. Ideal base for touring Connemara and Arran Islands. TV/beverages/all rooms ensuite. Breakfast menu. 20 mins city. Enjoy the Best of the West.
Open: Apr to Sep
091 553039 Mrs Joyce
mjoyce81@hotmail.com
D: Fr €25.50-€27.00 **S:** Fr €38.50
Beds: 1T 4D **Baths:** 4 En
ॐ 🅿 (8) ⌦ 📺 ✕ 📺 ▦ ▪ cc

Tuam

M4351

Kilmore House, *Kilmore, Galway Road, Tuam, Co Galway.* Registered and Approved B&B on farm. All rooms ensuite with TV & Fastext.
Open: All Year
093 28118 & 093 26525 Mrs O'Connor **Fax: 093 26525**
D: Fr €25.50
Beds: 2F 2D 2T 1S **Baths:** 7 En
ॐ 🅿 (15) 📺 🐾 ✕ ▦ ♿ ✳

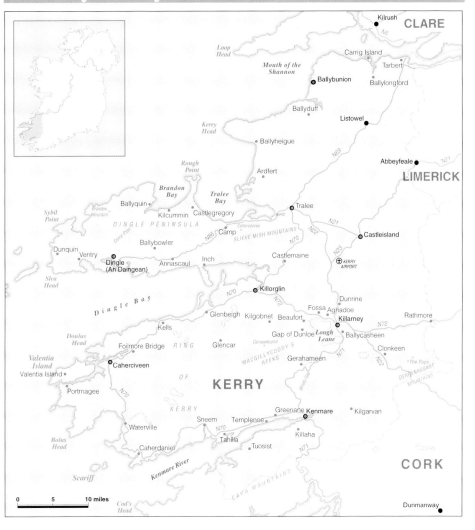

AIRPORTS ⊕
Kerry Airport - 066 9764644.

AIR SERVICES & AIRLINES ✈
Kerry to **London (Stansted)**.
Ryanair - in Republic, tel. 0818 303030; in UK, tel. 0871 2460000.

RAIL ⇌
Tralee and **Killarney** are at the end of a main line into **Dublin (Heuston)**.
You can also get to **Cork** from **Killarney**. Tel. **Irish Rail** on 01 8366222 for timetable details.

BUS 🚌
There are services from **Killarney** to **Tralee** and **Shannon Airport**; from **Tralee** to **Cork, Dingle** and **Limerick**.
Tel. **Bus Eireann** 01 8366111.

TOURIST INFORMATION OFFICES ℹ
RIC Barracks, **Caherciveen** (Jun to Sep), 066 9472589.
The Pier, **Dingle**, 066 9151188.
Kenmare Heritage Centre, **Kenmare** (Apr to Oct), 064 41233.
Beech Road, **Killarney** (open all year), 064 31633.
The Square, **Listowel** (Jun to Sep), 068 22590.
Denny Street, **Tralee** (open all year), 066 7121288.

Aghadoe
V9392

Glenmill House, *Nunstown, Aghadoe, Killarney, Co Kerry.* Luxurious new home, panoramic views lakes, McGillicuddy's Reeks, National Park. Orthopaedic beds, good breakfast.
Open: Mar to Oct
064 34391 Mrs Devane
glenmillhouse@eircom.net
D: Fr €28.00
Beds: 3D 1T **Baths:** 4 En
🄿 (6) 📺 ⅲ, ⚊

Carrowmore House, *Knockasarnett, Aghadoe, Killarney, Co Kerry.* Warm, welcoming, family-run B&B with panoramic views from bedrooms and lounge.
Open: Apr to Oct
064 33520 Mrs McAuliffe
D: Fr €27.00
Beds: 2F 2D 1T **Baths:** 5 En
🛏 🄿 (5) ⅙ 📺 Ⓥ ⅲ, ⚊

Annascaul
Q5902

Four Winds, *Annascaul, Dingle Peninsula, Co Kerry.* Scenic views. Ideal for touring Dingle Peninsula. Friendly village of Annascaul.
Open: All year **Grades:** BF Approv
066 9157168 Mrs O'Connor **Fax: 066 9157174**
D: Fr €26.00-€30.00 **S:** Fr €39.00
Beds: 2F 2T 2D **Baths:** 4 En 2 Sh
🛏 🄿 ⅲ, ⚊

The Old Anchor Guest House, *Annascaul, Tralee, Co Kerry.* Situated on Dingle Way. Painting and walking holidays arranged.
Open: Mar to Nov
066 9157382 Miss Kennedy
dropanchor@eircom.net
D: Fr €30.00 **S:** Fr €35.00
Beds: 10F **Baths:** 10 En
🛏 🄿 (4) ⅙ 🐾 ✗ Ⓥ ⅲ, ⅙ ⚊ cc

Ardfert
Q7821

Ardkeel House,
Brandonwell, Ardfert, Tralee, Co Kerry.
Open: All year **Grades:** BF Approv
066 7134288 Mrs Higgins
ardkeelhouse@oceanfree.net
D: Fr €26.50-€30.00 **S:** Fr €39.00-€42.00
Beds: 1F 1D 1T
🛏 🄿 (7) 📺 ✗ Ⓥ ⅲ, ❄
A distinctive modern luxurious family-run ITB approved B&B. Quiet central location off Ardfert/Fenit Road. Highly recommended for it's hospitality, good food, spacious rooms. Bars/restaurants walking distance. Tralee golf course 2.5 miles, Banna Beach 2 miles.

Ballybowler

Q4705

Bay View House, *Ballybowler, Dingle, Tralee, Co Kerry.* Situated on scenic tranquil Dingle Way. Spectacular views from bedrooms. Extensive breakfast menu.
Open: Easter to Oct
066 9151704 Mrs Barrett
D: Fr €24.00
Beds: 1F 1D 1T **Baths:** 3 En
ॐ (2) ▯ (5) ▣ ➤ ▣ ▥ ▪ **cc**

Ballybunion

Q8641

Greenmount Hotel, *Ballybunion, Listowel, Co Kerry.* Comfortable family operated hotel, overlooking beach, adjacent Ballybunion Golf Course.
Open: Jun to Sep
068 27147 Mr Purtill
D: Fr €23.00-€32.00 **S:** Fr €25.50-€32.00
Beds: 3F 3D 5T 1S **Baths:** 12 En
ॐ (1) **cc**

Gullane House, *Ballybunion, Listowel, Co Kerry.* Family run farmhouse on the coast road. Warm welcome.
Open: Jun to Sep
068 27132 Mrs O'Boyle
D: Fr €18.00-€20.50 **S:** Fr €25.50
Beds: 3T 1D **Baths:** 2 En
ॐ ▯ ⊬ ▣ ➤ ▥ ▪

Country Haven, *Tabart Car Ferry Road, Ballybunion, Listowel, Co Kerry.* Overlooking Atlantic near golf course. Own tennis court. Satellite TV in bedrooms - all ensuite.
Open: Easter to Nov
068 27103 Mrs Walsh **Fax: 068 27822**
eileenwalsh@eircom.net.
homepage.eircom.net/~eileenwalsh
D: Fr €35.00
Beds: 1F 2D 2T **Baths:** 5 Ensuite
ॐ ▯ (5) ⊬ ▣ ▣ ▥ ▪

B&B owners may vary rates – be sure to check when booking

Ballycasheen

V9790

Larkfield House, *Ballycasheen, Killarney, County Kerry.* Award-winning family-run Bed and Breakfast, 2km from town centre.
Open: Mar to Oct
064 34438 Mr & Mrs Ivory
jki@eircom.net www.larkfieldhouse.com
D: Fr €25.00 **S:** Fr €35.00
Beds: 2F 2D **Baths:** 4 En
ॐ ▯ (6) ⊬ ▣ ▥ ▪ **cc**

Ballyduff

Q8733

Shannon View, *Ferry Road, Ballyduff, Tralee, Co Kerry.* Chef-owned. Evening meals if required, located between Ballybunion and Ballyteigue.
Open: All Year
066 7131324 Mr & Mrs Sowden
gainescountryhouse@eircom.net
D: Fr €25.50
Beds: 2D 1T **Baths:** 2 En 2 Sh
ॐ ▯ (5) ▣ ✕ ▣ ▥

Ballyheigue

Q7528

Hillcrest, *Mountway, Ballyheigue, Tralee, Co Kerry.* Modern bungalow, large gardens, superb views of beach and mountains. Beside golf course.
Open: May to Oct
066 7133306 Mrs Collins
D: Fr €26.00 **S:** Fr €33.00
Beds: 1F 1D 1T **Baths:** 3 En
ॐ (2) ▯ (5) ▣ ▣ ▥ ▪

Ballylongford

R0045

Castle View House, *Carrig Island, Ballylongford, Listowel, Co Kerry.*
Open: All year (not Xmas)
Grades: BF Approv
068 43304 (also fax) Mrs Dee
castleviewhouse@eircom.net www.castleviewhouse.com
D: Fr €23.00 **S:** Fr €28.00
Beds: 3D 3T **Baths:** 6 En
ॐ ▯ (8) ▣ ➤ ✕ ▣ ▥ **cc**
Come and relax in a peaceful setting located on Carrig Island (entry by bridge), facing historical Carrigafoyle Castle. Scenic walks, fishing, Tarbert-Killimer car ferry, Ballybunion golf course nearby. Vouchers accepted. Good food, warm welcome.

Ballyquin

Q5213

Ard na Feinne B&B, *Ballyquin, Brandon, Tralee, Co Kerry.* Homely atmosphere on Dingle Way, mountains, angling, archaeological sites, beaches.
Open: May to Sep
066 7138220 (also fax) Mrs Nicholl
anfbandb@eircom.net
D: Fr €19.00-€23.00 **S:** Fr €25.50-€29.00
Beds: 1F 1D 1T **Baths:** 2 En
🛏 🅿 (6) 📺 Ⅴ �📶

Beaufort

V8682

Farmstead Lodge, *Shanara Cross, Kilgobnet, Beaufort, Killarney, Co Kerry.* Modern farmhouse nested at the foot of Irelands highest mountains.
Open: Apr to Nov
066 9761968 (also fax) Mr & Mrs O'Shea
D: Fr €20.50-€24.00 **S:** Fr €24.00-€28.00
Beds: 4F 1T 1D 2S **Baths:** 3 En 1 Sh
🛏 🅿 📺 🍴 ✕ Ⅴ �📶

The Invicta, *Tommes, Beaufort, Killarney, Co Kerry.* Charming home overlooking Killarney's Lakes. Fishing, boating, 9 and 18 hole golf courses.
Open: Easter to Oct
064 44207 (also fax) Ms Sweeney
D: Fr €21.50-€24.00 **S:** Fr €27.00-€32.00
Beds: 1F 2D 1T **Baths:** 4 En
🛏 �📶

Caherciveen

V4779

Ocean View Town & Country Home, *Renard Road, Caherciveen, Co Kerry.*
Open: All year (not Xmas)
066 9472261 (also fax)
Ms O'Donoghue
D: Fr €26.00 **S:** Fr €40.00
Beds: 2F 2D 2T **Baths:** 6 En
🛏 (4) 🅿 (6) 📺 🍴 �📶 ⚓
Luxury farmhouse overlooking Caherciveen Bay within walking distance of town. Bedrooms tastefully decorated, all with spectacular sea views, sunsets, islands, C15th castle. Peat/wood fires. Mountain climbing, sea sports, golf, pitch and putt. Skellig Rock nearby. Tea/coffee facilities in all bedrooms.

Iveragh Heights, *Carhan Road, Caherciveen, Co Kerry.* Highly recommended, golf, fishing, horse riding available. Sip a cool drink on the patio.
Open: All year
066 9472545 (also fax) Mrs O'Neill
www.kerryweb.ie/destination-kerry/cahirciveen/iveraghheights.html
D: Fr €20.50-€21.50 **S:** Fr €24.50
Beds: 7F 3D 3T 1S **Baths:** 9 En 7 Pr
🛏 🅿 (8) 📺 🍴 ✕ Ⅴ �📶 ❄ ⚓

Harbour Hill, *Knockeens, Caherciveen, Co Kerry.* Luxurious home, quiet, peaceful, panoramic views, Skellig trips and itineraries planned.
Open: Easter to Oct
066 9472844 (also fax) Mrs Curran
harbour_hill@hotmail.com
www.kerryweb.ie/destination-kerry/cahirciveen/harbourhill.html
D: Fr €20.50-€23.00 **S:** Fr €25.50-€30.50
Beds: 2F 2T 2D 1S **Baths:** 5 En 1 Pr
🛏 🅿 (6) ✁ 📺 🍴 ✕ Ⅴ �📶 ♿ ⚓ cc

Pine Crest, *Cappaghs, Caherciveen, Co Kerry.* country house, scenic surroundings, birdwatching, private car park.
Open: Jan to Sept
066 9472482 Mrs O'Shea
D: Fr €24.00-€25.50 **S:** Fr €24.00-€25.50
Beds: 1F 1D 1T **Baths:** 3 En
🅿 ✁ 📺 ✕ Ⅴ �📶 ❄ ⚓

Caherdaniel

V5459

Kerry Way B&B, *Caherdaniel, Killarney, County Kerry.* Family B&B on Kerry Way. Pub next door - traditional music/great food.
Open: Easter to Nov
066 9475277 Mr Sweeney **Fax: 066 9475280**
info@activity-ireland.com www.activity-ireland.com
D: Fr €25.00 **S:** Fr €30.00
Beds: 3T 3D **Baths:** 6 En
🅿 (3) ✁ 📺 �📶 ⚓ cc

B&B owners may vary rates – be sure to check when booking

Camp
Q6909

Suan na Mara, *Lisnagree, Camp, Tralee, Co Kerry.* Peaceful accommodation, highly recommended Laura Ashley style home. Superb breakfast menu.
Open: Mar to Oct
066 7139258 (also fax) Mrs Fitzgerald
suanmara@eircom.net www.kerryweb.ie/suanmara
D: Fr €25.50-€29.00 **S:** Fr €33.00-€58.50
Beds: 4D 2T 1S **Baths:** 7 En
⌂ 🅿 (8) ⅏ 📺 🎞. ♨

Carrig Island
Q9848

Castle View House, *Carrig Island, Ballylongford, Listowel, Co Kerry.* Peaceful setting, located on Carrig Island, facing historic Carrigafoyle castle.
Open: All year (not Xmas) **Grades:** BF Approv
068 43304 (also fax) Mrs Dee
castleviewhouse@eircom.net www.castleviewhouse.com
D: Fr €23.00 **S:** Fr €28.00
Beds: 3D 3T **Baths:** 6 En
⌂ 🅿 (8) 📺 🛏 ✕ Ⅴ 🎞. cc

Castlegregory
Q6113

Beenoskee B&B, *Conor Pass Road, Cappatigue, Castlegregory, Tralee, Co Kerry.*
Open: All year **Grades:** BF Approv
066 7139263 (also fax) Mrs Ferriter
beenoskee@eircom.net www.beenoskee.com
D: Fr €28.00-€30.00 **S:** Fr €40.00
Beds: 4D 1T **Baths:** 5 En
⌂ 🅿 (8) ⅏ 📺 ✕ 🎞. ✱ ♨ cc
Warm Irish hospitality, complimentary tea/home made cake. Tastefully decorated rooms directly overlooking ocean and long, safe, unspoilt sandy beach within walking distance. Spectacular views, mountains, islands and lake. Orthopaedic beds, extensive breakfast menu, home baking. Numerous recommendations, golf, fishing, surfing and tranquil walks.

The Shores Country House, *Conor Pass Road, Cappatigue, Castlegregory, Tralee, Co Kerry.*
Open: Feb to Nov
066 7139196 (also fax)
Mrs O'Mahony
theshores@eircom.net www.shores.main-page.com
D: Fr €28.00-€35.00 **S:** Fr €40.00-€60.00
Beds: 1F 4D 1T **Baths:** 6 En
⌂ (3) 🅿 (8) ⅏ 📺 ✕ Ⅴ 🎞. ♨ cc
Highest award winning AA 5 Diamond premises, luxurious spacious 'Laura Ashley' style decorated house. Magnificent panoramic sea view from almost all rooms. All rooms ensuite, some with bath, multi channel TV in all rooms. Recommended by many guides.

Sea Mount House, *Cappatigue Conor Pass Road, Castlegregory, Tralee, Co Kerry.*
Open: Apr to Nov **Grades:** AA 4 Diamond
066 7139229 (also fax) Mrs Walsh
seamount@unison.ie www.seamounthouse.com
D: Fr €28.00-€30.00 **S:** Fr €38.00-€40.00
Beds: 1F 1T 2D **Baths:** 3 En 1 Pr
⌂ 🅿 (4) ⅏ 📺 🛏 🎞. ♨ cc
Relax in our award-winning AA 4 Diamond stylishly decorated home on seafront overlooking Brandon Bay and miles of sandy beach. Outstanding seaviews. Rooms are spacious and luxurious. Golf, windsurfing, horse riding and restaurants nearby. 20 mins drive from Dingle Town.

Griffins Tip Top Country Farmhouse, *Goulane, Castlegregory, Tralee, Co Kerry.* Two storey farmhouse on the beautiful Dingle Peninsula. Fronted by safe, sandy beaches.
Open: Mar to Nov
066 7139147 (also fax) Mrs Griffin
D: Fr €32.00
Beds: 3F 3D 3T 1S **Baths:** 6 En 4 Sh
⌂ (5) 🅿 (10) 📺 🛏 Ⅴ 🎞.

Castleisland
Q9909

Beech Grove, *Camp Road, Castleisland, Co Kerry.* Relax in the sun lounge, stroll in the nature trail or Secret Garden.
Open: Easter to Oct 1
066 7141217 Mr & Mrs O'Mahony **Fax: 066 7142877**
www.irishfarmhoildays.com
D: Fr €25.50-€28.50 **S:** Fr €32.00-€35.00
Beds: 1F 2T 1D **Baths:** 4 En
⌂ (10) 🅿 ⅏ 📺 🎞. ♨ cc

The Gables, *Limerick Road, Dooneen, Castleisland, Co Kerry.* Luxurious house overlooking beautiful landscape and 18-hole golf course (1 minute drive). Ideal touring and golfing base. Large comfortable, ensuite bedrooms with orthopaedic beds and power showers. Extensive breakfast menu. Good restaurants nearby in Castleisland (2 miles). Warm welcome assured.
Open: All year (not Xmas/New Year)
066 7141060 (also fax) Mrs Dillon
D: Fr €25.50-€28.00 **S:** Fr €36.00-€38.50
Beds: 1T 1T 1D **Baths:** 3 En 1 Pr
ॐ 🅿 (6) ⅍ 🆅 ✕ 🆅 ⅏, 🛈 cc

Castlemaine
Q8303

Caher House, *Caherfilane, Keel, Castlemaine, Killarney, Co Kerry.* Comfortable bungalow overlooking mountains and Dingle Bay between Castlemaine & Inch.
Open: Apr to Oct
066 9766126 Mrs O'Sullivan
caherf1@eircom.net
D: Fr €21.50-€24.00 **S:** Fr €27.50-€30.00
Beds: 2F 2D 2T **Baths:** 5 En 1 Sh
ॐ 🅿 (6) ⅍ 🆅 ✕ ⅏, 🛈

Murphy's Farmhouse, *Boolteens, Castlemaine, Killarney, Co Kerry.* 300 yards off Dingle Road at Bole's village on south flank of Slieve Mirsh.
Open: All Year (not Xmas)
066 9767337 Ms Murphy **Fax: 066 9767839**
D: Fr €27.00
Beds: 14F 2D 10T 2S **Baths:** 14 En
ॐ 🅿 ⅍ ✕ ⅏, 🛈 cc

Palm Grove Farmhouse, *Ardcanaught, Castlemaine, Killarney, Co Kerry.* Gateway to Ring of Kerry and Dingle Peninsula. Two-storey farmhouse in peaceful surroundings.
Open: Easter to Mar
066 9767170 Mrs Nagle
D: Fr €27.00
Beds: 3D 1T **Baths:** 2 En 2 Sh
ॐ 🅿 ✕ 🆅 ⅏, 🛈 cc

BATHROOMS
En = Ensuite
Pr = Private
Sh = Shared

Tom & Eileen's Farm, *Castlemaine, Co Kerry.* Award-winning old style farmhouse nestling under Sliabh Mist mountains.
Open: May to Oct
066 9767373 Mrs Buckley
phenab@gofree.indigo.ie
D: Fr €21.50-€24.00 **S:** Fr €30.00-€32.50
Beds: 1F 3D 2T **Baths:** 5 En 1 Pr
ॐ 🅿 (6) ⅍ ⅏, 🛈 cc

Clonkeen
W0685

Woodgrove Farm, *Clonkeen, Killarney, Co Kerry.*
Open: Easter to Nov
064 53010
Mrs O'Donoghue
woodgrove@ gofree.indigo.ie
D: Fr €28.00 **S:** Fr €35.00
Beds: 3D **Baths:** 1 En 3 Pr
ॐ (11) 🅿 (4) ⅍ 🆅 ⅍ ✕ 🆅 ⅏, 🛈 cc
Get away from the rush & relax in this old world farm cottage. 'Woodgrove' nestles at the foot of the Crohane Mountains, 1 mile off the N22 Cork-Killarney road. A warm welcome is assured. Home cooking & friendly atmosphere.

The Glen, *Islandmore, Clonkeen, Killarney, Co Kerry.* Traditional C18th farmhouse, unspoilt mountain setting 10 mins Killarney on N22 Cork road.
Open: All year
064 53067 & 086 8535084 (M) Mrs Garner
theglen@esatclear.ie
D: Fr €25.00 **S:** Fr €28.00
Beds: 1F 1T **Baths:** 2 En
ॐ 🅿 (3) ⅍ ⅍ 🆅 ⅏, cc

Dingle
Q4401 🍴 *The Half Door, Beginish, Doyle's, Chart House, Paidi O'Shea, Murphy's Castle Bar*

Dingle View, *Connor Pass Road, Dingle, Tralee, Co Kerry.* New home overlooking Dingle Bay. Panoramic views of Conor Pass. Superb location. Beautiful beaches.
Open: All Year
066 9151662 Mr & Mrs Fitzgerald
D: Fr €33.00
Beds: 2T 2D **Baths:** 4 Ensuite

Conor Pass House, *Conor Pass Road, Ballybeg, Dingle, Tralee, Co Kerry.*
Open: All year (not Xmas/New Year)
066 9152184
K Hennessy
conorpasshouse@eircom.net www.conorpasshouse.com
D: Fr €30.00-€33.00
Beds: 4D **Baths:** 4 En
⌂ ▣ ⚲ ▥ Ⓥ ▥
A new house, ITB approved, tea/coffee on arrival, power showers, cable TV, hairdryers. Breakfast menu, panoramic views of Conor Pass/Dingle Bay, private parking, walking distance to town & all amenities. Highly recommended for its hospitality. Guest lounge.

The Hillgrove Inn, *Spa Road, Dingle, Tralee, Co Kerry.*
Open: May to Oct
066 9151131 & 069 9151441 & 086 6345424 (M)
Fax: 069 9151441
hillgrovedingle@eircom.net www.hillgrovedingle.com
D: Fr €35.00-€70.00 **S:** Fr €45.00-€80.00
Beds: 6T 6D **Baths:** 12 En
⌂ ▣ (60) ▥ ⊩ ⚓ cc
Family owned & managed, the Hillgrove is situated on the Spa Road, mins walk from Dingle's Main Street. All rooms are finished to a very high standard. We offer a perfect combination of professional service with cheerful & helpful staff.

The Lighthouse, *Ballinaboula, Dingle, Tralee, Co Kerry.* Spacious house, panoramic harbour views. Minutes walk to town centre.
Open: Feb to Nov
066 9151829 (also fax)
Mrs Murphy
info@lighthousedingle.com www.lighthousedingle.com
D: Fr €28.00-€35.00
Beds: 1F 4T 1D **Baths:** 6 En
⌂ ▣ ⚲ ▥ Ⓥ ▥ ⚓ cc

Bambury's Guest House, *Mail Road, Dingle, Tralee, Co Kerry.*
Open: All year
066 9151244
Mr Bambury
Fax: 066 9151786
info@bamburysguesthouse.com
D: Fr €35.00-€50.00 **S:** Fr €35.00-€70.00
Beds: 1F 3D 8T **Baths:** 12 En
⌂ (4) ▣ (12) ▥ ▥ ⅋ ⚓ cc
A family run guesthouse where people always come first. Situated 1 min walk from Dingle town. 12 recently refurbished bedrooms, all rooms ensuite with everything you need. The ideal base in the beautiful Dingle Peninsula be it for leisure or for business.

O'Shea's, *Conor Pass Road, Dingle, Tralee, Co Kerry.*
Open: Easter to Nov
066 9151368 Mrs O'Shea
celiaoshea@ireland.com
D: Fr €23.00-€27.00 **S:** Fr €32.00
Beds: 1F 1D 1T **Baths:** 3 En
⌂ (5) ▣ ▥ ▥ ⅋ ⚓
Perfectly situated for touring the Dingle Peninsula - 2 minute drive to Dingle Town, 10 minute walk - our home overlooks Dingle Bay with views of hills in the background. Peaceful surroundings almost guarantee a good night's sleep in our spacious bedrooms.

Bolands B&B, *Goat Street, Dingle, Tralee, Co Kerry.*
A warm welcome awaits you & your children of all ages.
Open: All year (not Xmas/New Year)
066 9151426 Mr & Mrs Boland
bolanddingle@eircom.net
homepage.eircom.net~bolanddingle
D: Fr €26.00-€40.00 **S:** Fr €30.00-€40.00
Beds: 1F 1T 6D **Baths:** 8 En
⌂ ▥ Ⓥ ▥ ⚓ cc

Kavanaghs, *Garfinny, Dingle, Tralee, Co Kerry.*
Family run, 3km Dingle town, golf, angling, boat trips, mountaineering.
Open: Apr to Sep
066 9151326 Mrs Kavanagh
mkavan@iol.ie
D: Fr €23.00-€28.00 **S:** Fr €30.00-€35.00
Beds: 1F 3D **Baths:** 3 En 1 Pr
⌂ ▣ (6) ▥ ✕ Ⓥ ▥ ⚓ cc

Garvey's Farmhouse, *Kilvicadownig, Ventry, Dingle, Tralee, Co Kerry.* Spacious house on dairy farm overlooking Ventry Bay in peaceful surroundings.
Open: Mar to Nov
066 9159914 Mrs Garvey **Fax: 066 9159921**
www.garveysfarmhouse.com
D: Fr €27.00-€30.00 **S:** Fr €36.00-€42.00
Beds: 2F 2D 1T **Baths:** 4 En 1 Pr
☎ 🅿 (6) 🆅 ✕ 🔲 cc

Alpine House, *Mail Road, Dingle, Co Kerry.* Delightfully furnished bedrooms with spacious private bathrooms. Rooms with excellent views of harbour and mountains. A menu of traditional and wholesome fare served in impressive breakfast room. Dingle, famous for seafood and traditional Irish music bars. Near bus stop.
Open: All year (not Xmas)
066 9151250 Mr O'Shea **Fax: 066 9151966**
alpinedingle@eircom.net www.alpineguesthouse.com
D: Fr €26.00-€38.00 **S:** Fr €31.75-€57.00
Beds: 2F 5D 5T **Baths:** 12 En
☎ (4) 🅿 (12) ⅍ 🆅 🔲 ⚓ cc

Duinin House, *Connor Pass Road, Dingle, Tralee, Co Kerry.* Superb location with magnificent views. Overlooking Dingle town and harbour.
Open: Easter to Feb
066 9151335 (also fax) Mrs Neligan
pandaneligan@eircom.net
D: Fr €29.00
Beds: 3D 2T **Baths:** 5 En
☎ (7) 🅿 (5) ⅍ 🆅 🔲 ⚓ cc

Doonshean View, *High Road, Garfinny, Dingle, Tralee, Co Kerry.* Dormer bungalow with fire safety certificate. Tranquil location. Surrounded by 'Slieve Mist' Mountains.
Open: Easter to Oct
066 9151032 Mrs O'Neill
doonsheanview@boinet.ie
homepage.eircom.net/~doonsheanview
D: Fr €24.00-€25.50 **S:** Fr €32.50-€34.50
Beds: 2F 1D 1T **Baths:** 4 En
☎ 🅿 (4) ⅍ 🆅 🆅 🔲 cc

Kirrary House, *Avondale St, Dingle, Tralee, Co Kerry.* Traditional family Irish home: nice atmosphere, open turf fires downstairs.
Open: All Year
066 9151606 Mrs Collins
collinskirrary@eircom.net
D: Fr €24.00-€28.00 **S:** Fr €30.00-€35.50
Beds: 1D 1T 1S **Baths:** 2 En 1 Sh 🆅 🆅 🔲

Connors, *Dykegate Street, Dingle, Tralee, Co Kerry.* Comfortable guest house in the heart of Dingle town.
Open: All Year (not Xmas)
066 9151598 (also fax) Mrs Connor
D: Fr €26.00
Beds: 2F 7D 5T 1S **Baths:** 15 En
☎ 🆅 🔲 ⚓ cc

Ard Na Greine House, *Spa Road, Dingle, Tralee, Co Kerry.* Luxury immaculate bungalow in a superb location 5 minutes' walk to town centre
Open: All Year (not Xmas)
066 9151113 Mrs Houlihan **Fax: 066 9151898**
D: Fr €32.00
Beds: 2D 2T **Baths:** 4 En
☎ (7) 🅿 (4) ⅍ 🆅 🔲 ⚓ cc

Barr na Sraide, *Goat Street, Dingle, Tralee, Co Kerry.* Newly refurbished, this is a charming, family-run bar/guest house in town centre.
Open: All Year (not Xmas)
066 9151331 Mrs Geaney
D: Fr €50.00-€55.00
Beds: 3F 6T 10D 3S **Baths:** 22 Ensuite
☎ 🅿 (25) 🆅 🆅 🔲 ⚓

Old Mill House, *3 Avondale Street, Dingle, Co Kerry.* Recently built family-run B&B. Located quiet residential street near bus stop. Ideal base. Open turf fires, complimentary hot whiskey. Spacious ensuite rooms (power shower), with TV, hairdryer. Breakfast menu (inc veg) and famous crepes suzettes (pancakes). Home-made brown bread and preserves. 10-min walk to Fungi. 1-min walk to traditional pubs.
Open: All year
066 9151120 & 066 9152349 Mrs O'Neil **Fax: 066 9151120**
verhoul@iol.ie www.iol.ie/~verhoul/index.html
D: Fr €15.00-€25.00 **S:** Fr €18.00-€23.00
Beds: 1F 2T 1D 1S **Baths:** 3 En 1 Pr
☎ ⅍ 🆅 🆅 🔲 cc

Cillfountain Farm, *Kilfountain, Dingle, Tralee, Co Kerry.* Beautiful tranquil location 2km west of Dingle off Ballyferriter Road R559.
Open: Easter to Nov & 26 Dec to 7 Jan
066 9151389 Mrs Lynch
D: Fr €30.00
Beds: 1F 2T 2D 1S **Baths:** 5 Ensuite 1 Private
☎ 🅿 (10) ⅍ 🆅 🆅 🔲 ⚓

Pax House, *Dingle, Tralee, County Kerry.*
Pax House has undeniably one of the most
spectacular views in the peninsula. All rooms
including suites beautifully appointed. Gourmet
breakfast includes local produce, home-made
breads and preserves. Enjoy a drink on the
balcony and watch the boats return with their
catch.
Open: Feb to Nov
066 9151518 Mrs Brosnan-Wright **Fax: 066
9152461**
paxhouse@iol.ie www.pax-house.com
D: Fr €45.00-€80.00 **S:** Fr €50.00-€70.00
Beds: 1F 7D 2S **Baths:** 13 En
🖵 (10) 📺 🛏 Ⅴ Ⅲ ☕ cc

Q3101

**Kruger's Guest
House,**
*Ballinaraha,
Dunquin, Dingle,
Tralee, Co Kerry.*
Open: Mar to Oct
066 9156127

Mrs O'Neill
D: Fr €27.00 **S:** Fr €27.00
Beds: 1F 3D 2T 1S **Baths:** 3 Sh
🛏 (10) 🖵 (50) 📺 🛏 ✕ Ⅲ
World-famous and popular traditional guest
house and lounge bar. Situated in heart of
spectacular Dingle Peninsula. Ideal for touring
popular scenic Dingle Way and Slea Head Way.
Two lovely sandy beaches nearby. Visit 'Ryan's
Daughter' film site nearby.

V9695

Beenoskee, *Tralee Road, Dunrine, Killarney, Co
Kerry.* Modern, comfortable family home, rural
setting, 5 minutes drive nearest town.
Open: Apr to Oct
064 32435 (also fax) Mrs Burke
scoolick@iol.ie
D: Fr €25.50
Beds: 3F 1D **Baths:** 4 En
🛏 🖵 ✂ 📺 ✕ Ⅴ Ⅲ ☕ cc

Planning a longer stay?
Always ask for any special rates

V5282

Fransal House, *Foilmore Bridge, Caherciveen,
Co Kerry.* Experience real Irish home hospitality in
peaceful, scenic surroundings away from noise
and traffic.
Open: All Year (not Xmas)
066 9472997 & 066 9473233 Mr & Mrs Landers
Fax: 066 9472997
D: Fr €25.00
Beds: 2F 1T 2D **Baths:** 4 Ensuite 1 Private
🛏 🖵 (6) 📺 🛏 ✕ Ⅴ Ⅲ ☕

V9191

Coffey s Loch Lein House, *Golf Course Road,
Fossa, Killarney, Co Kerry.* Uniquely situated
beside Killarney's lakes, magnificent family-run
hotel.
Open: Mar to Nov
064 31260 Mrs Coffey **Fax: 064 36151**
ecoffey@indigo.ie www.lochlein.com
D: Fr €35.00-€50.00 **S:** Fr €45.00-€60.00
Beds: 2F 14 D/T **Baths:** 16 En
🛏 🖵 (16) 📺 Ⅲ cc

Tuscar Lodge, *Golf Course Road, Fossa,
Killarney, Co Kerry.* Family-run guest house
overlooking Loch Lein. Magnificent view Kerry
Mountain Range.
Open: Mar to Oct
064 31978 (also fax) Mrs Fitzgerald
tuscar_lodge@irelanddot.com
D: Fr €20.50 **S:** Fr €21.50
Beds: 4D 10T **Baths:** 14 En
🛏 🖵 (14) 📺 🛏 Ⅴ Ⅲ ☕

Brookside Gortacollopa, *Fossa, Killarney, Co
Kerry.* Award-winning country home in farmland
setting. 1995 Country Rover B&B of the Year.
Open: Mar to Nov
064 44187 Mr & Mrs Moriarty
D: Fr €23.00-€25.50 **S:** Fr €32.00
Beds: 2F 1D 3T **Baths:** 5 En 1 Sh
🛏 🖵 (6) ✂ 📺 🛏 Ⅴ Ⅲ ☕

The Shady Nook, *Crohane, Fossa, Killarney, Co
Kerry.* Family home located in a scenic, peaceful
location 4km from Killarney town.
Open: Easter to Oct
064 33351 & 087 2359476 (M) Mrs O'Leary
D: Fr €25.50
Beds: 2F 1T **Baths:** 3 Ensuite 3 Private
🛏 ✂ 📺 ✕ Ⅴ Ⅲ ☕

Gap of Dunloe

V8787

Purple Heather, *Gap of Dunloe, Killarney, Co Kerry.*
Open: Mar to Oct
064 44266 (also fax)
Mrs Moriarty
purpleheather@eircom.net
homepage.eircom.net/~purpleheather
D: Fr €26.00-€30.00 **S:** Fr €38.00-€48.00
Beds: 1F 2D 2T 1S **Baths:** 6 En 5 Pr
➤ ⊞ (6) ⊡ ⊁ ✕ ⊞ ⚬ cc
Scenic area. All rooms with private bath/shower, toilet, TV, electric blankets, hairdryers, tea/coffee. Has its own pool room, free. Ideally centred for all scenic routes, golf, nature walks, mountain climbing, traditional Irish music restaurant 1km.

Holly Grove, *Gap of Dunloe, Killarney, Co Kerry.*
Spacious, comfortable bedrooms, one with 3 beds. Most rooms with private shower and toilet.
Open: Easter to Dec
064 44326 (also fax) Mrs Coffey
D: Fr €25.50
Beds: 1F 1D 2T **Baths:** 3 En 1 Pr
➤ ⊞ ⊁ ⊡ ⊁ ✕ ⊡ ⊞ ⚬ cc

Wayside, *Gap of Dunloe, Killarney, Co Kerry.*
Peaceful lake/mountain district. Restaurants, Irish music & dancing 1 km. Horseriding, fishing 1 km.
Open: All Year (not Xmas)
064 44284 Mrs Ferris
wayside@hotmail.com
www.dirl.com/.kerry/wayside.htm
D: Fr €23.00-€25.50 **S:** Fr €30.00-€32.50
Beds: 1F 2D 2D **Baths:** 2 En 1 Pr
➤ ⊞ ⊡ ⊞ cc

Shamrock Farmhouse, *Black Valley, Gap of Dunloe, Killarney, Co Kerry.* Modern farmhouse bungalow, peacefully situated at foot of McGillycuddy's Reeks overlooking Killarney's Upper Lake.
Open: All Year
064 34714 Mrs O'Sullivan
D: Fr €20.50-€23.00 **S:** Fr €20.50-€23.00
Beds: 1F 1D 2T **Baths:** 2 En 2 Pr 1 Sh
➤ ⊞ (4) ⊁ ⊡ ✕ ⊡ ⊞

All details shown are as supplied by B&B owners in Autumn 2002

Gerahameen

V8781

Hillcrest Farmhouse,
Gerahameen, Black Valley, Killarney, Co Kerry.
Traditional-style farmhouse, scenically situated on Kerry way walking route.
Open: Mar to Nov
064 34702 (also fax) Mrs Tangney
D: Fr €30.00 **S:** Fr €42.00
Beds: 1D 5T **Baths:** 6 En
➤ ⊞ ⊁ ⊡ ✕ ⊞ ⚬ cc

Glenbeigh

V6891

Village House,
Glenbeigh, Killarney, Co Kerry.
Open: All year
066 9768128
Mr Breen **Fax: 066 9768486**
breenvillage house@eircom.net
D: Fr €30.00-€40.00 **S:** Fr €40.00-€50.00
Beds: 2F 4D 3T **Baths:** 9 En 1 Sh
➤ ⊞ ⊡ ⊞ ⚼ ❋
A distinctive, modern two storey guest house. A modern conveniences including car park, drying room. Early breakfasts for early risers. On the Kerry Way walking route on Ring of Kerry. Central location for golfing in Kerry.

The Glenbeigh Hotel, *Glenbeigh, Killarney, Co Kerry.* This hospitable old house has welcomed visitors from all over the world.
Open: All Year (not Xmas)
066 9768333 Mrs Keary **Fax: 066 9768404**
glenbeighhotel@eircom.net www.kerryweb.ie
D: Fr €38.00-€57.00 **S:** Fr €44.50-€57.00
Beds: 6T 6B 2S **Baths:** All En
⊞ (15) ⊡ ✕ ⊡ ⊞ ⚬ cc

Rossbeigh Beach House, *Rossbeigh, Glenbeigh, Co Kerry.* Luxury furnished house overlooking sea - 5 mile walk of sandy beach.
Open: May to Sept
066 9168533 (also fax) Mrs Cahill
D: Fr €25.50 **S:** Fr €34.50
Beds: 1 T **Baths:** 6 En
➤ ⊞ ⊁ ⊡ ✕ ⊡ ⊞ ⚬

Woodside, *Curragh, Glenbeigh, Killarney, Co Kerry.* 2 km from Glenbeigh Village, 'Blue Flag' sandy beach, golf links, mountain walking, fishing.
Open: Easter to Oct
066 9768160 Mrs O'Shea
D: Fr €21.50 **S:** Fr €27.00
Beds: 1F 2D **Baths:** 3 En
⌕ � (6) 📺 🖙 🛏.

Mountain View, *Mountain Stage, Glenbeigh, County Kerry.* Modern-purpose built home set in quiet location, 200 yards off Ring of Kerry road.
Open: Easter to Oct
066 9768541 (also fax) Mrs O'Riordan
mountainstage@eircom.net
D: Fr €25.50
Beds: 3F 3D 2T **Baths:** 5 En 2 Sh
⌕ associated (20) ⅙ 🛏 ✕ 📺 🖙 ✳ 🍴 cc

Glencar

V7084

Climbers Inn, *Glencar, Killarney, Co Kerry.*
Open: Mar to Nov
066 9760101 Miss O'Sullivan
Fax: 066 9760104
climbers@iol.ie www.climbersinn.com
D: Fr €35.00 **S:** Fr €48.00
Beds: 10F **Baths:** 10 En
⌕ (10) 📶 ⅙ 📺 🖙 ✕ 📺 🖙. 🍴

Situated on the Kerry Way, Glencar - the Highlands of Kerry. Recognised as the oldest established country inn specialising in walking and climbing in Ireland. Superb food, wine and excellent accommodation. Walking books, maps, information. Ask about the Wilderness Walking Tour.

Blackstones House, *Glencar, Killarney, Co Kerry.* Old style farmhouse overlooking Caragh River, McGillicuddy Reeks. Forest walks.
Open: Feb to Nov
066 9760164 (also fax) Mrs Breen
blstones@iol.ie
D: Fr €28.00-€30.00 **S:** Fr €12.00
Beds: 3F 2D 2T **Baths:** 6 En 1 Pr
⌕ 📶 📺 ✕ 🖙. 🍴

Greenane

V8470

Greenane Heights, *Ring of Kerry Road, Greenane, Kenmare, Killarney, Co Kerry.* Enjoy our uniquely designed home, relax in friendly atmosphere, sample fine home cuisine.
Open: May to Sept
064 41760 (also fax) Mrs Topham
topham@iol.ie
www.kerry-insight.com/grenaneheights
D: Fr €25.50
Beds: 3F 1T 1D **Baths:** 5 En
⌕ 📶 📺 ✕ 📺 🖙. 🍴 🍴 cc

Inch

Q6501

Waterside, *Inch, Annascaul, Dingle Peninsula, Co Kerry.* Modern spacious friendly quality accommodation. Superb, central, scenic seaside setting.
Open: All Year
066 9158129 Mrs Kennedy
D: Fr €27.00
Beds: 1F 1T 2D **Baths:** 4 Ensuite
⌕ 📶 (6) ⅙ 🛏 ✕ 🖙.

Kells (Ring of Kerry)

V5788

Taobh Coille, *Gleesk, Kells, Killarney, Co Kerry.* Farmhouse Bed & Breakfast, overwhelming sea views, ideal location for walking the Kerry Way, fishing trips arranged.
Open: All year
066 9477626 Mrs O'Sullivan
D: Fr €25.00 **S:** Fr €25.00
Beds: 1F 1T 1D 1S **Baths:** 3 En 1 Pr
⌕ 📶 (10) ⅙ 📺 🛏 ✕ 🖙. ✳ 🍴

Sea View, *Kells Bay, Kells, Killarney, Co Kerry.* Family run, situated on sandy beach, relaxing atmosphere. Fishing, walking.
Open: Easter to October
066 9477610 Mrs Lynch
lynchbp@indigo.ie
D: Fr €21.50 **S:** Fr €21.50
Beds: 2F 1T 4D **Baths:** 5 En 2 Sh
⌕ 🐾 📶 📺 🛏 ✕ 📺 🖙.

Kenmare
V9070

Ardmore House,
Killarney Road,
Kenmare, Killarney,
Co Kerry.
Open: Mar to Nov
064 41406 (also fax)
Mr & Mrs Connor
D: Fr €28.00-€30.00 **S:** Fr €35.00-€40.00
Beds: 1F 1T 2D 1S **Baths:** 5 En
⌂ (1) 🄿 (6) ⚊ 📺 ⛿ 📺 🛏 ⬚ 🖧 ⚊ cc
Spacious house in quiet location adjoining
farmlands on Kerry Way & Beara Way. Ideal
location for touring Killarney, Ring of Kerry &
Ring of Beara. 2 18-hole courses nearby. Horse
riding and bicycles arranged.

Rose Garden Guest House & Restaurant, N70,
Kenmare, County
Kerry.
Open: Easter to
Nov
064 42288
Mr & Mrs Ringlever **Fax: 064 42305**
rosegard@iol.ie www.euroka.com/rosegarden
D: Fr €29.50-€39.50 **S:** Fr €45.50-€55.50
Beds: 4D 4T **Baths:** 8 En
🄿 (20) 📺 ⬚ ⚊ cc
The Rose Garden Guest House and Restaurant is
situated within a few minutes walk of Kenmare.
Set in 1 acre of landscaped garden with 350 roses.
3 and 7 day specials including breakfast and
dinner are available. Evening meals available.

O'Donnells of Ashgrove,
Kenmare, Killarney,
Co Kerry.
Open: Easter to Oct
064 41228 (also fax)
Mrs O'Donnell
D: Fr €28.00-€32.00
S: Fr €38.00-€42.00
Beds: 2D 2T **Baths:** 3 En
⌂ (8) 🄿 (6) 📺 🛏 ⬚ cc
Beautiful country home in peaceful setting
incorporating olde worlde charm, where guests
are welcomed as friends. Jacobean-style dining
room. Log fire. Spacious, elegant family lounge
with many antiques. Tea/coffee freely available.
Mature garden. Angling enthusiast.
Recommended 'Best 300 B&Bs'.

O Donnabhains Bar & Guest House, Henry Stree
Kenmare, Co Kerry.
Open: All year **Grades:** BF
Star
064 42106 Fax: 064 42321
info@odonnabhain-kenmare.com
www.odonnabhain-kenmare.com
D: Fr €34.00-€48.00 **S:** Fr €36.00-€54.00
Beds: 3F 2T 5D **Baths:** 10 En
🄿 ⚊ 📺 ✕ ⬚ ✳ ⚊ cc
Situated in the centre of Kenmare, Ireland's
tidiest town. Our accommodation opened in Ju
2000 and offers affordable accommodation in ou
hotel type bedrooms, with all mod cons. All ou
rooms are away from our popular bar,
guaranteeing no sleepless nights.

Hazelwood Stables,
Castletownbere Road,
Killaha, Kenmare, Co Kerry.
Open: All year
064 41420 & 086 4033489 (M
Mrs Frost-Jones
rawson@eircom.net
homepage.eircom.net/~hazelwood
D: Fr €22.00-€26.00 **S:** Fr €30.00
Beds: 2F 1T 1D **Baths:** 2 En 2 Pr
⌂ 🄿 📺 ✕ 📺 ⚊ cc
B&B & riding stables on the edge of Kenmare Ba
with beautiful sea views. Woodland & seashore
walks. Pony trekking on site, children's play area
Breakfast menu with vegetarian option. 2 miles
from Kenmare town.

Ard Na Mara, Pier Road,
Kenmare, Killarney, Co Kerry
Modern house, big garden.
Front view overlooking
Kenmare Bay. Five mins wal
to town.
Open: All year (not Xmas)
064 41399 (also fax) Mrs Dahm
D: Fr €26.00-€28.00 **S:** Fr €35.00
Beds: 2D 2T **Baths:** 4 Pr
⌂ 🄿 (4) ⚊

Avelow, Killarney Road, Kenmare, Killarney, Co
Kerry. Comfortable accommodation near town.
Ideal touring base for Ring of Kerry/Beara.
Open: Easter to Oct
064 41473 Pat Downing & Family
D: Fr €30.00
Beds: 1F 1D 2T **Baths:** 4 Ensuite
⌂ 🄿 ⚊ 📺 ⬚ ⚊

Inbhear Schein, *Dauros, Kenmare, Killarney, Co Kerry.* Perfectly situated for exploring the Beara and Iveragh Peninsulas. Tranquil surroundings.
Open: Apr to Oct
064 41210 Mr & Mrs O'Leary
ibhearschein@hotmail.com
D: Fr €22.00-€26.00 **S:** Fr €29.00-€33.00
Beds: 1F 2D **Baths:** 2 En 1 Sh
⟶ 🅿 📺 ✕ 📺 🛏, 🔌

Vander Inn, *Henry Street, Kenmare, Co Kerry.* Old-World style family-run hotel in the heart of Kenmare. Rooms furnished with beautiful antiques.
Open: All Year (not Xmas)
064 42700 B Keane **Fax: 064 42569**
vanderinn@eircom.net
D: Fr €32.00
Beds: 1F 7D 3T 0S **Baths:** 11 En
⟶ 🅿 (20) 📺 ✕ 🛏, cc

O'Shea's Guest House, *14 Henry Street, Kenmare, Killarney, Co Kerry.* Pleasing comfortable guest house in centre of town.
Open: Easter to Oct
064 41453 Mr O'Shea
D: Fr €19.00 **S:** Fr €19.00
Beds: 2F 2D 1T **Baths:** 1 En 2 Sh
⟶ (10) 🅿 (4) 📺 🛏 ✕ 🛏,

Annagry House, *Sneem Road, Kenmare, Killarney, Co Kerry.* Ideal location on Ring of Kerry, only 7 mins' walk Kenmare town centre.
Open: All Year (not Xmas/New Year)
064 41283 Mrs Carraher-O'Sullivan
anscottage@eircom.net
homepage.eircom.net/~inkenmare/index.html
D: Fr €25.50 **S:** Fr €34.50
Beds: 2F 2T 2D **Baths:** 6 En
📺 🛏, 🔌

Cherry Hill, *Killowen, Kenmare, Killarney, Co Kerry.* Located on R569. Beautiful views. Ideally situated for touring Kerry/Beara.
Open: May to Sep
064 41715 Mrs Clifford
cherryhill@eircom.net
D: Fr €21.50-€24.00
Beds: 2D 1T **Baths:** 2 En 1 Pr
⟶ 🅿 🛏, 🔌 cc

Rockvilla, *Templenoe, Kenmare, Killarney, Co Kerry.* Peaceful rural setting near Templenoe Pier. Relaxed friendly atmosphere. Large garden and parking area.
Open: Easter to Nov
064 41331 Mr & Mrs Fahy
rockvilla@esatclear.ie
D: Fr €21.50-€24.00 **S:** Fr €25.50-€32.00
Beds: 2F 1D 2T 1S **Baths:** 4 En 1 Sh
⟶ 🅿 (10) 📺 🛏 ✕ 📺 🛏, cc

Droumassig Bridge, *Kenmare, Killarney, Co Kerry.* On the N71 and Glengariff 3 miles from Kenmare. Relaxing.
Open: Easter to Oct
064 41384 & 087 2203691 (M) Mrs Foley
D: Fr €16.50-€19.00 **S:** Fr €19.00-€25.50
Beds: 3F 1T 1D **Baths:** 3 Sh
⟶ 🅿 ✂ 📺 🛏 ✕ 📺 🛏, ♿ ❄ 🔌 cc

Harbour View, *Castletown Berehaven Road, Dawros, Kenmare, Killarney, Co Kerry.* Luxurious home on seashore directly overlooking Kenmare Bay, panoramic views of harbour from bedrooms.
Open: Mar to Oct
064 41755 Ms McCarthy
D: Fr €32.00
Beds: 2F 2D **Baths:** 2 Ensuite 1 Private
⟶ (5) 🅿 (6) 📺 ✕ 🛏, 🔌

The Lodge, *Kilgarvan Road, Kenmare, Killarney, Co Kerry.* Luxury guest house in private gardens, elegantly furnished in period style, king size beds.
Open: Apr to Nov
064 41512 Mrs Quill **Fax: 064 41812**
D: Fr €45.00
Beds: 5F 2D 3T **Baths:** 10 En
⟶ 🅿 ✂ 📺 🛏, ♿ 🔌 cc

River Meadows House, *Sneem Road, Kenmare, Killarney, Co Kerry.* Modern house set in rustic surroundings with private road leading to sea shore.
Open: Easter to Nov
064 41306 (also fax) Mrs Ryan
D: Fr €24.00 **S:** Fr €32.00
Beds: 1F 1T 1D 1S **Baths:** 4 Pr
⟶ 🅿 (9) ✂ 📺 🛏 🛏, 🔌 cc

Planning a longer stay?
Always ask for any special rates

White Heather Farm, *Glengarriff Road, Kenmare, Killarney, Co Kerry.* Family farm on Kenmare-Glengarriff Road, N71. Easy to find at the Head of the Beara Peninsula and Ring of Kerry. Convenient, quiet location. Many animals. Spectacular mountain views. Ideal base for walking, touring, fishing. 'Le Guide du Routard' recommended.
Open: May to Oct
064 41550 & 087 6774468 (M) Mrs Lovett **Fax: 064 42475**
whiteheatherfarm@ireland.com
D: Fr €26.00-€28.00 **S:** Fr €29.00
Beds: 2F 2D 1T **Baths:** 4 En 4 Pr 1 Sh
⌂ ▣ ⅌ ☑ ☜ ✕ 🔲 ⬤ cc

O'Shea's Farmhouse, *Coel na nAbhaun, Killarney Road, Upper Gortamullen, Kenmare, Killarney, Co Kerry.* Ideal location on N71 Killarney Road, 1.5km from Kenmare. Warm, spacious ensuite rooms.
Open: Feb to Nov
064 41498 Mrs O'Shea
osheasfarmhouse@eircom.net www.neidin.net/oshea
D: Fr €25.00-€27.00 **S:** Fr €32.00-€37.00
Beds: 2F 2D 1T **Baths:** 5 En
⌂ ▣ (6) ☑ ☜ 🔲 ♿ ⬤ cc

Riverville House, *Gortamullen, Kenmare, Co Kerry.* Luxury B&B, Kenmare town. Antique pine furniture, ideal touring centre - Ring of Kerry.
Open: Feb to Nov
064 41775 Mrs Moore
rivervillehouse@eircom.net
D: Fr €32.00
Beds: 3D **Baths:** 3 En
▣ (4) ⅌ 🔲

Druid Cottage, *Sneem Road, Kenmare, Co Kerry.* C19th stone cottage situated on Ring of Kerry road.
Open: All Year (not Xmas)
064 41803 Mrs Goldrick
D: Fr €21.50-€25.50 **S:** Fr €30.00-€32.50
Beds: 1F 1D 1T **Baths:** 2 En 1 Pr
⌂ (11) ▣ (6) ☑ ☜ ✕ Ⓥ 🔲 ⬤

Island View, *Feorus West, Kenmare, Killarney, Co Kerry.* Panoramic view over Kenmare Bay. Spacious ensuite rooms. Ideal base for touring.
Open: Apr to Oct
064 41435 Mrs Sleator
D: Fr €28.00
Beds: 3F 1T 1D 1S **Baths:** 3 Ensuite 1 Shared
⌂ ▣ ⅌ ☑ ☜ ✕ Ⓥ 🔲 ⬤

Gaines Country Home, *Two Mile Bridge, Killarney Road N71, Kenmare, Killarney, County Kerry.* Gaines Country Home is superbly set on 137 acres of rugged mountain farmland.
Open: All Year (not Xmas)
064 42476 Ita & George Gaine
D: Fr €25.50
Beds: 2F 1D **Baths:** 3 Ensuite
⌂ ▣ (6) ☑ ✕

The White House, *Cappamore, Killarney Road, Kenmare, Killarney, County Kerry.* On Ring of Kerry after Killarney's 25,000 acres of lakes, waterfalls and highest peaks.
Open: All Year
064 42372 Mr McCabe
D: Fr €25.50
Beds: 2T/D 1D **Baths:** 2 Ensuite 1 Shared
▣ (4) ⅌ ☑ ✕ 🔲

Willow Lodge, *Convent Garden, Kenmare, Co Kerry.* Willow Lodge stands in the grounds of the famous Poor Clare's convent garden.
Open: All year
064 42301 Gretta Gleeson O'Byrne
willowlodgekenmare@yahoo.com
D: Fr €32.00-€38.00 **S:** Fr €38.00-€64.00
Beds: 8F/D/T **Baths:** 8 En
⌂ ▣ ⅌ ☑ ☜ Ⓥ 🔲 ✳ ⬤

The Caha's, *Hospital Cross, Kenmare, Killarney, Co Kerry.* Modern dormer bungalow in scenic peaceful location. Extensive breakfast menu.
Open: Easter to Oct
064 41271 (also fax) Mr & Mrs O'Shea
osheacahas@eircom.net
D: Fr €30.00
Beds: 2F 2D **Baths:** 4 En
⌂ (5) ▣ (4) ⅌ ☑ 🔲 ⬤

Kilcummin (Castlegregory)
Q5612

Kilcummin Farmhouse, *Kilcummin, Castlegregory, Tralee, Co Kerry.* Modern country house set between mountains and miles of sandy beach.
Open: Easter to Nov
066 7139152 Mrs O'Connor
D: Fr €25.50
Beds: 1F 2T 1D **Baths:** 3 Ensuite
⌂ (1) ▣ ☑ ☜ Ⓥ 🔲

ynch's Farm, *off Tralee Airport Road,*
ilcummin, Killarney, Co Kerry. Dairy farm 3 miles
*o*m Killarney. View of mountains and lakes.
Open: All Year
64 31637 Mrs Lynch
): Fr €24.00
Beds: 1F 2D 2T 1S **Baths:** 4 Ensuite
⬥ 🅿 ⌁ 📺 🏇 ✕ Ⓥ 🖩 ❋ ▪

Kilgarvan

V0073 🐟 *Paidi Kelliher*

Woodview House, *Kilgarvan, Killarney, Co*
Kerry. Modern family-run home, beautifully
*l*ocated in scenic surroundings. Large rose
*g*arden, excellent hospitality.
Open: June to Oct
64 85363 Mr & Mrs Kelleher
): Fr €21.50 **S:** Fr €28.00 ⬥ (12) 🅿 (6) ⌁ 📺 🖩

Conaberry House, *Church Street, Kilgarvan,*
Killarney, Kerry. 200-year-old modernised house.
*F*amily-run. Beautiful view of Roughty Valley and
*m*ountains.
Open: All Year
64 85323 Mrs Coffey
): Fr €18.00 **S:** Fr €18.00
Beds: 1F 2D **Baths:** 1 En 2 Pr
⬥ 🅿 (5) ⌁ 📺 🖩

Kilgobnet

V8191

Kingdom View, *Glencar Road, Kilgobnet,*
Beaufort, Killarney, Co Kerry. Welcoming family
*h*ome near the Gap of Dunloe on slopes of
*I*reland's highest mountains.
Open: Feb to Nov
64 44343 Mrs O'Sullivan
os@iol.ie
): Fr €25.50
Beds: 1F 3D 2T 5S **Baths:** 5 En 1 Pr
🅿 📺 🏇 ✕ Ⓥ 🖩 cc

RATES

) = Price range per person sharing
*i*n a double or twin room
S = Price range for a single room

Killaha

V8868

Hazelwood Stables, *Castletownbere Road,*
Killaha, Kenmare, Co Kerry. B&B & riding stables,
edge of Kenmare Bay, beautiful sea views.
Open: All year
064 41420 & 086 4033489 (M) Mrs Frost-Jones
rawson@eircom.net
homepage.eircom.net/~hazelwood
D: Fr €22.00-€26.00 **S:** Fr €30.00
Beds: 2F 1T 1D **Baths:** 2 En 2 Pr
⬥ 🅿 📺 ✕ Ⓥ ♿ ▪ cc

Killarney

V1992

**Kathleen's
Country House,**
Madam's Heights,
Tralee Road,
Killarney, Co Kerry.
Open: Mar to Nov
Grades: BF 4 Star,
AA 5 Diamond
064 32810 Ms Regan Sheppard **Fax: 064 32340**
info@kathleens.net www.kathleens.net
D: Fr €45.00-€65.00 **S:** Fr €45.00-€65.00
Beds: 3F 5D 9T **Baths:** 17 En
⬥ (5) 🅿 (17) ⌁ 📺 Ⓥ 🖩 ♿ ▪
Attentiveness, friendliness, traditional hospitality
make Kathleen's special. Romantic oasis on 3
acres of mature gardens. Antique pine bedrooms
with orthopaedic beds, large bathrooms. Non-
smoking, singles welcome. Ideal golf base. 3km
to town.

Gormans, *Tralee*
Road, Killarney, Co
Kerry.
Open: All year (not
Xmas/New Year)
Grades: BF Approv
064 33149 (also fax)
Mrs Gorman
mgormans@eircom.net
homepage.eircom.net/~gormanscountryhome
D: Fr €26.00-€30.00 **S:** Fr €26.00-€42.00
Beds: 1F 1T 2D **Baths:** 4 En 2 Pr 2 Sh
⬥ (3) 🅿 (6) ⌁ 📺 🏇 ✕ Ⓥ 🖩 ♿ ▪ cc
Set in large landscaped garden, including
waterfall in rockery. Former Bord Failte garden
prize winners. Family-run B&B 5km to Killarney
on N22, Killarney National Park & lakes, golf 6km.
Tea and scones on arrival.

Serenic View,
*Coolcorcoran,
Killarney, Co Kerry.*
Open: Mar to Nov
064 33434
Ms Murphy
Fax: 064 33578
serenic@eircom.net homepage.eircom.net/~serenic
D: Fr €30.00 **S:** Fr €45.00
Beds: 1F 3D 2T **Baths:** 6 En
♿ 🅿 (9) ⌦ 📺 ⊞, ☕ cc
Luxury, ground floor & balcony rooms with panoramic view. Quiet scenic area 5 mins drive from Killarney, on ring of Kerry. Breakfast menu, hairdryers, direct-dial telephones & large garden. Tours arranged, golf, fishing, horse riding, Muckross house and lakes nearby.

Killarney Villa,
*Cork/Mallow Road
N72, Killarney, Co
Kerry.*
Open: Easter to
Nov **Grades:** BF
Approv, AA 4
Diamond, RAC 4
Diamond, Sparkling
064 31878 (also fax) Mr & Mrs O'Sullivan
killarneyvilla@eircom.net www.killarneyvilla.com
D: Fr €28.00-€32.00 **S:** Fr €40.00-€45.00
Beds: 1F 3D 2T **Baths:** 6 En
♿ (6) 🅿 (10) ⌦ 📺 ✕ ⊞ 📺 ⊞, ☕ cc
Scenic, providing modern comforts. We pride ourselves on our roof top conservatory that overlooks magnificent gardens. Extensive breakfast menu. Visit our website for 'Holiday OFFER'.

Coffey s Loch Lein House, *Golf
Course Road, Fossa,
Killarney, Co Kerry.*
Open: Mar to Nov
064 31260
Mrs Coffey
Fax: 064 36151
ecoffey@indigo.ie www.lochlein.com
D: Fr €35.00-€50.00 **S:** Fr €45.00-€60.00
Beds: 2F 14 D/T **Baths:** 16 En
♿ 🅿 (16) 📺 ⊞, cc
Uniquely situated beside Killarney's lakes, Coffey's Loch Lein House is a magnificent family-run hotel. Guests can enjoy panoramic views from our luxurious rooms. Located on the Ring of Kerry route, it is perfect for golfing, walking, cycling, sightseeing & relaxing.

Glena House,
*Muckross Road,
Killarney, Co Kerry.*
Open: All year (no
Xmas/New Year)
064 32705
Mr Buckley
glena@iol.ie
www.glenahouse.com
D: Fr €35.00-€45.00 **S:** Fr €40.00-€60.00
Beds: 4F 10D 10T 2S **Baths:** 26 En
♿ 🅿 📺 ✕ 📺 ⊞, ♿, ☕
Award-winning guesthouse, AA 4 Diamond, RA⬤ Acclaimed, 5 mins walk from town centre, 15 mins to National Park. Ideal for walkers on the Kerry Way. Fantastic breakfast, home-baked breads & preserves. Wholesome food, wine bar Stay once. Return for ever.

Killarney View
House, *Muckross
Road, Killarney, Co
Kerry.*
Open: All year
064 33122 Ms Gueri⬤
*killarneyviewhouse@
eircom.net* www.killarneyviewhouse.com
D: Fr €30.00-€50.00 **S:** Fr €30.00-€50.00
Beds: 12F **Baths:** 12 En
♿ 🅿 📺 ✕ 📺 ⊞, ☕
Very reasonably priced, magnificent location overlooking our own river - your ideal base. Six mins' walk Killarney town, on main Muckross road, gateway to Killarney's mountain/lake are⬤ Wonderful river/mountain views from dining/lounge/bedroom areas. Guest lounge with open fire.

Slieve Bloom Manor,
*Muckross Road, Killarney, C⬤
Kerry.* Charming, friendly
guest house, prime location
Do check us out for yoursel⬤
Open: All year (not Xmas) **Grades:** BF 3 Star
064 34237 Ms Clery **Fax: 064 35055**
slievebloomanor@eircom.net
www.slievebloomkillarney.com
D: Fr €30.00-€35.00 **S:** Fr €35.00-€40.00
Beds: 4D 10T **Baths:** 14 En
♿ 🅿 (10) 📺 ⊞, ☕ cc

Please respect a B&B's wishes regarding children, animals and smoking

Nashville, *Tralee Road, Killarney, Co Kerry.*
Open: All year (not Xmas)
064 32924 (also fax) David & Vivienne Nash
ashville@eircom.net
ww.nashvillekillarney.com
D: Fr €28.00-€32.00 **S:** Fr €38.00-€42.00
Beds: 2F 2T 2D **Baths:** 6 Pr
⏂ (3) 🅿 (12) 📺 🛏, ♿ cc
Modern spacious family home, warm welcome.
Killarney 3km. Landscaped gardens, mountain/woodland surroundings. Golf, fishing, horseriding, restaurants and pubs, National Park all nearby. Excellent location for Ring of Kerry or Dingle. All tours arranged. Spacious parking - buses welcome.

Crystal Springs, *Ballycasheen, Killarney, Co Kerry.*
Open: All year
Grades: BF Approv, AA 4 Diamond
064 33272 & 064 35518 Mrs Brosnan
ax: 064 35518
rystalsprings@eircom.net
omepage.eircom.net/~doors/
D: Fr €28.00-€38.00 **S:** Fr €35.00-€58.00
Beds: 3F 2T 1D 1S **Baths:** 7 En 7 Pr
⏂ 🅿 (14) ⚡ 📺 🛏 ✕ 📺 🛏, ♿ cc
This luxury Bed & Breakfast is located on the banks of the peaceful River Flesk. It offers fishing in location. All spacious rooms are ensuite with tea/coffee making facilities, hairdryers, direct dial phones, trouser press & iron and refrigerators. Crystal Springs offers a friendly welcome and relaxed atmosphere situated in a quiet area, being only 10 minutes from Killarney town centre, where many fine traditional pubs and restaurants can be found. Close to all attractions like Killarney's lakes, mountains and National Park. Ample, safe parking.

National Grid References given are for villages, towns and cities – not for individual houses

Fair Haven, *Cork Road, Lissivigeen N22, Killarney, Co Kerry.*
Open: May to Sep
Grades: BF Approv
064 32542 Mrs Teahan
fairhavenbb@eircom.net
D: Fr €25.00-€30.00 **S:** Fr €40.00
Beds: 2D 2T **Baths:** 3 En 1 Pr
🅿 (5) ⚡ 🛏, ♿ cc
Country home in scenic location, warm, friendly welcome assured. Tea and coffee making facilities in TV lounge. breakfast menu. Pickup point for Ring of Kerry and other tours. Golf, fishing, horse riding locally. Convenient to Muckross House and gardens.

River Valley Farm House, *Minish, Killarney, Co Kerry.*
Open: Mar to Nov **Grades:** BF Approv
064 32411 Mrs O'Sullivan **Fax: 064 37909**
rivervalley.farmhouse@eircom.net
www.rivervalleyfarmbb.net
D: Fr €25.00-€27.00 **S:** Fr €32.00-€35.00
Beds: 6F 3D 1T 2S **Baths:** 6 Pr
⏂ 🅿 (8) ⚡ 📺 🛏 ✕ 📺 🛏, ♿ cc
A quiet, comfortable home. Beautiful view of the mountains. Surrounded by gardens. Lovely walks to the river. Highly recommended for food, atmosphere and has spacious rooms. Just 500 yds off N22.

Foley's Town House, *23 High Street, Killarney, Co Kerry.*
Open: Mar to Oct
064 31217 Mrs Hartnett **Fax: 064 34683**
info@foleystownhouse.com www.foleystownhouse.com
D: Fr €57.50-€60.00 **S:** Fr €64.00-€70.00
Beds: 12D 12T 4S **Baths:** 28 En
⏂ (3) 🅿 (60) ⚡ 📺 ✕ 📺 🛏, ♿ cc
Originally a C18th coaching inn, newly refurbished, now a 4 Star family-run guest house, located town centre. Downstairs an award-winning seafood and steak restaurant. Chef/owner Carol Hartnett supervises.

Friary View, *Dennehy's Bohereen, Killarney, Co Kerry.* House in quiet area close to town and all amenities. Breakfast menu.
Open: May to Sep
064 32996 Mrs Tuohy
D: Fr €24.00
Beds: 2D 2T **Baths:** 4 En
🅿 📺 🛏, ♿

Larkfield House,
Ballycasheen, Killarney, County Kerry. Award-winning family-run Bed and Breakfast, 2km from town centre.
Open: Mar to Oct
064 34438 Mr & Mrs Ivory
jki@eircom.net www.larkfieldhouse.com
D: Fr €25.00 **S:** Fr €35.00
Beds: 2F 2D **Baths:** 4 En
⌂ 🅿 (6) ⊁ 📺 ▥. ▪ cc

Leens, 22 Marian Terrace,
Killarney, Co Kerry.
Perfectly situated, 3-min walk to centre of town.
Open: All year
064 32819 Mrs Leen
siobhanleen@eircom.net www.stayatleens.com
D: Fr €28.00-€33.00 **S:** Fr €40.30-€44.00
Beds: 3F 1D **Baths:** 4 En
⌂ (1) 🅿 (4) 📺 ▣ ▥. ▪ cc

Tullyfern Villa, Woodlawn
Road, Killarney, Co Kerry.
Family-run B&B. Killarney walking distance. Ground floor rooms, quiet location.
Open: Easter to Oct
064 32413 Mrs O'Sullivan
tfvilla@oceanfree.net
D: Fr €23.00-€25.50 **S:** Fr €32.00
Beds: 1F 1D 1T **Baths:** 3 En
⌂ 🅿 (5) ⊁ 📺 ▣ ▥. ▪ cc

The Glen, Islandmore,
Clonkeen, Killarney, Co Kerry.
Traditional C18th farmhouse, unspoilt mountain setting 10 mins Killarney on N22 Cork road.
Open: All year
064 53067 & 086 8535084 (M) Mrs Garner
theglen@esatclear.ie
D: Fr €25.00 **S:** Fr €28.00
Beds: 1F 1T **Baths:** 2 En
⌂ 🅿 (3) ⊁ ♠ ▣ ▥. cc

Lime Court, Muckross Road, Killarney, Co Kerry.
Superb quality, great location, 10% discount on 3 night stays.
Open: Feb to Nov
064 34547 Mr Courtney **Fax: 064 34121**
limecrt@iol.ie www.kerry-insight.com/limecourt
D: Fr €29.00-€38.00 **S:** Fr €29.00-€48.50
Beds: 3F 3T 8d 7S **Baths:** 21 En
⌂ (3) 🅿 ⊁ 📺 ▥. ♿ ▪ cc

Direen House, Tralee Road, Killarney, Co Kerry
Award-winning and widely commended home. Five mins Killarney, 10 mins Kerry Airport. Ideal location for touring Ring of Kerry/Dingle Peninsula. With coach pick up/drop off, breakfast menu, home baking. Warm welcome with comfortable accommodation assured. Expanding views mountains/countryside.
Open: Mar to Nov
064 31676 (also fax) Mrs Casey
direenhouse@eircom.net
www.homepage.eircom.net/~direenhouse
D: Fr €25.50-€27.50 **S:** Fr €30.00-€35.00
Beds: 1F 1T 4D **Baths:** 5 En 1 Pr
⌂ (8) 🅿 ⊁ 📺 ♠ ✕ ▥. ▪ cc

Glebe Farmhouse, Tralee Road, Killarney, Co Kerry.
5 kms from Killarney, overlooking mountains. Ideal touring centre for Kerry.
Open: All Year
064 32179 Mr & Mrs O'Connor **Fax: 064 32039**
glebefarmhouse@eircom.net
D: Fr €19.00-€24.00 **S:** Fr €24.00-€28.00
Beds: 2F 2D 1T 1S **Baths:** 4 En 1 Pr 1 Sh
⌂ 🅿 (8) ⊁ 📺 ✕ ▥. ▪ cc

Avondale House, Tralee Road, Killarney, Co Kerry.
A distinctive, modern, two storey, family-run, ITB Approved B&B on the N22. Killarney: 4km. Surrounded by large landscaped gardens. Highly recommended for its hospitality, good food, hygiene and spacious rooms. Adjacent to riding stables, golf courses and walks. Panorami views.
Open: Feb to Nov
064 35579 (also fax) Ms Leahy
avondalehouse@eircom.net
www.kerry-insight.com/avondale
D: Fr €28.00-€30.00 **S:** Fr €38.00-€44.00
Beds: 4D 2T **Baths:** 6 En
🅿 (10) 📺 ▥. ▪ cc

Sunflower Cottage, Tralee Road, Killarney, C Kerry.
Excellent location offering superb accommodation with view of Kerry's mountains
Open: Mar to Nov
064 32101 Mrs O'Connor Wright
D: Fr €33.00
Beds: 1F 3D **Baths:** 4 En
⌂ (3) 🅿 (5) ⊁ 📺 ▥.

B&B owners may vary rates – be sure to check when booking

Wind Way House, *New Road, Killarney, Co Kerry.* Modern bungalow, all modern facilities, quiet area 5 mins' walk town centre, National Park.
Open: All year (not Xmas/New Year)
064 32835 Mrs Ahern **Fax: 064 37887**
D: Fr €25.50-€30.00 **S:** Fr €36.00-€38.50
Beds: 2T 4D **Baths:** 6 En
⌂ **P** (4) ⅍ ⊡ ▥, ▪

Doogary, *Lewis Road, Killarney, Co Kerry.* Select family-run B&B. Convenient to town. Beautiful walks.
Open: May to Oct
064 32509 Mrs O'Brien
D: Fr €35.00
Beds: 1F 1D 1T **Baths:** 3 En 1 Pr
⌂ **P** (4) ▥.

Mountain Dew, *3 Ross Road, Killarney, Co Kerry.* Modern town house situated 3 minute walk from town centre, rail and bus.
Open: All Year (not Xmas)
064 33892 Mrs Carroll **Fax: 064 31332**
mountain.dew@oceanfree.net
D: Fr €28.50
Beds: 1F 4D 1T **Baths:** 6 En
⌂ (3) **P** (6) ▣ ▥, **cc**

Shraheen House, *Ballycasheen, Killarney, Co Kerry.* Luxurious home set in 2 acres. Ideal touring base.
Open: All year (not Xmas/New year)
064 31286 Mrs Fleming **Fax: 064 37959**
info@shraheenhouse.com www.shraheenhouse.com
D: Fr €28.00-€31.00 **S:** Fr €40.00-€50.00
Beds: 4F 2D **Baths:** 6 En
⌂ (6) **P** (8) ⅍ ⊡ ▥, ▪

Redwood Country House and Apartments, *Rockfield, Tralee Road, Killarney, Co Kerry.* Large house and apartments on 15 acres, extensive breakfast menu.
Open: All Year
064 34754 Mrs Murphy **Fax: 064 34178**
redwd@indigo.ie
D: Fr €31.00
Beds: 2F 2D 2T **Baths:** 6 En 6 Pr
⌂ **P** (6) ▣ ▣ ▥, ▪ **cc**

B&B owners may vary rates – be sure to check when booking

Planning a longer stay?
Always ask for any special rates

Mulberry House, *Rookery Road, Ballycasheen, Killarney, Co Kerry.* Luxurious country home backing on to farmland, facing Killarney's mountain range.
Open: Feb to Nov
064 34112 Mrs Tarrant **Fax: 064 32534**
D: Fr €33.00
Beds: 2F 1T 2D **Baths:** 5 Ensuite
⌂ **P** ⅍ ⊡ ▣ ▥.

Sunrise Villa, *Mill Road, Flesk Castle, Killarney, Co Kerry.* Modern two-storey farmhouse situated in quiet scenic surroundings. Nature walks.
Open: May to Oct
064 32159 (also fax) Mrs O'Donoghue
sunrisevilla@tinet.ie
www.kerryweb.
ie/destination-kerry/killarney/sunrise-html
D: Fr €24.00
Beds: 2D 2T **Baths:** 4 En 1 Sh
P (4) ⊡ ▥, **cc**

Dromhall Heights, *Killarney, Co Kerry.* Family home, quiet scenic location. 7 minutes walk to town.
Open: Mar to Nov
064 32662 Mrs McCarthy
peggymccarthy@eircom.net
homepage.eircom.net/~peggymccarthy
D: Fr €23.00-€25.50 **S:** Fr €32.00-€38.00
Beds: 3F 1T 1D **Baths:** 2 En 1 Pr
P (4) ⊡ ▥, ▪ **cc**

Flesk Lodge, *Muckross Road, Killarney, Co Kerry.* Modern luxury bungalow, walking distance town centre. Beautiful gardens overlooking River Flesk & Killarney Lakes.
Open: All Year
064 9132135 (also fax) Mr & Mrs Mannix
D: Fr €24.00-€25.50 **S:** Fr €33.00
Beds: 1F 1D 4T **Baths:** 6 En
⌂ **P** ⊡ ✕ ▥, ▪

Countess House, *Countess Road, Killarney, Co Kerry.* Warm welcome luxurious house, 2 mins bus/rail and town centre.
Open: All year (not Xmas/New Year)
064 34247 Mrs Sheahan **Fax: 064 35542**
D: Fr €26.00-€32.00 **S:** Fr €32.00-€38.00
Beds: 2F 2T 2D **Baths:** 6 En
⌂ **P** (10) ⅍ ▣ ▥, ▪ **cc**

Killarney Town House, *31 New Street,*
Killarney, Co Kerry. Killarney town house ideally
situated in heart of Killarney town centre.
Open: All Year
064 35388 Mrs Hallissey **Fax: 064 35259**
D: Fr €29.00-€32.00 **S:** Fr €38.00-€44.50
Beds: 8D 3T **Baths:** 11 En
ॐ ⅟ 🖵 ▥ cc

Eagle View, *21 Woodlawn Park, Killarney, Co*
Kerry. Warm, friendly home from home. Walking
distance to all sightseeing and entertainment.
Open: Easter to Oct
064 32779 Mrs Brosnan
D: Fr €23.00 **S:** Fr €29.00
Beds: 1F 1T 1D **Baths:** 2 En 1 Pr
ॐ (7) 🄿 ♈ 🖵 ▥ ▪

Killorglin
V7796

Hillview Farm, *Milltown*
P.O., Killarney, Co Kerry.
Comfortable family-run sixth
generation dairy/sheep farm
in scenic countryside.
Open: Easter to Oct
066 9767117 Mrs Stephens **Fax: 066 9767910**
dstephens@eircom.net www.hillviewfarm.com
D: Fr €28.00-€30.00 **S:** Fr €35.00-€40.00
Beds: 1F 2D 1T **Baths:** 4 En
ॐ 🄿 ⅟ 🖵 ♈ ✕ �öᵛ ▥ cc

Carraig na Lamhna, *Killarney Road, Killorglin,*
Co Kerry. Friendly family home, central for touring
Kerry. Overlooking McGillicuddy Reeks.
Open: Easter to Oct
066 9761170 Mrs Brennan
leamhna@hotmail.com
D: Fr €26.00-€28.00 **S:** Fr €30.00-€35.00
Beds: 1F 1D 1T **Baths:** 2 En 1 Pr
ॐ 🄿 🖵 ♈ ✕ ▥

Fernrock, *Tinnahalla, Killorglin, Co Kerry.*
Excellent accommodation, superb view. Tours
arranged. Golf 5 km, horse riding close by.
Open: Jan 8th to Dec 20th
066 9761848 (also fax) Mrs Clifford
fernrock@eircom.net
D: Fr €24.00-€25.50 **S:** Fr €32.00
Beds: 2F 1D 1T **Baths:** 4 En 4 Pr
🄿 (8) ⅟ 🖵 ✕ �öᵛ ▥

Park House, *Laharn, Killorglin, Co Kerry.*
Luxurious country home, 0.5km Killorglin, ideal
touring, walking, cycling, golf.
Open: Apr to Oct
066 9761665 Mrs Woods
D: Fr €25.00
Beds: 2D 2T **Baths:** 2 Ensuite 2 Shared
ॐ 🄿 (6) 🖵 �öᵛ ▥ ▪

Dromin Farmhouse, *Milltown, Killorglin, Co*
Kerry. Friendly home, fantastic mountain views.
Welcoming tea and scones on arrival.
Open: Easter to Oct
066 9761867 Mrs Foley
D: Fr €27.00
Beds: 2F 2D **Baths:** 3 Ensuite 1 Shared
ॐ 🄿 (8) 🖵 ♈ ✕ �öᵛ ▥

Laune Bridge House, *Laune Bridge, Killorglin*
Road, Killorglin, Co Kerry. Comfortable modern
residence at bridge over river. Scenic location
overlooking town and mountains.
Open: Mar 1 to Dec 1
066 9761161 Mrs Evans
D: Fr €27.50
Beds: 6F **Baths:** 6 Ensuite
🄿 ⅟ 🖵 �öᵛ ▥ ▪

Riverside House, *Killorglin, Co Kerry.*
Riverside house. Luxury family-run residence.
Panoramic views from rooms overlooking River
Laune.
Open: Mar to Dec
066 9761184 (also fax) Mrs Mangan
D: Fr €27.50
Beds: 3F 1D 2T **Baths:** 4 En 2 Sh
ॐ 🄿 (6) 🖵 �öᵛ ▪

Listowel
Q9933

Millstream, *Greenville,*
Listowel, Co Kerry.
Peaceful and convenient
location. Fishing, golf and
quiet rural walks.
Open: All year (not Xmas/New Year)
068 21129 & 086 8555651 (M) Mrs Sheahan
millstreamhouse@holidayhound.com
D: Fr €25.00-€30.00 **S:** Fr €30.00-€40.00
Beds: 1F 1T 3D **Baths:** 5 En
ॐ 🄿 🖵 ▥ ♿ ✳ ▪

Aras Mhuire, *Ballybunion Road, Listowel, Co Kerry.* Near town centre on Ballybunion road R553, Ballybunion golf course and beach 9 km.
Open: All Year
068 21515 & 068 23612 Mrs Costello
marycos@eircom.net
D: Fr €35.00
Beds: 1F 1D 1T 1S **Baths:** 4 En 2 Pr
⌂ (1) **P** (4) ⌇ ▥ ▪ cc

Oakwood, *Tarbert Road, Cahirdown, Listowel, Co Kerry.* Tarbert, car ferry road. Modern country house. Spectacular view.
Open: All Year
068 22020 (also fax) Mrs Harnett
D: Fr €33.00
Beds: 1F 2D 1T **Baths:** 3 En 1 Sh
⌂ **P** (6) ▣ ⌇ ▥ ▪ cc

Milltown (Castlemaine)

Q8200

Shortcliff House, *Lyre Road, Milltown, Killarney, County Kerry.*
Open: Mar to Sep **Grades:** BF Approv
066 9767106 (also fax)
Mrs Short
D: Fr €25.00 **S:** Fr €35.00
Beds: 2F 1T 1D **Baths:** 4 En 1 Pr
⌂ (4) **P** (4) ⌇ ▥ ▪
Country home 1km off the N70 ring of Kerry route. Perfect base for touring Ring of Kerry, Dingle Peninsula, Gap of Dunloe. Minutes walk to local village, pubs, restaurants. Minutes drive to golf. Stables on site.

Hillview Farm, *Milltown P.O., Killarney, Co Kerry.* Comfortable family-run sixth generation dairy/sheep farm in scenic countryside.
Open: Easter to Oct
066 9767117 Mrs Stephens **Fax: 066 9767910**
dstephens@eircom.net www.hillviewfarm.com
D: Fr €28.00-€30.00 **S:** Fr €35.00-€40.00
Beds: 1F 2D 1T **Baths:** 4 En
⌂ **P** ⌇ ▣ ⌇ ✕ ▣ ▥ cc

Riverville, *Rathpook, Milltown, Killarney, Co Kerry.* Family-run two-storey house in peaceful setting near quaint village.
Open: May to Oct
066 9767108 Mrs Burke
D: Fr €25.00
Beds: 1F 1D 1T 1S **Baths:** 2 En 1 Sh
⌂ **P** ⌇ ▣ ⌇ ✕ ▥

Mangans Country Home, *Killarney Road, Milltown, Killarney, Co Kerry.* Hospitable and friendly country village. Location: Killarney-Dingle route R563.
Open: Mid-Mar to Oct
066 9767502 (also fax) Mrs Mangan
D: Fr €28.00
Beds: 1F 2D 1T **Baths:** 3 Ensuite
⌂ (5) **P** ⌇ ▣ ▣ ▥ ▪

Milltown (Dingle)

Q4301

Cill Bhreac, *Milltown, Dingle, Tralee, Co Kerry.* Spacious home overlooking Dingle Bay, Mount Brandon. All rooms satellite TV, hairdryer, electric blankets.
Open: Mar to Nov
066 9151358 Mrs McCarthy
cbhreac@iol.ie
D: Fr €24.00-€25.50 **S:** Fr €32.00-€33.00
Beds: 3F 2D 1T **Baths:** 6 En
⌂ **P** (8) ▣ ▣ ▥ ▪ cc

Muckross

V9886

Ardree House, *Muckross House, Muckross, Killarney, Co Kerry.* Situated on the N71, we are within 4 minutes' walking from town centre.
Open: All Year (not Xmas)
064 32374 Mrs King **Fax: 064 35877**
adreehouse@eircom.net
D: Fr €42.00
Beds: 2F 2D 2T **Baths:** 6 En
⌂ **P** (6) ▣ ⌇ ▥ ▪

Muckross Lodge, *Muckross Road, Muckross, Killarney, Co Kerry.* Non-smoking home situated one mile from Killarney town and adjacent to Muckross House.
Open: Mar to Oct
064 32660 (also fax) Mrs O'Sullivan
D: Fr €32.00
Beds: 1F 1D 3T **Baths:** 54 Ensuite
P ▣ ▥ ▪

Kiltrasna Farm, *Lough Guitane Road, Muckross, Killarney, Co Kerry.* Situated in Muckross Lakeland district, ideal for touring Kerry Way.
Open: Easter to Nov
064 31643 Mrs Looney
D: Fr €24.00 **S:** Fr €25.50
Beds: 3D 2T 1S **Baths:** 6 En
⌂ (3) **P** (8) ▣ ▣ ▥ ⌂

O'Donovans Farm/Muckross Riding Stables, *Mangerton Road, Muckross, Killarney, Co Kerry.* Modern farm dormer bungalow, panoramic view of National Park (oak forest with red deer).
Open: Mar to Nov
064 32238 Mrs O'Donovan
D: Fr €23.50 **S:** Fr €29.00
Beds: 2F 2D 2T **Baths:** 6 En
♿ (2) 🅿 ⌀ ✕ ▥ ▪

V3773

Harbour Grove Farmhouse, *Ahadda, Portmagee, Killarney, Co Kerry.* On scenic Skellig Ring, 6 km off Ring of Kerry N70. Private beach.
Open: Easter to Nov
066 9477116 & 087 2239933 (M) Mrs Lynch
Fax: 066 9477172
harbourlights@eircom.net
D: Fr €26.00
Beds: 2F 1D 1T 1S **Baths:** 3 En 1 Sh
♿ 🅿 ⌀ ▥ ✕ ▥ ▪

Reen Coast, *Reencaheragh, Portmagee, Co Kerry.* Breathtaking views of sea and mountains. 2 minutes from beach.
Open: All Year
066 9477247 Mrs O'Driscoll
D: Fr €19.00
Beds: 3F 1T 1D 1S **Baths:** 2 En 1 Pr
♿ 🅿 (6) ▥ ✕ ▥ ✳

W1792

Failte, *Shinnagh, Rathmore, Co Kerry.*
Peaceful rural atmosphere, spacious gardens, mountain climbing, quiet walks, panoramic views.
Open: Easter to Oct
064 58178 Ms O'Neill
D: Fr €20.00-€24.00 **S:** Fr €22.00-€26.00
Beds: 1F 1T 1D **Baths:** 2 En 1 Pr
♿ (0) 🅿 (8) ⌀ ▥ ✕ ▥ ▪

National Grid References given are for villages, towns and cities – not for individual houses

V6966

Rockville House, *Sneem, Kenmare, Killarney, Co Kerry.*
Open: Mar to Nov
064 45135 Mrs Drummond
rockville@oceanfree.net
D: Fr €26.00-€30.00 **S:** Fr €30.00-€35.00
Beds: 2T 2D **Baths:** 4 En
♿ 🅿 (7) ▥ ▥ ▥ ▪ cc
Luxurious dormer bungalow set in mature gardens, located on the famous Ring of Kerry. Ideally situated for exploring the most spectacular coastline and scenery in the Southwest. Every comfort provided for our guests. Breakfast menu including a fish dish.

Bank House, *North Square, Sneem, Kenmare, Killarney, Co Kerry.* Old Georgian home with magnificent collection of antique crystal and china.
Open: Apr to Nov
064 45226 Mrs Harrington
www.sneem.com.bankhouse.html
D: Fr €25.00-€27.00 **S:** Fr €33.00-€36.00
Beds: 2F 3D 1T **Baths:** 5 En
🅿 ▥ ▥

Derry East Farmhouse, *Sneem, Killarney, Co Kerry.* Luxury farmhouse, scenic area, riverside/mountain walks, golf, horseriding, tennis, fishing, beaches.
Open: Mar to Oct
064 45193 (also fax) Mrs Teahan
D: Fr €27.00
Beds: 1F 1D 2T **Baths:** 3 Ensuite 1 Private
♿ 🅿 ⌀ ▥ ✕ ▥ ▥

Heatherside, *Sneem, Killarney, County Kerry.*
A modern family-run country house nestling amongst the wild Kerry mountains with a panoramic view of the Beara peninsula. Just one mile east of the picturesque village of Sneem on the N70 Ring of Kerry road, 300 metres from the road.
Open: All year
064 45220 (also fax) Mr Smith
D: Fr €23.00-€25.00 **S:** Fr €30.00
Beds: 1F 2D 1T **Baths:** 3 En 1 Pr
♿ 🅿 (5) ⌀ ▥ ▥ cc

Tahilla

V7365

Brookvilla, *Ankail, Tahilla, Sneem, Killarney, Co Kerry.* Family-run B&B overlooking Kenmare Bay. Grid reference V725654.
Open: All year (not Xmas)
064 45172 (also fax) Mrs McCarthy
brookvilla2001@yahoo.co.uk
www.sneem.com/brookvilla.html
D: Fr €23.00 **S:** Fr €26.00
Beds: 2F 1D 1T **Baths:** 4 En
🛏 🅿 📺 🐾 ✕ Ⅴ 🖾 ❄ 🛢 cc

Tarbert

R0647

Dillanes Farmhouse, *Listowel Road, Tarbert, Listowel, Co Kerry.*
Open: Easter to Oct
Grades: BF Approv
068 36242 (also fax)
Mr & Mrs Dillane
dillanesfarmhouse@eircom.net www.dillanes.com
D: Fr €30.00 **S:** Fr €35.00
Beds: 1F 1T 1D **Baths:** 4 En
🛏 🅿 📺 🐾 🖾 🛢 cc
Comfortable modernised farmhouse, elevated site well back from Tarbert-Listowel Road. Overlooking farmland with views of River Shannon. 5 mins car ferry. Restaurants nearby. Musicians welcome. Golf & beaches 15 mins walk. Ideal base for touring.

Templenoe

V8369

Bay View Farm, *Templenoe, Kenmare, Killarney, Co Kerry.* Old style farm house overlooking Kenmare Bay on N70.
Open: Easter to Apr
064 41383 Mrs Falvey
D: Fr €26.00
Beds: 3F 1D 2T 1S **Baths:** 4 En 2 Sh
🛏 🅿 (8) 📺 🐾 ✕ Ⅴ 🖾 🛢 cc

Planning a longer stay?
Always ask for any special rates

Tralee

Q8413

Stonecrest Manor, *Country Lane, Manor Farm, Tralee, Co Kerry.*
Open: Feb to Oct
066 7120477 & 086 6019438 (M)
Mrs O'Loughlin
D: Fr €20.00-€25.00 **S:** Fr €23.00-€27.00
Beds: 1F 2D 1T **Baths:** 4 En
🛏 🅿 (4) 🕊 🐾 ✕ Ⅴ 🖾 🛢 cc
Quality good rate ensuite accommodation in scenic lane setting off N21/22 Tralee-Killarney road. Good breakfast. Close to town. TV, tea/coffee facilities in rooms. Public telephone. Central for Killarney, Dingle, Ring of Kerry. Registered with Family Homes of Ireland group.

2 Oakpark Drive, *Tralee, Co Kerry.* Luxurious, modern, family town house, 10 mins walk to town centre.
Open: June to Sep
066 7180123 Mr & Mrs O'Shea
Fax: 066 7180188
osheasofkerry@eircom.net
www.osheas-ok.com
D: Fr €28.00-€32.00 **S:** Fr €36.00-€40.00
Beds: 1T 3D **Baths:** 4 En
🛏 (10) 🅿 🕊 📺 🖾 cc

Ashlee House, *Manor West, Tralee, Co Kerry.* Modern town house 15 mins walk town centre.
Open: All year
066 7126492 Mrs O'Loughlin
ashlee@gofree.indigo.ie
D: Fr €23.00-€25.00 **S:** Fr €25.00-€30.00
Beds: 3D 3T **Baths:** 6 En
🛏 (6) 🅿 (7) 📺 🖾 cc

Coisli, *Leebrook, Tralee, Co Kerry.* Situated on the N21, adjacent to hotels. All rooms ground floor.
Open: All year (not Xmas)
066 7126894 Mrs Molyneaux
jmcoisli@gofree.indigo.ie
D: Fr €24.00-€28.00 **S:** Fr €32.00-€38.00
Beds: 4F 2D 2S **Baths:** 4 En 4 Pr
🛏 (6) 🅿 (4) 🕊 📺 Ⅴ 🖾 🛢 cc

The Grand Hotel, *Tralee, Co Kerry.* Situated in Tralee town centre. Our open fires, ornate ceilings and mahogany furnishings.
Open: All year (not Xmas) **Grades:** BF 3 Star
066 7121499 Fax: 066 7122877
info@grandhoteltralee.com
www.grandhoteltralee.com
D: Fr €30.00-€50.00 **S:** Fr €33.00-€70.00
Beds: 1F 8D 29T 7S **Baths:** 44 En
🛏 🗡 📺 ✗ 🖂 ▥ ☀ ♨ **cc**

Dormer Road, *Alderwood Road, Tralee, Co Kerry.* Situated 4 km from Tralee town, all rooms ensuite, private car park.
Open: Easter to Oct
066 7126768 Mrs Mitchell
D: Fr €28.00
Beds: 1F 1D 1T **Baths:** 3 En
🛏 (1) 🅿 (3) 📺 ▥ ♨

Rosedale Lodge, *Oak Park Road, Tralee, Co Kerry.* On N69 Listowel (car ferry) road, luxury accommodation, spacious bedrooms.
Open: Mar to Nov
066 7125320 Mrs Gleeson
D: Fr €24.00-€25.50 **S:** Fr €32.50
Beds: 2T 1D **Baths:** 3 En
🅿 🗡 📺 ▥ ♨ **cc**

Knockbrack, *Oakpark Road, Tralee, Co Kerry.* Bright, comfortable, family home in residential area. Ideal base for exploring County Kerry.
Open: Mar to Oct
066 9127375 Mrs Lyons
D: Fr €32.00
Beds: 1F 1T 1D **Baths:** 3 Ensuite
🛏 (5) 🅿 (6) 🗡 📺 ▥ ♨

Beech Grove, *Oak Park, Tralee, Co Kerry.* Picturesque bungalow, large gardens on N69. Ideal base touring Dingle, Ring of Kerry.
Open: All Year (not Xmas)
066 7126788 Mrs O'Neill **Fax: 066 7180971**
D: Fr €20.50-€25.50 **S:** Fr €22.50-€33.00
Beds: 2F 1T 1D **Baths:** 3 En 1 Pr
🛏 🅿 (6) 🗡 📺 ▥ ♨ **cc**

Barnakyle, *Clogherbrien, Tralee, Co Kerry.* Barnakyle is a family-run guest house situated 2km from Tralee.
Open: Mar to Oct
066 7125048 Mrs O'Connell **Fax: 066 7181259**
barnakyl@iol.ie
D: Fr €28.00
Beds: 3D 3T **Baths:** 6 Ensuite
🛏 (5) 🅿 (6) 🗡 📺 ▥ ♨

Brianville, *Feint Road, Tralee, Co Kerry.* Luxurious bungalow on spacious grounds, 1 mile from Tralee town, scenic view of mountain.
Open: All Year (not Xmas)
066 7126645 Mrs Smith
D: Fr €35.00
Beds: 2F 2D 1T **Baths:** 5 En
🛏 🅿 (10) 🗡 📺 ▥ ☀ ♨ **cc**

Bricriu, *20 Old Golf Links Road, Oakpark, Tralee, Co Kerry.* Comfortable bungalow close railway and all amenities. Also self-catering.
Open: Apr to Oct
066 7126347 Mrs Canning
D: Fr €24.00-€25.50 **S:** Fr €32.00
Beds: 1F 1T 1D **Baths:** 3 En
🛏 (8) 🅿 🗡 📺 ✗ ▥

Mountain View House, *Ballinorig West, Tralee, Co Kerry.* Real comfort and quality at Mountain View House. Own grounds and car park.
Open: All Year
066 7122226 Mrs Curley
D: Fr €21.50-€24.00 **S:** Fr €30.00-€32.50
Beds: 1F 2D 1T **Baths:** 4 En 1 Sh
🛏 (7) 🅿 (9) 📺 ▥ ♨

Crana Li, *Curragraigue, Blennerville, Tralee, Co Kerry.* Looking for peace & tranquillity? All available 1 mile off N86 at Blennerville Village.
Open: Easter to Sep
066 7124467 Mrs Ryle
cottages@loveless.co.uk
D: Fr €25.50
Beds: 2F 1D 2T **Baths:** 3 En 1 Sh
🛏 🅿 🗡 📺 ▥ ♨

Ashville House, *Ballyard, Tralee, Co Kerry.* Architect-designed house in country setting off Dingle road (N86).
Open: All Year
066 7123717 Mrs O'Keefe **Fax: 066 7125698**
tokeeffe@leestrand.ie
D: Fr €28.00
Beds: 2F 2D 2T **Baths:** 6 En
🛏 🅿 (8) 🗡 📺 ▥ ☀ ♨ **cc**

Manor Lodge, *Killarney Road, Tralee, Co Kerry.* Hospitable warm house, good breakfasts. 10-minute walk to town centre.
Open: All Year
066 7124372 Mrs Lacey
D: Fr €25.50
Beds: 1T 3D **Baths:** 4 Ensuite
🛏 🅿 📺 ✗ ▥ ♨

Planning a longer stay?
Always ask for any special rates

Curraheen House, *Curraheen, Tralee, Co Kerry.*
Traditional style farmhouse situated between
mountains and sea, on Tralee-Dingle Road.
Open: Feb to Nov
066 7121717 Mrs Keane **Fax: 066 7128362**
D: Fr €24.00 **S:** Fr €32.00
Beds: 1F 2D 1T **Baths:** 4 En
🖪 (6) ⅍ ♍ ✕ Ⅲ, ■ cc

Ballingowan House, *Mile Height, Killarney
Road, Tralee, Co Kerry.* Purpose-built 2-storey
house detached on Killarney road. All spacious
rooms ensuite and interchangeable with TV and
tea/coffee. Breakfast menu, large private car
park. Approaching Tralee on N21/N22 - on left
before McDonald's Restaurant. Opposite Kerry
Motor Works.
Open: Easter to Oct
066 7127150 Mrs Kerins **Fax: 066 7120325**
ballingowan@eircom.net
www.kerryview.com/ballingowanhouse
D: Fr €26.00 **S:** Fr €38.00
Beds: 4F 2T 2D **Baths:** 4 En
ᵗᴥ (4) 🖪 (6) ⅍ Ⅳ Ⅲ, ■

V7962

Lake House, *Cloonee, Tuosist, Kenmare,
Killarney, Co Kerry.*
Open: Easter to Oct
064 84205 Ms O'Shea
mary@clooneelakehouse.com
www.clooneelakehouse.com
D: Fr €26.00 **S:** Fr €26.00
Beds: 3D 2T **Baths:** 2 Sh
🖪 (20) Ⅳ Ⅲ, &
Country house with full bar and restaurant. On
Cloonee Lakes with boats and fly-fishing.

B&B by the Sea, *Cloonee, Tuosist, Kenmare,
Killarney, Co Kerry.* Unique and peaceful C18th
waterside farmhouse with mountain/sea/wildlife
lookout cabin.
Open: All Year
064 84211 & 087 4118972 (M) Mr Wyles
D: Fr €23.00 **S:** Fr €23.00
Beds: 1T 3D **Baths:** 4 En
ᵗᴥ 🖪 (5) ♍

V3675 ◀ *The Ring Lyne, Boston Bar, Royal Pier*

Spring Acre, *Knightstown, Valentia Island, Co
Kerry.* Located on seafront beside village,
restaurant, pubs, scenic walks, fishing.
Open: Easter to Nov
066 9476141 Mrs Foran **Fax: 066 9476377**
rforan@indigo.ie
D: Fr €24.00-€25.00 **S:** Fr €26.00-€28.00
Beds: 2F 2T 1D **Baths:** 5 En
ᵗᴥ 🖪 (8) Ⅳ Ⅲ, ■ cc

Q3800

Garvey's Farmhouse, *Kilvicadownig, Ventry,
Dingle, Tralee, Co Kerry.* Spacious house on dairy
farm overlooking Ventry Bay in peaceful
surroundings.
Open: Mar to Nov
066 9159914 Mrs Garvey **Fax: 066 9159921**
www.garveysfarmhouse.com
D: Fr €27.00-€30.00 **S:** Fr €36.00-€42.00
Beds: 2F 2D 1T **Baths:** 4 En 1 Pr
ᵗᴥ 🖪 (6) Ⅳ ✕ Ⅲ, cc

Ard Na Mara, *Ballymore, Ventry, Dingle, Tralee,
Co Kerry.* Situated 3 miles from Dingle on the Slea
Head scenic drive.
Open: Easter to Oct
066 9159072 Mrs Murphy
D: Fr €23.00-€24.00 **S:** Fr €25.50-€32.00
Beds: 4F 2D 1S **Baths:** 4 En 4 Pr 1 Sh
ᵗᴥ (7) Ⅳ ♍ Ⅳ Ⅲ, ■ cc

Moriarty's Farmhouse, *Rahanane, Ventry,
Tralee, Co Kerry.* Family-run home overlooking
Ventry Harbour 8km west of Dingle. Signposted
at Ventry Church.
Open: All Year
066 9159037 (also fax) Mrs Moriarty
mrty@eircom.net
D: Fr €25.50
Beds: 3F 2D 1T **Baths:** 6 En
ᵗᴥ 🖪 (6) Ⅳ ✕ Ⅳ Ⅲ, ■ cc

Please respect a B&B's wishes
regarding children, animals and
smoking

Ballymore House, *Ballymore, Ventry, Dingle, Tralee, Co Kerry.* Friendly, family, no-smoking home in peaceful surroundings. Sea view, breakfast/dinner menu.
Open: All Year
066 9159050 Mr & Mrs O'Shea
ballyhse@iol.ie
D: Fr €29.00
Beds: 3F 3D 1T **Baths:** 5 En 2 Pr
🛏 🅿 (7) ⌇ 📺 ✕ 🛏 ⋆ ▪

Mount Eagle Lodge, *Clahane, Ventry, Dingle, Co Kerry.* Designer house. Fantastic sea, beach and mountain views. Acclaimed breakfasts.
Open: Easter to Oct
066 9159754 (also fax) Mr Prestage
ventry@irishcroft.iol.ie
D: Fr €40.00
Beds: 2F 2T **Baths:** 4 Ensuite 1 Private
🛏 (2) 🅿 (6) ⌇ 📺 ✕ 🛏 ♿ ▪

Waterville

V5066

The Old Cable House, *Cable Station, Waterville, Killarney, Co Kerry.*
Open: All year (not Xmas) **Grades:** BF Approv
066 9474233
Mr & Mrs Brown **Fax: 066 9474869**
mbrownn@iol.ie www.oldcablehouse.com
D: Fr €20.00-€36.00 **S:** Fr €25.00-€45.00
Beds: 6F 4D 2T **Baths:** 4 En
🛏 🅿 (15) ⌇ 📺 ♨ ✕ 📺 🛏 ▪ cc
Century-old house traces origins to first Transatlantic Telegraph Cable, laid 1866 from Europe to USA. Exhibit on view at the house. Bright spacious rooms, full private facilities. Skelligs/golf/fishing/walks/riding all nearby. Excellent seafood restaurant at the house, fully licensed.

O'Grady's, *Spunkane, Waterville, Killarney, Co Kerry.* Spacious family-run accommodation. Centrally located. Breakfast menu. Warm welcome.
Open: Easter to Nov
066 9474350 Mrs O'Grady **Fax: 066 9474730**
paogrady@eircom.net
D: Fr €26.50-€30.00 **S:** Fr €39.00-€42.50
Beds: 1F 2D 3T **Baths:** 6 En
🛏 🅿 (6) 📺 🛏 ▪ cc

National Grid References given are for villages, towns and cities – not for individual houses

Clifford's B&B, *Main Street, Waterville, Killarney, Co Kerry.* Golfing, fishing, sea-angling locally. Ideal base for walking/cycling. Skellig Island trips arranged.
Open: Mar to Nov
066 9474283 (also fax) Mrs Clifford
cliffordbandb@eircom.net
D: Fr €23.00-€25.00 **S:** Fr €25.00-€30.00
Beds: 2F 2D 2T **Baths:** 6 En
🛏 🅿 📺 🛏 🛏 ▪ cc

Golf Links View, *Murreigh, Waterville, Killarney Co Kerry.* Family-run B&B, comfortable ensuite rooms with TV, tea/coffee making facilities.
Open: Mar to Oct
066 9474623 (also fax) Mrs Barry
jbar@eircom.net
D: Fr €25.00-€30.00 **S:** Fr €35.00-€42.00
Beds: 1F 2T 3D **Baths:** 6 En
🛏 🅿 ⌇ 📺 ✕ 🛏 ▪ cc

Silver Sands, *Waterville, Killarney, Co Kerry.* Family-run guest house and restaurant in centre of Waterville village.
Open: All year (not Xmas)
066 9474161 Fax: 066 9474537
silversandswaterville@eircom.net www.silversands.com
D: Fr €19.00-€28.00 **S:** Fr €20.50-€43.50
Beds: 2F 4D 3T 1S **Baths:** 7 En 3 Sh
🛏 🅿 (4) ⌇ 📺 🛏 ✕ 📺 🛏

Klondyke House, *New Line Road, Waterville, Killarney, Co Kerry.* Luxurious home situated on main Ring of Kerry road N70, breakfast menu.
Open: All Year (not Xmas)
066 9474119 Mrs Morris **Fax: 066 9474666**
D: Fr €25.50
Beds: 1F 2D 2T 1S **Baths:** 6 En
🛏 🅿 (8) 📺 🛏 ✕ 📺 🛏 ▪ cc

RATES

D = Price range per person sharing in a double or twin room
S = Price range for a single room

RAIL ⇌
Kildare town is well-served by the railway. Trains run into **Dublin (Heuston)** every half an hour. The **Waterford, Cork, Limerick** & **Athlone** lines all run through **Kildare.**
Tel. **Irish Rail** on 01 8366222 for details.

BUS 🚌
Kildare to **Dublin** (every half hour) - tel. **Bus Eireann** on 01 8366111.

TOURIST INFORMATION OFFICE 🛈
Main Square, **Kildare** (Mar to Oct), 045 521240.

Allen
N7621

Sammax House, Allen Cross Roads, Allen, Naas, Co Kildare. Hospitable home where we do our utmost to ensure visitors comfort and enjoyment.
Open: All year
045 860089 & 087 9307790 (M)
Tom & Phil Geoghegan
sammax2@eircom.net
D: Fr €25.00-€30.00 **S:** Fr €30.00
Beds: 1T 1D 1S **Baths:** 1 En 1 Pr 1 Sh
🅿 (5) ⅙ 📺 🅗 ✕ 🔲, 🖭 cc

Athy
S6894

Ardscull Farm, Dublin Road, Athy, Co Kildare.
Open: Mar to Dec
Grades: BF Approv
0507 26188 (also fax) Mr & Mrs Flood
D: Fr €28.00-€32.00
S: Fr €40.00-€44.00
Beds: 2F 2D/T **Baths:** 4 En
🛏 🅿 (6) 📺 🅗 🔲, & 🖭
On Dublin's doorstep, Anne & Noel invite you to their home at this prestigious location on the N78; 45 mins from Dublin, airport & ferry port. Close to National Stud, Japanese Gardens, Curragh & Punchestown Races. Warm, spacious rooms, tea/scones on arrival.

Ballindrum
S7398

Ballindrum Farm, Ballindrum, Athy, Co Kildare. National Agri-Tourism Award winner. National award of excellence.
Open: Apr to Oct
0507 26294 (also fax) Mrs Gorman
ballindrumfarm@eircom.net
D: Fr €25.50
Beds: 1F 1D 2T 1S **Baths:** 4 Ensuite 1 Private
🛏 🅿 (20) ⅙ 📺 🅥 🔲, 🖭

Ballytore
S8095

Griesemount, Ballytore, Athy, Co Kildare. Comfortable historic Georgian country house overlooking river, relaxed family atmosphere.
Open: Feb to Nov **Grades:** BF Approv
0507 23158 Mr & Mrs Ashe **Fax:** 0507 41687
griesemount@eircom.net
D: Fr €32.00-€44.50 **S:** Fr €38.00-€51.00
Beds: 3D **Baths:** 2 En
🛏 🅿 ⅙ 📺 🅗 🅥 🔲, 🖭

Carragh
N8422

Setanta Farmhouse, Mondello Road, Carragh, Naas, Co Kildare. Working farm centrally located for N7/N4 (both routes connect with M50).
Open: Mar to Sep
045 876481 Mrs McLoughlin
setantafarmhouse@eircom.net
D: Fr €26.00 **S:** Fr €26.00
Beds: 1F 1T 1D 2S **Baths:** 3 En 2 Sh
🅿 (5) ⅙ 📺 🔲, 🖭

Castledermot
S7885

Kilkea Lodge, Castledermot, Athy, Co Kildare. Kilkea Lodge has belonged to the family since 1740. Lots of character and charm.
Open: All year (not Xmas)
0503 45112 (also fax) Mrs Greene
D: Fr €45.00 **S:** Fr €51.00
Beds: 1F 3D 1T **Baths:** 3 Pr 2 Pr
🛏 (8) 🅿 🅗 ✕ 🅥 🔲, 🖭 cc

All details shown are as supplied by B&B owners in Autumn 2002

Doyle's School House, *Main Street, Castledermot, Athy, Co Kildare.* Converted old school, with restaurant and four bedrooms.
Open: Easter to Oct
0503 44282 (also fax) Mr Doyle
D: Fr €35.00 **S:** Fr €35.00
Beds: 2D 2T **Baths:** 4 En
⊞ (20) 📺 ⚡ ✕ Ⅴ ▥

Celbridge

N9733

Green Acres, *Dublin Road, Celbridge, Co Kildare.* 1km Castletown House. Garden for visitors use.
Open: All year
01 6271163 Mrs McCabe
ptmcbe@indigo.ie
D: Fr €30.00 **S:** Fr €35.00
Beds: 1F 3D 2T **Baths:** 6 En
⚡ ⊞ 📺 ▥ ⚡ ■

Kildare

N7212

Castleview Farm, *Lackaghmore, Kildare, Co Kildare.* Working dairy farm, peaceful, historical setting, airport, ferries 1 hour.
Open: Mar to Nov
045 521816 (also fax) Mrs Fitzpatrick
castleviewfarmhouse@oceanfree.net
D: Fr €23.00-€30.00 **S:** Fr €35.00-€39.00
Beds: 1F 1D 1T 1S **Baths:** 3 En 1 Pr
⚡ ⊞ (6) 📺 ⚡ Ⅴ ▥ ■ cc

Kilgowan

N8202

Sandlands, *Kilgowan, Kilcullen, Curragh Camp, Co Kildare.* Home from home on main Dublin/ Carlow road.
Open: Jan to Dec
045 485246 Mrs Sutton
D: Fr €27.00
Beds: 2D 1T 1S **Baths:** 2 Shared

Kill

N9322

Olthove House, *Newtown, Kill, Naas, Co Kildare.* Modern, on four acres with river, mature trees and beautiful gardens.
Open: All Year (not Xmas)
045 877022 Mr Meagher
D: Fr €35.00
Beds: 3F **Baths:** 3 Ensuite
⚡ (4) ⊞ (8) ▥ ■

Maynooth

N9338

Ballygoran Lodge, *Old Celbridge Road, Maynooth, Co Kildare.*
Open: All year (not Xmas/New Year)
01 6291860 (also fax) Mrs Connolly
D: Fr €35.00 **S:** Fr €35.00
Beds: 2F 1T 1D **Baths:** 4 En
⚡ ⊞ 📺 Ⅴ ▥ ■ cc
Bally G will give an opportunity to sample Irish hospitality at its best. Adjacent to N4. Dublin 30 minutes. Dublin Airport 40 minutes. Nearby Intel, Hewlett Packard, Maynooth College, Carton House, Castletown House, home of the Lennox sisters 1740-1832.

Monasterevin

N6309

The Gables, *Coole, Monasterevin, Co Kildare.* The Venice of Ireland - adjacent to canal, riverside walks. Airport, ferries 1 hour.
Open: Easter to Oct
045 525564 Mr & Mrs Cullen **Fax: 045 525244**
owen@weuait.isl.ie
D: Fr €30.00
Beds: 1F 2D 1T **Baths:** 2 En 2 Sh
⚡ ⊞ ⚡ 📺 ⚡ ▥ ■ cc

Please respect a B&B's wishes regarding children, animals and smoking

Naas

N8919

Setanta Farmhouse, *Mondello Road, Carragh, Naas, Co Kildare.* Working farm centrally located for N7/N4 (both routes connect with M50).
Open: Mar to Sep
045 876481 Mrs McLoughlin
setantafarmhouse@eircom.net
D: Fr €26.00 **S:** Fr €26.00
Beds: 1F 1T 1D 2S **Baths:** 3 En 2 Sh
🅿 (5) ⅍ 📺 ▦ ☞

Newbridge

N8014

Bronville, *Ladytown, Newbridge, Co Kildare.*
Open: All year (not Xmas)
045 434024 Mr Wheeler **Fax: 045 866494**
D: Fr €32.50 **S:** Fr €35.00-€45.00
Beds: 2F 1T 2D **Baths:** 5 En
⏴ 🅿 (6) ⅍ 📺
Bronville Country home is situated halfway between Naas and Newbridge.

Rathmore

N9619

Springfield, *Rathmore, Naas, Co Kildare.* Set in scenic countryside, off the N7 at Rathcoole.
Open: Apr to Sep
045 862116 Margaret Gillespie
D: Fr €25.00-€30.00 **S:** Fr €33.00-€38.00
Beds: 1F 1T 1d **Baths:** 1 Sh
⏴ 🅿 (6) ⅍ 📺 ▦ ☞

Moatefield, *Rathmore, Naas, Co Kildare.* Country home set 10 km from Wicklow Mountains. Dublin 25 km.
Open: Easter to Oct
045 862121 Mrs Sargent
D: Fr €25.00-€28.00 **S:** Fr €30.00-€35.00
Beds: 1D 2T **Baths:** 1 En 1 Sh
⏴ (4) 🅿 (5) 📺 🐾 ▦ ☞

BATHROOMS

En = Ensuite

Pr = Private

Sh = Shared

RAIL ⇌

Kilkenny town is on the **Dublin** to **Waterford** line (4 trains per day).

tel. **Irish Rail** on 01 8366222 for timetable details.

BUS 🚌

Kilkenny to **Dublin** *(4 per day)* -

Tel. **Bus Eireann** on 01 8366111.

TOURIST INFORMATION OFFICE 🛈

Rose Inn Street, **Kilkenny** (open all year), tel. 056 7751500.

Bennettsbridge
S5549

Norely Theyr, *Barronsland, Bennettsbridge, Kilkenny.*
Open: All year **Grades:** BF Approv
056 7727496 Mrs Cole

norelytheyr@eircom.net
D: Fr €24.50-€30.00 **S:** Fr €37.00-€42.50
Beds: 2F 2D **Baths:** 2 En 1 Sh
🛌 🅿 ⅍ 📺 ✕ 🔲 ✳ ♨

Comfortable, spacious modern home set in quiet, rural but central location. Relaxing, friendly & hospitable 'home from home'. Large, secluded garden. Adjacent to village and craft studios. Golf courses nearby include Mount Juliet. Horse riding & fishing facilities local.

Callan
S4143

Moonarch, *Mullinahone Road, Callan, Kilkenny.* Charming family home set in scenic woodland countryside on R692 just off N76.
Open: All Year
056 7725810 Mrs Treacy
moonarch@indigo.ie
D: Fr €29.00
Beds: 5F 1D 1T **Baths:** 2 En 4 Pr 1 Sh
🛌 🅿 (8) ⅍ 📺 ✕ 🔲 🔲 ⅙ ☎ cc

Crosspatrick
S2668

Bayswell House, *Crosspatrick, Johnstown, Co Kilkenny.* Georgian farmhouse, historic features, gardens, 2 hours Dublin, Rosslare, Galway, Kilarney.
Open: May to Oct
056 8831168 Mrs Delaney
D: Fr €25.00
Beds: 3F **Baths:** 3 Ensuite
🛌 🅿 📺 ✕ 🔲

Freshford
S4064

Pomadora House, *Clinstown, Freshford, Kilkenny.* Country home on small Hunter stud, in pretty village of Freshford. Personal service guaranteed.
Open: All year
056 8832256 Mrs Flanagan
D: Fr €33.00-€35.00 **S:** Fr €40.00-€45.00
Beds: 1F 1D 1T **Baths:** 3 En
🛌 🅿 (6) 📺 ✕ ✕ 🔲 🔲 ✳

Gowran
S6253

Whitethorns, *Flagmount, Clifden, Gowran, Kilkenny.* Rural bungalow in two acres. Panoramic scenery.
Open: Easter to Sep
056 7726102 (also fax) Mrs Kenny
D: Fr €26.00
Beds: 2D 1T **Baths:** 1 Ensuite 1 Shared
🛌 🅿 (6) 📺 ✕ 🔲 ⅙

Inistioge
S6337

Grove Farm House, *Ballycocksuist, Inistioge, Thomastown, County Kilkenny.* 200-year-old country home with breathtaking views of scenic countryside.
Open: Easter to Oct
056 7758467 Mrs Cassin
grovefarmhouse@unison.ie
D: Fr €25.50 **S:** Fr €35.00
Beds: 1F 2T 1D **Baths:** 3 En 1 Sh
🅿 ⅍ ✕ 🔲 cc

Ashville, *Kilmacshane, Inistioge, Thomastown, Co Kilkenny.* Modern family home, situated in beautiful Nore Valley. Lovely views.
Open: Mar to Oct
056 7758460 Mrs Naddy
D: Fr €26.00
Beds: 1F 1D 1T **Baths:** 3 Ensuite 1 Private
⌂ (1) 🅿 (5) ⌇ 📺 ▥.

Nore Valley Villa, *Inistioge, Thomastown, Co Kilkenny.* Georgian villa overlooking River Nore. Ideal location for fishing, walking, hill climbing.
Open: Mar to Oct
056 7758418 (also fax) Mr & Mrs Rothwell
D: Fr €24.00 **S:** Fr €28.00
Beds: 1F 1D 2T **Baths:** 1 En 3 Pr 1 Sh
⌂ 🅿 (6) 📺 ▥. ▪ cc

Cullintra House, *The Rower, Inistioge, Thomastown, Co Kilkenny.* C18th 'Hidden Ireland' country house serving dinner by candlelight at 9pm.
Open: All Year
051 423614 Miss Cantlon
D: Fr €40.00
Beds: 7D **Baths:** 3 Ensuite
⌂ (4) 🅿 (12) ✕ 📺 ▥. ❋ ▪

Norebridge House, *Inistioge, County Kilkenny.* Norebridge House, situated just above the bridge, overlooks the River Nore.
Open: All Year
056 7758158 & 056 7758117 Mrs Storie
info@norebridgehouse.com
D: Fr €32.50
Beds: 3D 1T **Baths:** 4 En 1 Sh
🅿 (6) 📺 🏂 ✕ ▥. & ❋ ▪ cc

Kilkenny

S5156

Burwood, *Waterford Road, Kilkenny.* Modern bungalow on the Waterford Road N10 just 10 mins walk from city centre.
Open: Easter to Sep
056 7762266 Mrs Flanagan
D: Fr €28.00-€30.00 **S:** Fr €40.00
Beds: 1F 2D 1T **Baths:** 3 En 1 Pr
⌂ 🅿 (10) ⌇ 📺 🏂 ✕ 📺 ▥. ▪ cc

Kilkenny Bed & Breakfast, *Dean Street, Kilkenny.* Beautiful new house in centre of Kilkenny. Surrounded by historical monuments, pubs, restaurants.
Open: All year
056 7764040 Mrs Heffernan
kilkennybandb@eircom.net
D: Fr €20.00-€40.00 **S:** Fr €30.00-€40.00
Beds: 1F 1T **Baths:** 2 Sh
⌂ 🅿 📺 🏂 ✕ 📺 ▥. ❋

Lacken House, *Dublin Road, Kilkenny.* Beautiful Victorian house originally built as a Dower house in 1847.
Open: All Year
056 7761085 Fax: 056 7762435
www.lackenhouse.ie
D: Fr €44.50-€51.00 **S:** Fr €51.00-€58.50
Beds: 1F 5D 3T **Baths:** 9 En
⌂ (1) 🅿 (30) 📺 ✕ 📺 ▥. ▪ cc

Churchview, *Cuffsgrange, Callan Road, Kilkenny.* Luxury, quiet house 6 minutes' drive from the medieval city of Kilkenny (N76).
Open: All Year
056 7729170 (also fax) Mr & Mrs Banahan
D: Fr €27.00
Beds: 2F 3D 1T **Baths:** 3 Ensuite 1 Shared
⌂ 🅿 (6) 📺 🏂 📺 ▥. ❋ ▪

Danville House, *Kilkenny.* 200-year-old Georgian house. Delightful welcome awaits you with relaxed atmosphere and comfortable accommodation. At the back of house there is an old garden with croquet on lawn. Situated 1.5km from Kilkenny City on New Ross R700 road, 0.2km past roundabout on right hand side.
Open: Mar to Nov
056 7721512 (also fax) Mrs Stallard
treecc@iol.ie
D: Fr €23.00-€30.00 **S:** Fr €31.00-€38.00
Beds: 2F 1T 2D **Baths:** 4 En 1 Pr
⌂ 🅿 ▥.

Glen View, *Castlecomer Road, Kilkenny.* Warm friendly welcome assured. Walking distance medieval city, theatre, golf, activity centre.
Open: All Year (not Xmas)
056 7762065 (also fax) Mrs Dowling
glenvew@iol.ie
D: Fr €32.00
Beds: 1F 1D 1T **Baths:** 3 Ensuite
⌂ 🅿 ⌇ 📺 📺 ▥. & ▪

Dunboy, *10 Parkview Drive, Freshford Road, Kilkenny City.* Beautiful detached modern B&B convenient to castle, greyhound racing track, city centre.
Open: Mar to Nov
056 7761460 (also fax) Mrs Dunning
dunboy@eircom.net www.dunboy.com
D: Fr €19.00 **S:** Fr €24.00
Beds: 1F 1T 2D **Baths:** 4 En
🅿 ⅄ 📺 🛏, ⚊ cc

Ashleigh, *Waterford Road, Kilkenny.* Friendly, comfortable home on Kilkenny-Waterford road (N10). Convenient to city, castle etc.
Open: All Year (not Xmas)
056 7722809 Mrs Flannery
D: Fr €30.00
Beds: 2F 1D **Baths:** 2 Ensuite 1 Private
🅿 (4) ⅄ 📺 📺 🛏, ⚊

Viewmount House, *Castlecomer Road, Kilkenny.* Friendly family home between Newpark Hotel and Kilkenny Golf Club.
Open: All Year (not Xmas)
056 7762447 (also fax) Mrs Hennessy
D: Fr €30.00
Beds: 2F 1D 1T **Baths:** 4 Ensuite
🅿 (4) 📺 📺 🛏, ⚊

Rodini, *Waterford Road, Kilkenny.* Ideal base from which to tour the beautiful historic south east region.
Open: All Year (not Xmas)
056 7721822 Mrs Lawlor
rodini@eircom.net
D: Fr €24.00-€27.00 **S:** Fr €32.50-€33.00
Beds: 1F 2D 1T 1S **Baths:** 5 En
🐾 (2) 🅿 (5) 📺 🛏, ⚊ cc

SURE STAY Kilkenny, *5 Lower Patrick's Street, Kilkenny.* A warm welcome awaits you here at Berkeley House, a fine period residence located in the centre of the city. All rooms are ensuite TV, tea/coffee facilities. We also provide private car parking.
Open: All year (not Xmas)
01726 890770 (UK) Fax: 056 7764829
berkeleyhouse@eircom.net www.surestay.com
D: Fr €35.00-€48.00 **S:** Fr €44.50-€57.50
Beds: 4F 3T 3D **Baths:** 10 En
🐾 🅿 (10) 📺 🛏, ⚊ cc

'The Meadows', *6 Greenfields Road, Bishops Meadows, Kilkenny.* Quiet area off R693. Home baking. Walking distance city. Comfortable.
Open: All Year (not Xmas/New Year)
056 7721649 (also fax) Ms Ryan
kryan@indigo.ie www.themeadows.bizland.com
D: Fr €25.50 **S:** Fr €32.00-€34.50
Beds: 2F 1D **Baths:** 2 En 1 Pr
🐾 (3) 🅿 (3) ⅄ 🛏, ⚊ cc

Ashling, *39 Glendine Heights, Castlecomer Road, Kilkenny.* Family home with friendly welcome. Home baking. Tea/coffee on arrival. American Express/Visa.
Open: All year
056 7765709 Mrs Shortis
ashlinghouse@oceanfree.net
D: Fr €23.00 **S:** Fr €30.00
Beds: 1F 1D 1T **Baths:** 3 En
🐾 🅿 (3) 📺 🛏, cc

Kilmanagh
S3851

Hartford House, *Graigue, Kilmanagh, Kilkenny.* Family home, traditional music, home baking, walks, golf and horse riding. Close to Ballykeefe Amphitheatre. Musicians welcome.
Open: All year (not Xmas)
056 7769215 Mrs Butler
marypbutler@eircom.net www.kilmanagh.com
D: Fr €22.00-€25.00 **S:** Fr €32.00
Beds: 1F 1D 1T **Baths:** 3 En
🐾 🅿 ⅄ 📺 🐎 🛏, 🔥 ⚊

Knocktopher
S5337

Cushlawn House, *Castlecolumb, Knocktopher, Kilkenny.* Warm welcome to our comfortable Georgian home on N9 Dublin-Waterford road.
Open: All Year (not Xmas)
056 7768601 Mrs Coady
D: Fr €21.50-€23.00 **S:** Fr €21.50-€25.50
Beds: 1F 2D 2T **Baths:** 5 En
🐾 🅿 📺 🛏, cc

All details shown are as supplied by B&B owners in Autumn 2002

Piltown

S4522

Kildalton House, *Piltown, Carrick-on-Suir, Co Tipperary.* Peaceful bungalow in the countryside with beautiful garden.
Open: Jul to Sept
051 643196 Mrs Maddock
D: Fr €18.00 **S:** Fr €18.00
Beds: 2T 1D **Baths:** 1 Sh
🅿 (6) ⅍ 🖾

Stoneyford

S5242

Oldtown Farmhouse, *Oldtown, Stoneyford, Thomastown, Co Kilkenny.* Comfortable, friendly farmhouse, scenic views, working farm with ancient ring fort.
Open: All year (not Xmas) **Grades:** BF Approv
056 7728224 Mrs Fitzgerald **Fax: 056 7728481**
pfitz@iol.ie
D: Fr €26.50-€30.00 **S:** Fr €37.00-€40.00
Beds: 2D 1T 1F **Baths:** 4 En
🏠 🅿 ⅍ 🖾 🕇 🖾 ⅍ cc

Tober Mogue, *Ennisnag, Stoneyford, Kilkenny.* Home from home. Tranquil rural setting. Dairy farm. Crafts, amenities.
Open: All year (not Xmas)
056 7728155 Mrs Wallace
fwallace@oceanfree.net
D: Fr €20.00-€25.00 **S:** Fr €20.00
Beds: 2T 1D **Baths:** 1 Sh
🅿 (4) ⅍ 🖾 🖾

The Rower

S7034

Charlefield Farmhouse, *Charlefield, The Rower, Thomastown, Co Kilkenny.* 200-year-old farmhouse set in beautiful gardens overlooking the River Barrow on the R700. Ideal base for touring the South East. 1 hour to Rosslare Ferry. 10 minutes to New Ross. 35 mins to Kilkenny.
Open: All year
051 422386 Mrs Grace
D: Fr €25.00-€30.00 **S:** Fr €25.00-€30.00
Beds: 1F 1D 1S **Baths:** 2 En 1 Pr
🏠 🅿 ⅍ 🖾

Thomastown

S5842

Oldtown Farmhouse, *Oldtown, Stoneyford, Thomastown, Co Kilkenny.*
Open: All year (not Xmas)
Grades: BF Approv
056 7728224 Mrs Fitzgerald **Fax: 056 7728481**
pfitz@iol.ie
D: Fr €26.50-€30.00 **S:** Fr €37.00-€40.00
Beds: 2D 1T 1F **Baths:** 4 En
🏠 🅿 ⅍ 🖾 🕇 🖾 ⅍ cc
Comfortable, friendly farmhouse, scenic views, working farm with ancient ring fort and propagation nursery. Kilkenny 10 mins; Mount Juliet Golf Course, Kells, Jerpoint Abbey 5 mins; Rosslare 1 hour. Signposted on N10 1m south of Stoneyford; on N9 2m south of Thomastown.

Carrickmourne House, *New Ross Road, Thomastown, Co Kilkenny.* Picturesque split-level house on elevated site surrounded by breathtaking scenic views.
Open: All year (not Xmas)
056 7724124 (also fax) Mrs Doyle
D: Fr €26.50-€38.00 **S:** Fr €39.00-€50.00
Beds: 2F 2D 1T **Baths:** 5 En
🅿 (10) ⅍ 🖾 🖾 ▪ cc

Abbey House, *Jerpoint Abbey, Thomastown, Co Kilkenny.* Georgian house standing in 20 acres on the banks of the Little Arrigle river.
Open: Dec to Dec
056 7724166 Mrs Blanchfield **Fax: 056 7724192**
D: Fr €28.57-€44.44 **S:** Fr €32.00-€50.79
Beds: 2T **Baths:** 7 En
🏠 🅿 🖾 🕇 🖾 cc

BATHROOMS

En = Ensuite

Pr = Private

Sh = Shared

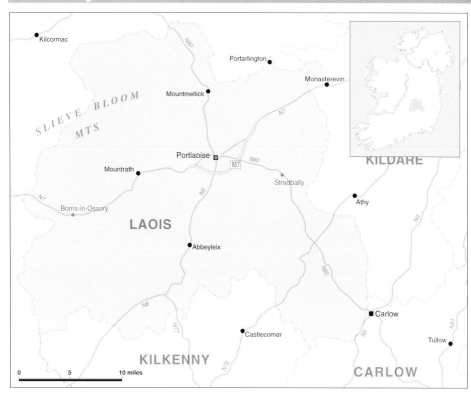

LAOIS

RAIL ⇌

Portlaoise is on the main lines from **Dublin** to **Limerick** and **Cork**.
Tel. **Irish Rail** on 01 8366222 for timetable details.

BUS 🚌

Portlaoise to **Dublin** (6 a day).
Tel. **Bus Eireann** on 01 8366111.

TOURIST INFORMATION OFFICE 🛈

James Fintan Lawlor Avenue,
Portlaoise (May to Sep), 0502 21178.

Borris-in-Ossory

S2487

Castletown House, *Donaghmore, Rathdowney, Co Laois.* Award-winning beautiful C19th family home on working farm.
Open: All year **Grades:** BF Approv
0505 46415 & 087 6868558 (M) Mrs Phelan **Fax: 0505 46415**
castletown@eircom.net
www.castletownguesthouse.com
D: Fr €27.00-€30.00 **S:** Fr €32.00-€35.00
Beds: 2F 2D 1S **Baths:** 5 En
🛏 🅿 (20) ⌕ 📺 🛏 🛏 ♨ cc

S4698

Rosedene, Limerick Road, Portlaoise, Co Laois.
Centre of Ireland, just off N7, nestling at the foot
of Slieve Bloom mountains.
Open: All Year (not Xmas)
0502 22345 (also fax) Mrs Saunders
rosedene@gofree.indigo.ie
D: Fr €25.50
Beds: 1F 2D 1T **Baths:** 2 En 2 Sh
⌂ (4) 🅿 (4) ⚲ 📺 🛏 ▣

# BATHROOMS
En = Ensuite
Pr = Private
Sh = Shared

S5796

Park House, Stradbally, Portlaoise, Co Laois.
200-year-old farmhouse. Large garden. One
hour's drive from Dublin.
Open: May to Oct
0502 25147 Mrs Cushen
D: Fr €26.00-€28.00 **S:** Fr €32.00-€34.00
Beds: 1F 2D **Baths:** 1 Sh
⌂ 📺 🛏 ✕

Talltrees, Cork Road, Stradbally, Portlaoise, Co
Laois. Warm, friendly family home on Euro-Route
N80 to Midlands and West.
Open: All year
0502 25412 & 086 8533264 (M) Mrs Condon
epcon@dol.ie
D: Fr €25.00 **S:** Fr €25.00
Beds: 1F 2D 1S **Baths:** 4 En
⌂ 🅿 (4) 📺 Ⓥ ▥

RAIL ⇌

Carrick-on-Shannon is on the **Sligo to Dublin (Connolly)** line (3 trains daily).

Tel. **Irish Rail** on 01 8366222 for timetable details.

TOURIST INFORMATION OFFICE
i

The Quay, **Carrick-on-Shannon** (May to Sep), 071 9620170.

Ballinamore

H1211

Riversdale Farm Guest House, Ballinamore, Co Leitrim.
Open: All year (not Xmas)
071 9644122
Ms Thomas **Fax: 071 9644813**
riversdaleguesthouse@eircom.net
D: Fr €38.00-€45.00 **S:** Fr €45.00-€52.00
Beds: 4F 3D 2T 1S **Baths:** 10 En
🛏 (5) 🅿 (12) 📺 ⚓ ✕ Ⓥ ▥, cc
Comfortable spacious residence in parkland setting alongside Shannon-Erne Waterway. Indoor heated swimming pool, squash, sauna, table tennis, fitness suite on premises. Local golf, horse-riding, boat trips. Good touring centre. Brochure available. Weekly terms. Canal barge holidays.

Carrick-on-Shannon

M9499

The Shannon Valley, Carrick-on-Shannon, Co Leitrim. Superb old house. Fine dining, own wooded grounds. Night club.
Open: All Year
071 9620103 Fax: 071 9650876
D: Fr €71.00-€91.50 **S:** Fr €71.00-€91.50
Beds: 4F 6D **Baths:** 10 En
🛏 🅿 (200) 📺 ✕ Ⓥ ▥, cc

Corbally Lodge, Dublin Road N4, Carrick-on-Shannon, Co Leitrim. Country peacefulness, antique furnishings, laundry, breakfast service. Fishing and walking.
Open: All Year (not Xmas)
071 9620228 (also fax) Mr & Mrs Rowley
D: Fr €19.50
Beds: 1D 3T **Baths:** 3 En
🛏 🅿 📺 ⚓ ✕ Ⓥ ▥.

Moyrane House, Dublin Road, Carrick-on-Shannon, Co Leitrim. A truly Irish family home. Peaceful setting. Highly recommended.
Open: Apr to Oct
071 9620325 Mrs Shortt
eleanorhotel@eircom.net
D: Fr €24.00
Beds: 4F 2D/T 1S **Baths:** 3 En
🛏 🅿 (5) 📺 ✕ Ⓥ ▥.

Gortmor House, Lismakeegan, Carrick-on-Shannon, Co Leitrim. Modern quiet scenic area. Fishing facilities.
Open: Feb to Nov
071 9620489 Mrs McMahon **Fax: 071 9621439**
gortmorhouse@oceanfree.net
D: Fr €25.00 **S:** Fr €38.00
Beds: 1F 2T **Baths:** 4 En 4 Pr
🛏 🅿 (6) 📺 ⚓ ✕ Ⓥ ▥, cc

Carrigallen

H2303

Hartes Arms, Main Street, Carrigallen, Cavan. Family business located in the picturesque lakeland village of Carrigallen.
Open: All Year
049 4339737 C Harte **Fax: 049 4339152**
cima@indigo.ie
D: Fr €25.50 **S:** Fr €32.00
Beds: 5T 7D **Baths:** 12 En
🛏 📺 ⚓ ✕ Ⓥ ▥, ■ cc

Cornafest House, Carrigallen, Cavan. Charming country residence beside lake. Ideally located for touring week.
Open: Easter to 15 Nov
049 4339643 (also fax) Mrs McGerty
cornafest@10free.ie
D: Fr €20.50-€23.00 **S:** Fr €23.00-€25.50
Beds: 1F 1T 1D 1S **Baths:** 1 En 2 Sh 1 Pr
🛏 (1) 🅿 (8) 📺 ✕ Ⓥ ▥.

Dromod

N0590

Tooman House, *Dromod, Carrick-on-Shannon, Co Leitrim.* Family-run farmhouse B&B. Beautiful location for fishing, walking, golf.
Open: All year (not Xmas/New Year)
043 24119 (also fax) Mrs Herbert
D: Fr €30.00 **S:** Fr €30.00
Beds: 2F 1D 1T **Baths:** 1 En 3 Pr
🛏 🅿 ✕ 📺 ▪ cc

Drumshanbo

G9710

Mooney's B&B, *2 Carick Road, Drumshanbo, Carrick-on-Shannon, Co Leitrim.* Stone two-storey house, home from home, scenic area in lovely Leitrim.
Open: All year (not Xmas)
071 9641013 Mrs Mooney **Fax: 071 9641237**
D: Fr €20.00 **S:** Fr €25.00
Beds: 2D 2S **Baths:** 1 Sh
🛏 (12) ⅍ 📺 🖾

Fenagh

H1007

The Old Rectory, *Fenagh, Ballinamore, Co Leitrim.* Beautifully restored Georgian house on 50 acres of wooded parkland overlooking Fenagh Lake.
Open: Jan 10 to Dec 15
071 9644089 Mr & Mrs Curran
theoldrectoryleitrim@eircom.net
D: Fr €25.50 **S:** Fr €32.00
Beds: 2D 1T 1F **Baths:** 3 En 1 Sh
🛏 🅿 (6) 📺 ➤ ✕ 📺 🖾 cc

Mohill

N0897

Travellers Rest, *Glebe Street, Mohill, Co Leitrim.* Traditional Irish pub and 3 Star guest house. Situated in lovely Leitrim.
Open: All year
071 9631174
D: Fr €28.00 **S:** Fr €32.00
Beds: 1F 5T **Baths:** 6 En
🛏 📺 ✕ 📺 🖾 ▪

Laheen House, *Eslin Bridge, Mohill, Carrick-on-Shannon, Co Leitrim.* Beautiful farmhouse in excellent fishing area. Close to the river Shannon & Canal.
Open: Easter to Oct
071 9631232 Mrs Duignan
D: Fr €21.00-€23.50 **S:** Fr €21.00-€23.50
Beds: 1F 1S 1T **Baths:** 2 En 1 Sh ▪ cc

Coolabawn House, *Station Raod, Mohill, Carrick-on-Shannon, Co Leitrim.* Highly recommended, friendly accommodation. Beautiful gardens to relax in.
Open: Apr to Dec
071 9631033 Mrs Slevin
D: Fr €27.00
Beds: 1F 2D **Baths:** 2 Ensuite 1 Private 1 Shared
🛏 🅿 (5) ⅍ 📺 🖾

Planning a longer stay?
Always ask for any special rates

County Limerick

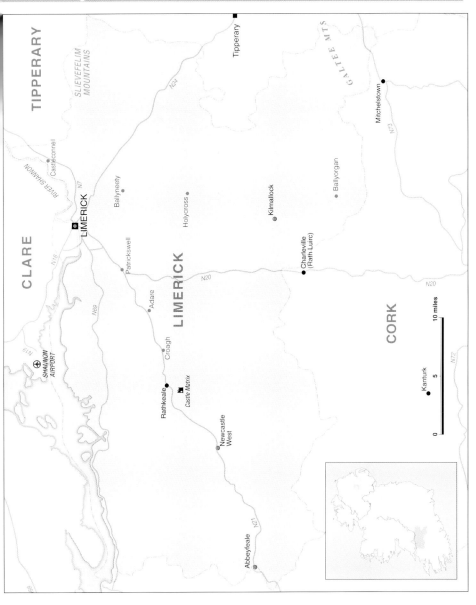

TIPPERARY

CLARE

LIMERICK

CORK

SLIEVEFELIM MOUNTAINS

GALTEE MTS

RIVER SHANNON

Castleconnell

Ballyneety

LIMERICK

Patrickswell

Holycross

Kilmallock

Ballyorgan

Tipperary

Mitchelstown

Charleville
(Rath Luirc)

Adare

Croagh

Rathkeale

Castle Matrix

Newcastle
West

Abbeyfeale

Kanturk

SHANNON
AIRPORT

N18

N7

N24

N20

N20

N69

N21

N72

N73

10 miles

0   5

AIRPORTS

Shannon Airport (in ***County Clare***) is 10 miles away from ***Limerick City***.

Tel. 061 471444.

AIR SERVICES & AIRLINES

Shannon *to* ***London Heathrow*** **-**

Aer Lingus. In Ireland tel. 0818 365000; in Britain tel. 0845 0844444.

Shannon *to* ***London Stansted*** **-**

Ryanair. In Ireland tel. 0818 303030; in Britain tel. 0871 2460000.

Shannon *to* ***Manchester*** **-**

British Airways (for **Manx Airlines**). In the Republic tel. (freefone): 1800 626747; in Northern Ireland & the UK tel. (local rate): 08705 511155.

RAIL

Limerick City is well-served by railway lines. 12 trains a day run to ***Dublin***, via ***Nenagh*** and ***Portlaoise***.

Limerick is also on the ***Rosslare*** line (via ***Limerick Junction***).

Tel. **Irish Rail** on 01 8366222.

TOURIST INFORMATION OFFICES

Heritage Centre, **Adare** (Mar to Oct), 061 396255.

Arthur's Quay, **Limerick** (open all year), 061 317522.

Adare

R5857

Ivy House, *Graigue, Adare, Co Limerick.*
Open: Apr to Oct
061 396270 (also fax) Mrs Hickey
D: Fr €30.00-€33.00
S: Fr €45.00
Beds: 1F 1D 1T **Baths:** 3 En
(7)
Beautifully restored C18th country home, surrounded by gardens, lawns, furnished with antiques and objets d'art. Homely atmosphere, TV lounge for guests, tea/coffee making facilities. ITB approved.

Avona, *Kildimo Road, Adare, Co Limerick.*
Highly recommended, well-appointed bedrooms. Breakfast menu, lounge for guests.
Open: Mar to Nov
061 396323 (also fax) Mrs Harrington
avona@eircom.net adareaccommodation.com
D: Fr €30.00-€32.00 **S:** Fr €40.00-€45.00
Beds: 1F 1T 2D **Baths:** 4 En
(5) cc

Berkeley Lodge, *Station Road, Adare, Co Limerick.*
Open: All year
061 396857 (also fax) Mr & Mrs Donegan
berlodge@iol.ie www.adare.org
D: Fr €28.00-€32.00 **S:** Fr €38.00-€51.00
Beds: 2 F 1T 3D **Baths:** 5 En 1 Pr
cc
Deluxe, warm, spacious, friendly home adjacent to hotels, churches, restaurants, Heritage Centre. Golfers dream. Breakfast menu. Ideal touring base for the South and West of Ireland. Shannon 30 minutes. Turn at roundabout in centre of village, 5th house on right after Texaco filling station.

Carrabawn House, *Killarney Road, Adare, Co Limerick.* Multi-recommended house, select area, dining room and sun lounge overlooking picturesque gardens.
Open: All Year (not Xmas)
061 396067 Mr & Mrs Lohan **Fax: 061 396925**
D: Fr €45.00
Beds: 2F 4D 2T **Baths:** 8 En
(14) cc

Sycamore View, *Beabus, Adare, Co Limerick.*
Open: Mar to Oct
061 396074 Mrs Ryan
D: Fr €23.00
Beds: 1F 1D **Baths:** 2 En

ॐ 🅿 (4) ⌘ 📺 Ⅴ 🖾.

Enjoy a warm welcome. Peaceful country setting off N21, signposted Ballingarry R519 on entry to Adare village from Killarney side. Complimentary refreshments, home cooking, tasty home-made breads and jams. Comfortable beds assured - situated 7 mins from village and 35 minutes from Shannon.

Hillcrest House,
Clonshire, Croagh, Adare, Co Limerick. Charming home, set amidst beautiful, tranquil pastures. Frommer Travel Guide recommended.
Open: Mar to Nov
061 396534 (also fax) Mr & Mrs Power
hillcrest_irl@hotmail.com
www.dirl.com/limerick/hillcrest.htm
D: Fr €29.50-€30.50 **S:** Fr €44.50
Beds: 1F 1D 2T **Baths:** 4 En

ॐ 🅿 (12) ⌘ 📺 ⋔ ✕ 🖾. ▪ cc

Elm House, *Mondelihy, Adare, Co Limerick.*
Elegant, restored 1892 Georgian home 'Lonely Planet' recommended. Shannon Airport - 30 mins.
Open: All year (not Xmas/New Year)
061 396306 (also fax) Mrs Hedderman
D: Fr €28.00 **S:** Fr €33.00-€38.00
Beds: 1T 2D **Baths:** 1 En 2 Pr

ॐ 🅿 ⌘ 📺 ⋔ 🖾. cc

Coatesland House, *Killarney Road, N21, Adare, Co Limerick.* Modern, warm Mansard home. AA Award (4 Q) 1993-1998. Many extras as standard.
Open: All Year (not Xmas)
061 396372 Mrs Hogan **Fax: 061 396833**
coatesfd@indigo.ie
D: Fr €32.00
Beds: 2F 2D 1T 1S **Baths:** 6 Ensuite

ॐ 🅿 (15) 📺 ⋔ 🖾. ▪

B&B owners may vary rates – be sure to check when booking

R6249

Bridge House Farm, *Grange, Holycross, Bruff, Co Limerick.*
Open: Mar to Nov
061 390195 (also fax) Mr & Mrs Barry
grange@esatclear.ie www.iolfree.ie/~grange
D: Fr €28.00-€30.00 **S:** Fr €28.00-€35.00
Beds: 1F 1D 1T 1S **Baths:** 2 En 1 Sh

ॐ (6) 🅿 (10) ⌘ 📺 🖾. ▪ cc

Welcome to our 200-year-old home by Camogue River. Convenient to Limerick City and Shannon Airport. Archaeological Laugh Gur nearby. Limerick County Golf Club at Ballyneety, 5 mins drive. Ideal touring base for South and West, e-mail facilities.

Four Seasons, *Ballyneety, Limerick.*
Superb residence, view of golf course from conservatory. TV, hairdryers, tea/coffee in bedrooms.
Open: All Year (not Xmas)
061 351365 (also fax) Mary Conway Ryan
D: Fr €25.50
Beds: 2F 1D 2T **Baths:** 5 En

ॐ 🅿 (10) 📺 ✕ Ⅴ 🖾. ₺ ▪

R6718

Lantern Lodge, *Ballyorgan, Kilfinnane, Kilmallock, Co Limerick.* Modern comfortable farmhouse, foot of Ballyhouse Hills.
Open: All Year (not Xmas)
063 91085 Mrs O'Donnell
D: Fr €26.00
Beds: 1F 1T 2S **Baths:** 4 Ensuite

ॐ 🅿 📺 ⋔ ✕ Ⅴ 🖾.

R4142

Meadowview, *Kiltannon, Croagh, Rathkeale, Co Limerick.* Modern bungalow on family-run dairy farm, 6 minutes from Adare - off N21 Killarney road.
Open: Easter to Oct
069 64820 Mrs Piggott
D: Fr €23.00
Beds: 3F 2D 1S **Baths:** 1 En 1 Sh

ॐ (3) 🅿 ⌘ 📺 ✕ 🖾. ₺ ▪

Please respect a B&B's wishes regarding children, animals and smoking

Castleview, *Clonshire, Adare, Co Limerick.*
Beautiful warm home, award-winning gardens.
Beside Clonshire Equestrian Centre, off N21.
Open: All Year
061 396394 (also fax) Mrs Glavin
castleview@eircom.net
D: Fr €25.50 **S:** Fr €34.50
Beds: 4F 2D 2T **Baths:** 4 En 3 Pr 1 Sh
P (6) ⚹ TV ⋔ ✕ V ▥ ⚍ cc

Holycross
R6340

Bridge House Farm, *Grange, Holycross, Bruff,
Co Limerick.* Welcome to our 200-year-old home
by Camogue River. Convenient Limerick,
Shannon Airport.
Open: Mar to Nov
061 390195 (also fax) Mr & Mrs Barry
grange@esatclear.ie www.iolfree.ie/~grange
D: Fr €28.00-€30.00 **S:** Fr €28.00-€35.00
Beds: 1F 1D 1T 1S **Baths:** 2 En 1 Sh
☎ (6) P (10) ⚹ TV ▥ ⚍ cc

Kilmallock
R6028

Ash Hill, *Kilmallock, Co
Limerick.* Large Georgian
house set in farmland, self-
catering flat also available.
Open: All year (not Xmas/
New Year)
063 98035 Mr Johnson **Fax: 063 98752**
ashhill@iol.ie www.ashhill.com
D: Fr €40.00-€50.00 **S:** Fr €50.00-€60.00
Beds: 1D 2F **Baths:** 3 En
☎ P ⋔ ✕ V cc

Flemingstown House, *Kilmallock, Co
Limerick.* 250-year-old house situated at the
intersection of three counties on R512 Kilmallock-
Kilfinane road.
Open: Feb to Nov
063 98093 Mrs Sheedy-King **Fax: 063 98546**
keltec@iol.ie
D: Fr €40.00
Beds: 1F 2D 2T **Baths:** 5 En
P (20) TV ⋔ ✕ V ▥ ⚍

Hillgare House, *Uregare, Kilmallock, Co
Limerick.* Family farm with pony for children's
use. Ideal base for touring the south.
Open: Easter to Oct
061 382275 Mrs Power
D: Fr €25.50
Beds: 1F 2T **Baths:** 2 Ensuite 1 Private
☎ P ✕ V ▥ ⚍

Limerick
R7185

Clonmacken Guest House, *Clonmacken, of
Ennis Road, Limerick.*
Open: All year (not Xmas)
061 327007 Ms McDonald **Fax: 061 327785**
clonmac@indigo.ie
www.euroka.com/limerick/clonmacken
D: Fr €35.00 **S:** Fr €50.00
Beds: 6F 3D 1T **Baths:** 10 En
☎ P (30) TV V ▥ ⚍ cc
Purpose-built family-run guest house, 5 mins
drive city centre, 10 mins Shannon Airport and
Bunratty Castle. All rooms ensuite with
telephone, TV, tea/coffee, hairdryer etc. Perfect
base for golfing, fishing, horseriding, shopping,
touring historic and beautiful Mid-West.

Santolina, *Coonagh, Ennis Road, Limerick.*
Open: All year (not Xmas) **Grades:** BF Approv
061 451590 & 061 328321 Mrs Keane
patriciackeane@eircom.net
homepage.eircom.net/~santolina
D: Fr €27.00-€30.00 **S:** Fr €39.00-€42.50
Beds: 3F 2D 1T **Baths:** 6 En
☎ P (8) TV ⋔ V ▥ ⚍
Spacious home in rural setting 3km from
Limerick city. 12km Shannon Airport. All
bedrooms on ground floor. Driving range 1km.
Advice on day tours, restaurants and bars.
Reductions for off season/3 nights' stay/senior
citizens. Ideal location Bunratty Castle and Folk
Park.

Clifton Guest House,
Ennis Road, Limerick. 1 acre
landscaped gardens. Multi-
channel TV. Trouser press,
hair dryer. Direct dial
telephone.
Open: All year (not Xmas)
061 451166 Mr Powell **Fax: 061 451224**
D: Fr €35.00 **S:** Fr €50.00
Beds: 3F 3D 4T 6S **Baths:** 16 En
☎ P (22) TV ▥ cc

Trebor, *Ennis Road, Limerick.* Near city centre, bus stop for airport/Bunratty at door.
Open: Apr to Nov
061 454632 (also fax) Mrs McSweeney
reborhouse@eircom.net
D: Fr €27.00-€30.00 **S:** Fr €39.00-€42.50
Beds: 1F 2D 2T **Baths:** 5 En
⌂ P (6) ☒ ☒ ▥, ▪ cc

Acacia Cottage, *2 Foxfield, Dooradoyle Rd, Limerick, Co Limerick.* Cosy, comfortable cottage-style home. Spacious rooms.
Open: All Year
061 304757 (also fax) Mrs Dundon
D: Fr €29.00
Beds: 2D 1T 1S **Baths:** 2 Ensuite
⌂ (4) P (4) ⌯ ☒ ☒ ▥, ▪

Railway Hotel, *Limerick.* Family-run hotel with restaurant, adjacent to rail and bus station.
Open: All Year (not Xmas)
061 413653 Ms Collins **Fax: 061 419762**
D: Fr €37.00-€38.00
Beds: 1F 8D 7T 8S **Baths:** 24 Ensuite 3 Shared
⌂ P (6) ☒ ⼤ ✕ ☒ ▥, ▪

Coonagh Lodge, *Coonagh East, Limerick.* Family run home. Quiet river setting, spacious gardens and parking.
Open: All Year (not Xmas)
061 327050 Mrs Carroll
coonagh@iol.ie
D: Fr €28.00
Beds: 3F 2D 1T **Baths:** 6 En ☒ ▥, ▪ cc

Ennis House, *2 Inagh Drive, Caherdavin, Limerick.* Comfortable house on Shannon/Bunratty Castle Road, beside Green Hills Hotel.
Open: All Year (not Xmas)
061 326257 (also fax) Noreen O'Toole
D: Fr €23.00-€25.50 **S:** Fr €29.00-€32.00
Beds: 2F 1T 1D 1S **Baths:** 4 En 1 Pr 1 Sh
⌂ P (5) ☒ ⼤ ▥, ⅋ ▪ cc

Dromatha, *Ennis Road, Limerick.* Large detached house in 1 acre of gardens with pond and waterfall.
Open: April to Nov
061 326302 Mrs O'Driscoll
D: Fr €23.00 **S:** Fr €25.50
Beds: 2D 1T 1S **Baths:** 1 En 2 Pr
⌂ P (12) ⌯ ☒ ⼤ ▥,

Moyrhee, *Phares Road, Meelick, Limerick.* Quiet bungalow, elevated site, off main Limerick-Shannon road. All bedrooms look onto Clare hills.
Open: All Year (not Xmas)
061326300 & 087 2696615 (M) Mrs Callinan
D: Fr €29.00
Beds: 1F 1D 1T **Baths:** 3 Ensuite
⌂ P ⌯ ☒ ⼤ ✕ ☒ ▥, ▪

Newcastle West

R2833

Ballingowan House, *Gortroe, Newcastle West, Co Limerick.* Luxurious pink Georgian house. N21 - halfway stop between Shannon/Killarney.
Open: All Year (not Xmas)
069 62341 Mrs O'Brien
D: Fr €25.50
Beds: 2F 2D 1T 1S **Baths:** 6 Ensuite
⌂ P (6) ☒ ▥,

Patrickswell

R5249

Laurel Lodge, *Adare Rd, Newboro, Patrickswell, Limerick.* Pamper yourself in our luxurious country home. Award-winning gardens.
Open: Apr to Oct
061 355059 (also fax) Mrs Buckley
D: Fr €28.00
Beds: 1F 1D 1T 1S **Baths:** 3 En
⌂ P ☒ ⼤ ▥, ▪

Carnlea House, *Caher Road, Patrickswell, Limerick.* Spacious bungalow - 3 km from Patrickswell. Ideal stopover. Friendly atmosphere. Highly recommended.
Open: Easter to Oct
061 302902 Mr Geary
gearydavid@tinet.ie
D: Fr €21.50-€24.00 **S:** Fr €32.00-€38.00
Beds: 1F 2D 1T 1S **Baths:** 2 En 1 Sh
P ⌯ ☒ ▥, & cc

RATES

D = Price range per person sharing in a double or twin room

S = Price range for a single room

Lurriga Lodge, *Patrickswell, Limerick.*
Delightful country house set in secluded
landscaped gardens. Excellent restaurants,
music pubs.
Open: Apr to Oct
061 355411 (also fax) Mrs Woulfe
woulfe@esatclear.ie
D: Fr €28.00
Beds: 2F 1D 1T **Baths:** 4 En
🛏 🅿 (8) ⊁ 📺 🍴 Ⓥ ⏷ ₺ ☕

Rockhill

R5230

Ballyteigue House, *Rockhill, Bruree,*
Kilmallock, Co Limerick. Georgian country house
set in parkland. Gracious living. Warm welcome
Open: Mar to Nov
063 90575 (also fax) Mrs Johnson
ballyteigue@eircom.net
D: Fr €35.00 **S:** Fr €35.00
Beds: 3D 1T 1S **Baths:** 4 En 1 Pr
🛏 🅿 ⊁ 📺 ✕ Ⓥ ⏷ ₺ ☕ **cc**

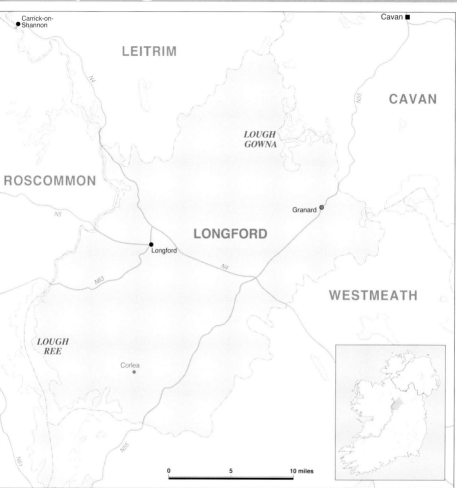

Corlea

N0862

Derrylough, *Corlea, Ballymahon, Longford.*
Comfortable farmhouse, tranquil surroundings,
spacious gardens, food from farm and garden.
Open: Easter to Sep
043 22126 Mr & Mrs Gerety **Fax:** 043 22040
D: Fr €29.00
Beds: 1D 1T 1S **Baths:** 1 Shared
⌖ P TV ✕ V ▥ ☎ cc

BEDROOMS

D = Double   S = Single

T = Twin   F = Family

RAIL ⇌

Longford is on the *Sligo to Dublin (Connolly)* line.
For timetable details phone **Irish Rail**: 01 8366222.

BUS 🚌

Longford to Dublin (3 daily) -
tel. **Bus Eireann** on 01 8366111.

TOURIST INFORMATION OFFICE
i

Market Square, **Longford** (Jun to Aug), 043 46566.

Granard

N3381

Toberphelim House, *Granard, Longford.*
Georgian family home situated 2km from Granard
on working farm.
Open: Mar to Sep
043 86568 (also fax) Mr & Mrs Smyth
tober@eircom.net
D: Fr €40.00
Beds: 2F 1T **Baths:** 2 En 1 Pr
🛏 🅿 (5) 📺 ✕ 🆅 ▦ **cc**

Bellurgan

0910

Daru, *Old Road, Bellurgan, Dundalk, Co Louth.*
Welcoming home close to Ballymascanlon Hotel,
olf course, Fitzpatrick's pub/restaurant.
Open: All year (not Xmas)
42 9371408 & 087 6481117 (M) Mrs Roddy
arubandb@eircom.net
: Fr €23.00-€26.00 **S:** Fr €25.00-€27.00
Beds: 2D 1T **Baths:** 3 En
(4) 🗲 📺 🛏 🔌 cc

Carlingford

J1811 🍴 *Village Inn, Fitzpatrick's, Carlingford Arms*

Viewpoint Guest House, *Omeath Road,*
Carlingford, Dundalk, Co Louth. Viewpoint - motel-
style guest house, spectacular mountain and sea
views. Highly recommended.
Open: All Year
042 9373149 Mr Woods **Fax: 042 9373733**
D: Fr €35.00
Beds: 2F 2D 2T **Baths:** 8 En
🐕 🅿 (9) 🗲 🛏 🔌 cc

RAIL ⇌

Dundalk & **Drogheda** are both on the main **Dublin (Connolly) to Belfast** line. For details phone **Irish Rail** on 01 8366222.

BUS 🚌

There are regular services to **Dublin** & **Belfast** from both **Dundalk** & **Drogheda**. Tel. **Bus Eireann** on 01 8366111.

TOURIST INFORMATION OFFICE ℹ

Jocelyn St, **Dundalk** (open all year), 042 9335484.

Mourne View, Belmont, Carlingford, Dundalk, Co Louth. Spacious family run home. Tranquil location. Panoramic views of mountains.
Open: All year
042 9373551 (also fax) Mrs Grills
info@mourneviewcarlingford.com
www.mourneviewcarlingford.com
D: Fr €27.00-€32.00 **S:** Fr €32.00-€42.50
Beds: 2F 1D 3T **Baths:** 6 En
⌂ 🅿 (5) ⅟ 🛏 ⚓ cc

Shalom, Ghan Road, Carlingford, Dundalk, Co Louth. Situated in medieval town overlooking Cooley Mountains beside the shores of Carlingford Lough.
Open: All year (not Xmas)
042 9373151 Mrs Woods
kevinwoods@eircom.net www.jackiewoods.com
D: Fr €26.00 **S:** Fr €38.50
Beds: 2F 4D **Baths:** 6 En
⌂ 🅿 (9) 📺 🛏 ⚓

RATES

D = Price range per person sharing in a double or twin room

S = Price range for a single room

O1684

The Cross Garden, Ganderstown, Clogherhead, Drogheda, Co Louth. Overlooking Irish sea, dormer on elevated site. All rooms private facilities. Warm welcome.
Open: All year
041 9822675 Mrs McEvoy
D: Fr €25.50 **S:** Fr €36.00
Beds: 3F **Baths:** 2 En 1 Pr
⌂ 🅿 (8) 📺 🛏 ⚓

J0407

Failte, Dublin Road, Dundalk, Co Louth.
Open: All year (no Xmas/New Year)
Grades: BF Appro
042 9335152
www.failteguesthouse.eircom.net
D: Fr €30.00 **S:** Fr €40.00
Beds: 3T 7D 2S **Baths:** 7 En 1 Sh
⌂ 🅿 (15) 📺 ✕ 🅥 🛏 ⚓ cc
Central location in Dundalk town centre. Golf & beach 4 km.

Inisfree Guest House, Carrick Road, Dundalk, Co Louth. Early C20th town house. Close to town centre and train station.
Open: All year (not Xmas)
042 9334912 Rosie Bell
info@innisfreeguesthouse.com
D: Fr €27.00-€35.00 **S:** Fr €35.00-€45.00
Beds: 3F 4D **Baths:** 5 En
⌂ 🅿 (9) ⅟ 📺 🅥 🛏 ⚓ cc

Daru, Old Road, Bellurgan, Dundalk, Co Louth. Welcoming home close to Ballymascanlon Hotel, golf course, Fitzpatrick's pub/ restaurant.
Open: All year (not Xmas)
042 9371408 & 087 6481117 (M) Mrs Roddy
darubandb@eircom.net
D: Fr €23.00-€26.00 **S:** Fr €25.00-€27.00
Beds: 2D 1T **Baths:** 3 En
🅿 (4) ⅟ 📺 🛏 ⚓ cc

Lynolan House,
Muhaharlin Road, Dundalk, Co Louth. Family-run home - ideal base for touring North East region.
Open: All year
042 9336553 **(also fax)** Mrs Carolan
lynolan@indigo.ie www.indigo.ie/~lynolan
D: Fr €26.00-€28.00 **S:** Fr €28.00-€37.00
Beds: 4T 2D **Baths:** 5 En
🖃 (8) ✗ 📺 🛏 🔟, ■ cc

Pinewoods, *Dublin Road, Dundalk, Co Louth.*
Friendly welcome in modern comfortable surroundings.
Open: All Year
042 9321295 Mrs Murphy
almurphy@eircom.net
D: Fr €25.50-€33.00 **S:** Fr €32.00-€44.50
Beds: 1F 3D 2D **Baths:** 5 En 1 Pr
🖢 🖃 📺 🔟, ■ cc

Riverstown Farmhouse, *Ballygoley, Riverstown, Dundalk, Co Louth.* Situated on the Tain Walk in the Cooley Mountains. Children's playground.
Open: All year
042 9376300 Mrs Breen
riverstownfarmhouse@eircom.net
D: Fr €23.00-€26.00 **S:** Fr €28.00-€30.00
Beds: 2F 2D **Baths:** 3 En 1 Pr
🖢 🖃 (4) ✗ 📺 🔟, 🕭 ■ cc

Rosemount,
Dublin Road, Dundalk, Co Louth. Luxury designer home on N1, prize winning garden, convenient to Fairways Hotel and Dundalk Golf Course, Dublin Airport 45 mins. New Grange 20 mins. Good breakfast, large private parking, warm hospitality extended.
Open: All year **Grades:** AA 4 Diamond
042 9335878 **(also fax)** Mrs Meehan
D: Fr €30.00 **S:** Fr €40.00
Beds: 2F 1T 6D **Baths:** 9 En
🖢 🖃 🛏 📺 🔟, 🕭 ✳ ■

Monasterboice
O0382

Tullyesker Country House, *N1, Dundalk Road, Monasterboice, Drogheda, Co Louth.*
Major guides recommended, extensive breakfast menu, Dublin Airport 25 miles.
Open: Feb to Nov
041 9830430 **&** 041 9832624 Mrs McDonnell **Fax:** 041 9832624
D: Fr €33.00
Beds: 1F 2D 2T **Baths:** 5 En
🖢 (10) 🖃 (20) 📺 🔟, ■

L7399

St Annes, *Achill Sound, Westport, Co Mayo.*
5 mins from House of Prayer. Close to scenic
drives, Blue Flag beaches.
Open: All Year
098 45821 Ms McHugh
D: Fr €23.00-€25.50 **S:** Fr €20.50-€23.00
Beds: 2F 2T 1D **Baths:** 4 En 1 Sh
☎ (4) 🅿 (5) ⚹ 📺 🛏 ✕ Ⓥ ▥ 🕁 ☎ cc

F6904

The Grove, *Bunnacurry, Achill Island, Westport
Co Mayo.* Georgian house in centre of Achill.
Close to Blue Flag beaches.
Open: Easter to Oct
098 47108 (also fax) Mrs McHugh
D: Fr €19.00-€23.00 **S:** Fr €21.50-€25.50
Beds: 2F 2T **Baths:** 1 En 1 Sh
☎ (1) 🅿 (8) ⚹ 📺 🛏 ✕ Ⓥ ▥ ☎

AIRPORTS ⊕

Knock Airport - 094 67222.

RAIL ⇌

Ballina, Castlebar and *Westport* are all on lines that go to *Dublin (Heuston)*. Tel. **Irish Rail** on 01 8366222.

AIR SERVICES & AIRLINES ✈

Knock to Manchester -

British Airways (for **Manx Airlines**). In the Republic tel. (freefone): 1800 626747. In Northern Ireland & the UK tel. (local rate): 08705 511155.

Knock to London (Stansted) -

Ryanair. In the Republic tel. 0818 303030; in the UK tel. 0871 2460000.

TOURIST INFORMATION OFFICES 🛈

Cathedral Road, **Ballina** (Apr to Sep), 096 70848.

Linenhall Street, **Castlebar**, 094 9021207.

Knock (May to Sep), 094 88193.

James Street, **Westport** (open all year), 098 25711.

ACHILL ISLAND — Dooagh

F6005

West End, *Dooagh, Achill Island, Westport, Co Mayo.* West End - famous for its breakfast in conservatory with ocean & mountain views.
Open: All year (not Xmas/New Year)
098 43204 Mrs McNeill
maymcneill@unison.ie
D: Fr €25.00 **S:** Fr €32.00
Beds: 2F 1T 1D **Baths:** 3 En
🛏 🅿 (5) ⊬ 📺 🎇 Ⅴ ▥ ♨ cc

Teach Cruachan, *Dooagh, Achill Island, Westport, Co Mayo.* Warm welcome guaranteed, near Europe's highest sea cliffs. Enjoy great food in our seafront restaurant. Home-baking and seafood from our own nets our speciality. Short stroll to pubs. Choice of breakfasts. Bus terminus 200m. Guided tour of Achill Island arranged.
Open: All year (not Xmas)
098 43301 Mrs Lavelle
rlavelle@esatclear.ie www.achill-island.com
D: Fr €22.50-€27.50 **S:** Fr €27.50-€34.00
Beds: 3D 2T **Baths:** 4 En 1 Sh
🛏 🅿 (20) ⊬ 📺 ✗ Ⅴ ▥ ♿ cc

ACHILL ISLAND — Keel

F6305

Achill Isle House, *Newtown, Keel, Achill Island, Westport, Co Mayo.*
Open: Apr to Nov
098 43355 Mrs Mangan
achillisle@eircom.net
D: Fr €25.00-€30.00 **S:** Fr €36.00-€40.00
Beds: 4F 3D 1T **Baths:** 7 En 1 Sh
🛏 (2) 🅿 (12) 📺 ▥
Modern purpose-built B&B. Fantastic views overlooking Keel Bay area. Ideal location for painting, golf, hillwalking, sea/lake fishing, relaxing on any of the Blue Flag beaches. Choice of breakfasts. On main bus route. Packed lunches available on request.

Groigin Mor, *Pollagh, Keel, Achill Island, Westport, Co Mayo.* Bungalow with breathtaking Atlantic views, 5-min walk Keel and Dooagh, pubs, music.
Open: All year **Grades:** BF Approv
098 43385 & 086 3821764 (M) Mrs Quinn
groigin_mor@hotmail.com
D: Fr €30.00 **S:** Fr €40.00
Beds: 2D 1T **Baths:** 3 En
🛏 🅿 (6) ⊬ 📺 🎇 ✗ Ⅴ ▥ ♨ cc

Achill Head Hotel, *Keel, Achill Island, Westport, Co Mayo.* Close blue flag beaches. Outdoor activities on lake close by. 9-hole golf course.
Open: All Year (not Xmas)
098 43108 & 098 43131 Mrs Heaney **Fax: 098 43388**
D: Fr €40.00
Beds: 3F 14D 7T 1S **Baths:** 25 Ensuite
🛏 🅿 TV ⊼ ✕ Ⅴ ▥ ▪

Aghagower
M0380

St Catherine's, *Lugrevagh, Aghagower, Westport, Co Mayo.* Modern bungalow in peaceful country, located overlooking Croagh Patrick. Close to Westport town.
Open: Mar to Oct
098 26812 & 087 2052160 (M) Mrs Moran
stcatherinesbandb@eircom.net
D: Fr €28.00-€30.00 **S:** Fr €38.00-€40.00
Beds: 2F 2D **Baths:** 3 En 1 Pr
🛏 🅿 TV Ⅴ ▥ ▪

Balla
M2584

Forest View, *Station Road, Balla, Castlebar, Co Mayo.* A beautiful home situated in a picturesque and scenic area.
Open: All Year
094 9365181 Mrs Rogers
D: Fr €23.00 **S:** Fr €25.50
Beds: 1T 4D **Baths:** 2 En 1 Pr 1 Sh
🛏 🅿 (5) TV Ⅴ ▥ ⅋ ✳ ♨ ▪

Ballina
G2418

Hogans American House, *Station Road, Ballina, Co Mayo.* Beautifully restored town centre hotel, private garden, 2 mins bus/rail stations.
Open: All Year (not Xmas/New Year)
096 21350 Mr Hogan **Fax: 096 71882**
D: Fr €25.50-€38.00 **S:** Fr €32.00-€51.00
Beds: 4D 8T 4S **Baths:** 16 En
🛏 (10) 🅿 (6) TV ✕ Ⅴ ▥ ▪ cc

The Rocks, *Foxford Road, Ballina, Co Mayo.*
Open: All year
096 22140
Mrs Cumiskey
therocks@eircom.net
www.therocks.net
D: Fr €25.00 **S:** Fr €35.00
Beds: 2F 4T **Baths:** 6 En
🛏 (1) 🅿 (20) ⅋ TV ⊼ Ⅴ ▥ 🚻 ✳ ▪
Designed and built by the present owners offering hospitality and atmosphere. All rooms ensuite with hairdryers and TV. Tea-coffee room and guest lounge. Large landscaped gardens, barbecue. Fishing arranged on Lough Conn & River Moy. Sea Fishing. Touring North West.

Ashley House, *Ardoughan, Ballina, Co Mayo.* Highly recommended: peaceful country surroundings, landscaped gardens, 1km Ballina Town.
Open: All Year
096 22799 & 088 2141889 (M) Mrs Murray
D: Fr €25.50
Beds: 1F 2D 1T **Baths:** 4 En
🛏 🅿 (6) TV ▥ ▪

Moy Call, *Creggs Road, Ballina, Co Mayo.* A warm welcome awaits you at Moy Call, overlooking the River Moy.
Open: May to Oct
096 22440 Mrs O'Toole
D: Fr €23.00-€25.50 **S:** Fr €30.50-€33.00
Beds: 3F 1D **Baths:** 3 En 1 Pr
🛏 🅿 (5) ⅋ TV ✕ Ⅴ ▥ ▪ cc

Belvedere House, *Foxford Road, Ballina, Co Mayo.* Georgian style home, 10 mins walking distance to town, bus, train. Cable TV.
Open: All Year (not Xmas)
096 22004 Mrs Reilly
D: Fr €25.50
Beds: 2F 3D 2T 1S **Baths:** 4 Ensuite 1 Shared
🅿 ⅋ TV ⊼ ▥ ▪

Errigal, *Killala Road, Ballina, Co Mayo.* Modern bungalow, walking distance from town. 30km from the famous Ceide Fields.
Open: Apr to Oct
096 22563 Mrs Treacy **Fax: 096 70968**
D: Fr €25.50
Beds: 2F 1T **Baths:** 3 Ensuite 1 Private
🛏 🅿 (4) TV ⊼ Ⅴ ▥ 🚻 ▪

Ballinrobe

M1964

Hillcrest, *Clonbur Road, Ballinrobe, Co Mayo.* Modern bungalow, peaceful location beside Mask, Carra and Corrib lakes.
Open: All year (not Xmas)
094 9541456 Mrs O'Donnell
D: Fr €25.00-€30.00 **S:** Fr €35.00
Beds: 1D 2T **Baths:** 2 En 1 Sh
🄿 (4) ⅍ 📺 ⅏. 🖦

Friars Quarter House, *Convent Road, Ballinrobe, Co Mayo.* Elegant house in spacious gardens, period furnishings. 0.75km from town, N84.
Open: All Year (not Xmas)
094 9541154 Mr & Mrs Kavanagh
D: Fr €25.50
Beds: 4F 1D 2T **Baths:** 1 En
🌜 🄿 📺 🐾 ⅏. 🕭 cc

Ballycastle

G1037

Suantrai, *Ballycastle, Ballina, Co Mayo.* Olde worlde-style cottage incorporating all modern conveniences within.
Open: Jun to Aug
096 43040 Mr & Mrs Chambers
D: Fr €21.50 **S:** Fr €25.50
Beds: 1F 2D **Baths:** 3 En
🌜 🄿 (4) ⅍ 📺 🅥 ⅏.

Ballyhaunis

M5079

Errit, *Carrowbehy, Ballyhaunis, Co Mayo.* Lakeland District. Coarse and game fishing. Off N60.
Open: Apr to Sep
0907 49015 Mrs Regan
D: Fr €20.50 **S:** Fr €23.00
Beds: 1T 2D **Baths:** 3 En
🌜 🄿 (8) 📺 🐾 ⅏.

Please respect a B&B's wishes regarding children, animals and smoking

Bangor Erris

F8523

Hillcrest, *Main Street, Bangor Erris, Ballina, Co Mayo.* Fishing locally - Carrowmore Lake, Owenmore River. Carne golf club 13m, Ceade Fields 2m.
Open: All Year
097 83494 Mrs Cosgrove
D: Fr €27.00
Beds: 2D 2T **Baths:** 2 En 2 Sh
🌜 🄿 📺 ✕ 🅥 ⅏. cc

Belderrig

F9940

The Yellow Road B&B, *Belderrig, Ballina, Co Mayo.* Situated 10km west of Ceide Fields.
Open: All Year
096 43125 Mrs McHale
D: Fr €22.00
Beds: 1F 1T 2D **Baths:** 2 Ensuite 1 Private
🄿 📺 🐾 ✕ 🅥 ⅏. ⅖

Belmullet

F7032

Highdrift, *Ballina Road, Belmullet, Co Mayo.* Modern bungalow in quiet scenic surroundings overlooking Broadhaven Bay.
Open: Apr to Oct
097 81260 (also fax) Mrs Reilly
D: Fr €25.50
Beds: 2F 2D 1T **Baths:** 3 En 1 Sh
🌜 (3) 🄿 (6) 📺 🐾 ✕ 🅥 ⅏. 🕭

Castlebar

M1490

Dun Mhuire, *5 Quinn's Row, Westport Road, Castlebar, Co Mayo.* Modern, comfortable and welcoming - ideal touring base for the West.
Open: Easter to Oct
094 9021395 Mrs Quinn
D: Fr €26.00-€28.00 **S:** Fr €36.00-€38.00
Beds: 2D 3T **Baths:** 5 En
🌜 (4) 🄿 (6) ⅍ 📺 ⅏. 🕭

Windermere House, *Westport Road, Castlebar,*
Co Mayo. Luxurious spacious home between
Westport/Castlebar. Bilberry lake 1km - boat hire.
Open: All year
094 9023329 Mrs McGrath
windermerehse@eircom.net
D: Fr €25.00-€27.00 **S:** Fr €38.00-€40.00
Beds: 2F 1D 1T 1S **Baths:** 4 En
🛏 🅿 📺 ✕ 🏚 🔌 cc

Millhill House, *Westport Road, Castlebar, Co*
Mayo. Comfortable accommodation. Guest
lounge with TV. Tea/coffee making facilities.
Open: May to Oct
094 9024279 Mrs Scahill
millhill@eircom.net homepage.eircom.net/~millhill
D: Fr €23.00-€25.50 **S:** Fr €33.00-€35.00
Beds: 1T 2D **Baths:** 2 En 1 Pr
🛏 🅿 📺 🏚 🔌

Devard, *Westport Road, Castlebar, Co Mayo.*
Bungalow with award-winning gardens. TV,
coffee/tea, hairdryers in bedrooms.
Open: All Year
094 9023462 (also fax) Mrs Ward
devard@esat.clear.ie
D: Fr €18.00-€24.00 **S:** Fr €24.00-€32.00
Beds: 1F 2D 2T **Baths:** 5 En
🛏 🅿 📺 🐎 🏚 ♿ 🔌

Rocksberry B&B, *Ballymacragh, Westport*
Road, Castlebar, Co Mayo. Rocksberry also do
boat hire on local lakes. Within 1 hour of a drive
you can visit Knock shrine, Achill Island,
Ballintuber Abbey, Cong and on to Galway. A day
trip by boat to Clare Island is a dream.
Open: Feb to Nov
094 9027254 (also fax) Mrs Walsh
D: Fr €23.00-€25.50 **S:** Fr €38.50
Beds: 1F 2D 1T **Baths:** 4 En
🛏 🅿 ✂ 📺 📹 🏚 🔌 cc

G1112

Kilmurray House, *Castlehill, Crossmolina,*
Ballina, Co Mayo. Large country house, scenic
area. Cycling, angling, walking, music. Pub and
restaurant food locally.
Open: Apr to Oct
096 31227 Mrs Moffat
D: Fr €27.00
Beds: 3F 1D 1T 1S **Baths:** 4 Ensuite 2 Shared
🛏 🅿 📺 ✕ 📹 🏚 ♿ 🔌

M1554

Hill View Farm, *Drumsheel, Cong, Co Mayo.*
Open: Feb to Nov
094 9546500 (also fax) Mrs O'Toole
hillviewcong@hotmail.com
D: Fr €26.50-€30.00 **S:** Fr €39.00-€42.00
Beds: 1F 2T/D **Baths:** 3 En
🛏 🅿 (6) ✂ 📺 🏚 🔌
Warm welcome in a modern farmhouse situated
between Loughs Corrib/Mask, in a quiet, peaceful
scenic location with magnificent views of
Connemara Mountains and old castle, 2 km from
Cong. Signposted in Cong Village near Esso
petrol/diesel station. Home baking.

Villa Pio, *Gortacurra Cross, Cong, Claremorris,*
Co Mayo. Near 'Quiet Man' film locations,
Ashford Castle, Cong/Ballintubber Abbeys,
Ashford Castle, Giant's Cave.
Open: All Year
094 9546403 (also fax) Mrs Holian
D: Fr €25.50
Beds: 1F 1D 1T 1S **Baths:** 2 En 1Private 1 Sh
🛏 (1) 🅿 (4) ✂ 📺 📹 🏚 🔌

Breezy Heights, *Houndswood Cross, Cong,*
Claremorris, Co Mayo. Modern country home
situated in scenic area overlooking Lough Corrib
and Connemara Mountains.
Open: All Year (not Xmas)
094 9546212 (also fax) Mrs Moran
D: Fr €26.00
Beds: 2T 2D **Baths:** 4 Ensuite
🛏 🅿 (4) 📺 ✕ 📹 🏚 🔌

G1317

Shalom House, *Gortnor Abbey, Crossmolina,*
Ballina, Co Mayo. Nice bungalow close to Loughs
Conn & Moy. Excellent fishing area.
Open: May to Sep
096 31230 (also fax) Mrs Cowman
D: Fr €22.00-€24.00 **S:** Fr €25.00-€30.00
Beds: 1T 2D **Baths:** 2 En
🛏 🅿 (10) ✂ 📺 🐎 ✕ 🏚 🔌 cc

Planning a longer stay?
Always ask for any special rates

Doocastle

G5808

Rossli House, *Doocastle, Ballymote, Co Sligo.*
Family-run country home. Laundry facilities.
Open: All Year
071 9185099 Mrs Donoghue
D: Fr €25.50
Beds: 1F 5D 1T 1S **Baths:** 4 Ensuite 1 Shared
⌂ 🅿 📺 ⊁ ✕ Ⅴ 🔲 ·

Facefield

M3080

Valley Lodge, *Castlebar Road, Facefield, Claremorris, Co Mayo.* Working farm. Peaceful location with animals. Ideal touring base. Golf nearby.
Open: All year (not Xmas/New Year)
094 9365180 Mrs Barrett
valleylodge@eircom.net
homepage.eircom.net/~vlodge/index.htm
D: Fr €25.00-€30.00 **S:** Fr €30.00-€35.00
Beds: 5F **Baths:** 5 En
⌂ 🅿 📺 🔲 ℔ · cc

Foxford

G2703

Scenic Drive, *Pontoon Road, Foxford, Ballina, Co Mayo.* Excellent location for keen anglers close to town.
Open: All Year (not Xmas)
094 9256614 Mr & Mrs O'Connell
D: Fr €22.50-€25.50
Beds: 2D 2T **Baths:** 2 En 1 Sh
⌂ 🅿 (5) ⊁ 📺 ✕ 🔲 ·

Killala

G2030   🍺 *Anchor Bar*

Garden Hill Farmhouse, *Killala, Ballina, Co Mayo.* Family farmhouse in quiet surroundings near river, lakes, seaside and fishing.
Open: Jun to Sep
096 32331 (also fax) Mr Munnelly
D: Fr €24.00
Beds: 4F 2D 2T **Baths:** 4 En
⌂ 🅿 (10) Ⅴ 🔲 ·

Avondale House, *Pier Road, Killala, Ballina, Co Mayo.* Beautiful dormer bungalow, newly refurbished, overlooking Killala Bay, landscaped garden for visitors. Barbecue can be used to cook your catch after fishing. Recommended as one of top ten favourite B&Bs in the 'Best Bed & Breakfast Guide to Ireland'.
Open: All year (not Xmas/New Year)
096 32229 Ms Bilbow
bilbow@eircom.net
D: Fr €21.50-€23.49 **S:** Fr €25.93-€27.93
Beds: 1F 2D 1T **Baths:** 2 En 2 Sh
⌂ 🅿 (2) ⊁ 📺 ℔ ✕ 🔲

Kilmeena

L9689

Seapoint House, *Kilmeena, Westport, Co Mayo.* Large country house overlooking the sea. Quiet location. Signposted on N59 Westport-Newport road.
Open: May to Oct
098 41254 & 098 41903 O'Malley Family **Fax: 098 41903**
D: Fr €28.00-€32.00 **S:** Fr €35.00-€40.00
Beds: 2F 2D 2T **Baths:** 6 En

Kilsallagh

L8581

Achill View, *Kilsallagh, Westport, Co Mayo.* Early C20th working farmhouse with interior renovated to top standard.
Open: All Year (not Xmas/New Year)
098 66433 Mrs Gannon
margannon@hotmail.com
D: Fr €19.00-€23.00 **S:** Fr €23.00-€25.50
Beds: 1F 1T 2D **Baths:** 2 En 1 Pr 1 Sh
⌂ 🅿 ⊁ 📺 ✕ Ⅴ 🔲 ℔ ·

Kiltimagh

M3489

Hillcrest, *Kilkelly Road, Kiltimagh, Claremorris, Co Mayo.* Modern bungalow. Spacious grounds, peat fire. Five minutes' drive Knock shrine, international airport.
Open: All Year (not Xmas)
094 9381112 Mrs Carney
D: Fr €25.50
Beds: 6T **Baths:** 6 Ensuite
⌂ 🅿 ⊁ 📺 ℔ ✕ Ⅴ 🔲 ·

Knock

M3983

Burren, *Kiltimagh Road, Knock, Claremorris, Co Mayo.* 1km west on R323 off N1Y. All ground floor rooms.
Open: June to Sep
094 9388362 (also fax) Mrs Carney
carneymaureene@eircom.net
D: Fr €25.00-€30.00 **S:** Fr €30.00-€40.00
Beds: 2F 1T 1D **Baths:** 4 En
⌂ 🅿 (4) 📺 📹 🖥 cc

Windermere, *Churchfield, Knock, Claremorris, Co Mayo.* Quiet country location, yet 2 mins' drive from Knock Shrine.
Open: Easter to Oct
094 9388326 & 087 2927723 (M) Mrs Morris
D: Fr €24.00-€25.00 **S:** Fr €28.00-€35.00
Beds: 2D 1T 1F **Baths:** 3 En 1 Sh
⌂ 🅿 (6) 📺 🍴 ✕ 📹 🖥 ♿

Eskerville, *Claremorris Road, Knock, Claremorris, Co Mayo.* Dormer bungalow. Family run. Mature gardens, private car park. Situated on N17.
Open: All Year
094 9388413 Mr & Mrs Taaffe
D: Fr €25.50
Beds: 1F 2D 1T 2S **Baths:** 4 Ensuite 1 Shared
⌂ (1) 🅿 (8) 📺 🍴 ✕ 📹 🖥 ♿ ❊ ▪

Liscarney

L9876

Moher House, *Liscarney, Westport, Co Mayo.* Award-winning gardens, breakfast, dinner menu, lakeside, warm hospitality, fishing, walking.
Open: Oct
098 21360 Mrs O'Malley
D: Fr €27.00
Beds: 2F 2D 2T **Baths:** 3 En 2 Pr 1 Sh
⌂ 🅿 (6) 📺 🍴 ✕ 📹 🖥 ♿ cc

Oughty Lodge, *Oughty, Drummond, Liscarney, Westport, Co Mayo.* Modern comfortable bungalow in Drummin valley, adjacent to Western Way.
Open: May to Sep
098 21929 Mrs Friel
D: Fr €25.00
Beds: 2D 1T **Baths:** 2 Ensuite 1 Shared
⌂ (4) 🅿 (3) ⚬ 📺 ✕ 📹 🖥 ♿

Louisburgh

L8080

Whitethorns, *Bunowen, Louisburgh, Westport, Co Mayo.* Bungalow in scenic location off R335 opposite Roman Catholic church.
Open: May to Sep
098 66062 Mrs McNamara
D: Fr €26.00
Beds: 1F 2D 1T **Baths:** 4 Ensuite
🅿 📺 🖥

Rivervilla, *Shraugh, Louisburgh, Westport, Co Mayo.* Secluded riverside farmhouse in scenic area. Ideal touring centre for Mayo/Galway.
Open: May to Nov
098 66246 (also fax) Miss O'Malley
D: Fr €26.00
Beds: 5F 2D 1T 2S **Baths:** 3 En 2 Pr 3 Sh
⌂ 🅿 (8) 📺 🍴 📹 🖥 ▪

Cuaneen House, *Carramore, Louisburgh, Westport, Co Mayo.* 3 mins' walk to Blue Flag beach. Views from windows.
Open: Apr to Oct
098 66460 Mrs Sammon
D: Fr €24.00-€27.00 **S:** Fr €18.00-€27.00
Beds: 1F 1T 1D 2S **Baths:** 2 En 1 Pr 1 Sh
⌂ 🅿 ✕ 🖥

Mulranny

L8296

Moynish Guest House, *Mulranny, Westport, Co Mayo.* Spectacular location, ideal for golf, fishing, walking holidays.
Open: All year (not Xmas)
098 36116 Mr Moran
D: Fr €25.50-€32.00 **S:** Fr €25.50-€32.00
Beds: 2F 2D 2T 2S **Baths:** 6 En 2 Sh
⌂ 🅿 (10) 📺 🍴 ✕ 📹 🖥 ▪ cc

Murrisk

L9282

Highgrove, *Murrisk, Westport, Co Mayo.* Peaceful scenic area at Croagh Patrick. Restaurants, bars 2 mins.
Open: May to Sep
098 64819 (also fax) Mrs Churchill-Gavin
mgavin@unison.ie
D: Fr €27.00-€29.00 **S:** Fr €29.00-€32.00
Beds: 1F 1T 1D 1S **Baths:** 2 En 1 Pr 1 Sh
⌂ (8) 🅿 (6) 📺 🖥 ▪ cc

Bertra House, *Thornhill, Murrisk, Westport, Co Mayo.* Seaside family-run farmhouse 3 minutes' walk to long sandy award-winning Blue Flag beach.
Open: Easter to mid-Nov
098 64833 Mrs Gill
D: Fr €28.00
Beds: 2F 1T 2D **Baths:** 4 Ensuite 1 Private
☺ (5) 🅿 (6) 🍴 📺 ⬛, ⚓

L9894

Anchor House, *The Quay, Newport, Westport, Co Mayo.* Modern home overlooking river on the Clew Bay. Private parking, nice garden.
Open: All year (not Xmas)
098 41178 (also fax) Mrs McGovern
maureenanchorhouse@hotmail.com
D: Fr €25.50-€32.00 **S:** Fr €36.00-€44.50
Beds: 2T 4D 1S **Baths:** 5 En 2 Sh
🅿 📺 ⬛, ⚓ cc

De Bille House, *Main Street, Newport, Westport, Co Mayo.* Beautifully restored Georgian house with antique furnishings in Newport town.
Open: Jun to Oct
098 41145 Mrs Chambers **Fax: 098 41777**
pchambers@onu.ie
D: Fr €25.50
Beds: 5F **Baths:** 4 En 1 Sh
☺ 🅿 (8) 📺 ✕ ⬛, ⚓

M0084

Cedar Lodge, *Kings Hill, Newport Road N59, Westport, Co Mayo.*
Open: Feb to Dec
098 25417 Mr & Mrs Flynn
mflynn@esatclear.ie www.cedarlodgewestport.com
D: Fr €28.00-€30.00 **S:** Fr €40.00-€45.00
Beds: 1F 1D 2T **Baths:** 3 En 1 Pr
☺ (10) 🅿 (4) 🍴 📺 📺 ⬛, ⚓ cc
Enjoy Irish hospitality with Peter and Maureen at their peaceful bungalow, landscaped gardens awards 1997, relax on the patio, 6 min walk to town, ideal base for golf, touring etc. Breakfast menu, recommended Frommer Best B&B, Guide du Routard, vouchers accepted.

Brook Lodge, *Deerpark East, Newport Road, Westport, Co Mayo.*
Open: Mar to Oct
098 26654 Mrs Reddington
brooklodgebandb@eircom.net
homepage.eircom.net/~brooklodgebandb
D: Fr €26.00-€28.00 **S:** Fr €38.00
Beds: 3F 1D **Baths:** 4 Pr
☺ (6) 🅿 📺 📺 ⬛, cc
Modern house in quiet residential area, 5 mins' walk from town centre. A warm welcome awaits you with tea or coffee on arrival - ideal base for touring West Coast. Listed in '400 Best B&Bs in Ireland'.

Hazelbrook, *Deerpark East, Newport Road, Westport, Co Mayo.*
Open: All year
098 26865 & 086 8647148 Mr & Mrs Cafferkey
hazelbrookhouse@eircom.net
D: Fr €26.00-€28.00 **S:** Fr €38.00-€40.00
Beds: 2F 2D 1T 1S **Baths:** 6 En
☺ 🅿 (6) 📺 📺 ⬛, ⚓ cc
Luxurious guest house in quiet residential area. Bedrooms ensuite with TV. Tea/coffee facilities. Massage and reflexology available. Five mins' walk town centre. Ideally situated for touring West Coast. Vouchers and credit cards accepted. Garden available to guests. Golf, angling, taxis etc organised.

Two Views, *Carrawn, Westport, Co Mayo.* Friendly accommodation in peaceful surroundings. Home baking a speciality.
Open: July to Oct
098 26441 Mr & Mrs Vahey
twoviews@eircom.net
D: Fr €24.00-€26.00
Beds: 1T 2D **Baths:** 1 En 1 Pr
☺ 🅿 🐾 📺 ⬛,

Lui Na Greine, *Castlebar Road, Westport, Co Mayo.* Comfortable bungalow. Panoramic views, Clew Bay and Mountains. Spacious gardens.
Open: Easter to Oct
098 25536 Mrs Doherty
D: Fr €25.50 **S:** Fr €32.00-€33.00
Beds: 2F 2D 2T **Baths:** 4 En 2 Sh
🅿 (7) 🍴 📺 📺 ⬛, ♿ cc

Hillside Lodge, *Castlebar Road, Westport, Co Mayo.* Warm friendly family home just a short distance from Westport on N5.
Open: All Year (not Xmas/New Year)
098 25668 Mrs English
veraandjohn@unison.ie
homepage.eircom.net/~hillsidelodge
D: Fr €21.50-€24.00 **S:** Fr €28.00-€30.50
Beds: 1F 1D 1T **Baths:** 2 En 2 Pr
🛏 🅿 (8) ⚞ 📺 ✕ Ⓥ 🏮 ♿ cc

Glenderan, *Rosbeg, Westport, Co Mayo.* Luxurious, warm, comfortable house perfectly situated exploring West of Ireland.
Open: Mar to Oct
098 26585 & 098 27352
glendaran@ano.ie
www.anv.ie/glenderan/index.html
D: Fr €28.00-€29.00 **S:** Fr €40.00
Beds: 2F 2T 2D **Baths:** 4 En 2 Pr
🅿 (6) 📺 Ⓥ 🏮 ⚓ cc

Riverbank House, *Rosbeg, Westport, Co Mayo.* Peaceful country home, home baking, walking distance restaurants/pubs. T39/R335.
Open: Easter to Oct
098 25719 Mrs O'Malley
D: Fr €28.00
Beds: 1F 5D 2T **Baths:** 6 Ensuite 1 Private
🅿 (8) 📺 🏮 ⚓

Emania, *Castlebar Road, Sheeaune, Westport, Co Mayo.* Impressive two-storey dwelling in own grounds - friendly hospitable atmosphere.
Open: May to Sep
098 26459 & 098 28751 Mrs O'Reilly
piaras@anu.ie
D: Fr €25.50
Beds: 2D 1T **Baths:** 2 En
🛏 🅿 (6) ⌁ ✕ 🏮

Woodside, *Golf Course Road, Westport, Co Mayo.* Modern town house. Spacious landscaped gardens. Private car park. 10 mins' walk town centre.
Open: Mar to Oct
098 26436 Mrs Hopkins
D: Fr €24.00-€25.50 **S:** Fr €38.00
Beds: 2F 2D 1T **Baths:** 5 En
🛏 (8) 🅿 (8) ⚞ 📺 🏮 ⚓ cc

Ceol na Mara, *Lower Quay, Westport, Co Mayo.* Two storey town house. All amenities nearby. Car parking facilities.
Open: All Year (not Xmas)
098 26969 Mrs McGreal **Fax: 091 565201**
D: Fr €23.00-€25.50 **S:** Fr €25.50-€32.00
Beds: 1F 2T 3D
🛏 🅿 (8) 📺 🏮 cc

Woodview House, *Buckwaria, Westport, County Mayo.* Hospitality and comfort awaits you in modern home. Peaceful wooded area.
Open: All Year (not Xmas)
098 27879 Ms Ruane
truane@iol.ie
D: Fr €29.00
Beds: 1F 3T 1D **Baths:** 6 Ensuite
🛏 (4) 🅿 📺 🏮 ⚓

Linden Hall, *Altamount Street, Westport, Co Mayo.* Warm welcomes, good humour and a relaxed atmosphere in our spacious Edwardian town house.
Open: All Year (not Xmas)
098 27005 (also fax) Mr & Mrs Breen
lindenhall@iol.ie www.iol.ie/~lindenhall
D: Fr €21.50-€28.00 **S:** Fr €29.00-€38.00
Beds: 1F 3D **Baths:** 4 En 📺 Ⓥ 🏮 ⚓

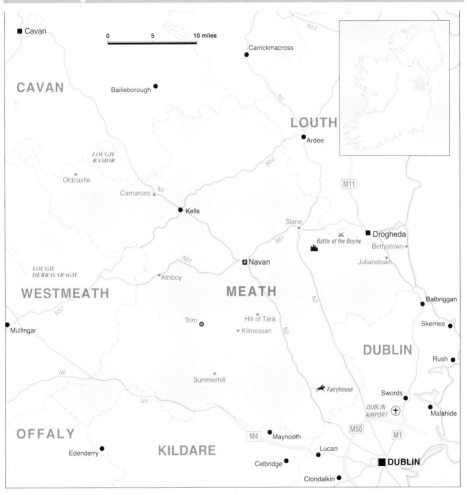

Athboy

RAIL ⇌

Navan to *Dublin* *(once an hour).*

Tel. **Irish Rail** on 01 8366222.

TOURIST INFORMATION OFFICES
i

Railway Street, **Navan,** 046 9073426.

Mill Street, **Trim** (May to Sep), 046 9437111.

Athboy

N7163

Woodtown House, *Athboy, Co Meath.*
Early Georgian house, built 1725. Fabulous
atmosphere. Comfortable bedrooms. No TV,
phones - what bliss!
Open: April to Sept
046 9435022 (also fax) Ms Finnegan
woodtown@iol.ie www.iol.ie/~woodtown
D: Fr €25.50-€32.00 **S:** Fr €32.00-€38.00
Beds: 2T 1D **Baths:** 2 En 1 Pr
ॐ (12) **P** (3) ⊁ ⊡ ✕ Ⅴ ⊞ ≥ cc

Bettystown

O1573

Eleventh Tee House, *Golf Links Road, Bettystown, Drogheda, Co Louth.* Modern house in beautiful garden setting overlooking golf course. 5 minutes' walk large beach.
Open: All Year (not Xmas)
041 9827613 Mrs Nallen **Fax: 041 9828150**
D: Fr €32.00
Beds: 1F 1T 1D 1S **Baths:** 3 Ensuite 1 Private
⛺ (10) 🅿 (5) ⅙ 📺 ⬛ ⬛

Carnaross

N6978

Lennoxbrook, *Carnaross, Kells, Co Meath.* Wonderful homely old country house. Trees and garden stream complete the idyllic setting.
Open: All Year (not Xmas)
046 9245902 (also fax) Mrs Mullen
D: Fr €32.00
Beds: 1F 2D 2T **Baths:** 2 En 1 Pr 1 Sh
⅙ 📺 ✕ �V ⬛ cc

Hill of Tara

N9159

Hillside, *Old Ross Road, Hill of Tara, Navan, Co Meath.* 1 km Hill of Tara. 15 km Newgrange. 35 km airport.
Open: May to Oct
046 9025571 Mrs Bowden-O'Keeffe
hillsidebandb@oceanfree.net
D: Fr €23.00 **S:** Fr €29.00 ⛺ 🅿 (4) ⅙ �V ⬛ ⬛ cc

Julianstown

O1370

Barden Lodge, *Whitecross, Julianstown, Drogheda, Co Louth.* Quiet country home off main N1 Dublin-Belfast road, close amenities, hotels, country pub/restaurant.
Open: All Year (not Xmas)
041 9829369 & 041 9829910 Mr & Mrs Kington **Fax: 041 9829369**
kington@eircom.net
www.dirl.com/meath/barden-lodge.htm
D: Fr €25.50-€32.00 **S:** Fr €32.00-€38.00
Beds: 3F **Baths:** 4 En 1 Pr
⛺ 🅿 ⅙ 📺 �V ⬛ ⬛

Kilmessan

N8957

The Station House, *Kilmessan, Navan, Co Meath.* Old railway junction with signal box, platforms, etc.
Open: All Year
046 9025239 Mr Slattery **Fax: 046 9025588**
stnhouse@indigo.ie
D: Fr €63.50
Beds: 2F 6D 2T 2S **Baths:** 4 Ensuite 2 Private 6 Shared
⛺ 🅿 📺 🐕 ✕ �V ⬛ ♿

Navan

N8667

Boyne Dale, *Donaghmore, Navan, Co Meath.* Comfortable warm home in the heart of the Boyne Valley.
Open: Mar to Oct
046 9028015 Ms Casserly **Fax: 046 9075862**
boynedale@iolfree.ie
D: Fr €24.50-€30.00 **S:** Fr €37.00-€40.00
Beds: 2D 3T **Baths:** 3 En 2 Pr
⛺ 🅿 (6) ⅙ 📺 ⬛ ⬛

Lios Na Greine, *Athlumney, Duleek Road, Navan, Co Meath.* Luxurious home 1km off N3 on Dunleek/Ashbourne airport road (R153).
Open: All Year
046 9028092 Mrs Callanan
D: Fr €30.00
Beds: 3F 1D **Baths:** 3 En
⛺ 🅿 ⅙ 📺 🐕 ✕ �V ⬛ ✳

Bothar Alainn House, *Trim Road, Balreask, Navan, Co Meath.* Spacious, modern farmhouse. Ideal base for touring Boyne Valley. Golf and fishing nearby.
Open: All Year
046 9028580 Mrs McKeigue
D: Fr €32.00
Beds: 1F 1T 1D **Baths:** 3 Ensuite
⛺ 🅿 ⅙ 📺 ⬛

All details shown are as supplied by B&B owners in Autumn 2002

Oldcastle

N5680

Ross Castle, *Mount Nugent, Oldcastle, Kells, Co Meath.*
Open: All year
049 8540237 & 086 8242206 (M) Mrs Liebe-Harkort
book@rosscastle.com www.ross-castle.com
D: Fr €40.00 **S:** Fr €50.00
Beds: 2F 2D **Baths:** 4 En
➳ 🅿 (5) ♞ ▥ ▩ cc
Find exclusive retreat in C16th castle on the shores of Lough Sheelin. Magnificent view. Ancient history combined with modern comfort. Neighbouring accommodation approved Ross House Equestrian House with the use of its facilities, 30 fence cross-country-course, boats, tennis courts.

Slane

N9674

Mattock House, *Balfeddock, Slane, Navan, Co Meath.* Situated 3 miles east of Slane. Half price vouchers available for Newgrange.
Open: All Year
041 9824592 (also fax) Mrs Gough
D: Fr €29.00
Beds: 1F 1D 1T **Baths:** 2 Ensuite 1 Private
➳ 🅿 (4) 📺 ♞ 📺 ▥

Trim

N8056

Brogan's Guest House,
High Street, Trim, Co Meath.
Open fires, traditional music in our cosy lounge/bar. Picturesque location.
Open: All year
046 9431237 Fax: 046 9437648
brogangh@iol.ie
D: Fr €32.00 **S:** Fr €40.00
Beds: 2F 1T 8D 4S **Baths:** 14 En 1 Pr
➳ 🅿 ✂ 📺 📺 ▥ ♿ ❋ ▪ cc

White Lodge, *New Road, (Navan Road), Trim, Co Meath.* Spacious town house, friendly atmosphere, rural setting. Convenient airport, Dublin, Boyne Valley. Warm welcome.
Open: All Year (not Xmas)
046 9436549 (also fax) Mrs O'Loughlin
D: Fr €32.00
Beds: 3F 2D 1T **Baths:** 5 Ensuite 1 Shared
➳ 🅿 (9) 📺 ▥ ▪

National Grid References given are for villages, towns and cities – not for individual houses

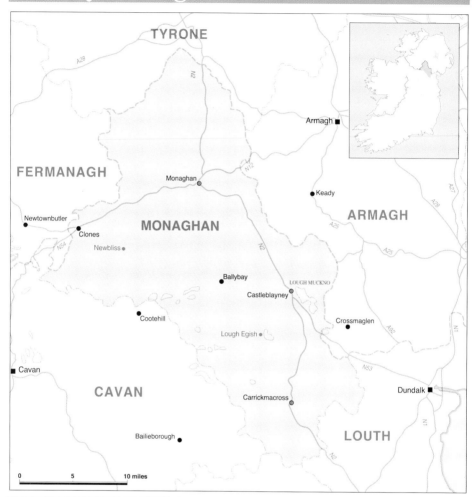

TYRONE

A28

N2

Armagh ■

FERMANAGH

Monaghan ○

Keady ●

ARMAGH

A27

A28

Newtownbutler ●

Clones ■

MONAGHAN

N54

Newbliss ●

N12

N2

A25

A25

Ballybay ●

LOUGH MUCKNO

Castleblayney ●

Cootehill ●

Crossmaglen ●

A32

N1

Lough Egish ●

N53

Cavan ■

CAVAN

Carrickmacross ●

Dundalk ■

N1

Bailieborough ●

LOUTH

N2

0   5   10 miles

RAIL ⇌

Monaghan to *Belfast* (7 daily).
Monaghan to *Dublin* (7 daily).

Tel. Irish Rail on 01 8366222.

TOURIST INFORMATION OFFICE ℹ

Market House, **Monaghan**
(open all year), 047 81122.

Carrickmacross

H8403

Lisanisk House, *Dundalk Road,
Carrickmacross, Co Monaghan.* Beautiful lakeside
country house, many rooms overlooking lake
beside town.
Open: Easter to Nov
042 9661035 & 087 2382917 (M) Mrs Haworth
D: Fr €25.50-€29.50 **S:** Fr €32.00
Beds: 1D 1T 1S **Baths:** 2 En 2 Sh
🛏 🅿 (20) 📺 🛏 ✗ 🆅 ▥ ⅙

Castleblaney

H8219

Hillview, *Bree, Castleblaney, Co Monaghan.*
Beautiful country view from guest rooms. Only 10 min walk into town.
Open: Jan to Dec
042 9746217 Mrs Wilson
D: Fr €20.50 **S:** Fr €21.50
Beds: 1F 1D 2T 1S **Baths:** 3 Pr
ॐ 🅿 (8) 📺 ✕ 🆅 🛏.

Lough Egish

H7913

Palm Grove Lodge,
Drumlane, Lough Egish, Castleblayney, Co Monaghan.
Modern country house, warm welcome, tea/coffee on arrival, 5 mins Ballybay/ Castleblaney.
Open: All year
042 9745170 Mrs Gorman **Fax: 042 9745554**
D: Fr €30.00-€35.00 **S:** Fr €30.00-€35.00
Beds: 1F 1D 2T **Baths:** 3 En 1 Pr 1 Sh
ॐ 🅿 (6) 📺 🛏 ✕ 🆅 🛏.

Monaghan

H6733

Willow Bridge Lodge, *Armagh Road, Monaghan.* Motel style facilities in secluded location with panoramic views over surrounding countryside.
Open: All Year (not Xmas)
047 81054 (also fax) Ms Holden
thelodge@eircom.net
www.homepage.eircom.net/billh/index.html
D: Fr €32.00-€38.00 **S:** Fr €32.00-€38.00
Beds: 1F 1D 1T **Baths:** 3 En
ॐ (5) 🅿 (8) ⅟ 📺 🛏 🛏. ▪

Newbliss

H5623

Glynch House, *Newbliss, Clones, Monaghan.*
Antique furniture, fresh vegetables, truly an Irish welcome.
Open: Mar to Sep
047 54045 Mrs O'Grady **Fax: 047 54321**
mirth@eircom.net
D: Fr €25.50-€32.00 **S:** Fr €25.50-€38.00
Beds: 2F 1D 2T 1S **Baths:** 3 En 1 Pr 2 Sh
ॐ 🅿 📺 🛏 ✕ 🆅 🛏. ♿

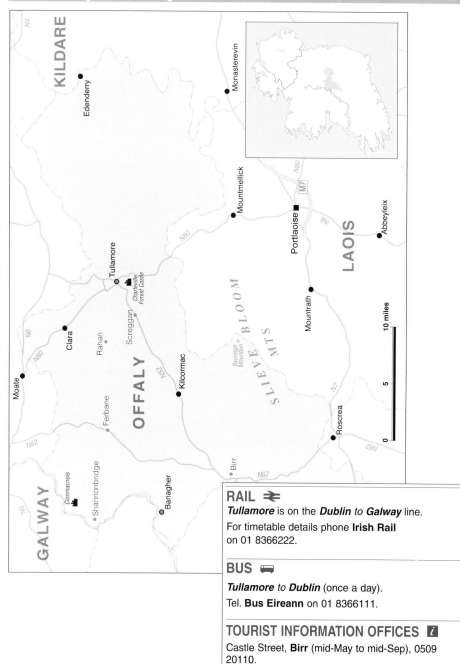

RAIL ⇌

Tullamore is on the **Dublin to Galway** line.

For timetable details phone **Irish Rail** on 01 8366222.

BUS 🚌

Tullamore to Dublin (once a day).

Tel. **Bus Eireann** on 01 8366111.

TOURIST INFORMATION OFFICES ℹ

Castle Street, **Birr** (mid-May to mid-Sep), 0509 20110.

Planning a longer stay?
Always ask for any special rates

N0015

Sleepy Hollow, *Taylors Cross, Banagher, Birr, Co Offaly.* Comfortable, friendly country home, good food, private parking, bait stockist.
Open: Easter to Oct
0509 51273 Mrs Kelleher
D: Fr €23.50
Beds: 2F 1T **Baths:** 1 Sh
⌂ 🅿 (8) ✕ Ⓥ ▥.

The Old Forge, *West End, Banagher, Birr, Co Offaly.* The Old Forge is a town house in the heart of Banagher, just 200m from River Shannon. We have on site a fishing tackle shop which can supply the angler with all he needs to fish the Shannon. Boat hire available.
Open: All year (not Xmas)
0509 51504 Mrs Duthie
D: Fr €20.00-€25.00 **S:** Fr €20.00-€25.00
Beds: 3F 1T 1S **Baths:** 5 En
⌂ 🅿 (5) Ⓥ ▥. ▪

N0504

Spinners Town House & Bistro, *Castle Street, Birr, County Offaly.* Homely ambience. Traditional, with exciting new features, e.g. new Medieval rooms.
Open: All year
0509 21673 Mr & Mrs Breen **Fax: 0509 21672**
spinners@indigo.ie www.spinners-townhouse.com
D: Fr €32.00-€45.00 **S:** Fr €32.50-€60.00
Beds: 4F 5T 4D 1S **Baths:** 12 En 2 Pr
⌂ ✕ ✕ Ⓥ ▥. ✳ ▪ cc

N1124

Highfield House, *Rosfaraghan, Ferbane, Birr, Co Offaly.* Just off the N62, 2km from Ferbane on Clara Road. Tranquillity abounds.
Open: All Year (not Xmas)
090 6454387 Mrs Moore
D: Fr €22.00
Beds: 1F 1T 1S **Baths:** 1 Ensuite 1 Shared
⌂ 🅿 Ⓥ ✕ Ⓥ ▥. ✳ ▪

Daragh, *Ballyclare, Ferbane, Birr, Co Offaly.* Bungalow ideally situated for touring. Warm welcome, ample parking, gardens.
Open: All year
090 6454196 Mrs Mitchell
D: Fr €17.00 **S:** Fr €20.00
Beds: 3F 2T 1D **Baths:** 1 En 2 Pr
✕ Ⓥ ▥.

N2525

Rahan Lodge, *Rahan, Tullamore, County Offaly.* Country retreat dating from 1740, set in 17 acres of wood and farmland.
Open: Apr to Oct
0506 55796 Ms McDermott **Fax: 0506 55606**
mail@rahanlodge.com www.rahanlodge.com
D: Fr €45.00-€55.00 **S:** Fr €45.00-€55.00
Beds: 4D 1T **Baths:** 3 Pr
🅿 ✕ Ⓥ ✕ Ⓥ ▥. ▪ cc

Canal View, *Killina, Rahan, Tullamore, Co Offaly.* Dormer bungalow overlooking Grand Canal.
Open: All Year (not Xmas)
0506 55868 Mrs Keyes **Fax: 0506 55034**
canalview@eircom.net
D: Fr €26.00
Beds: 3F 1D **Baths:** 4 Ensuite
⌂ 🅿 ✕ Ⓥ ✕ Ⓥ ▥. ▪

N2921

Shepherds Wood, *Screggan, Tullamore, Co Offaly.* 1930s period house in 50 acres forest, a wildlife sanctuary.
Open: May to Sep
0506 21499 (also fax) Mr & Mrs MacSweeney-Thieme
jgott@esatclear.ie
www.dirl.com/offaly/shepherdswood.htm
D: Fr €32.00-€35.50 **S:** Fr €42.00-€46.00
Beds: 2D 1T **Baths:** 2 En 1 Pr
⌂ (12) 🅿 (10) 🐾 ▥. ▪

BATHROOMS
En = Ensuite
Pr = Private
Sh = Shared

Shannonbridge

M9725

Laurel Lodge, *Garrymore, Shannonbridge, Athlone, Co Westmeath.* Modern farmhouse situated in peaceful surroundings 2km from Shannonbridge.
Open: All Year
0905 74189 Mrs McManus
D: Fr €26.00
Beds: 2F 2D 2T **Baths:** 6 Ensuite
ॐ 🄿 🆅 🛏 ✕ 🖵 ▦.

Tullamore

N3324

Pine Lodge Country Home, *Tullamore, Co Offaly.*
Open: Apr to Oct
0506 51927 (also fax) Mrs Krygel

pinelodge@holidayhound.com
www.pinelodgecountryhome.com
D: Fr €38.00 **S:** Fr €51.00
Beds: 2D 2T **Baths:** 4 En
ॐ (12) 🄿 (6) ⅍ 🆅 ▦. ⚲
A peaceful haven in a sylvan setting offering a delicious breakfast menu plus use of heated indoor pool, sauna, steam room and sunbed (charged extra). Massage and reflexology also available. A number of excellent restaurants in nearby Tullamore - 4 miles away.

Rahan Lodge, *Rahan, Tullamore, County Offaly.*
Open: Apr to Oct
0506 55796 Ms McDermott
Fax: 0506 55606
mail@rahanlodge.com www.rahanlodge.com
D: Fr €45.00-€55.00 **S:** Fr €45.00-€55.00
Beds: 4D 1T **Baths:** 3 Pr
🄿 ⅍ 🆅 ✕ 🆅 ▦. ⚲ cc
Country retreat dating from 1740, set in 17 acres of wood and farmland. A place to enjoy comfort and seclusion away from the hustle and bustle of city life. Good food and open fires. Located off N52, for Birr out of Tullamore.

Daracorr, *Arden Road, Tullamore, Co Offaly.* Friendly Home. Dublin 65 miles. Championship golf courses. Bog train.
Open: Easter to Nov
0506 41347 Mrs Corroon
D: Fr €20.50-€23.00 **S:** Fr €21.50-€27.00
Beds: 2D 2T **Baths:** 2 En 2 Pr
ॐ (5) 🄿 🆅 🛏 🆅 ▦. ♿ ⚲

Gormagh, *Durrow, Tullamore, Co Offaly.* The use of natural materials throughout the house are in harmony with the countryside.
Open: All Year
0506 51468 Mrs O'Brien
D: Fr €24.00 **S:** Fr €32.50
Beds: 2T 2D **Baths:** 4 En
🄿 🆅 ▦.

RAIL ⇌

Boyle is on the **Sligo** to **Dublin (Connolly)** line, while **Roscommon** has 3 daily trains on the **Westport** to **Dublin (Heuston)** line. For timetable details phone **Irish Rail** on 01 8366222.

TOURIST INFORMATION OFFICES
i

Particle Street, **Boyle** (Jun to Sep), 071 9662145. The Museum, **Roscommon** (Jun to Sep), 090 6626342.

Boyle
G8002

Forest Park House, *Carrick-on-Shannon Road, Boyle, Co Roscommon.* A country house beside forest park. Noted for friendly service.
Open: All year
071 9662227 Mrs Kelly **Fax: 091 565201**
forestparkhse@hotmail.com
www.bed-and-breakfast-boyle.com
D: Fr €30.00 **S:** Fr €35.00
Beds: 2T 4D 1S **Baths:** 7 En
🅿 (15) 📺 ✕ Ⓥ 🏠 ⚫ cc

Cesh Corran, *Sligo Road, Boyle, County Roscommon.* A beautifully-restored Edwardian BF Approved town house. Many amenities.
Open: Feb to Nov
071 9662265 (also fax) Mrs Cooney
cooneym@iol.ie www.marycooney.com
D: Fr €26.50-€35.00 **S:** Fr €39.00-€45.00
Beds: 2D 1T **Baths:** 3 En
🛏 🅿 (100) 📺 🐾 Ⓥ 🏠 ⚫ cc

Hillside House, *Doon, Corrigeenroe, Boyle, Co Roscommon.* Attractive country house, more than 100 years old, in woodland area beside Lough Key.
Open: All Year (not Xmas)
071 9666075 Mrs Taylor
D: Fr €21.50-€24.00 **S:** Fr €20.50
Beds: 1F 1D 2T **Baths:** 2 En 2 Sh
🛏 🅿 📺 🐾 🏠

All details shown are as supplied by B&B owners in Autumn 2002

Planning a longer stay? Always ask for any special rates

Castlerea
M6779

Williamstown Road, *Castlerea, Co Roscommon.* Town house on edge of town in country setting, lovely views.
Open: All year (not Xmas)
0907 20431 Mrs Ronane
D: Fr €21.50-€25.50 **S:** Fr €21.50-€25.50
Beds: 1F 2D 1T 1S **Baths:** 4 En 1 Sh
🛏 🅿 🐾 ✕ 🏠

Croghan
M8596

Rushfield, *Croghan, Boyle, Co Roscommon.* Rushford house a Georgian farmhouse, set in the centre of a prize-winning dairy farm.
Open: Easter to Sep
071 9662276 Mr & Mrs Graham
D: Fr €25.50 **S:** Fr €25.50-€30.50
Beds: 2F 1D 1T **Baths:** 4 En
🛏 🅿 📺 🐾 Ⓥ 🏠 ⚫

Kiltoom
M9847

Castleside, *Moyvannion, Kiltoom, Athlone, Co Westmeath.* Quiet country home on N61. Fishing golf & water sports.
Open: All Year
090 6489195 (also fax) Mrs Hegarty
D: Fr €30.00
Beds: 1F 2T 1D 1S **Baths:** 4 Ensuite 2 Shared
🛏 🅿 (10) 📺 🐾 ✕ Ⓥ 🏠 ⚫ ♿ ⚫

Monksland
N0141

Woodville, *Monksland, Athlone, Co Westmeath.* Modern bungalow on quiet road 3 km from Athlone Town. Ideal touring base.
Open: Easter to Oct **Grades:** BF Approv
090 6494595 Mrs McCam **Fax: 090 6498789**
D: Fr €26.00 **S:** Fr €36.00
Beds: 1D 2F **Baths:** 3 En
🛏 🅿 (3) 📺 🏠 ⚫

Rahara

M9152

Lacken House, *Rahara, Athlone, Co Roscommon.* C19th cutstone manor on 5 acres in rural setting; peaceful and quiet.
Open: All Year
090 6623449 (also fax) Mr Cammeraat
info@lackenhouse.findhere.com
D: Fr €32.00
Beds: 4D 2T **Baths:** 6 En
⊇ (6) ⊁ ✕ ▥ cc

Rooskey-on-Shannon

N0487

Avondale House, *Rooskey-on-Shannon, Carrick-on-Shannon, Co Leitrim.* Luxury two-storey house. Beside River Shannon. Family-run home.
Open: All Year
071 9638095 Mrs Davis
D: Fr €25.50
Beds: 2F 2D 2T **Baths:** 5 Ensuite
⌖ ▣ (6) ⊁ ▼ ★ ✕ Ⓥ ▥ ⅙ ▄

Roscommon

M8764

Riverside House, *Riverside Ave, Roscommon.* Modern dormer bungalow set in mature grounds. Ameneties within walking distance.
Open: All Year
090 6626897 Mrs Hynes
D: Fr €25.50
Beds: 3F 2D 1S **Baths:** 3 En 3 Sh
⌖ ▣ (6) ★ ✕ Ⓥ ▥ ✱

Strokestown

M9381

Church View House, *Strokestown, Roscommon.* Country house in peaceful surroundings. Strokestown Historical House and Famine Museum 5 km.
Open: June to Sept
071 9633047 A Cox-Mills
D: Fr €23.00-€25.50 **S:** Fr €25.50-€28.00
Beds: 3D 2T 1S **Baths:** 3 En
⌖ ▣ ⊁ ▼ ★ Ⓥ ▥

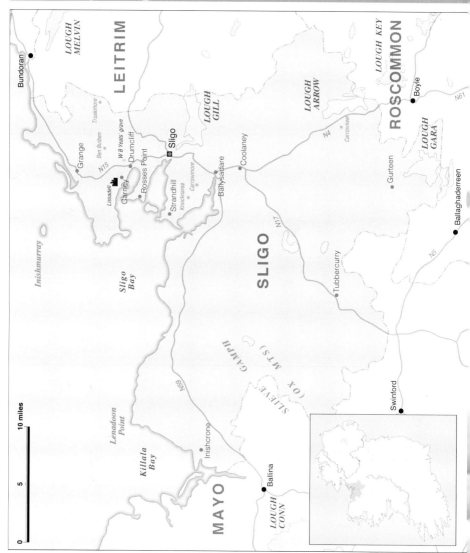

AIRPORT ⊕

The nearest international airport is **Knock** (see Co Mayo chapter).

RAIL ⇌

Sligo is on the main line to **Dublin (Connolly)**, via **Boyle** and **Carrick-on-Shannon**.
There are 3 trains daily. For timetable details phone **Irish Rail** on 01 8366222.

TOURIST INFORMATION OFFICE 🅸

Temple Street, **Sligo** (open all year), 071 9161201.

Ballysadare

56629

Seashore, *Off Balina Road (N59), Lisduff, Ballysadare, Co Sligo.*
Open: All year
071 9167827 & 086 2224842
(M) Ann Campbell **Fax: 071 9167827**
eashore@oceanfree.net www.seashoreguests.com
D: Fr €32.50-€35.00 **S:** Fr €40.00-€45.00
Beds: 1F 1D 2T 1S **Baths:** 4 En 1 Pr
🅿 (6) ✻ 📺 🞓. ⬛ cc
Country home ideally situated for touring Yeats Country, Carrowmore megalithic tombs. Sample breakfast in our conservatory/dining room with panoramic views of Ox Mountains, Ballysadare Bay, Knocknarea. Access to shore walk with eye-catching view for enthusiastic birdwatchers. Birdwatching facility, tennis court, jacuzzi.

Carney

56543

Mountain View, *Carney, Drumcliffe, Sligo.*
High standard of accommodation with a view of Benbulben Mountain.
Open: Easter to Nov
71 9163290 Mrs Murphy
D: Fr €24.00-€25.50 **S:** Fr €32.00
Beds: 3F 1T 1D **Baths:** 5 En
🖫 🅿 (6) ✻ 📺 🞓. ⬛

Coolaney

G6025

Mountain Inn, *Lipsetts of Coolaney, Co Sligo.* Bar/restaurant with comfortable rooms. N4/N17/N59 10 mins by car.
Open: All year (not Xmas/New Year)
071 9167225 & 071 9167329 Fax: 071 9167228
info@mountaininn.net www.mountaininn.net
D: Fr €35.00-€37.50 **S:** Fr €32.00-€40.00
Beds: 1F 3T 2D **Baths:** 4 En 2 Sh
🖫 📺 ✕ 🞓. ⬛ cc

Drumcliffe

G6742

Castletown House, *Drumcliffe, Sligo.*
Spectacular panoramic mountain view. W B Yeats grave nearby. Waterfalls, peaceful location.
Open: Mar to Oct
071 9163204 Mrs Rooney
f_rooney_ie@yahoo.co.uk
D: Fr €24.00 **S:** Fr €23.00
Beds: 1F 1D 1T 2S **Baths:** 3 En
🖫 (10) 🅿 ✻ 📺 🛏 ✕ 📹 🞓. ⬛

Benbulben Farm, *Barnaribbon, Drumcliffe, Sligo.* Working farm, wonderful location, scenic, unspoilt, relaxing - Sligo 10 mins' drive.
Open: Apr to Sep
071 9163211 Mrs Hennigan **Fax: 071 9173009**
D: Fr €23.00-€25.00 **S:** Fr €32.00
Beds: 1T 3D 1S
🖫 🅿 ✻ 📺 ✕ 🞓. ⬛ cc

Thurmore, *Donegal Road, Tully, Drumcliffe, Sligo.* Comfortable country home. Panoramic views of Benbulben Mountain and Drumcliffe Bay.
Open: Easter to Sep
071 9143890 Mrs Feeney
D: Fr €23.00-€24.00 **S:** Fr €25.50-€28.00
Beds: 1F 2D **Baths:** 2 En 1 Pr
🖫 🅿 📺 🞓. ⅙ ⬛

Lissadell View, *Tullyhill, Rathcormac, Drumcliffe, Sligo.* Spacious home overlooking Yeats country, Benbulben Mountain, Drumcliffe Bay.
Open: Mar to Nov
071 9143892 Mrs Feeney
D: Fr €30.00
Beds: 1F 1T 2D **Baths:** 4 Ensuite
🅿 (6) 📺 🛏 🞓. ⬛

Grange

G6649

Armada Lodge, *Donegal Road, N15, Grange, Sligo.* Beautiful tranquil location overlooking sea/ mountains off Donegal road.
Open: Apr to Sep
071 9163250 (also fax) Mrs Brennan
armadalodge@eircom.net
D: Fr €28.00
Beds: 2F 1D 3T **Baths:** 7 Ensuite 1 Shared
☜ 🅿 (6) 📺 🐾 🖳 ♨

Rosswick, *Grange, Sligo.* Family home; beaches, mountains, Yeats Country close by. Breakfast menu.
Open: Easter to Oct
071 9163516 Mrs Neary
rosswick@eircom.net
D: Fr €21.50-€24.00 **S:** Fr €27.00-€29.00
Beds: 1D 3T **Baths:** 2 En 1 Sh
☜ (6) 🅿 (3) ⌦ 📺 📺 🖳 cc

Gurteen

G6704

San Giovanni, *Gurteen, Ballymote, Co Sligo.* Modern farmhouse situated in peaceful surroundings offering high standard of accommodation.
Open: All Year (not Xmas)
071 9182038 Mrs O'Grady
sangiovanni@eircom.net
D: Fr €24.00 **S:** Fr €31.00
Beds: 1D 2T **Baths:** 3 En
☜ 🅿 (6) ⌦ 📺 🐾 📺 🖳 cc

Inishcrone

G2830

Smiths Lodge, *Pier Road, Inishcrone, Ballina, Co Mayo.* Georgian family-run town house adjacent to all amenities.
Open: Easter to Oct
096 36414 Mrs Casey
D: Fr €30.00
Beds: 1F 1D 1T **Baths:** 3 Ensuite
☜ 🅿 (4) 📺 🐾 🖳 ♿ ♨

Please respect a B&B's wishes regarding children, animals and smoking

Rosses Point

G6341

Sea Park House, *Rosses Point Road (R291), Rosses Point, Sligo.* Modern bungalow. Choice breakfast menu. Orthopaedic beds. Super scenic area.
Open: All Year
071 9145556 (also fax) Mrs Fullerton
D: Fr €21.50-€25.50 **S:** Fr €25.50-€32.00
Beds: 1F 3D 2T **Baths:** 4 En 1 Sh
☜ (2) 🅿 (10) ⌦ 📺 📺 🖳 ♨ cc

Sligo

G6936

Aisling, *Cairns Hill, off N4, Sligo.* Overlooking gardens and sea. Rooms on ground floor, lounge, hospitality.
Open: All year (not Xmas)
071 9160704 (also fax)
Mr & Mrs Faul
aislingsligo@eircom.net
D: Fr €26.50-€30.00 **S:** Fr €39.00-€45.00
Beds: 2F 2D 1T **Baths:** 3 En 2 Sh
🅿 (6) ⌦ 📺 🖳 cc

Belvoir House, *Holywell Road, Sligo.* Beautiful scenery. Complex with heated pool/ gym. Nearby Sligo, 1 km.
Open: Apr to Oct
071 9169136 Mrs Brady
D: Fr €30.00 **S:** Fr €35.00 ☜ 🅿 (6) ⌦ 📺 🖳 ♨

Stonecroft (off Donegal Road), *Kintogher, Sligo.* 'Stonecroft' signposted N15 Donegal Road Spacious home. Living room and five guest bedrooms.
Open: Feb to Dec
071 9145667 Mrs Conway
stonecroft_sligo@yahoo.com
D: Fr €32.00-€35.00 **S:** Fr €40.00-€46.00
Beds: 2F 2D 1T **Baths:** 5 En
☜ (2) 🅿 (5) 📺 🖳 ♿ ♨

Ard Cuilinn Lodge, *Drumiskabole, Sligo.* Country home in tranquil scenic surroundings. Home cooking a speciality.
Open: Apr to Oct
071 9162925 Mrs Carroll
ardcuilinn@esatclear.ie
D: Fr €24.00-€25.50
Beds: 1F 2D 1T **Baths:** 2 En 1 Sh
☜ (6) 🅿 (4) ⌦ 📺 🖳 cc

athnashee, Teesan, *Donegal Road (N15),*
igo. Bungalow in scenic location near pitch and
utt. Beaches. Golf club.
pen: All Year (not Xmas)
71 9143376 Mrs Haughey **Fax: 071 9142283**
: Fr €25.50
eds: 3T **Baths:** 2 Ensuite 1 Private
5 (7) **P** (4) 📺 ✕ Ⅴ 🛏,

'ree Tops, *Cleveragh Road off N4, Sligo.*
minutes' walk Sligo town centre. Ideal base for
xploring Yeats country.
pen: All Year (not Xmas)
71 9160160 Mrs MacEvilly **Fax: 071 9162301**
eetops@iol.ie
: Fr €29.50
eds: 2F 2D 1T **Baths:** 3 En
5 (6) **P** (5) ✂ 📺 🛏, ■ **cc**

osscahill, *19 Marymount, Pearse Road, Sligo.*
omfortable home in quiet cul-de-sac. Walking
istance Sligo town.
pen: Apr to Nov
71 9161744 Mrs O'Halloran
: Fr €29.50
eds: 1F 1D 1T **Baths:** 3 Ensuite
✂ 📺 🛏, ■

Lar-Easa', *12 Kestrel Drive, Kevensfort,*
trandhill Road, Sligo. Modern family-run B&B set
*r*ithin 6 acres of parkland 1km from Sligo.
Dpen: All Year (not Xmas)
71 9169313 Mr Kilfeather **Fax: 071 9168593**
ir-easa@esatclear.ie
: Fr €29.50
eds: 1F 1D 1T 1S **Baths:** 4 En
5 (6) **P** (6) 📺 Ⅴ 🛏, ■

nnagh Bay, *Ballinode, Sligo.* Special, friendly
velcome. 5 minutes from town centre, beaches
vithin five mile radius.
Dpen: All Year
71 9162255 Miss Holmes
D: Fr €30.00
eds: 2F 1T 1D **Baths:** 2 Ensuite 1 Private 1
hared
5 **P** (6) 📺 Ⅴ 🛏, ■

bercorn B & B, *Rathbraughan Line, Sligo.*
*M*odern bungalow in quiet location; golf,
eaches, fishing within 5 km.
Dpen: All Year
71 9146087 Mrs Jenkins
D: Fr €24.00-€25.50 **S:** Fr €24.00-€35.50
eds: 1D 1T 1S **Baths:** 2 En 1 Pr
a (10) ✂ 🛏, ■

Beach House, *Strandhill,*
Sligo.
Open: May to Oct
071 9168500 & 071 9168140
Mrs Byrne
D: Fr €30.00 **S:** Fr €35.00
Beds: 1F 3D 1T 1S **Baths:** 4 En 2 Sh
P (6) 📺 🛏, ■
Large Georgian house. Homely atmosphere,
comfortable. 100 metres from Atlantic.

**Cruckawn
House,** *Ballymote-
Boyle Road (off N17
on R294),
Tubbercurry, Co
Sligo.*
Open: Apr to Nov
Grades: BF Approv,
AA 3 Star
071 9185188 (also fax) Mrs Walsh
cruckawn@esatclear.ie
www.sligotourism.com/cruckawn
D: Fr €28.00-€32.00 **S:** Fr €39.00-€42.00
Beds: 2F 1D 2T **Baths:** 5 En 5 Pr
⅗ **P** (7) 📺 🛏 ✕ Ⅴ 🛏, ■ **cc**
Award-winning home, set in peaceful suburb
overlooking golf course. AIB 'Best Hospitality'/
Frommer/Guide du Routard/Dillard/Causin,
many recommendations. Facilities: fishing, hill-
walking, cycling, horse-riding, archaeology,
excellent pubs, Irish music, food. Sun lounge,
gardens, laundry. Breakfast menu. Ideal touring
base. Yeats country, Ox Mountain Trail, Museum
of Country Life, Knock Sligo airports 15-25 mins.
Town & Country Homes Assoc.

Cawley's Guest House, *Tubbercurry, Co Sligo.*
Cawley's, a 3-storey family-run guest house. We
offer high standards in accommodation.
Open: All Year (not Xmas)
071 9185025 Fax: 071 9185963
D: Fr €32.50
Beds: 4F 9T 7D **Baths:** 10 Ensuite
P 📺 ✕ Ⅴ 🛏, ■

Eden Villa, *Ballina Road, Tubbercurry, Co Sligo.*
Quiet, friendly, luxury family home, located off the
N17 (the main Sligo-Galway road). On N294 road,
Edenvilla is 25 mins from Sligo, Ballina,
Inishcrone, Castlebar and Boyle. 15 mins from
Knock Airport, making it an ideal base to share in
the tradition of rural Ireland.
Open: All year (not Xmas/New Year)
071 9185106 (also fax) Mrs Brennan
edenvilla@ireland.com sligotourism.com
D: Fr €25.50 **S:** Fr €33.00
Beds: 1F 2T 1D **Baths:** 3 En
⌂ ▣ ⊬ 🖵 ✕ Ⓥ ▥ ▪ cc

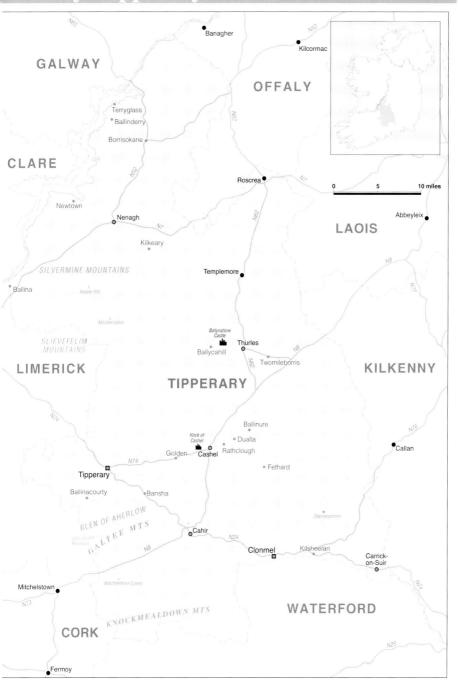

GALWAY

Banagher

Kilcormac

OFFALY

Terryglass
Ballinderry

Borrisokane

CLARE

Roscrea

N7

0   5   10 miles

Newtown

Nenagh

Kilkeary

N7

LAOIS

Abbeyleix

SILVERMINE MOUNTAINS

Templemore

Ballina

Keeper Hill

Mauherslieve

SLIEVEFELIM
MOUNTAINS

Ballynahow
Castle

Thurles

LIMERICK

Ballycahill

Twomileborris

KILKENNY

TIPPERARY

N62

N8

Ballinure

Rock of
Cashel

Dualla

Callan

Golden

Cashel

Rathclough

N74

Fethard

Tipperary

N76

Ballinacourty

Bansha

GLEN OF AHERLOW

Slievenamon

GALTEE MTS

Galtymore
Mountain

Cahir

N24

Clonmel

Kilsheelan

Carrick-
on-Suir

N8

Mitchelstown

Mitchelstown Caves

N73

KNOCKMEALDOWN MTS

WATERFORD

CORK

N25

Fermoy

AIRPORTS ⊕

The nearest airport is **Shannon Airport** (see Co Clare chapter).
Tel. 061 471444.

RAIL ⇛

Thurles is on the main *Cork* and *Tralee* line into *Dublin (Heuston)*.
For timetable details phone **Irish Rail** on 01 8366222.

TOURIST INFORMATION OFFICES ℹ

Cahir (Apr to Sep), 052 41453.
Main Street, **Cashel**, 062 61133,
Sarsfield Street, **Clonmel**
(open all year), 052 22960.
James Street, **Tipperary**
(open all year), 062 51457.

Ballina
R7173

Rathmore House, *Ballina, Killaloe, Co Clare.*
Family home on R494, between Birdhill (N7) and
Killaloe on the River Shannon.
Open: All year (not Xmas)
061 379296 (also fax) Mrs Byrnes
rathmorebb@oceanfree.net www.rathmorehouse.com
D: Fr €24.50-€30.00 **S:** Fr €37.00-€42.50
Beds: 4F 2D **Baths:** 4 En 2 Sh
⌂ (1) 🅿 (8) 📺 🛏 ⅙ ☕ cc

Arkansas, *Lakedrive Road, Ballina, Killaloe, Co
Clare.* Modern bungalow within 5 minutes' walk of
Ballina, Killaloe villages. Lovely scenic area.
Open: All Year (not Xmas)
061 376485 Mrs Boner
D: Fr €25.00
Beds: 1F 2D 1T **Baths:** 4 En
⌂ (3) 🅿 (2) 📺 🛏 ☕ cc

B&B owners may vary
rates – be sure to check when
booking

RATES

D = Price range per person sharing
in a double or twin room
S = Price range for a single room

Ballinacourty
R8529

Homeleigh Farmhouse, *Ballinacourty, Glen*
Aherlow, Tipperary. Luxurious farmhouse.
Residential riding holidays, hill/mountain walks
evening meals.
Open: All year **Grades:** BF Approv
062 56228 Mr & Mrs Frewen
homeleighfarmhouse@eircom.net
www.homeleighfarmhouse.com
D: Fr €32.00 **S:** Fr €40.00
Beds: 2F 2D 1T **Baths:** 5 En
⌂ 🅿 (10) 📺 🛏 ✕ 📺 🛏 ⅙ ☀ cc

Ballinacourty House & Restaurant, *Glen*
Aherlow, Tipperary. Stable complex in courtyard
setting. Beautiful views of Galty Mountains.
Walking maps available.
Open: Feb to Nov
062 56000 The Stanley Family **Fax: 062 56230**
info@ballinacourtyhse.com
www.ballinacourtyhse.com
D: Fr €25.50 **S:** Fr €36.00
Beds: 3D 2T **Baths:** 5 En
⌂ 🅿 (8) 📺 ✕ 📺 🛏 ☕ cc

Ballinderry
R8597

Coolangatta B&B, *Brocka, Ballinderry,*
Nenagh, Co Tipperary. Spectacular lake views,
breakfast menu, garden, quiet location. Irish
music nights.
Open: All year
067 22164 Mrs McGeeney
coolangatta@eircom.net
D: Fr €27.00 **S:** Fr €35.00
Beds: 1F 2D 1T **Baths:** 3 En 1 Sh
⌂ 🅿 (10) 📺 🛏 ✕ 📺 🛏 ☕ cc

Planning a longer stay?
Always ask for any special rates

Ballinure

1545

Derrynaflan,
Ballinure, Cashel,
Thurles, Co
Tipperary.
Open: Mar to Dec
052 56406
Mrs O'Sullivan

naflan@iol.ie www.tipp.ie/derrynaf.htm
D: Fr €28.00-€32.00 **S:** Fr €30.00
Beds: 1F 3T 3D 1S **Baths:** 4 En 1 Sh
⌂ (1) 🅿 (10) 📺 ⊱ ✕ Ⓥ ⠇⠇⠇ ☕

18th farmhouse set in scenic location, 600 metre tree-lined avenue on site of C16th castle. Antique furniture throughout. Prize-winning farmhouse. Light and evening meals also available. Cashel nearby has plenty of entertainment in pubs, etc.

Ballycahill

0759

Ballynahow Castle Farm, *Ballycahill, Thurles, Co Tipperary.* Barley for Guinness grown on the farm. 200-year-old house in shadow of castle.
Open: Easter to Oct
504 21297 (also fax) Mr & Mrs Finn
nnfamily@eircom.net
D: Fr €32.00
Beds: 1F 1D 1T **Baths:** 2 Ensuite 1 Private Shared
⌂ 🅿 ⊱ 📺 ✕ Ⓥ ⠇⠇⠇

Bansha

9533

Cooleen House, *Ardane, Bansha, Tipperary.* Steeped in history - St Benisons Kiel, St Pecan's, ruins of C12th church.
Open: All Year (not Xmas)
62 54392 Mrs Farrell
pp@iol.ie
D: Fr €24.00
Beds: 4F 2D 1T 1S **Baths:** 4 En
⌂ 🅿 (6) 📺 ⠇⠇⠇ ☕

Foxford Farm House, *Foxford, Bansha, Co. Tipperary.* Comfortable friendly home. Central location for touring. All amenities close by.
Open: All Year (not Xmas/New Year)
62 54552 Mr & Mrs Russell
D: Fr €23.00 **S:** Fr €25.50
Beds: 1T 1F 2D **Baths:** 1 En 3 Pr
⌂ 🅿 ⊱ 📺 ⊱ ✕ Ⓥ ⠇⠇⠇ ☕ cc

Borrisokane

R9193

Dancer Cottage,
Borrisokane, Nenagh, County
Tipperary.
Open: Jan to Dec
067 27414 (also fax) Mr & Mrs Roedder

dcr@eircom.net dancercottage.cjb.net
D: Fr €28.00-€32.00 **S:** Fr €35.00
Beds: 1F 3D **Baths:** 4 En
⌂ 🅿 ⊱ 📺 ⊱ ✕ Ⓥ ⠇⠇⠇ ⚘ ☕ cc
Comfortable Tudor-style house. Quiet rural location by the ruin of an old castle, large garden area for guests. Ideal to relax, spend restful days. Fresh delicious home-cooking, baking. German, some French spoken, bicycles. Lough Derg, golf, sailing nearby.

Cahir

S0524 🍴 *Galtee Inn*

Ashling, *Dublin Road, Cahir, Co Tipperary.* Ground level family home, smoke free, electric blankets.
Open: All Year
052 41601 Mrs Fitzgerald
D: Fr €25.50 **S:** Fr €38.00
Beds: 1T 2D **Baths:** 3 En
🅿 (6) ⊱ 📺 ⠇⠇⠇ ☕

Hollymount House, *Upper Cahir Abbey, Cahir, Co Tipperary.* Country home in peaceful woodlands via mountain road. Walkers' paradise.
Open: All year
052 42888 & 087 2769641 (M) Ms Neville
D: Fr €23.00-€25.50 **S:** Fr €36.00-€38.50
Beds: 2F 1D 1T **Baths:** 2 En 1 Pr 2 Sh
⌂ 🅿 (6) 📺 ⠇⠇⠇ ☕

The Homestead, *Mitchelstown Road, Cahir, Co Tipperary.* Spacious bungalow, near town centre, all rooms ensuite plus TV. Car park.
Open: Jan to Nov
052 42043 Mrs Duffy
D: Fr €24.00 **S:** Fr €32.50
Beds: 1F 2D 1T **Baths:** 4 En
⌂ 🅿 (10) 📺 ⠇⠇⠇

Please respect a B&B's wishes regarding children, animals and smoking

All details shown are as supplied by B&B owners in Autumn 2002

S4021

The Grand Inn, *Nine Mile House, Carrick-on-Suir, Co Tipperary.* An old historic house restored in old style. Antique furnishings, private gardens. Personal supervision.
Open: All year **Grades:** BF Approv
051 647035 (also fax) Mr Coady
thegrandinn9@eircom.net
D: Fr €25.00-€30.00 **S:** Fr €35.00-€40.00
Beds: 2F 2D 2T **Baths:** 2 En 2 Sh
🛏 🅿 (5) ⅟ 📺 🐾 📺 🛏, ♨

S0740

Ladyswell House, *Ladydwell Street, Cashel, Co Tipperary.*
Open: All year (not Xmas)
062 62985 (also fax) K J Leahy

ladyswellhouse@eircom.net
www.tipp.ie/ladyswella.htm
D: Fr €27.00-€45.00 **S:** Fr €35.00-€55.00
Beds: 2F 2D 1T **Baths:** 5 En
🛏 📺 🐾 🛏, ♨ cc
Experience bygone charm with modern comforts 500 yards under Ireland's premier monument. We invite you to share a memorable visit to Tipperary with us. Ladyswell House has gained an outstanding reputation for service. Chauffeur service Mercedes S320 available for tours.

The Chestnuts, *Dualla Road, Rathclough, Cashel, Co Tipperary.* Award-winning farm residence, nestled amidst 170 acres. Landscaped scenic gardens.
Open: All year (not Xmas)
062 61469 (also fax) Mrs O'Halloran
bookings@thechestnuts.com www.thechestnuts.com
D: Fr €30.00 **S:** Fr €35.00-€40.00
Beds: 1F 2D 1T **Baths:** 4 En
🛏 🅿 (10) ✗ 🛏,

Dualla House, *Dualla, Cashel, Co Tipperary.*
Open: Mar to Nov
Grades: BF Appro
AA 4 Diamond
062 61487 (also fax) Mrs Power

duallahse@eircom.net www.tipp.ie/dualla-house.htn
D: Fr €32.00-€40.00 **S:** Fr €45.00-€55.00
Beds: 2F 1D 1T **Baths:** 4 En 1 Pr
🛏 🅿 (6) ⅟ 📺 🐾 🛏, ♨ cc
Elegant Georgian manor house on 300-acre sheep/grain farm. Splendid views of rolling parkland and mountains. Recommended in several guides. Spacious rooms with every comfort. Relax in front of peat fire. Garden, farr walks, ideal for relaxing break, golfing, racing e touring.

Rockside House B&B, *Rock Villas, Cashel, Co Tipperary.* Modern town house located at foot of world-famous Rock of Cashel.
Open: Mar to Nov
062 63813 (also fax) R & J Joy
D: Fr €28.00-€32.00 **S:** Fr €45.00
Beds: 1F 2T 1D **Baths:** 4 En
🛏 🅿 (5) ⅟ 📺 🛏, ♨

Indaville, *Cashel, Co Tipperary.* Centrally locate on the N8 at the southern end of Main Street.
Open: Mar to Nov
062 62075 Mrs Murphy
indaville@eircom.net
D: Fr €25.50-€28.00 **S:** Fr €32.00-€38.00
Beds: 1F 2T 2D **Baths:** 5 En
🛏 (3) 🅿 (8) ⅟ 📺 🐾 🛏, cc

Abbey House, *1 Dominic Street, Cashel, Co Tipperary.* Town house opposite Dominic's Abbey, 150m to Rock of Cashel.
Open: All Year (not Xmas)
062 61104 (also fax) Ms Ryan
D: Fr €25.50 **S:** Fr €32.00-€38.00
Beds: 1F 2D 1T 1S **Baths:** 3 En 2 Sh
🛏 🅿 (5) 📺 🛏, ♨ cc

Please respect a B&B's wishes regarding children, animals and smoking

Clonmel

S2021

Brighton House, *1 Brighton Place, Clonmel, Co Tipperary.* Family-run three storey Georgian guest house. Hotel ambience.
Open: All Year (not Xmas)
052 23665 Mrs Morris
brighton@iol.ie
D: Fr €38.00
Beds: 1F 3D 2S **Baths:** 3 En 1 Pr 2 Sh
ॐ (7) ▣ (6) 🖵 Ⅴ 🎹, ☎

Edermine House, *Fethard Road, Rathronan, Clonmel, Co Tipperary.* Spacious bungalow overlooking farm, close to equestrian centre.
Open: All Year (not Xmas)
052 23048 Mrs Cox
mike1@esatclear.ie
D: Fr €25.50
Beds: 1F 1D 2T **Baths:** 2 En 1 Sh
ॐ ▣ (10) 🖵 ★ 🎹.

Beentee, *Cahir Road, Ballingarrane, Clonmel, Co Tipperary.* Comfortable family bungalow, quiet cul-de-sac on main Limerick-Rosslare, Cork, Waterford road, N24. Private parking.
Open: Jan to Dec
052 21313 Mrs Deely
deelymartin@hotmail.com
D: Fr €23.00-€25.50 **S:** Fr €27.00-€29.50
Beds: 4F 1T 2D 1S **Baths:** 3 Pr 1 Sh
▣ (6) 🖵 ★ 🎹, ☎ cc

Benuala, *Marlfield Road, Clonmel, Co Tipperary.* Family bungalow. Ideal base for touring. Vegetarian breakfast available. Quiet location.
Open: All year
052 22158 Mrs O'Connell
benuala@indigo.ie
D: Fr €20.00 **S:** Fr €20.00
Beds: 3D 4T **Baths:** 5 En 2 Sh
ॐ ▣ ⊬ 🖵 ★ Ⅴ 🎹, ৬ ☎ cc

Carrodun, *Kilmacomma, Dungarvan Road, Clonmel, Co Tipperary.* Warm welcome assured, home baking. Close to all amenities.
Open: All year (not Xmas)
052 24349 Mrs Cliffe
D: Fr €18.00 **S:** Fr €18.00
Beds: 2F 1S **Baths:** 2 Sh
ॐ ▣ (4) ⊬ 🖵 ★ Ⅴ 🎹, ৬ ☎

Please respect a B&B's wishes regarding children, animals and smoking

Dualla

S1243

Tir Na Nog, *Dualla, Cashel, Co Tipperary.*
Open: All year (not Xmas/New Year)
062 61350 Mrs Brett-Moloney
Fax: 062 62411
tnanog@indigo.ie www.tirnanogbandb.com
D: Fr €28.00-€38.00 **S:** Fr €36.00-€45.00
Beds: 2F 2T 2D **Baths:** 6 En
ॐ (1) ▣ ⊬ 🖵 ★ 🎹, ☎ cc
Award-winning friendly country home. Landscaped gardens, peaceful surroundings, home-baking, orthopaedic beds. 3 miles from the Rock of Cashel. Ideal base for touring the south east. Tir Na Nog is a home away from home.

Dualla House, *Dualla, Cashel, Co Tipperary.* Elegant Georgian manor house on 300-acre sheep/grain farm. Splendid views.
Open: Mar to Nov **Grades:** BF Approv, AA 4 Diamond
062 61487 (also fax) Mrs Power
duallahse@eircom.net www.tipp.ie/dualla-house.htm
D: Fr €32.00-€40.00 **S:** Fr €45.00-€55.00
Beds: 2F 1D 1T **Baths:** 4 En 1 Pr
ॐ ▣ (6) ⊬ 🖵 ★ 🎹, ☎ cc

Fethard

S2034

The Gateway, *Rocklow Road, Fethard, Clonmel, Co Tipperary.* Town house in centre of Fethard.
Open: Apr to Oct
052 31701 Mr & Mrs Nevin
D: Fr €28.00
Beds: 1T 1D 2S **Baths:** 4 Ensuite
ॐ ▣ 🖵 🎹.

# BEDROOMS
D = Double   S = Single
T = Twin   F = Family

Please respect a B&B's wishes regarding children, animals and smoking

Golden
S0238

White Villa,
Mantle Hill, Golden, Cashel, Co Tipperary.
Open: All year
062 72323
Mrs Blundell **Fax: 062 72041**

whitevilla@unison.ie
D: Fr €21.00 **S:** Fr €24.00
Beds: 4F 1T 2D **Baths:** 7 En
🛏 🅿 (10) ⅓ 📺 ▥ 🐾 cc
Spanish-style home, country view. Excellence Award winner 2001. Situated on N74 from Cashel to Golden, where a warm welcome awaits you. Spacious bedrooms. Close to famous Rock of Cashel and many leisure facilities: horseriding, golf, pitch and putt, tennis, driving range, cart racing. 5 min drive from Cashel town. Families welcome.

Kilkeary
R9475

The Country House, Thurles Road, Kilkeary, Nenagh, Co Tipperary. Luxurious residence. Recommended in Frommer Guide. Rooms have tea/coffee facilities.
Open: All Year
067 31193 Mrs Kennedy
D: Fr €25.50
Beds: 1F 1T 2D **Baths:** 4 Ensuite
🛏 🅿 📺 ▣ ▥ ⅙ ▪

Kilsheelan
S2823

Nagles Bar, Kilsheelan, Clonmel, Co Tipperary. Modern bar and accommodation in scenic area, adjacent to River Suir and mountains.
Open: All Year
052 33496 Mr & Mrs Gleeson
D: Fr €25.00
Beds: 5D 1T **Baths:** 6 En
🛏 🅿 (20) 📺 🐾 ✕ ▣ ▥ ▪ cc

Nenagh
R8779

Ashley Park House,
Nenagh, Co Tipperary.
Friendly welcome, C17th country house overlooks Lough Ourna. Boating and fishing, walled garden.
Open: All year
067 38223 Mr & Mrs Mounsey **Fax: 067 38013**
margaret@ashleypark.com www.ashleypark.com
D: Fr €40.00-€50.00 **S:** Fr €50.00-€60.00
Beds: 2F 2D 1T **Baths:** 5 En
🛏 🅿 (10) 📺 🐾 ✕ ▣ ▥ ▪

Williamsferry House,
Fintan Lawlor Street, Nenagh Co Tipperary.
Located centrally. Ideal for touring. Private car park. Warm welcome.
Open: Jan to Dec **Grades:** BF Approv, AA 3 Diamond
067 31118 Mr & Mrs Devine **Fax: 067 31256**
willamsferry@eircom.net
D: Fr €27.00-€30.00 **S:** Fr €39.00-€43.00
Beds: 2F 2D 2T **Baths:** 6 En
🛏 🅿 (12) 📺 ▥ ▪ cc

Newcastle-on-Suir
S1213

Kilmaneen Farmhouse, Newcastle-on-Suir, Clonmel, Co Tipperary. National Rural Tourism Award Winner. The complete rural experience.
Open: Easter to Nov
052 36231 (also fax) Mrs O'Donnell
kilmaneen@eircom.net
www.dirl.com.tipperary/kilmaneen.htm
D: Fr €28.50 **S:** Fr €38.00
Beds: 2D 1T **Baths:** 3 En
🛏 (4) 🅿 (5) ⅓ 📺 ✕ ▣ ▥ ▪ cc

Newtown (Nenagh)
R8081

Curraghbawn House, Lake Drive, Newtown, Nenagh, Co Tipperary. Spacious period residence on Lough Derg Way, lake boat available extra.
Open: All Year (not Xmas)
067 23226 Mrs O'Callaghan
D: Fr €19.00-€25.50 **S:** Fr €25.50-€32.00
Beds: 2F 1D 1T **Baths:** 1 En 1 Pr 1 Sh
🛏 🅿 (8) 📺 🐾 ✕ ▣ ▥ ▪

RATES

D = Price range per person sharing in a double or twin room

S = Price range for a single room

S1042

The Chestnuts, *Dualla Road, Rathclough, Cashel, Co Tipperary.* Award-winning farm residence, nestled amidst 170 acres. Landscaped scenic gardens.
Open: All year (not Xmas)
062 61469 (also fax) Mrs O'Halloran
bookings@thechestnuts.com www.thechestnuts.com
D: Fr €30.00 **S:** Fr €35.00-€40.00
Beds: 1F 2D 1T **Baths:** 4 En
⑤ ☐ (10) ✕ ▥

S1389

Cregganbell, *Birr Road, Roscrea, Co Tipperary.* Comfortable bungalow, electric blankets, just off N7, central for touring midlands.
Open: Easter to Oct
505 21421 Mrs Fallon
cregganbell@eircom.net
D: Fr €24.00 **S:** Fr €24.00
Beds: 3D 1T **Baths:** 4 En
⑤ ☐ (8) ⌦ ▥ ♁ ▥ ▪

18600

Coolangatta B&B, *Brocka, Ballinderry, Nenagh, Co Tipperary.* Spectacular lake views, breakfast menu, garden, quiet location. Irish music nights.
Open: All year
067 22164 Mrs McGeeney
coolangatta@eircom.net
D: Fr €27.00 **S:** Fr €35.00
Beds: 1F 2D 1T **Baths:** 3 En 1 Sh
⑤ ☐ (10) ⌦ ▥ ♁ ✕ ▥ ▥ ▪ cc

S1258

Culin House, *Templemore Road, Thurles, Co Tipperary.* Beautiful family home, good breakfasts. World wide guest recommendations. Ideal touring base.
Open: Mar to Nov
0504 23237 Mrs Cavanagh **Fax: 0504 26075**
thurlesbandb@eircom.net
homepage.eircom.net/~thurlesbandb/bord.html
D: Fr €25.50 **S:** Fr €32.50-€38.00
Beds: 2F 1D 1T **Baths:** 3 En 1 Sh
⑤ ☐ (10) ▥ ♁ ▥ ▥ ▪ cc

R8935

Homeleigh Farmhouse, *Ballinacourty, Glen of Aherlow, Tipperary.* Luxurious farmhouse. Residential riding holidays, hill/mountain walks, evening meals.
Open: All year **Grades:** BF Approv
062 56228 Mr & Mrs Frewen
homeleighfarmhouse@eircom.net
www.homeleighfarmhouse.com
D: Fr €32.00 **S:** Fr €40.00
Beds: 2F 2D 1T **Baths:** 5 En
⑤ ☐ (10) ▥ ♁ ✕ ▥ ▥ ♿ ✻ cc

Purt House, *Emly Road, Bohercrow, Tipperary.* R515 to Killarney: it's not a long way to Tipperary.
Open: Apr to Nov
062 51938 Mrs Collins
D: Fr €24.00-€28.00 **S:** Fr €32.00-€36.00
Beds: 2F 2D 2T **Baths:** 5 En 1 Pr
⑤ ☐ (10) ⌦ ▥ ✕ ▥ ▥ ▪ cc

Teach Gobnathan, *Golf Links Road, Tipperary.* Modern home beside Tipperary golf course, on scenic route to Aherlow, warm welcome.
Open: Jan to Nov
062 51645 Mrs Merrigan
D: Fr €25.50
Beds: 3T 1D 1S **Baths:** 3 Ensuite 2 Shared
☐ (6) ▥ ✕ ▥ ▥ ▪

Planning a longer stay?
Always ask for any special rates

Villa Maria, *Limerick Road, Bohercrowe,*
Tipperary. Modern family home on Limerick Road
(N24). Leisure facilities, golf nearby.
Open: May to Sep
062 51557 Mrs O'Neill
D: Fr €26.50
Beds: 1F 1D 1T **Baths:** 2 Ensuite 1 Private
1 Shared
❧ 🅿 ⅍ 📺 �.

Twomileborris
S1857

Dunboy House, *Cork Dublin Road N8 Turnpike*
Twomileborris, Thurles, Co Tipperary.
Bungalow farmhouse, farm animals, ponies, fowl
large garden front and rear.
Open: All Year
0504 44343 Mrs Healy
D: Fr €29.00
Beds: 3F 1T **Baths:** 4 En
❧ (1) 🅿 (15) ⅍ 📺 🐾 Ⅴ III. ▪

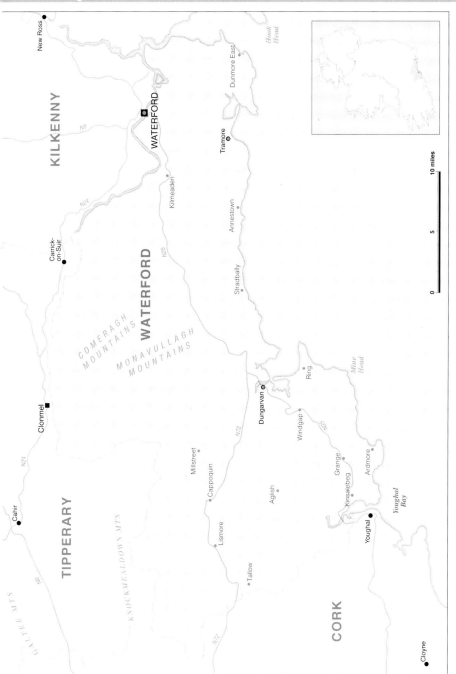

AIRPORT ⊕

The nearest international airport is at
Cork (see Co Cork chapter).

RAIL ⇌

Waterford is on the main lines to **Dublin
(Connolly), Limerick Junction** and
Rosslare.

For timetable details phone
Irish Rail on 01 8366222.

BUS 🚌

Waterford to **Dublin** *(8 daily).*
Tel. **Bus Eireann** on 01 8366111.

TOURIST INFORMATION OFFICES 🄸

Gratton Square, **Dungarvan** (mid-Jun to
Aug), 058 41741.

Railway Square, **Tramore**, 051 381572.

41 The Quay, **Waterford** (open all year),
051 875823.

Cork Road, **Waterford** (open all year),
051 332500.

Aglish

X1290

Aglish House, *Aglish, Cappoquin, Co Waterford.*
Relax in our old world-style home. Resident chef.
Open: All Year
024 96191 T & T Moore **Fax: 024 96482**
aglishhouse@eircom.net www.aglishhouse.com
D: Fr €38.00-€44.50 **S:** Fr €51.00-€57.00
Beds: 2F 1T 1D **Baths:** 3 En 1 Pr
🐕 🅿 📺 🛏 ✕ 🖿

Annestown

X4898

Annestown House,
Annestown, Co Waterford.
Open: All year
051 396160 Mr & Mrs
Galloway **Fax: 051 396474**
relax@annestown.com www.annestown.com
D: Fr €47.50-€60.00 **S:** Fr €65.00-€75.00
Beds: 3D 2T **Baths:** 5 En
🅿 (20) 📺 ✕ 🆅 🖿 ▪ cc
A country house of character on Waterford's
renowned Copper Coast. A place for unfussy
relaxation - grass tennis court, croquet lawn,
billiard table and several sitting rooms. Private
path to beach, Waterford, Comeragh Mountains,
8 golf courses, caves, fishing harbours all nearby.

Benvoy, *Annestown, Waterford.*
Beautiful peaceful countryside. Large guest
rooms overlooking sea with TV tea/coffee makin
facilities.
Open: All Year
051 396340 (also fax) Mrs Fiorani-Fitzpatrick
pfiorani@hotmail.com
D: Fr €20.50-€25.50 **S:** Fr €27.00-€32.00
Beds: 3F 1D **Baths:** 3 En
🐕 🅿 ⅄ 📺 ✕ 🆅 🖿 ☀ ▪ cc

Ardmore

X1877

Newtown Farm Guest House, *Grange,
Ardmore, Youghal, Co Cork.* Tudor-type house,
private garden with views of the river and the
mountains.
Open: All year (not Xmas)
024 94143 & 086 2600799 Mrs O'Connor **Fax: 02
94143**
newtownfarm@eircom.net www.newtownfarm.com
D: Fr €30.00-€36.00 **S:** Fr €30.00-€40.00
Beds: 3F 2D 2T **Baths:** 7 Pr
🐕 🅿 (8) ⅄ 📺 🛏 🖿 ▪ cc

Planning a longer stay?
Always ask for any special rates

Summerhill Farm House, *Kinsalebeg, Youghal, Co Cork.*
Modern farm bungalow with panoramic view of Atlantic Ocean.
Open: Mar to Dec
024 92682 (also fax) Mrs Budds
summerhillfm@eircom.net www.summerhillfm.com
D: Fr €30.00 **S:** Fr €40.00
Beds: 6F 1D 2T **Baths:** 5 En
⌂ P ⌱ TV ▥

Cappoquin
X1099

Coohilla, *Ballyhane, Cappoquin, Co Waterford.*
Ambassador of Tourism' winner. Ideal for walking, fishing, golfing. Highly recommended.
Open: All Year (not Xmas)
058 54054 (also fax) Mrs Scanlon
D: Fr €25.50 **S:** Fr €31.00
Beds: 1F 1D 1T **Baths:** 3 En
⌂ ⌱ TV ✕ V ▥ ❄ ▪ cc

Dungarvan
X2693

Ballyguiry Farm, *Dungarvan, Co Waterford.*
Open: Apr to Oct
058 41194 (also fax)
Mrs Kiely
katkiely@eircom.net
D: Fr €30.00 **S:** Fr €38.00
Beds: 2F 1D 1T **Baths:** 1 Pr 1 Sh 3 En
⌂ P ⌱ TV ✕ ▥ cc
Georgian house overlooking the beautiful Brickey Valley with Monavullagh Mountains in the background. Signposted on N25 road, south of Dungarvan, 10 mins to town centre. Dairy farm, pony, play area for children. Small tennis court, garden with various heathers, roses and shrubs.

Ashley, *Waterford Road, Dungarvan, Co Waterford.* Country home on the N25. Adjoining Dungarvan Golf Club. 1km town.
Open: Easter to Oct
058 42064 Mrs Dwane
D: Fr €25.00
Beds: 3F 2T 1D **Baths:** 1 Ensuite 2 Private
⌂ P ⌱ TV V ▥ ⚴

Cairbre House, *Strandside North, Abbeyside, Dungarvan, Co Waterford.*
Open: Easter to Oct
Grades: BF Approv
058 42338
Mr Wickham & Family
cairbrehouse@eircom.net
D: Fr €26.00-€32.00 **S:** Fr €32.00-€38.00
Beds: 1F 2D 1T **Baths:** 3 En 1 Pr 1 Sh
⌂ P (6) TV V ▥ cc
Relaxing home built in 1819. Award-winning B&B with old world charm, scenic setting and beautiful gardens. Home and local produce used for delicious breakfasts. Ideal touring/walking base. Excellent pubs, traditional music less than 1km away. Located 150m off N25.

Rosebank, *Coast Road, Dungarvan, Co Waterford.*
Open: Mar to Dec
Grades: BF Approv
058 41561
Mrs Sleator
msleator@eircom.net www.rosebankhouse.com
D: Fr €26.50-€30.00 **S:** Fr €39.00-€42.00
Beds: 1F 2D 1T **Baths:** 3 En 1 Sh
⌂ (6) P (6) ⌱ TV ✕ ▥ ▪ cc
Enjoy warm hospitality in our home situated on the R675 Coast Road, 2 miles from Dungarvan. Uninterrupted mountain views. Blue Flag beach, 2 18-hole golf courses 1 mile. Firm beds, electric blankets. Gourmet breakfast menu. Tea/coffee facilities in lounge.

Ard Na Coille Farm, *Clonmel Road R672 off N72, Dungarvan, Co Waterford.*
Charming farm residence, breathtaking views, surrounded by prize-winning gardens, excellent food. Many recommendations, a walkers' paradise, horseriding locally.
Open: All year (not Xmas) **Grades:** BF Approv
058 68145 Mrs Kennedy
kencol&iol.ie www.waterfordfarms.com/ardnacoille
D: Fr €27.00-€29.00 **S:** Fr €32.00-€35.00
Beds: 2F 1D **Baths:** 3 En
⌂ P (6) ⌱ TV ⌖ ✕ V ▥ ⚴ ▪ cc

Planning a longer stay? Always ask for any special rates

Farm Lodge, *Clonea Road (R675), Dungarvan, Co Waterford.*
Open: All year (not Xmas/New Year)
058 42574 & 087 9228307 (M)
Mrs Dwane
fdwane@queallygrp.com www.farmlodge.com
D: Fr €27.00-€28.00 **S:** Fr €40.00
Beds: 1F 2T **Baths:** 3 Pr
꜒ 🅿 (5) ⚹ 📺 Ⓥ 🏠, ♨ cc
Enjoy warm, friendly welcome in our comfortable home. Panoramic views of the sea and mountains convenient to town, beach and local amenities, prestigious golf courses. Ideal for bird watchers. Highly recommended by German Consul. 'Let our home be your home'.

Abbeyhouse, *Friars Walk, Abbeyside, Dungarvan, Co Waterford.* Luxury bungalow by the sea with exceptionally warm welcome. Breathtaking views in tranquil surroundings.
Open: All Year (not Xmas)
058 41669 Mrs Phelan
D: Fr €23.00-€28.00 **S:** Fr €32.00
Beds: 12F 1T **Baths:** 2 En 1 Pr
꜒ 🅿 📺 🐾 Ⓥ 🏠, ♨

The Old Rectory, *Waterford Road, Dungarvan, Co Waterford.* Situated on 2.5 acres, cable TV, tea/coffee facilities in bedrooms.
Open: All year (not Xmas)
058 41394 & 086 2501410 (M) Mrs Prendergast
Fax: 058 41394
theoldrectory@cablesurf.com
homepage.eircom.net/~1108
D: Fr €26.00-€30.00 **S:** Fr €32.00-€35.00
Beds: 1F 2D 1T **Baths:** 4 En
꜒ 🅿 📺 ✕ 🏠, ♨

Failte House, *Youghal Road, Dungarvan, Co Waterford.* Lovely town house, overlooking sea. Nice restful garden. Quiet location, good parking.
Open: Easter to Oct
058 44170 Mrs Spratt **Fax:** 058 44343
D: Fr €38.00
Beds: 2D 2T **Baths:** 4 Ensuite
🅿 (5) 📺 Ⓥ 🏠, ♨

An Bohreen, *Killineen West, Dungarvan, Co Waterford.* Quarter mile off N25. Sea and mountain views. Fine dining.
Open: Mar to Oct
051 291010 A and J Mulligan **Fax:** 051 291011
mulligan@anbohreen.com www.anbohreen.com
D: Fr €32.00 **S:** Fr €50.00
Beds: 1T 3D **Baths:** 4 En
🅿 (4) ⚹ ✕ 🏠, cc

Dunmore East

S6800

Church Villa, *Dunmore East, Waterford.*
Open: All year (not Xmas)
051 383390 Mr & Mrs Lannon **Fax:** 051 383023
churchvilla@eircom.net
homepage.eircom.net/~churchvilla
D: Fr €28.00 **S:** Fr €30.00
Beds: 1F 3D 1T 1S **Baths:** 5 En
꜒ (4) 📺 Ⓥ 🏠, ♨ cc
Beautiful Victorian town house B&B in centre of picturesque village. Idyllic surroundings. Coves, sheltered harbours, cliff walks. Blue Flag beach, sailing, angling and diving. Five golf courses within twenty minutes. Horseback riding nearby. Excellent restaurants and pubs, all within walking distance.

Foxmount Country House, *Passage East Road, Dunmore East, Waterford.* Beautiful C17th country house on 200 acres with log fires and antique furnishings.
Open: Mar to Nov **Grades:** BF Approv
051 874308 Mrs Kent **Fax:** 051 854906
foxmouth@iol.ie www.iol.ie/tipp/foxmount.htm
D: Fr €45.00-€50.00 **S:** Fr €60.00
Beds: 1F 2T 2D **Baths:** 5 En
🅿 ⚹ 📺 ✕ Ⓥ 🏠,

Ashgrove, *Dunmore East, Waterford.* Country house near seaside in peaceful scenic surroundings.
Open: Mar to Nov
051 383195 Mrs Battles
D: Fr €24.00-€25.50 **S:** Fr €32.00-€33.00
Beds: 1F 2D 1T **Baths:** 4 En
꜒ 🅿 (10) 📺 🐾 🏠, ♨ cc

Please respect a B&B's wishes regarding children, animals and smoking

Lakefield House, *Rosduff, Dunmore East, Waterford.* Beautiful house by the lakeside. Superb home cooking guaranteed.
Open: Mar to Oct
051 382582 & 051 382305 Mrs Carney **Fax: 051 382582**
D: Fr €32.00
Beds: 1F 2D 2T **Baths:** 5 Ensuite
ॐ 🅿 ⅍ 📺 🛏 ✕ Ⓥ ▥ ♿

Creaden View, *Dunmore East, Waterford.* Charming, friendly home in centre of village, overlooking the sea.
Open: Mar to Nov
051 383339 (also fax) Mrs Martin
D: Fr €29.00
Beds: 1F 3D 1T **Baths:** 5 En
ॐ (6) 📺 ▥ ▪

Copper Beach, *Dock Road, Dunmore East, Waterford.* Modern bungalow in beautiful location overlooking harbour and sailing club.
Open: Easter to Oct
051 383187 Mrs Hayes
D: Fr €29.00
Beds: 2F 1D 1T **Baths:** 4 En 1 Pr 1 Sh
ॐ 🅿 (6) ⅍ 📺 ▥ ▪ cc

Grange
X1782

Newtown Farm Guest House, *Grange, Ardmore, Youghal, Co Cork.* Tudor-type house, private garden with views of the river and the mountains.
Open: All year (not Xmas)
024 94143 & 086 2600799 Mrs O'Connor **Fax: 024 94143**
newtownfarm@eircom.net www.newtownfarm.com
D: Fr €30.00-€36.00 **S:** Fr €30.00-€40.00
Beds: 3F 2D 2T **Baths:** 7 Pr
ॐ 🅿 (8) ⅍ 📺 🛏 ▥ ▪ cc

Kilmeaden
S5110

Dawn B&B, *Kildarmody, Kilmeaden, Waterford.* Modern bungalow in a peaceful quiet area - Waterford Crystal nearby.
Open: Mar to Oct
051 384465 Mrs Fitzgerald
dawnbabdb@esactclear.ie
D: Fr €25.50
Beds: 1F 1D 1T **Baths:** 3 En
ॐ 🅿 (10) ⅍ 📺 ✕ ▥ cc

Kinard, *Adamstown, Kilmeaden, Waterford.* Just off N25, ideal for visiting Waterford crystal factory.
Open: Easter to Oct
051 384505 Mr & Mrs Walsh
kinard@eircom.net
D: Fr €26.00
Beds: 1D 3T **Baths:** 4 En
ॐ 🅿 ⅍ 📺 🛏 ▥ ♿ ▪ cc

Kinsalebeg
X1280

Gables, *Rath, Kinsalebeg, Youghal, Co Cork.* Modern home on N25 Route. Two miles from beach.
Open: March to Nov
024 92739 Mrs Cliffe
D: Fr €23.00 **S:** Fr €27.50-€30.00
Beds: 4F 1T 1D **Baths:** 1 En 1 Pr 1 Sh
ॐ 🅿 ⅍ 🛏 ▥ cc

Lismore
X0498

Pine Tree House, *Ballyanchor, Lismore, Co Waterford.* Situated on outskirts of Lismore. Walking distance to Lismore Castle.
Open: All year
058 53282 Mrs Power
pinetreehouse@oceanfree.net
www.pinetreehouselismore.com
D: Fr €25.50-€28.00 **S:** Fr €36.50-€38.50
Beds: 1F 1T 1D **Baths:** 3 En
ॐ 🅿 (10) ⅍ 📺 🛏 ▥ Ⓥ ▪ cc

Millstreet
S1601

The Castle, *Cappagh, Millstreet, Dungarvan, Co Waterford.* Award-winning restored wing of C15th castle set between Comeragh and Knockmealdown Mountains.
Open: Easter to Nov
058 68049 Mrs Nugent **Fax: 058 68099**
D: Fr €42.00
Beds: 5F 2D 2T **Baths:** 5 En 5 Pr
ॐ (2) 🅿 📺 🛏 ✕ Ⓥ ▥ ▪ cc

Ring

X2988

Helvick View, *Ring, Dungarvan, Co Waterford.*
Open: Apr to Sep
058 46297 Mrs Maher
D: Fr €26.00
Beds: 4D **Baths:** 4 En

🅿 ✕ 🖵, 🐾 cc

Seaside bungalow with ensuite rooms overlooking Dungarvan Bay and Helvick Harbour and view of Comeragh Mountains. Rose garden for guest use. Three golf courses nearby. Also pony trekking. Pubs and restaurants nearby. Sea- and river-fishing nearby.

Gortnadiha House, *Ring, Dungarvan, County Waterford.* Gracious country home with sea views on a working dairy farm.
Open: Mar to Nov
058 46142 Mrs Harty **Fax: 058 46538**
ringcheese@eircom.net
D: Fr €35.00
Beds: 2F 1T **Baths:** 2 En 1 Pr
⛱ (10) 🅿 📺 🐾 🔽 🖵, 🐾 cc

Stradbally

X3697

Park House, *Stradbally, Kilmacthomas, Co Waterford.* Superb C19th farmhouse with amazing garden where our guests can sit and relax.
Open: Easter to Nov
051 293185 (also fax) Mrs Connors
www.waterfordfarms.com/parkhouse
D: Fr €23.50-€25.50 **S:** Fr €25.00-€27.00
Beds: 1D 1S **Baths:** 2 En 1 Sh
⛱ (10) 🅿 (20) 🍴 📺 🐾 🔽 🖵,

Tallow

W9993 🍺 *Brideview Bar, Kenny's, Glencairn Inn*

Sunlea, *Chapel Street, Tallow, Co Waterford.*
Dormer bungalow in quiet neighbourhood. Good breakfasts. Very friendly hosts.
Open: Apr to Sep
058 56150 Mrs Power
D: Fr €22.50 **S:** Fr €25.50
Beds: 1F 1T 1D **Baths:** 3 En
⛱ 🅿 (5) 🐾 🖵, 🐾

Devonshire Arms, *Tallow, Co Waterford.*
Open: All year (not Xmas/ New Year) **Grades:** BF 3 Star
058 56128 & 058 56170
J Clancy
seanclancy90@hotmail.com
D: Fr €28.00 **S:** Fr €28.00
Beds: 4F 1T 2D **Baths:** 7 En
🅿 (10) 📺 ✕ 🖵, 🐾 cc

Noted C18th coach house situated on main Youghal-Fermoy Road N72 (L36). Family run, home cooking. Trout fishing on River Bride (1km), salmon fishing on Blackwater River (8km), selection of golf courses within 30km.

Tramore

S5801

Cloneen, *Love Lane, Tramore, Co Waterford.*
Open: All year
051 381264 (also fax) Mrs Skedd
cloneen@iol.ie
www.cloneen.net
D: Fr €30.00-€32.00 **S:** Fr €50.00
Beds: 2F 2D 1T **Baths:** 5 En
⛱ 🅿 (5) 🍴 📺 ✕ 🖵, 🐾 cc

Family-run detached home set in landscaped gardens. Quiet location with private off-street parking. Close to beach, Splashworld, golf, tennis & Waterford Crystal. Guest conservatory. All rooms ensuite with TV, tea/coffee facilities. Master/Visa cards accepted.

Sea Court, *Tivoli Road, Tramore, Co Waterford.*
Open: All year (not Xmas)
Grades: BF Approv
051 386244 Mr Moran
www.tramore.net/tramore/seacourt.htm
D: Fr €30.00-€35.00 **S:** Fr €45.00
Beds: 1F 2T 3D **Baths:** 6 En
⛱ (9) 🅿 (7) 🍴 📺 🐾 🔽 🖵, ♿ 🐾 cc

Luxurious home in the heart of Tramore. All rooms ensuite with multi-channel TV, tea/coffee etc. Guest lounge, extensive breakfast menu, secure parking, credit cards accepted, home from home, Town & Country Approved.

Chetwynd, *7 Spring Mount, Tramore, Co Waterford.*
Open: May to Sep
051 386230 P Hassett
D: Fr €22.00-€25.00 **S:** Fr €30.00
Beds: 1F 2D 1T **Baths:** 2 En 2 Sh
⌂ ▣ (4) TV Ⓥ ▥ ▪ cc
Highly-recommended modern bungalow, FHI Approved, rooms ensuite. Friendly family home situated in quiet residential area cul-de-sac, overlooking Tramore Bay, safe parking, pleasant gardens, adjacent to racecourse, Splashworld, beach, tennis, 18-hole championship golf course 5 mins drive.

Belair, *Racecourse Road, Tramore, Co Waterford.*
Open: Apr to Oct
051 381605 & 051 386265 Mary Curran **Fax: 051 386688**
belair@holidayhound.com www.belairtramore.com
D: Fr €40.00-€50.00
Beds: 3F 1T 2D **Baths:** 6 En
⌂ ▣ ▣ TV ✕ ▥ ⅊ ▪
Belair is a lovely Georgian house, featuring delightful enclosed gardens, overlooking Tramore Bay and miles of beach, offering safe parking. Fishing, tennis, surfing, horseriding, golf and Splashworld all at hand. Waterford Crystal & six golf courses within 8 miles radius.

Seamist, *Newtown, Tramore, Co Waterford.*
Luxurious, spacious home. Renowned generous breakfast, on coastal historical walk.
Open: Feb to Nov **Grades:** BF Approv
051 381533 (also fax) Mrs McCarthy
annflor@iol.ie www.tramore.net/seamist
D: Fr €26.50-€30.00 **S:** Fr €39.00-€45.00
Beds: 1F 1D 1T **Baths:** 3 En
⌂ (8) ▣ (3) ⅊ TV Ⓥ ▥ ▪ cc

Avanti, *Pickardstown, Tramore, Co Waterford.*
Large modern bungalow with spacious bedrooms. Recommended for its hospitality.
Open: June to Sep
051 381671 Mrs
avantibb@eircom.net
D: Fr €28.00-€30.00
Beds: 1F 2T 1D **Baths:** 4 En
⌂ ▣ (6) ⅊ TV ▥ ▪ cc

Oban, *1 Eastlands, Pond Road, Tramore, Co Waterford.*
Spacious, luxurious home. Walking distance to beach, golf, races, tennis, Splashworld, restaurants and pubs.
Open: All year (not Xmas)
051 381537 Mrs McCarthy
D: Fr €25.00-€30.00 **S:** Fr €37.00-€42.50
Beds: 2F 2D **Baths:** 4 En
⌂ (3) ▣ (4) TV Ⓥ ▥ ▪ cc

Ard Mor House, *Doneraile Drive, Tramore, Co Waterford.*
Centrally-located overlooking Bay. Walking distance beaches, Splashworld, pubs, restaurants.
Open: Apr to Oct
051 381716 & 086 3797943 (M) Ms McGrath
D: Fr €28.00-€35.00
Beds: 1F 2D **Baths:** 3 En
⌂ (6) ▣ (2) Ⓥ ▥ ▪

Knockville, *Moonvoy, Tramore, Co Waterford.*
Country home situated in rural area on R682. Owner chef, excellent cuisine.
Open: Mar to Dec
051 381084 Mr & Mrs O'Meara
D: Fr €25.50
Beds: 1F 3D 1T **Baths:** 3 En 2 Sh
⌂ ▣ (6) ✝ ✕ ▥ ▪ cc

Glenorney, *Newtown, Tramore, Co Waterford.*
Luxurious home and gardens with panoramic view of Tramore Bay.
Open: Feb to Nov
051 381056 (also fax) Mrs Murphy
Glenoney@iol.ie
D: Fr €35.00
Beds: 2F 2D 2T **Baths:** 6 En
⌂ ▣ ⅊ TV ✝ Ⓥ ▥ ⅊ ▪ cc

Ardview House, *Lower Branch Road, Tramore, Co Waterford.* Georgian house overlooking sea. View from all windows, very central location.
Open: All Year (not Xmas)
051 381687 Mrs O'Connor
D: Fr €20.50-€25.50 **S:** Fr €25.50-€32.00
Beds: 2F 3D **Baths:** 5 En 2 Pr
⌂ TV ✝ ▥ ▪ cc

Cliff House, *Cliff Road, Tramore, Co Waterford.*
Luxury home with panoramic view of Tramore
Bay. Breakfast - extensive menu, beautiful dining
room.
Open: Feb to Nov
051 381497 (also fax) Mrs O'Sullivan
cliffhouse@tramore.net
D: Fr €32.00
Beds: 3F 3D **Baths:** 6 Ensuite 1 Shared
⛱ (6) 🅿 (10) ⌇ 📺 📶 🛏 ⬛

Radharc na Mara, *Westown, Tramore, Co
Waterford.* Panoramic sea view pitch and putt
opposite situated on designated scenic route.
Open: Easter to Sept
051 381606 Mrs Power
D: Fr €20.50-€23.00 **S:** Fr €25.50
Beds: 1F 1T 1D **Baths:** 2 En 1 Sh
🅿 (6) 📺 ⬥ 📶 🛏 ⬛ cc

Glenart House, *Tivoli Road, Tramore, Co
Waterford.* Elegant restored 1920s detached
residence convenient to Splash World.
Open: Easter to Nov
051 381236 Mr & Mrs Heraughty **Fax: 051 391236**
tourismse@eircom.net
D: Fr €35.00
Beds: 4F 4T **Baths:** 4 En
⛱ 🅿 (8) ⌇ 📺 📶 🛏 ⬛ cc

Waterford

S6011

Sion Hill House,
*Rosslare Road,
Ferrybank,
Waterford City.*
Open: All year (not
Xmas)
051 851558
Mrs Kavanagh **Fax:**
051 851678
sionhill@eircom.net
D: Fr €38.00-€55.00 **S:** Fr €47.00-€70.00
Beds: 3F 1D **Baths:** 4 En
⛱ 🅿 (15) ⌇ 📺 📶 🛏 ⬛ cc
Charming Listed Georgian manor on 5 acres of
park and woodland overlooking the River Suir. An
oasis of tranquillity within 10 mins walk of the city
centre, wonderful old gardens containing many
rare plants, TV and tea/coffee facility in each
room, highly recommended.

**The Coach
House,**
*Butlerstown Castle,
Butlerstown,
Waterford.*
Open: Feb to Dec
Grades: BF 3 Star,
AA 4 Diamond
051 384656 Mr O'Keeffe **Fax: 051 384751**
coachhse@iol.ie www.iol.ie/~coachhse
D: Fr €37.50-€47.50 **S:** Fr €50.00-€60.00
Beds: 5D 2T **Baths:** 7 En
⛱ 🅿 (15) ⌇ 📺 📶 ⬛ cc
An elegantly-restored C19th house, 3 miles from
Waterford city (Waterford Crystal 5 minutes
away). Historic, tranquil, romantic setting (C13th
castle in grounds). Excellent pubs, restaurants
nearby. Five golf courses within 6 miles radius.
Best Magazine's No 1 in Ireland.

**Foxmount Country
House,** *Passage East Road,
Dunmore East, Waterford.*
Beautiful C17th country
house on 200 acres with log
fires and antique furnishings.
Open: Mar to Nov **Grades:** BF Approv
051 874308 Mrs Kent **Fax: 051 854906**
foxmouth@iol.ie www.iol.ie/tipp/foxmount.htm
D: Fr €45.00-€50.00 **S:** Fr €60.00
Beds: 1F 2T 2D **Baths:** 5 En
🅿 ⌇ 📺 ✕ 📶 🛏

24 Morley Terrace, *Gracedieu, Waterford.*
Victorian town house, with Waterford Crystal, golf
courses & beaches nearby.
Open: May to Sep
051 855879 Mrs Murphy
D: Fr €23.00-€25.00 **S:** Fr €23.00-€25.00
Beds: 1F 1T 1S **Baths:** 1 En 1 Sh
⛱ (4) 📺

Rice Guest House, *Barrack Street, Waterford.*
Rice guest house is purpose built, with hotel
surroundings and guest house prices. 21 ensuite
bedrooms, cable TV and DD telephones, a
comfortable stay is guaranteed. Located in
Waterford's city centre, it's positioned close to all
the amenities Waterford has to offer.
Open: All year (not Xmas)
051 371606 & 051 351352 Mr
info@riceguesthouse.com www.rkguesthouse.com
D: Fr €40.00-€45.00 **S:** Fr €50.00-€60.00
Beds: 21D **Baths:** 21 En
⛱ 🅿 ⌇ 📺 ✕ 📶 cc

Loughdan, *Dublin Road, Waterford.* Situated 1 mile from Waterford on main Dublin-Limerick road.
Open: All year (not Xmas/New Year)
051 876021 Mrs Dullaghan
info@loughdan.net www.loughdan.net
D: Fr €26.00-€28.00 **S:** Fr €38.00-€40.00
Beds: 1F 3T 2D **Baths:** 5 En 1 Pr
☎ ▣ (7) ⅙ ▦ ▥, ▪

Marsuci Country Home, *Olivers Hill, Butlerstown, Waterford.* In a rural location, not far from Waterford Crystal.
Open: All Year (not Xmas/New Year)
051 370429 Mr & Mrs Ostinelli **Fax: 051 350983**
marsuci@indigo.ie
D: Fr €33.00
Beds: 2F 2D 1T 1S **Baths:** 6 Ensuite
☎ (3) ▣ (8) ▦ ✕ ▥ ▦, ▪

Abhaile, *Cork Road, Butlerstown, Waterford.* Modern purpose built accommodation set in 3 acres 5 minutes from crystal factory.
Open: Easter to Oct
051 384590 Mrs O'Donnell
D: Fr €18.00 **S:** Fr €20.50
Beds: 1F 2D 3T **Baths:** 3 En 3 Sh
☎ ▣ (10) ⅙ ▦ ▥ ▦, ⅙

Dunroven, *Cork Road (N25), Ballinaneesagh, Waterford.* Modern home. Cork/Waterford N25. 2 mins crystal factory. Cable TV in bedrooms.
Open: All Year
051 374743 & 051 377050 Mrs Power **Fax: 051 377050**
D: Fr €26.00
Beds: 2F 2D 1T 1S **Baths:** 6 En
☎ ▣ ⅙ ▦ ▦, ▪ cc

Brown's Town House, *29 South Parade, Waterford.* Fine Victorian town house, Waterford city centre, beautifully restored, modernised.
Open: All Year (not Xmas)
051 870594 Mr Brown **Fax: 051 871923**
info@brownstownhouse.com
D: Fr €45.00
Beds: 2F 3D 1T **Baths:** 6 En
☎ ▦ ▦, ▪

Brookdale House, *Carrigrue, Ballinaneeshagh, Waterford.* Modern home, quiet location, landscaped surrounding 400m of Cork/Waterford (N25).
Open: Jan to Nov
051 375618 Mrs Harrington
D: Fr €24.00-€25.50 **S:** Fr €32.50
Beds: 4F 2D 2T **Baths:** 4 En
▣ (4) ⅙ ▦ ▥ ▦, ▪

Janeville, *Newtown Park, Newtown, Waterford.* Situated in a quiet cul-de-sac where our mature gardens overlook the River Suir.
Open: All Year (not Xmas)
051 874653 (also fax) Mr & Mrs Mouire
D: Fr €32.00 **S:** Fr €38.00
Beds: 1F 1D 2T **Baths:** 4 En
☎ ▣ (4) ⅙ ▦ ✕ ▥ ▦, ▪

Beechwood, *7 Cathedral Square, Waterford.* Four-storey Georgian house situated in a tree-lined, pedestrianised area.
Open: Jan to Nov
051 876677 Mrs Ryan
D: Fr €21.50 **S:** Fr €32.00
Beds: 1D 2T **Baths:** 1 Sh
☎ (6) ▣ (6) ⅙ ▦ ✕ ▦,

Windgap
X2289

Maple Leaf, *Cork Road, Windgap, Dungarvan, Co Waterford.* Beautiful country house 6 km Dungarvan. 200 metres off N25 overlooking Bay and mountains.
Open: Mar to Nov
058 41921 O Fennell
onra@esatclear.ie
D: Fr €24.00-€28.00 **S:** Fr €25.50-€32.00
Beds: 1F 1T 1D 1S **Baths:** 3 En 3 Pr 1 Sh
☎ ▣ (6) ▦ ⌐ ✕ ▦, ▪ cc

Planning a longer stay?
Always ask for any special rates

County Westmeath

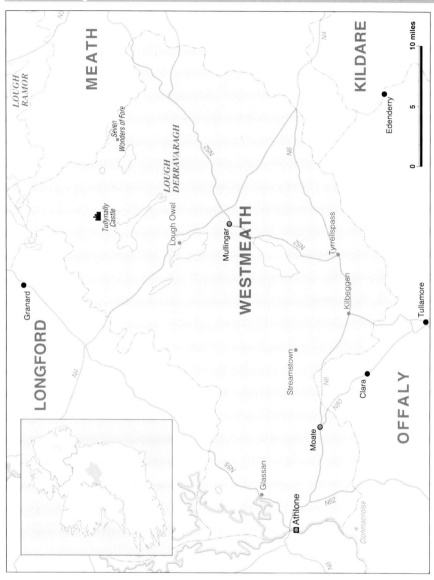

RAIL ⇌

Mullingar is on the *Sligo to Dublin (Connolly)* line; *Athlone* is on the *Galway to Dublin (Heuston)* line. For timetable details phone **Irish Rail** on 01 8366222.

BUS ⇌

Mullingar to Dublin (2 daily). *Athlone to Dublin* (6 daily). Tel. **Bus Eireann** on 01 8366111.

TOURIST INFORMATION OFFICES *i*

Athlone Castle, **Athlone** (Jun to Aug), 0902 94630. Dublin Road, **Mullingar** (open all year), 044 48650.

Athlone
N0441

Woodville,
Monksland, Athlone, Co Westmeath.
Open: Easter to Oct
Grades: BF Approv
090 6494595
Mrs McCam **Fax:**
090 6498789
D: Fr €26.00 **S:** Fr €36.00
Beds: 1D 2F **Baths:** 3 En
⛺ 🅿 (3) 📺 ⅲ, ♨
Modern bungalow on quiet road 3 km from Athlone Town. Ideal touring base - Athlone is situated on River Shannon. Clonmacnoise Monastic Site. Bog rail tour, 4 golf courses, pet farm, cruising on Shannon River, 18 hole mini golf 1 km, castles.

BATHROOMS

En = Ensuite

Pr = Private

Sh = Shared

The Holly Bush,
Hillquarter, Athlone, Co Westmeath. Country setting, walking distance to Lough Ree - fishing, sailing etc. Warm welcome.
Open: Mar to Nov
090 645955 & 087 2797764 (M) Mrs Skelly
hollybush@holidayhound.com
D: Fr €25.00
Beds: 1F 2T 1D **Baths:** 2 En 1 Sh
⛺ 🅿 (10) 📺 ★ 🆅 ⅲ, ♿ cc

Stone Lodge B&B,
Glassan, Athlone, County Westmeath. Beautiful house with comfortable spacious bedrooms set in quaint village, traditional pubs.
Open: Mar to Dec
090 6485004 Ms
glassonstonelodge@eircom.net
www.glassonstonelodge.com
D: Fr €35.00-€45.00 **S:** Fr €45.00-€55.00
Beds: 2D 3T **Baths:** 5 En
🅿 (12) 📺 ⅲ, ♨

Riverview House, *Summerville, Athlone, Co Westmeath.* On N6, close to restaurants, pubs, Shannon, lake, golf, fishing.
Open: Feb to Dec
090 6494532 (also fax) Mr & Mrs Corbett
riverviewhouse@hotmail.com
D: Fr €26.00
Beds: 2F 1D 1T 1S **Baths:** 5 En 5 Pr
⛺ (2) 🅿 (10) 📺 ⅲ, ♨ cc

Harbour House, *Ballykeeran, Athlone, Co Westmeath.* Luxurious quiet country home by Lough Ree, 200 metres to award-winning restaurant.
Open: All Year (not Xmas)
090 6485063 (also fax) Mrs Meade
ameade@indigo.ie
D: Fr €25.50
Beds: 1F 2D 3T **Baths:** 6 En
⛺ 🅿 (12) 📺 ⅲ, ♨ cc

Cluain Inis, *N6, Galway Road, Summerhill, Athlone, Co Westmeath.* Friendly, family-run B&B close to fishing, golf and historic sites.
Open: Easter to Oct
090 6494202 Mrs Shaw
D: Fr €25.50
Beds: 1F 1D 1T **Baths:** 1 En 2 Sh
⛺ (1) 🅿 (3) 📺 ⅲ, ♨ cc

BEDROOMS

D = Double	S = Single
T = Twin	F = Family

Shelmalier House, *Retreat Road, Catrontroy, Athlone, Co Westmeath.* Town house in quiet location. Beautifully appointed bedroom with all in room facilities.
Open: All Year (not Xmas)
090 6472245 Mrs Denby **Fax: 090 6473190**
shelmal@iol.ie
D: Fr €23.00-€24.00 **S:** Fr €32.00
Beds: 1F 5D 1T **Baths:** 7 En
🛏 🅿 📺 ▥, ■ cc

Shannonside House, *Westlodge Road, Athlone, Co Westmeath.* Town house situated in Athlone with own beautiful gardens and private car park.
Open: All Year (not Xmas)
090 6494773 (also fax) Mr & Mrs Egan
shannonside@eircom.net
homepage.eircom.net/shannonside
D: Fr €32.00
Beds: 4F 1T
🛏 🅿 (10) 📺 ✕ 📺 ▥, ■

Cornamagh House, *Cornamagh, Athlone.* Country living on the edge of town. Tea/coffee on arrival. Dog friendly.
Open: All Year
090 6474171 Mr & Mrs Fagg
fagg@indigo.ie
D: Fr €25.00
Beds: 2F 1D 1T 1S **Baths:** 2 En 1 Sh
🛏 🅿 ⅍ 📺 🐾 ▥, ■ cc

Innyside Lodge, *Finea, Mullingar, Co Westmeath.* Situated on the banks of the Luny river and beside Lough Sheelin.
Open: All Year
043 81124 Mrs O'Reilly
D: Fr €20.50-€23.00 **S:** Fr €23.00
Beds: 6F 1T 2S **Baths:** 3 Pr 📺 ✕ 📺 ▥, ♿

Stone Lodge B&B, *Glassan, Athlone, County Westmeath.* Beautiful house with comfortable spacious bedrooms set in quaint village, traditional pubs.
Open: Mar to Dec
090 6485004 Ms
glassonstonelodge@eircom.net
www.glassonstonelodge.com
D: Fr €35.00-€45.00 **S:** Fr €45.00-€55.00
Beds: 2D 3T **Baths:** 5 En
🅿 (12) 📺 ▥, ■

Benown House, *Glassan, Athlone, Co Westmeath.* Beautiful bungalow beside picturesque village 'Glassan'. Choice reaturants, pubs, golf.
Open: All Year
090 6485406 Mrs Byrne **Fax: 090 6485776**
benownhouse@glassan.com
D: Fr €31.50
Beds: 1F 2D 1S 2T **Baths:** 5 Ensuite
🛏 🅿 (6) 📺 📺 ▥, ✳ ■

Seber House, *Kilbeggan, Co Westmeath.*
Delightful purpose-built B&B halfway between Dublin and Galway. Golfing, racing and Locke's Distillery museum minutes away.
Open: All year (not Xmas/New Year)
0506 32113 S and B Guilfoyle
D: Fr €25.00 **S:** Fr €33.00
Beds: 1F 1T 2D **Baths:** 4 En
🅿 (4) ⅍ 📺 ▥, ■ cc

Lough Owel Lodge, *Cullion, Lough Owel, Mullingar, Co Westmeath.* Situated in pleasant grounds overlooking Lough Owel. Tennis court, games room, lakeshore walks.
Open: Mar to Nov
044 48714 Mrs Ginnell **Fax: 044 48771**
aginnell@hotmail.com
D: Fr €30.00
Beds: 1F 3D 1T **Baths:** 5 En
🛏 🅿 (7) 📺 ✕ ▥,

Mullingar

N4352

Newbury Hotel, Dominick
*Street, Mullingar, Co
Westmeath.* Cosy family-run
hotel situated in centre of
Mullingar. You are assured a
warm welcome.
Open: All year
044 42888 Mr McGinley
newburyinfo@eircom.net www.thenewburyhotel.com
D: Fr €51.00-€70.00 **S:** Fr €42.00-€70.00
Beds: 5F 20D **Baths:** 27 En 1 Pr 2 Sh
⑊ ▣ (20) 📺 🛏 ✕ Ⓥ ▥ ▪ cc

Aisling B&B, Tullaniskey
*(Rochford Bridge Road),
Mullingar, Co Westmeath.*
Very central for touring. Ideal
for golf, fishing and
equestrian activities.
Open: Apr to Nov
044 40677 Mrs Munnelly
info@family-homes.ie
D: Fr €26.50 **S:** Fr €26.50
Beds: 1F 1T 1D 1S **Baths:** 2 En 1 Sh
⑊ ▣ ⅒ 📺 🛏 Ⓥ ▥ cc

Avondale, Dublin Road,
*Marlinstown, Mullingar, Co
Westmeath.* Set in own
grounds in quiet area.
Convenient Lakes, golf
course, sporting amenities.
Open: All year (not Xmas)
044 48814 Mrs Rowan
D: Fr €28.00-€30.00 **S:** Fr €35.00-€40.00
Beds: 2D 2T **Baths:** 3 En 1 Pr 1 Sh
⑊ ▣ (10) 📺 🛏 Ⓥ ▥

Hilltop, Delvin Road N52, Rathconnell,
Mullingar, Co Westmeath. Unique modern
country house. Award-winning garden. Tranquil
setting.
Open: Feb to Nov
044 48958 Mr and Mrs Casey **Fax:** 044 48013
hilltopcountryhouse@eircom.net
D: Fr €30.00 **S:** Fr €40.00
Beds: 2T 3D **Baths:** 5 En
▣ (6) ⅒ 📺 Ⓥ ▥ cc

Petitswood House, Dublin Road, Mullingar,
Co Westmeath. Beautiful house, friendly
atmosphere, tree-lined avenue, all bedrooms
overlooking gardens, comfortable beds.
Open: All Year (not Xmas)
044 48397 Mrs Farrell
D: Fr €24.00-€25.50 **S:** Fr €30.50-€32.00
Beds: 1F 1D 1T **Baths:** 3 En
⑊ ▣ (8) ⅒ 📺 ▥ ▪

Keadeen, Longford Road, Irishtown, Mullingar,
Co Westmeath. Lovely bungalow situated in a
peaceful location near the town.
Open: Easter to October
044 48440 Mrs Nolan
D: Fr €23.00 **S:** Fr €25.50
Beds: 1F 1D 1T **Baths:** 2 En 1 Pr
⑊ ▣ (6) ⅒ 📺 Ⓥ ▥

Streamstown

N2643

Woodlands Farm, Streamstown, Mullingar, Co
Westmeath. Charming old country house
surrounded by ornamental trees on 120-acre
farm.
Open: Mar to Oct
044 26414 Mrs Maxwell
D: Fr €28.00
Beds: 1F 2D 2T 1S **Baths:** 3 Ensuite 3 Private
⑊ ▣ 📺 🛏 ✕ ▥ ♿

Tyrrellspass

N4137

Cornagher House, Tyrrellspass, Mullingar, Co
Westmeath. 300-year-old Georgian house set on
an organic farm.
Open: All Year
044 23311 (also fax) Mrs Treacy
rtreacy@eircom.net
homepage.eircom.net/~westmeath/
D: Fr €23.00-€32.00 **S:** Fr €32.00
Beds: 6F 1T 5D **Baths:** 6 En 6 Pr
⑊ ▣ (40) 📺 🛏 ✕ Ⓥ ▥ ♿ ▪ cc

County Wexford

RAIL ⇌

Wexford and **Rosslare Harbour** are on the East Coast line into **Dublin (Connolly)**; **Rosslare** is also on direct lines for **Waterford** and **Limerick Junction**, with connections for many other parts of the country. For timetable details phone **Irish Rail** on 01 8366222.

BUS 🚌

Rosslare Harbour to **Cork** *(4 daily)*, to **Dublin** *(5 daily)*, to **Limerick** *(3 daily)*. **Wexford** to **Dublin** *(5 daily)*. Tel. **Bus Eireann** on 01 8366111.

FERRIES ⚓

Rosslare Harbour to **Fishguard** *(3¹/₂ hrs)*. **Stena Sealink** - in Republic tel. 053 33115,

in UK 0870 5707070.
Rosslare Harbour to **Pembroke** *(4¹/₄ hrs)*. **Irish Ferries** - in Republic, tel. 01 6610511, in UK, tel. 0870 5171717.

TOURIST INFORMATION OFFICES *i*

Gorey (open all year), 055 21248.

Enniscorthy (mid-Jun to Aug), 054 34699.

Kennedy Centre, **New Ross** (mid-Jun to Aug), 051 421857.

Kilrane, **Rosslare**, 053 33232.

The Crescent, **Wexford** (open all year), 053 23111.

Arthurstown

S7110

Glendine Country House, Arthurstown, New Ross, Co Wexford.
Open: All year (not Xmas)
Grades: BF Approv, AA 4 Star
051 389258 Mrs Crosbie **Fax: 051 389677**
glendinehouse@eircom.net www.glendinehouse.com
D: Fr €35.00-€40.00 **S:** Fr €45.00-€55.00
Beds: 2F 1D 1T **Baths:** 5 En
🛏 🅿 (15) 📺 🐾 Ⓥ 🛏, ♨ cc

1830 Georgian home overlooking sweeping views of Barrow Estuary, set in 50 acres peaceful landscape, home to rare breeds of animals. Elegant rooms furnished with antiques. Rosslare 30 miles (early breakfast served). Waterford Glass 7 miles. S/C also available.

Arthurs Rest, *Arthurstown, New Ross, Co Wexford.* Situated in beautiful riverside village, thoroughly refurbished, real home-from-home comforts.
Open: All year
051 389192 Mrs Murphy **Fax: 051 389362**
arthursrest@hotmail.com
D: Fr €27.50-€32.50 **S:** Fr €35.00-€40.00
Beds: 2F 2D 1T **Baths:** 5 En
🛏 🅿 (5) ⚘ 📺 🛏, ♨ cc

Boolavogue

S9949

Ballyorley House,
Boolavogue, Ferns, Enniscorthy, Co Wexford. Family-owned since 1530, Georgian residence surrounded by woodland. Working farm.
Open: All year
054 66287 Mrs Gough-Jordan
D: Fr €25.50-€32.00
Beds: 4F **Baths:** 4 En
🛏 (6) 🅿 📺 🐾 ✕ Ⓥ 🛏, ♨

Carrig-on-Bannow

S8610

Carrig House, Carrig-on-Bannow, Wexford.
Carrig House is situated in a quite country village 1.5 miles from Atlantic Ocean.
Open: All year (not Xmas)
051 561101 (also fax) Ms Howlin
n.howlin@eircom.net www.bandbwexford.com
D: Fr €26.00-€32.00 **S:** Fr €39.00
Beds: 1F 2D 1T **Baths:** 3 En
🛏 🅿 (10) 📺 Ⓥ 🛏, ♨ cc

Castlebridge

T0526

Troon Lodge, *Ballycrane, Castlebridge, Wexford.*
Beautiful country house set in maturing gardens with tennis court.
Open: All Year
053 59012 Mr & Mrs O'Connor **Fax: 053 59200**
info@troon.ie
D: Fr €32.00
Beds: 2F 1D 1T **Baths:** 3 En 1 Pr
🛏 🄿 ⅍ 📺 Ⅴ 🖳 ◼ cc

Coolgreaney

T1969

Ballykilty House,
Coolgreaney, Arklow, Co Wicklow. Homely, old world farmhouse, mature gardens, tennis court, log fires.
Open: Easter to Oct **Grades:** BF Approv
0402 37111 Mrs Nuzum **Fax: 0402 37272**
ballykiltyfarmhouse@eircom.net
D: Fr €32.00-€35.00 **S:** Fr €45.00-€48.00
Beds: 1F 2D 2T **Baths:** 5 En
🛏 (5) 🄿 (7) 📺 🖳 ◼

Drinagh

T0518

The Elms, *Rosslare Harbour Road, Drinagh, Co Wexford.* Modernised country home with warm & friendly welcome. All rooms tastefully decorated.
Open: All Year
053 58058 Mrs Stafford
theelmsbnb@iegateway.net www.irish-bnb.com
D: Fr €21.50 **S:** Fr €34.50
Beds: 1F 1T 5D **Baths:** 7 En
🛏 (9) 🄿 (9) ⅍ 📺 Ⅴ 🖳 ᕃ cc

Enniscorthy

S9740

9 Main Street, *Enniscorthy, Co Wexford.*
Open: All year (not Xmas) **Grades:** BF Approv
054 33522 & 054 37837 Mrs Murphy
mauramurphybb@eircom.net
D: Fr €24.00-€25.00 **S:** Fr €26.00-€30.00
Beds: 2F 2D 2T 1S **Baths:** 4 En 2 Sh
🛏 🄿 (7) 📺 Ⅴ 🖳 ◼
Large red brick town house, late C18th, central position close to beautiful Pugin cathedral. Orthopaedic beds, private car park for 7 cars, refurbished bar with sunny beer garden, historic town.

Lemongrove House, *Blackstoops, Enniscorthy, Co Wexford.*
Open: All year (not Xmas)
054 36115 Mr & Mrs McGibney
lemongrovehouse@iolfree.ie
D: Fr €30.00-€38.00 **S:** Fr €35.00-€45.00
Beds: 6F 2D 1T **Baths:** 9 En
🛏 🄿 (12) ⅍ 📺 🍴 Ⅴ 🖳 ᕃ ◼ cc
Luxury home set in mature gardens with private parking. Recommended by 'Guide du Routard', AA & other leading guides. Within walking distance of a choice of restaurants, pubs & new pool & leisure centre. Locally, we have beaches, golf, horseriding, walking & quad track.

St Judes, *Munfin, Tommalosset, Enniscorthy, Co Wexford.* Peaceful family-run country house. Tea-making facilities, TV in rooms, hairdryers. Visa cards accepted.
Open: Jan to Dec
054 33011 Mrs Delany **Fax: 054 37831**
D: Fr €25.50
Beds: 5F 2D 1T **Baths:** 4 En 1 Pr 1 Sh
🛏 🄿 ⅍ 📺 ✕ 🖳 ◼ cc

Ivella, *Rectory Road, Enniscorthy, Co Wexford.* Friendly welcome, home cooking in peaceful, historic scenic clean environment.
Open: All Year
054 33475 Miss Heffernan
D: Fr €21.50-€25.50
Beds: 3F 1D 2T **Baths:** 1 Pr 1 Sh
🛏 (2) 🄿 (3) 📺 🖳 ◼

Vale View Farmhouse B&B, *St John's, Enniscorthy, County Wexford.* Modern bungalow situated in quiet rural area, with scenic views of surrounding countryside.
Open: Marc to Oct
054 35262 Mrs Keogh
D: Fr €25.50
Beds: 1F 1T 1D **Baths:** 2 Ensuite 1 Shared
🄿 (6) ⅍ 📺 ✕ 🖳 ᕃ ◼

All details shown are as supplied by B&B owners in Autumn 2002

Ferns

T0149

Glencarra, *Crory, Ferns, Enniscorthy, Co Wexford.* Situated on N11, tea on arrival, very clean, good value.
Open: Apr to Sep
054 66106 Mrs Brennan
D: Fr €20.50-€23.00 **S:** Fr €23.00-€28.00
Beds: 2D 2S **Baths:** 1 En 1 Sh
⛺ (6) 🅿 (3) ⑃ 📺 Ⓥ ▥ ▪

Clone House, *Ferns, Enniscorthy, Co Wexford.* C17th working farm guest house in South East Ireland.
Open: Mar to Oct
054 66113 Mrs Breen **Fax: 054 66225**
dbreen@e-merge.ie
www.homepage.eircomnet/~clonehouse
D: Fr €29.00-€35.00 **S:** Fr €37.00-€43.00
Beds: 4F 1T **Baths:** 5 En
⛺ (3) 🅿 (35) 📺 ✕ ▥

Ferrycarrig

T0124

Tara, *Kitestown Cross, Ferrycarrig, Wexford.* A warm welcome at 'Tara' overlooking the River Slaney and a full Irish breakfast.
Open: Feb to Dec
053 20133 & 087 2805242 (M) Mr & Mrs Shovlin
D: Fr €25.50-€32.00 **S:** Fr €32.00-€38.00
Beds: 3D 3T 1S **Baths:** All En
⛺ 🅿 (6) ⑃ 📺 ▥ ▪

Gorey

T1559

Riverfield Farmhouse, *Inch, Gorey, Co Wexford.* Tea/coffee on arrival, riverside gardens, dinner, wines, log fire, tennis, local pub.
Open: All year (not Xmas)
0402 37232 Mr & Mrs Anderson-Proby **Fax: 0402 37884**
riverfieldfarmhouse@eircom.net
www.riverfieldfarmhouse.ie
D: Fr €30.00 **S:** Fr €45.00
Beds: 4F 1D 1T **Baths:** 6 En
⛺ 🅿 (6) 📺 ⚡ ✕ Ⓥ ▥ ♿ ▪

Woodlands Country House, *Killinierin, Gorey, Co Wexford.* 1836 award-winning house on 1.5 acres of gardens and courtyard of stone buildings.
Open: Mar to Oct
0402 37125 Mrs O'Sullivan **Fax: 0402 37133**
woodlands@iol.ie www.woodlandscountryhouse.com
D: Fr €35.00-€42.00 **S:** Fr €55.00
Beds: 3F 2D 1T **Baths:** 6 En
⑃ 📺 ▥ ▪

St Thereses, *Mount Alexander, Gorey, Co Wexford.* Set in its own private grounds St Thereses offers you a complete break.
Open: All Year (not Xmas)
055 21793 Mrs Kenny
D: Fr €30.00
Beds: 2F 4T **Baths:** 6 Ensuite
⛺ (10) 🅿 (12) ⑃ 📺 ✕ ▥ ▪

Kirwan's Farm, *Kilmuckridge, Gorey, Co Wexford.* Our home is located on the R742 coast road between Blackwater and Kilmuckridge. 30 mins from Rosslare ferryport. 2 hrs from Dublin. It nestles in a peaceful countryside landscape. Adjacent to miles of sandy beaches. We offer you a warm friendly atmosphere. Good food and facilities.
Open: Apr to Nov
053 30168 Mr and Mrs Kirwan
kirwansfarmhouse@eircom.net
D: Fr €26.00 **S:** Fr €38.00
Beds: 2F 1T **Baths:** 3 En
⛺ 🅿 📺 ⚡ ✕ ▥ ▪

Inch

T1867

Riverfield Farmhouse, *Inch, Gorey, Co Wexford.* Tea/coffee on arrival, riverside gardens, dinner, wines, log fire, tennis, local pub.
Open: All year (not Xmas)
0402 37232 Mr & Mrs Anderson-Proby **Fax: 0402 37884**
riverfieldfarmhouse@eircom.net
www.riverfieldfarmhouse.ie
D: Fr €30.00 **S:** Fr €45.00
Beds: 4F 1D 1T **Baths:** 6 En
⛺ 🅿 (6) 📺 ⚡ ✕ Ⓥ ▥ ♿ ▪

National Grid References given are for villages, towns and cities – not for individual houses

Perrymount, *Inch, Gorey, Co Wexford.*
Breakfast provided. 1-min walk from other pubs and restaurants.
Open: All year
0402 37418 Mrs Byrne
perrymont@eircom.net
D: Fr €25.00-€28.00 **S:** Fr €35.00-€40.00
Beds: 1F 2T 1D **Baths:** 4 Pr
☼ 🄿 📺 ✕ 🏛, 🚗

T1566

Woodlands Country House, *Killinierin, Gorey, Co Wexford.* 1836 award-winning house on 1.5 acres of gardens and courtyard of stone buildings.
Open: Mar to Oct
0402 37125 Mrs O'Sullivan **Fax: 0402 37133**
woodlands@iol.ie www.woodlandscountryhouse.com
D: Fr €35.00-€42.00 **S:** Fr €55.00
Beds: 3F 2D 1T **Baths:** 6 En
⊁ 📺 🏛, 🚗

S9725

Healthfield Manor, *Killurin, Wexford.* To visit Healthfield is to step back into the gracious living of the past.
Open: All Year (not Xmas)
053 28253 Mrs Colloton
D: Fr €35.00
Beds: 1D 3T **Baths:** 1 En 3 Pr
☼ (10) 🄿 (10) 🐴 📺 🏛,

RATES

D = Price range per person sharing in a double or twin room

S = Price range for a single room

S9906

Ballyhealy House, *Kilmore, Wexford.*
Open: All year
Grades: BF Approv
053 35035
Mrs Maher-Caulfield
Fax: 053 35038
bhh@gofree.indigo.ie gofree.indigo.ie/~bhh
D: Fr €30.00-€35.00 **S:** Fr €35.00-€40.00
Beds: 3F **Baths:** 3 En
☼ 🄿 (20) 📺 🐴 🏛, ❋ 🚗
Recently restored large C18th country house 500 metres from miles of sandy beach. The Burrow hinterland offers a paradise for birdwatchers and walkers. Self-catering apartment on site also an AIRE approved riding school specialising in beach rides.

S9603

Groveside, *Ballyharty, Kilmore Quay, Wexford.*
You are very welcome to 'Groveside' Farm Guest House, spacious modern house, peaceful surroundings.
Open: May to Sep
053 35305 & 088 2785558 (M) Mrs Cousins
Fax: 053 35305
Groveside@infowing.ie
D: Fr €25.50
Beds: 1F 1D 1T **Baths:** 2 Ensuite 1 Shared
☼ 🄿 (10) 📺 📺 🏛, 🚗

S7227

Carbery, *Mountgarrett, New Ross, County Wexford.*
Open: Apr to Oct
051 422742 Mrs Casey
caseycolin@eircom.net
D: Fr €27.00-€30.00 **S:** Fr €27.00-€30.00
Beds: 3F 2D 1T **Baths:** 3 En
☼ 🄿 📺 📺 🏛, 🚗
Tudor-type I.T.B. approved on edge of town. Waterford 24 km, Kilkenny 41 km. Private garden, views of river & mountains. Walking distance to town, lovely pub close by. Good food, hospitality, hygiene, comfortable rooms. Close to golf courses, boating and fishing.

Greenpark,
Creakan Lower, New Ross, Co Wexford.
Open: Feb to Nov
051 421028 (also fax) Ms Kinsella
D: Fr €25.00-€30.00
S: Fr €40.00-€50.00
Beds: 1T 2D **Baths:** 2 En 1 Pr
⌂ 🅿 (4) ⌖ 📺 💻, ▪

Greenpark is an 'Olde Worlde' country house, 4km from New Ross, just off the R 733, close to the J F Kennedy Homestead, the National Arboretum and the Hook Lighthouse. Golf, fishing and horseriding nearby. 45 mins' drive from Rosslare. No weddings or parties.

Ossory, *Mountgarrett, New Ross, Co Wexford.*
Modern comfortable select bungalow with scenic views of Blackstairs Mountains.
Open: All year
051 422768 Mr & Mrs Neve
D: Fr €23.00-€25.00 **S:** Fr €23.00-€25.00
Beds: 1F 2D 1T **Baths:** 2 En 2 Pr
⌂ 🅿 (6) 📺 💻, ▪

Killarney House, *The Maudlins, New Ross, Co Wexford.* Peaceful setting, ground floor bedrooms, reduction for more than one night.
Open: April to Sept
051 421062 Mrs Fallon SRN, SCM
noreenfallon@eircom.net
D: Fr €21.50-€24.00 **S:** Fr €30.00-€32.50
Beds: 1D 2T **Baths:** 2 En 1 Sh
⌂ 🅿 (3) 📺 💻, cc

Rosville House, *Knockmullen, New Ross, Co Wexford.* Modern home. Peaceful surroundings. Warm welcome. Dishing, golfing nearby. Ferry 40 mins.
Open: Mar to Nov
051 421798 Mrs Gallagher
rosvillehouse@oceanfree.net www.rosville.com
D: Fr €23.00-€25.50 **S:** Fr €36.00
Beds: 3F 1D 1T **Baths:** 4 En 1 Sh
⌂ 🅿 (7) 📺 ⍆ 📺 💻, ▪ cc

Oakwood House, *Ring Road, New Ross, County Wexford.* Purpose-built home with view over landscaped gardens, warm welcome.
Open: Apr to Oct
051 425494 (also fax) Mrs Halpin
susan@oakwoodhouse.net www.oakwoodhouse.net
D: Fr €30.00-€32.00 **S:** Fr €35.00-€40.00
Beds: 1F 1T 2D **Baths:** 4 En
⍆ 📺 💻, ▪ cc

Newbawn

S8222

Woodlands House,
Carrigbyrne, Newbawn, County Wexford.
Open: Mar to Oct **Grades:** BF Approv, AA 3 Diamond, RAC 3 Diamond
051 428287 (also fax) Mr Campbell
woodwex@eircom.net
D: Fr €30.00 **S:** Fr €35.00-€42.50
Beds: 3D 1T 1S **Baths:** 4 En 1 Pr
⌂ (5) 🅿 (6) 📺 ✕ 📺 💻, ▪ cc

Beautifully situated in a quiet location on the Rosslare-Waterford road (N25), 30 mins from Rosslare. An ideal base for Wexford, Waterford, Wicklow and Kilkenny. Golf, fishing, riding nearby. Refurbished to a high standard. Guest lounge, early breakfast. Private parking.

Cypress House, *Newbawn, Wexford.*
Large gardens, hard tennis court, pleasant peaceful surroundings. Hotel pub restaurant 5 mins.
Open: All year
051 428335 Mrs Wall **Fax: 051 428148**
wallnjc@hotmail.com
D: Fr €25.00-€28.00 **S:** Fr €31.00
Beds: 2F 2D **Baths:** 4 En
🅿 ⍆ 📺 📺 💻, ▪ cc

Rosslare

T1015

Eurolodge, *Rosslare Harbour, Co Wexford.*
Close to excellent golf courses, sandy beaches & numerous outdoor activities.
Open: Mar to Oct
053 33118 Ms Sinnott **Fax: 053 33120**
eurolodge@eircom.net www.euro_lodge.com
D: Fr €38.00-€48.00 **S:** Fr €70.00-€80.00
Beds: 30T 8D **Baths:** 38 En
⌂ 🅿 (50) ⍆ 📺 💻, ⅙ ▪ cc

All details shown are as supplied by B&B owners in Autumn 2002

Ballybro Lodge, *Rosslare, Wexford.*
Modern home in over 3 acres of peaceful gardens, close to safe sandy beaches.
Open: All Year (not Xmas)
053 32333 Mrs Stewart
ballybrolodge@oceanfree.net
D: Fr €24.00 **S:** Fr €33.00
Beds: 1D 3T 1S **Baths:** 5 En
❄ 🅿 (6) ⌀ 📺 Ⅴ ▥, ▪ cc

Rosslare Harbour
T1312

Ailsa Lodge, *Rosslare Harbour, Wexford.*
Edwardian house on private grounds overlooking the sea and ferry port.
Open: All year (not Xmas)
053 33230 Fax: 053 33581
ailsalodge@eircom.ie www.ailsalodge.com
D: Fr €30.00-€40.00 **S:** Fr €30.00-€45.00
Beds: 1F 2D 2T 1S **Baths:** 6 En
❄ 🅿 (15) 📺 Ⅴ ▥, ▪ cc

Cloverlawn, *Kilrane, Rosslare Harbour, Wexford.*
Highly-recommended comfortable home. Ferry port, golf, beaches 1km, vouchers accepted.
Open: Mar to Nov
053 33413 Mrs Lonergan
cloverlawn@eircom.net
homepage.eircom.net/~cloverlawn
D: Fr €25.00-€30.00 **S:** Fr €35.00-€50.00
Beds: 1F 1D 1T 1S **Baths:** 2 En 2 Sh
❄ 🅿 (6) ⌀ 📺 ▥, ▪ cc

Ailesbury, *The Moorings, Rosslare Harbour, Wexford.*
Comfortable home. Closest B&B on N25 to Ferryport, bus/rail terminals. Early breakfast.
Open: Mar to Nov **Grades:** BF Approv
053 33185 (also fax) Mrs O'Dwyer
ailesb@eircom.net homepage.eircom.net/~ailesbury
D: Fr €25.00-€30.00 **S:** Fr €32.00-€42.00
Beds: 1F 1T 1D 1S **Baths:** 3 En 1 Pr
🅿 (2) ⌀ 📺 ▥, ▪

Clifford House, *Rosslare Harbour, Wexford.* The house is overlooking the sea, surrounded by beautiful landscaped gardens.
Open: All year (not Xmas)
053 33226 Michael Delaney & Margaret Hartigan
cliffordhouse@eircom.net
D: Fr €25.50-€29.50 **S:** Fr €27.00-€38.00
Beds: 1F 4D 2T 1S **Baths:** 5 En 3 Sh
❄ 🅿 (8) 📺 ↟ ✕ Ⅴ ▥, ⅙ cc

Oldcourt House, *Rosslare Harbour, Wexford.*
Modern house situated in centre of Rosslare Harbour Village, overlooking Rosslare Bay. Scenic views.
Open: Feb to Nov **Grades:** BF Approv, AA 4 Diamond
053 33895 Mrs McDonald
oldcrt@gofree.indigo.ie
D: Fr €27.50-€30.00 **S:** Fr €35.00
Beds: 1F 3D **Baths:** 4 En 1 Pr
❄ 🅿 (10) 📺 Ⅴ ▥.

Hotel Rosslare, *Rosslare Harbour, Wexford.*
Rosslare Harbour's oldest hotel. Home of the famous award-winning 'Portholes Bar'.
Open: All Year (not Xmas)
053 33110 Fax: 053 33386
D: Fr €50.00-€60.00
Beds: 6F 10D 7T **Baths:** 25 Ensuite
❄ 🅿 📺 ↟ ✕ Ⅴ ▥.

Glenville, *St Patricks Road, Rosslare Harbour, Wexford.* Modern detached bungalow in seaside setting on N25, 3 miles to ferry.
Open: Easter to Oct
053 33142 Mrs Barry
glenville@oceanfree.net
D: Fr €21.50 **S:** Fr €23.00
Beds: 1D 1T 1S **Baths:** 1 En 1 Pr
🅿 (5) 📺 ↟ Ⅴ ▥, ▪

O'Leary's Farm, *Killilane, Kilrane, Rosslare Harbour, Wexford.* Overlooking St Helens beach. Comfortable old farmhouse. Convenient for ferries.
Open: All Year (not Xmas)
053 33134 Mrs O'Leary
D: Fr €25.50
Beds: 2F 4D 2T 2S **Baths:** 7 Ensuite 2 Shared
❄ (3) 🅿 ⌀ 📺 ↟ ✕ Ⅴ ▥.

Kilrane House, *Kilrane, Rosslare Harbour, Wexford.* Lovely 1830 house with immense character and charm, homely attractive bedrooms.
Open: All Year (not Xmas)
053 33135 Mrs Whitehead **Fax: 053 33739**
D: Fr €28.00
Beds: 2F 2D 2T **Baths:** 6 En
⌂ ▣ (8) ⌿ Ⓥ ▥ ▪ cc

Ballygillane House, *Cawdor Road, Rosslare Harbour, Wexford.* Ballygillane House. Quiet, comfortable home in village centre within 5 mins of ferries. Early breakfast served - walking distance to beach, restaurants, bars and supermarket. Satellite TV all rooms. Private off-road parking - 8 spaces. Golf: 10 mins to championship courses.
Open: Jun to Sep
053 33899 (also fax) Mr & Mrs Drennan
D: Fr €24.00 **S:** Fr €30.00
Beds: 2F 1T **Baths:** 3 En
⌂ (5) ▣ (8) ⌿ Ⓣ Ⓥ ▥ ▪

Loranda Lodge, *Ballygillane Beg, Rosslare Harbour, Co Wexford.* Warm friendly family home 5 minutes from Rosslare ferry port.
Open: All Year
053 33804 (also fax) Mrs Brennan
loranda@esatclear.ie
D: Fr €24.00 **S:** Fr €25.50-€32.00
Beds: 1F 1T 1D **Baths:** 3 En 1 Pr
⌂ ▣ ⌿ Ⓣ ▥ ▪ cc

Laurel Lodge, *Rosslare Harbour, Co Wexford.* Quiet location. Convenient ferry port, rail and bus. Golf and beach nearby.
Open: Mar to Oct
053 33291 Mr & Mrs O'Donoghue
D: Fr €25.50 **S:** Fr €38.50
Beds: 1F 2D 1T **Baths:** 4 En
⌂ ▣ (4) ⌿ Ⓣ Ⓥ ▥ ▪ cc

Saltmills

S7908

Grove Farm, *St Kearns, Saltmills, Fethard-on-Sea, New Ross, Co Wexford.* Attractive farmhouse overlooking sea, located 2km off 733 road. 1km from Fethard-on-Sea.
Open: Mar to Oct
051 562304 Mrs Power
D: Fr €25.50
Beds: 1D 1T 1S **Baths:** 2 Ensuite
⌂ ▣ ⌿ Ⓣ × ▥

Screen

T0830

Avondale, *Ballyfarnogue, Screen, Enniscorthy, Co Wexford.* Excellent touring area. Beautiful Curracloe beach. Visit our working dairy farm.
Open: Easter to Nov
053 37197 Mrs Corrigan
D: Fr €22.50-€25.50 **S:** Fr €28.00-€32.00
Beds: 1F 2D **Baths:** 1 En 2 Pr
⌂ ▣ (5) Ⓣ ↟ × ▥ ♿

Tagoat

T1011

Padua, *Kilscoran, Tagoat, Rosslare, Wexford.* Friendly Irish home on N25, 2km from Rosslare Harbour, near all facilities.
Open: All year
053 31373 (also fax) Helen Farrell
D: Fr €27.50 **S:** Fr €40.00
Beds: 1F 1T 1D **Baths:** 3 En
⌂ ▣ ⌿ Ⓣ ↟ ▥ ▪

Wellington Bridge

S8513

River Valley Farm House, *Ballylannon, Wellington Bridge, Wexford.* Trout fishing river available free to guests.
Open: All year
051 561354 (also fax) Mrs Breen Murphy
rivervalley@oceanfree.net
D: Fr €23.00 **S:** Fr €29.50
Beds: 1F 2D 1T **Baths:** 4 En
⌂ Ⓣ × ▥ ▪

Wexford

T0421

Darrel House, *Spawell Road, Wexford.*
Open: Jan to Dec
053 24264 Mrs Nolan **Fax: 053 24284**
D: Fr €32.50-€40.00 **S:** Fr €45.00-€55.00
Beds: 3F 1D **Baths:** 4 En
▣ ⌿ Ⓣ ▥ ▪ cc
Beautiful period house. Luxury accommodation. Fine high ceilings a feature of elegant sitting and dining room. Owner, chef Sean and his wife Kathleen, offer a wide choice for breakfast, including fresh fruit, fish and other tempting dishes. A memorable stay guaranteed.

South View House,
Coolballow, Wexford.
Open: June to Sep
Grades: BF Approv
053 45592
Mrs Redmond

southview2000@eircom.net
D: Fr €27.50
Beds: 3D **Baths:** 3 En
🅿 ⌁ 📺 ▥, ♨ **cc**

A modern, two-storey , ITB-approved B&B. 2 miles south of Wexford Town just off the N25 with panoramic views of South Wexford & Rosslare Harbour. Adjacent to all amenities, Johnstown Castle & gardens, National Heritage Park. Rosslare ferry only 15 minutes.

The Gallops, Bettyville,
Newtown Road, Wexford.
Open: All year (not Xmas/New Year)
053 44035
Mrs Murphy

Fax: 053 44950
info@thegallopswexford.com
www.thegallopswexford.com
D: Fr €32.00-€35.00 **S:** Fr €38.00-€44.00
Beds: 2F 2D **Baths:** 4 En
🛏 🅿 (10) ⌁ 📺 ▥ ▥, ♨ **cc**

Beautiful home, architecturally-designed and offering excellent accommodation. All guest rooms are ensuite with tea/coffee facilities, TVs and hairdryers, and all overlook gardens. Most enjoy scenic views. Private off-road parking. One mile from town centre. Early breakfasts on request.

Clonard House, *Clonard Great, Wexford.*
Clonard Country House offers superior accommodation, warm hospitality and an excellent breakfast menu.
Open: Mar to Nov
053 43141 Mrs Hayes
clonardhouse@indigo.ie www.indigo.ie/~khayes
D: Fr €32.00-€35.00 **S:** Fr €40.00
Beds: 1F 3T 4D 1S **Baths:** 9 En
🛏 🅿 (20) ⌁ 📺 ▥ ▥, ♨ **cc**

O'Brien's Auburn House,
Auburn Terrace, Redmond Road, Wexford.
Open: All year (no Xmas)
053 23605
Mr & Mrs O'Brien **Fax: 053 42725**
mary@obriensauburnhouse.com
www.obriensauburnhouse.com
D: Fr €30.00-€35.00 **S:** Fr €35.00-€50.00
Beds: 2F 2D 1T **Baths:** 4 En 1 Pr
🛏 🅿 (5) ⌁ 📺 ▥ ▥, ♨ **cc**

In the heart of Wexford town, this listed late-Victorian town house offers superb accommodation throughout. Spacious, tasteful, friendly, antique furniture, breakfast menu, secure parking, river views only go part of the way to describe the overall experience.

McMenamin's Town House, *3 Auburn Terrace, Wexford.*
Open: Jan to Dec
053 46442 Mr & Mrs
McMenamin
mcmem@indigo.ie
www.wexford-bedandbreakfast.com
D: Fr €30.00-€40.00 **S:** Fr €50.00
Beds: 1F 3D 2T **Baths:** 6 En
🛏 🅿 (7) ⌁ 📺 ▥ ▥, ♨ **cc**

Large Victorian town house, guest rooms are individually furnished with antiques, including brass and canopy beds. One of the '100 Best Places to Stay in Ireland', Allied Irish Bank 'B&B of the Year' and one of the 'Ten Best Breakfasts'

Slaney Manor, *Ferrycarrig, Wexford.*
1820s Georgian manor house & courtyard in 30 hectares, overlooking River Slaney.
Open: All Year (not Xmas)
053 20051 Mr Caulfield **Fax: 053 20510**
slaneymanor@eircom.net
www.new-zealands.com/slaney
D: Fr €32.00-€57.00 **S:** Fr €44.50-€70.00
Beds: 8F 20D 12T **Baths:** 40 En
🛏 🅿 (40) ⌁ 📺 ✕ ▥ ▥, ♨ **cc**

National Grid References given are for villages, towns and cities – not for individual houses

Faythe Guest House, *Swanview, The Faythe, Wexford.* Wexford's oldest guest house, set in a quiet part of the old town.
Open: All Year (not Xmas)
053 22249 Mr Lynch **Fax: 053 21680**
faythhse@iol.ie
D: Fr €40.00
Beds: 1F 6D 2T 1S **Baths:** 10 Ensuite
ॐ (7) P (30) TV ✕ V ▦ & ▪

Rathaspeck Manor, *Rathaspeck, Wexford.* Restored C17th Georgian house in quiet location. All rooms ensuite.
Open: Jun to Nov
053 42661 Mrs Cuddihy www.iol.ie/~ecuddihy
D: Fr €32.00 **S:** Fr €32.00
Beds: 3F 1D 2T **Baths:** 6 En
ॐ (3) P (10) TV ▦ ▪

Shanora Lodge, *Newtown Road, Wexford.* Comfortable modern home, friendly hosts. Panoramic views of Wexford Harbour, Slaney Valley, Blackstairs Mountains.
Open: All year (not Xmas)
053 41414 Mr & Mrs O'Brien
D: Fr €25.50-€32.00 **S:** Fr €25.50-€32.00
Beds: 2F 2D 1T 1S **Baths:** 4 En 1 Pr 1 Sh
ॐ P (8) TV ⊨ ▦ & ▪ cc

Bedford House, *Ballymorris, Clonard, Wexford.* Large dormer home on R733. Private parking, lovely garden. Adjacent to national heritage park.
Open: All Year (not Xmas)
053 45643 Mrs Toomey
bedford@eircom.net
D: Fr €28.50
Beds: 1F 1T 2D **Baths:** 4 Ensuite
ॐ P (6) TV ▦ ▪

The Blue Door, *18 Lower George Street, Wexford, Co Wexford.* 200-year-old Georgian house situated in the heart of Wexford town.
Open: All Year (not Xmas)
053 21047 I Scallan
bluedoor@indigo.ie indigo.ie/~bluedoor
D: Fr €23.00-€32.00 **S:** Fr €32.00-€38.00
Beds: 1F 2T 1D **Baths:** 4 En
ॐ ⊬ TV ▦ ▪ cc

BEDROOMS
D = Double   S = Single
T = Twin   F = Family

T1799

Carmels, *Annamoe, Glendalough, Co Wicklow.*
Well-established home in the heart of the
Wicklow Mountains.
Open: Mar to Nov
0404 45297 (also fax) Mrs Hawkins
carmelsbandb@eircom.net
D: Fr €27.50-€31.00 **S:** Fr €31.00
Beds: 2F 1D 1T **Baths:** 4 En
🛏 🅿 (5) ⚥ ✕ Ⅴ ▥.

T2473   🛥 *Arklow Bay Hotel, Kitty's, Golf Club, Woodbridge Hotel*

Swanlake, *Sea Road, Arklow, Co Wicklow.*
Bungalow overlooking Beach, ideal for touring,
Ballykissangel and Wicklow Mountains.
Open: Mar to Oct
0402 32377 Mrs Hendley
D: Fr €25.50-€28.00 **S:** Fr €32.00
Beds: 2F 1D **Baths:** 1 En 3 Sh

RAIL ≇

Wicklow and *Arklow* are on the East Coast line from *Rosslare to Dublin (Connolly)*.
For timetable details phone **Irish Rail** on 01 8366222.

BUS 🚌

Arklow to Dublin & Wicklow to Dublin (4 daily).
Tel. **Bus Eireann** on 01 8366111.

TOURIST INFORMATION OFFICES 🇮

Main Street, **Arklow** (open all year), 0402 32484.
Fitzwilliam Square, **Wicklow** (open all year), 0404 69117.

Moneylands Farm, *Arklow, Co Wicklow.*
Georgian-style farmhouse, 2 km south of Arklow town on R772.
Open: Feb to Nov
0402 32259 Mrs Byrne **Fax: 0402 32438**
land@eircom.net
D: Fr €32.00
Beds: 1F 2D 1T **Baths:** 3 En 1 Pr
🛏 (5) 🅿 (8) 📺 📹 🛏. ■ cc

Snug Harbour, *Abbeylands, Arklow, Co Wicklow.* Family home overlooking golf links and beach. Located in town.
Open: Easter to Oct
0402 32059 Mrs English
D: Fr €25.00 **S:** Fr €25.00
Beds: 1F 3D 1T **Baths:** 2 En 2 Pr
■ (5) 📺 🛏 🛏. ■

Plattenstown House,
Coolgreaney Road, Arklow, Co Wicklow. Period residence in beautiful gardens, near sea, forests and mountains.
Open: All Year (not Xmas) **Grades:** BF Approv
0402 37822 (also fax) Mr & Mrs McDowell
cdpr@indigo.ie www.wicklow.ie/farm/f-plattn.htm
D: Fr €33.00-€38.00 **S:** Fr €38.00-€42.00
Beds: 3D 1T **Baths:** 3 En 1 Pr
🛏 (7) 🅿 (10) ⊬ 📺 ✕ 📹 🛏. ■

Planning a longer stay?
Always ask for any special rates

T2398

Bel Air, *Conroe, Ashford, County Wicklow.*
Family-run hotel, holiday village and equestrian club, set in farm and parkland.
Open: All year (not Xmas)
0404 40109 Ms Freeman **Fax: 0404 40188**
belairhotel@eircom.net www.ncl.ie
D: Fr €35.00-€45.00 **S:** Fr €40.00-€53.00
Beds: 1F 4T 4D 1S **Baths:** 10 En
🛏 🅿 📺 ✕ 🛏. ■ cc

Ballyknocken House, *Glenealy, Ashford, Wicklow.* Charming 1850s farmhouse, furnished old style. Extensive breakfasts, splendid dinner.
Open: March to Nov
0404 44627 Mrs Fulvio **Fax: 0404 44696**
cfulvio@ballyknocken.com www.ballyknocken.com
D: Fr €32.00-€37.50 **S:** Fr €56.00-€61.50
Beds: 2F 4T 2D **Baths:** 8 En
🛏 🅿 (8) 📺 ✕ 📹 🛏. ■ cc

Ballylusk Farm, *Ashford, Wicklow.*
Old farmhouse in beautiful Wicklow Mountains. Near N11.
Open: Easter to Apr
0404 40141 Mrs Kelly
D: Fr €26.00
Beds: 2F 2D **Baths:** 4 En
🛏 🅿 (4) 📺 🛏 🛏.

Carrig Lodge Guest House, *Ballylusk, Ashford, Co Wicklow.* Spacious country home. Dublin/Rosslare one hour. Dun Laoghaire half hour.
Open: All Year (not Xmas)
0404 40278 (also fax) Mrs Joynt
D: Fr €30.00
Beds: 2F 2D **Baths:** 3 Ensuite 1 Private
🛏 🅿 (6) 📺 🛏. ■

T2080

Ashdene, *Knockanree Lower, Avoca, Arklow, Co Wicklow.* Award-winning home, peaceful location, ideal touring base
1.5 hours Dublin/Rosslare.
Open: Apr to Oct **Grades:** BF Approv
0402 35327 (also fax) Mrs Burns
burns@ashdeneavoca.com www.ashdeneavoca.com
D: Fr €28.00-€30.00 **S:** Fr €38.00-€40.00
Beds: 3D 2T **Baths:** 4 En 1 Pr
🛏 🅿 (5) ⊬ 📺 📹 🛏. ■ cc

Keppels Farmhouse,
Ballanagh, Avoca, Arklow, Co Wicklow.
Open: Apr to Oct
0402 35168 Mrs Keppel **Fax: 0402 30950**
keppelsfarmhouse@eircom.net keppelsfarmhouse.com
D: Fr €30.00-€32.50 **S:** Fr €50.00
Beds: 2D 2T **Baths:** 5 En 1 Pr
🛏 (12) 🅿 (8) ⅍ 📺 🏠, ⚘ cc
Traditional-style C19th farmhouse, set amidst tranquil, scenic countryside, on dairy farm 2 km from Avoca (Ballkissangel). 5 km from N11. Golf, heritage sites, gardens, mountains & beaches all nearby. B&B home hospitality awards. Breakfast menu, Rosslare/Dunlaoghaire ports 75 mins.

Koliba, *Beech Road, Avoca, Arklow, Co Wicklow.*
Open: Mar to Oct
0402 32737 (also fax)
Mrs Gilroy
koliba@eircom.net www.koliba.com
D: Fr €28.00-€30.00
Beds: 1F 2D **Baths:** 3 En
🛏 🅿 📺 🏠, ⚘ cc
Widely-recommended country house, on 2 acres of landscaped gardens, midway between Arklow town and Avoca village of 'Ballykissangel' fame. Breathtaking and panoramic views of sea and countryside. 1 hour drive from Dublin/Rosslare Ports and airport. Ground floor bedrooms, Lonely Planet recommended.

Rockfield, *Avoca, Arklow, Co Wicklow.* 'Award-winning Guest House' - delicious food, picturesque views - 2km 'Ballykissangel'.
Open: Apr to Oct
0402 35273 Mrs Crammond **Fax: 0402 35530**
ecrammond@eircom.net
www.familyhomes.
ie/countyfilesold2/entries/ww20.htm
D: Fr €32.50 **S:** Fr €40.00
Beds: 1F 1D **Baths:** 2 En
🛏 🅿 (12) ⅍ 📺 ✕ Ⓥ 🏠, ⚘ cc

Cherrybrook, *Avoca, Arklow, Co Wicklow.* Set in 1 acre of gardens with sun, minutes' walk Ballykissangel Fitzgerald's Bar.
Open: All Year
0402 35179 (also fax) Mrs Ivers
cherrybandb@eircom.net www.cherrybrookhouse.com
D: Fr €25.50 **S:** Fr €25.50
Beds: 1F 2D 2T **Baths:** 3 En 1 Pr 1 Sh
🛏 🅿 (6) 📺 ✕ Ⓥ 🏠, ⚘ cc

Ballinaclash
T1785

Brookvale House, *The Straight Mile, Ballinaclash, Rathdrum, Co Wicklow.*
Modern bungalow, quiet area.
Open: May to Sep
0402 35272 (also fax) Mrs Corrigan
D: Fr €29.50
Beds: 1F 1D 1S **Baths:** 2 Ensuite 1 Private
🛏 🅿 (10) ⅍ 📺 ✕ ✕ Ⓥ 🏠,

Ballinahinch
T2697

Carriglen Glen, *Ballinahinch, Ashford, Wicklow.*
Modern bungalow 1km from Ashford, 45 mins from Dublin, close to Devil's Glen, Glendalough
Open: All Year
0404 40627 (also fax) Mrs Shannon
D: Fr €27.50
Beds: 1F 2T **Baths:** 3 Ensuite
🛏 🅿 ⅍ 📺 ✕ ✕ 🏠, ✻ ⚘

Blessington
N9814

Shalimar, *Crosscool Harbour, Blessington, Co Wicklow.* Country home in scenic location in mature gardens, 2km north of Blessington.
Open: All Year (not Xmas)
045 865259 Mrs Corley
D: Fr €32.00
Beds: 2F 1T **Baths:** 2 Ensuite 1 Private
🛏 (4) 🅿 (4) ⅍ 📺 ✕ 🏠, ⚘

Bray
O2718

Loyola, *Vevay Road, Bray, Co Wicklow.*
Open: Mar to Oct
01 2863757 (also fax) Mrs Loughman
D: Fr €30.00-€33.0
Beds: 1F 1T 2D **Baths:** 3 En
🅿 📺 🏠, ⚘
Warm, homely & friendly-run B&B, breakfast menu, convenient base for touring, Powerscourt House & Gardens, Kilneddery House & Gardens and famous cliff walk. Bray Head and many golf courses.

Ulysses Guest House, *Centre Esplanade, Bray, Co Wicklow.* Overlooking Bray seafront, convenient to Dublin and Wicklow Hills.
Open: Feb to Dec
01 2863860 Mr Jones
Fax: 01 2865114
ojo@indigo.ie
D: Fr €35.00-€37.00 **S:** Fr €40.00
Beds: 2F 6D **Baths:** 8 En
(8) **cc**

Brittas Bay

T3083

Ballinclea House, *Brittas Bay, Wicklow.* Georgian-style farmhouse. Spacious rooms with a view. Good breakfast.
Open: Apr to Sep
0404 47118 Mrs Doyle
D: Fr €30.00
Beds: 1F 2T 1D **Baths:** 2 Ensuite 2 Private

Donard

S9396

Beech Lodge, *Irishtown, Donard, Dunlavin, Co Wicklow.* Beech Lodge 1.6km off N81.
Open: Apr to Oct
045 404651 Mrs Hanbridge
D: Fr €30.50
Beds: 1F 1T 1D **Baths:** 1 Ensuite 1 Shared
(4)

Dunlavin

N8701

Tynte House, *Dunlavin, Co Wicklow.* Period farmhouse in picturesque village.
Open: All Year (not Xmas)
045 401561 Mrs Lawler **Fax: 045 401586**
clawler@iol.ie
D: Fr €30.00
Beds: 2F 4D **Baths:** 6 Ensuite
(15)

Please respect a B&B's wishes regarding children, animals and smoking

Enniskerry

O2217

Powerscourt Arms, *Enniskerry, Bray, Co Wicklow.* Snuggling in the foothills of Wicklow Mountains - ideal base for touring expeditions.
Open: All Year (not Xmas)
01 2828903 Fax: 01 2864909
D: Fr €41.00-€44.50 **S:** Fr €44.50-€48.50
Beds: 2F 4T 8D 1S **Baths:** 5 En 2 Sh

Summerhill House Hotel, *Enniskerry, Bray, Co Wicklow.* Period country house situated at the foot of the Sugar Loaf Mountain.
Open: All Year
01 2867928 Mrs Sweeney
D: Fr €51.00-€70.00 **S:** Fr €51.00-€70.00
Beds: 3F 20D 29T 5S
cc

Cherbury, *Monastery, Enniskerry, Bray, Co Wicklow.* Large bungalow. Ideal base for touring Wicklow. Beside Powerscourt Gardens.
Open: All Year
01 2828679 Mrs Lynch
cherbury@eircom.net
D: Fr €35.00
Beds: 1D 2T **Baths:** 3 En
(6)

Glendalough

T1296

Pinewood Lodge, *Glendalough, Co Wicklow.* **Open:** All year **Grades:** BF Approv, AA 4 Diamond
0404 45437 (also fax) Mr & Mrs Cullen
pwlodge@gofree.indigo.ie
D: Fr €26.00-€30.00 **S:** Fr €41.00
Beds: 2F 2D 2T **Baths:** 6 En
(6) **cc**
Situated in tranquil forest setting on Wicklow Way in Ireland's garden county. Convenient to ferries and airport, only 5 mins' walk to pub and restaurants, lovely ensuite accommodation, breakfast menu, guest TV lounge, off-road parking, friendly family atmosphere, warm welcome.

Doire Coille House, *Glendalough,*
Cullentragh, Rathdrum, Co Wicklow.
Open: All year (not Xmas)
0404 45131 (also fax) Mrs Byrne
marybyrne@esatclear.ie
D: Fr €26.50-€30.00 **S:** Fr €39.00
Beds: 3D 1T **Baths:** 4 En
⌂ 🄿 (10) ⌘ Ⅴ 🎟 **cc**
Lovely farmhouse in one acre of gardens on
working dairy and sheep farm.

Carmels, *Annamoe,*
Glendalough, Co Wicklow.
Well-established home in the
heart of the Wicklow
Mountains.
Open: Mar to Nov
0404 45297 (also fax) Mrs Hawkins
carmelsbandb@eircom.net
D: Fr €27.50-€31.00 **S:** Fr €31.00
Beds: 2F 1D 1T **Baths:** 4 En
⌂ 🄿 (5) ⌘ ✕ Ⅴ 🎟.

Greystones
O2912

Butler's B&B, *83 Rathdown*
Park, Greystones, Co Wicklow.
Seaside town bedside Dublin
(bus/rail). All amenities,
rooms ensuite.
Open: All year (not Xmas)
01 2875518 Mrs Butler
butlersbandb@eircom.net
www.geocities.com.butlersbab
D: Fr €28.00-€30.00 **S:** Fr €45.00-€50.00
Beds: 1F 1T 2D **Baths:** 4 En
⌂ 🄿 (7) ⌘ 🎟 Ⅴ 🎟. **cc**

Hollywood
N9405

Rosannas, *Bannagroe,*
Hollywood, Blessington, Co
Wicklow. Fantastic country
house close to Dublin, golf
courses, racecourses,
fishing, Glendalough.
Open: Mar to Dec **Grades:** BF Approv
045 864225 Mrs Byrne
D: Fr €20.00-€28.00 **S:** Fr €30.00-€40.00
Beds: 1T 2D 1S **Baths:** 2 En 1 Sh
🄿 (8) ⌘ 🎟 ✕ Ⅴ 🎟.

Heathers, *Poulaphouca, Hollywood,*
Blessington, Co Wicklow. Bungalow beside lakes
national stud, Japanese Gardens, Glendalough,
Russborough House, Punchestown Racecourse
golf, angling.
Open: All Year (not Xmas/New Year)
045 864554 Mrs Curley
theheathers@eircom.net
D: Fr €25.50 **S:** Fr €33.00-€38.00
Beds: 2D 1F 1T **Baths:** 2 En 1 Sh
⌂ 🄿 (6) 🎟 ✕ Ⅴ 🎟. ▪ **cc**

Kilbride (Blessington)
O0217

Beechwood House,
Kilbride, Blessington, Co
Wicklow. Country house
convenient to Dublin and
Wicklow. Dinner by
arrangement only.
Open: All year (not Xmas/
New Year)
01 4582802 Ms McCann
amccann@beechwoodhouse.ie
www.beechwoodhouse.ie
D: Fr €32.00-€64.00 **S:** Fr €45.00-€64.00
Beds: 2F 2T 2D **Baths:** 6 En
⌂ 🄿 ⌘ ✕ Ⅴ 🎟. **cc**

Moyne
T0279

Jigsaw Cottage,
Moyne, Tinahely,
Arklow, Co Wicklow
Open: Mar to Oct
0508 71071 (also
fax) Mr More-
O'Ferrall
jigsaw@wickloway.com
www.wickloway.com
D: Fr €28.00-€35.00 **S:** Fr €40.00
Beds: 2D 2T **Baths:** 1 En 1 Sh
🄿 (8) 🎟 ✕ 🎟. ▪ **cc**
Cosy stone and timber farmstead in gently rolling
countryside, spectacular mountain backdrop.
Hill-walking, golf, horse-riding. Glendalough
monastic site, beautiful gardens, historic houses
pubs from the past, beaches all easily reached.
Quality home-cooking, transport arranged,
mountain navigation courses conducted.

Newtownmountkennedy

)2606

Primrose Lodge, *Kilquade Hill, Kilquade, Newtownmountkennedy, Greystones, Co Wicklow.* Country home, Mediterranean-designed, snooker, tennis, close to golf, sea.
Open: Easter to Oct
1 2877291 Mrs Toolan **Fax: 01 2873677**
D: Fr €25.50-€32.00 **S:** Fr €29.00-€35.50
Beds: 1F 1D 1T **Baths:** 2 En 1 Pr
� (1) 🅿 (4) ⊁ 📺 🛏 ⬛ 👜 ≡ cc

Rathdrum

*1888

St Bridgets, *Corballis, Rathdrum, Co Wicklow.* Adjacent to Avondale, Avoca, Glendalough. Travel agents.
Open: All year (not Xmas)
404 46477 Mrs Scott
t.bridgets@eircom.net
D: Fr €27.50-€30.00 **S:** Fr €40.00
Beds: 3F 1D 2T **Baths:** 3 En
⊃ (3) 🅿 ⊁ 📺 📺 🛏 ≡

The Hawthorns, *Corballis, Rathdrum, Wicklow.* Modern bungalow with award-winning garden, km from village. Near Avondale Forest Park.
Open: All Year (not Xmas)
404 46217 & 0404 46683 Mrs Sheehan **Fax: 0404 6217**
D: Fr €28.00
Beds: 1F 3D 2T **Baths:** 4 En 1 Sh
⊃ 🅿 (10) ⊁ 📺 🐕 🛏 👜 ≡ cc

Wicklow

3194

Greenfields, *Blainroe, Wicklow.*
Open: All year
404 68309 Mr Moloney
D: Fr €23.00 **S:** Fr €26.00
Beds: 2F 2D 1T **Baths:** 5 En
⊃ 🅿 (15) 📺 🐕 🛏 ≡ cc
Dormer bungalow with two acres of mature gardens, next door to Blainade Golf Course. Seven golf courses within 20 minute radius, snooker room and sun room available. Beaches within easy reach.

Lissadell House, *Ashtown Lane, Wicklow.*
Open: Mar to Nov
0404 67458 Mrs Klaue
lissadellhse@eircom.net
D: Fr €30.00-€34.00 **S:** Fr €40.00-€50.00
Beds: 4F 1D 1T **Baths:** 2 En 2 Pr 2 Sh
⊃ 🅿 ⊁ 📺 🛏 ✕ ⬛
Lissadell House, one mile from Wicklow Town, Wicklow/Wexford route, first turn off Marlton Road (L29A) signposted. Two miles off Dublin/Wexford Road (N11). Exit at Beehive Pub, junction for Marlton Road (L29A) (R751). First turn left - see signpost.

Rospark, *Silverstrand Road, Dunbur, Wicklow.* Spacious bungalow, ideal base for touring Wicklow. 1.5 hours Dublin and Rosslare.
Open: Easter to Oct
0404 69615 & 086 8333285 (M) Mrs Naughton
Fax: 0404 69615
Rospark@gofree.indigo.ie
D: Fr €26.00 **S:** Fr €30.00
Beds: 2F 2D **Baths:** 4 En
⊃ 🅿 ⊁ 📺 🛏 📺 ⬛ cc

Glen Na Smole, *Ashtown Lane, Wicklow.* Cosy family home with individual style. Each room tastefully decorated. Equidistant Dublin/Rosslare.
Open: Easter to Nov
0404 67945 Mrs Byrne
byrne.wicklow@indigo.ie
D: Fr €27.00-€30.00 **S:** Fr €35.00-€40.00
Beds: 2F 1D 1T **Baths:** 4 En
⊃ 🅿 (5) 📺 🛏 ✕ 📺 ⬛ ≡

Thomond House, *St Patrick's Road Upper, Wicklow.* Thomond House is situated on an elevated site with panoramic views of the sea.
Open: Apr to Oct
0404 67940 (also fax) Mrs Gorman
D: Fr €28.00
Beds: 2T 2D 2S **Baths:** 2 Ensuite 2 Shared
🅿 ⊁ 📺 ⬛

Silver Sands, *Dunbar Road, Wicklow.* Welcoming home overlooking Wicklow Bay. 1 km town centre. Ideal touring base.
Open: March to Nov
0404 68243 Mrs Doyle
lyladoyle@eircom.net
D: Fr €28.00
Beds: 5F **Baths:** 5 En
⊃ 🅿 📺 🛏 📺 ⬛ ≡

Location Index

The cities, towns, villages and hamlets listed in this index all have entries in **Stilwell's ireland: Bed & Breakfast** under their respective county heading. If there is no listing for the place you wish to stay in, the section map for that particular county will show you somewhere else to stay close by.

Location Index